RHYTHM AND NOISE

AN AESTHETICS OF ROCK

Theodore Gracyk

DUKE UNIVERSITY PRESS   Durham and London 1996

© 1996 Duke University Press
All rights reserved
Printed in the United States of America on
acid-free paper ∞
Typeset in Sabon by Keystone Typesetting, Inc.
Library of Congress Cataloging-in-Publication Data
appear on the last printed page of this book.

RHYTHM AND NOISE

Contents

Preface

Architecture in general is frozen music.
— Friedrich W. J. von Schelling, 1809

Writing about music is like dancing about architecture.
— Elvis Costello, 1983

⬤ About the time I was born, hula hoops were the new rage. Eddie Cochran's "Summertime Blues" was a hit, and it cost a nickel to hear it on a jukebox. In many southern states, segregation laws meant that Cochran could not appear on stage with the Coasters, then riding the charts with Leiber and Stoller's "Yakety Yak." Tin Pan Alley plotted its revenge against rock and roll; Elvis was in the army, and Fabian, Frankie Avalon, and Paul Anka commanded a disproportionate share of time on Dick Clark's *American Bandstand*. In Liverpool, the members of the Quarry Men renamed themselves Johnny and the Moondogs and watched Eddie Cochran on the Saturday evening television program *Oh Boy!*

Earlier that decade, John Passmore complained about the dreariness of aesthetics. The antidote, he thought, was to ground aesthetics in "the real differences between the works of art themselves."[1] It seems never to have occurred to him to include popular culture. Because rock has always proclaimed its difference, its special status in opposition to the rest of our music, it invites us to reflect on its differences. But I do not believe that this means rejecting aesthetics. Until recently, most rock was produced by Americans and Europeans influenced by aesthetic assumptions that helped shape and define modern culture. At the same time that they have shaped rock, the practices of rock music constitute a challenge to the hegemonic impulses of high culture.

In attempting to map out an aesthetics of rock, I find it necessary to wrestle with its identity conditions. What do musicians, critics, and fans count as a finished work in rock? As a successful work? As original? By what processes are works created, disseminated, and known by the audience? What medium and what perceptual qualities are most central to the presence of meaning? In recent years, a further level of self-reflection has been added. To what extent do the questions themselves reflect prevailing ideologies?

My own thinking was crystallized by Paul Williams's admirable *Performing Artist: The Music of Bob Dylan* (1990). As the title indicates, Williams contends that Dylan is less a songwriter than a performing artist. Dylan became a writer out of necessity, because he needed a closer connection between his own emotions and the songs he performed, a connection that could not be sustained with the existing rock-and-roll repertoire. Williams embarks on a two-volume discussion of Dylan's life as an artist, comparing alternative performances of major songs over the years and linking those performances to events in Dylan's personal life. Williams argues that we cannot analyze the songs apart from specific performances of them. But as the first volume proceeds, it becomes clear that Williams is not discussing *performances* at all. As he recognizes in the second volume of his Dylan study, he is discussing *recordings*. Williams defends himself by saying that concert tapes give "direct" access to Dylan in performance.[2] But he is not consistent on this matter.

With some recorded performances, Williams notes, there is "a sound that is mysterious in its perfection."[3] In addition to the magnificence of the performance, the recording features "just the right mix, just the right fade, just the right echoes in the room, and the result is you can listen to the track over and over and over." So what is Williams reviewing? When he comes to "Can You Please Crawl Out Your Window?" Williams denigrates the digital mix on *Biograph* and warns us that the sublime effect he is discussing "depends on the perfection of the sound," which in this case "only happens on the mono mix (as heard on the original single and certain bootleg albums)."[4] As the book proceeds and Williams critiques specific performances at specific shows, it turns out that Williams's test for "perfection" is a recording that reveals new facets and nuances on playing after playing. But doesn't he thus admit that the standards for a great live performance and for a recording are quite different? A powerful live performance does not always come across on a recording, just as the qualities that infuse a recording with "perfection" are often ones that do not exist during the live performance.

If a critic of this stature is not clear on whether he is evaluating a performance or a recording, attention to the distinction is long past due. Insofar as there can be a rock aesthetic, a general theory about rock music as an object of critical attention, I propose that it must focus on recorded music. But Williams is hardly alone in taking the principal signifier to be a song even as he analyzes a recording. Wilfrid Mellers waffles over the distinction in his own Dylan study, *A Darker Shade of Pale*. Critic Dave Marsh often refers to recordings as "performances," seemingly endorsing the thesis that recordings transparently convey performances. Or consider George Lipsitz's exemplary discussions of popular music as the repository of our history and ideals. In some respects, his thesis is an elaboration of Greil Marcus's *Mystery Train*. As Lipsitz puts it, "popular music depends upon the recovery and reaccentuation of previous works."[5] But what are we to count as "works" here? Where Greil Marcus was clearly interpreting recordings, Lipsitz almost always characterizes the object of his interpretation as songs.

For instance, Lipsitz analyzes a recording made nearly forty years ago as if it were simply a matter of a song and its arrangement:

> Little Richard's "Good Golly Miss Molly" provides the quickest introduction to the vocabulary of rock-and-roll music. . . . Throughout *the song,* instrumental bursts "answer" and "respond" to the vocalist's "call." . . . "Good Golly Miss Molly" also displays rhythmic properties of African derivation.[6]

The song, we should note, is not Little Richard's. It was composed by Robert "Bumps" Blackwell and John Marascalco, who contributed much of the "playful wit" valued by Lipsitz. Blackwell also produced the Specialty recording sessions and was largely responsible for the arrangements. (Not simply the repository of African American music, Blackwell studied advanced composition at UCLA.) But how many of these traits are present in *other* versions of "Good Golly Miss Molly"? Many rock fans are more likely to know Creedence Clearwater Revival's 1969 cover version, which eliminates falsetto from the vocal and is rhythmically less sophisticated.

In short, the song does not have all of the properties that Lipsitz finds significant. The object of critical attention is a recording. Occasionally he seems to acknowledge this; writing about "Jackie Wilson Said" as done by Kevin Rowland and Dexy's Midnight Runners, he notes that "Van Morrison wrote and recorded the original" in 1971.[7] How does this square with Fredric Jameson's claim that popular songs have copies but no originals, as approvingly cited by Lipsitz?[8] Yet the concept of the original recording is central to rock ideology. Robert Walser's lengthy analysis of Van Halen's "Runnin' with the Devil" is the linchpin of his book on heavy metal, and Walser talks about "the songs" and "musical works" featured on Van Halen's first album. But he is discussing specific recordings.[9]

It is crucial to the arguments of these writers that we can listen to the very *same* recordings. Yet Little Richard went from being a traveling performer of popular music to a figure of mass culture precisely because he provided the vocals for a series of hit recordings. Like many early rock and rollers, his success depended on making the transition from performing artist to recording artist. Within popular music, rock is significantly dependent on a shift in ontological category, in *what* counts as a unit of significance or an object of critical attention. Most writers who've addressed the distinction between songs and recordings as the primary works and signifiers in rock music have been interested in the music *industry* and its history. Here, the distinction is examined as one supporting differences in what can and cannot be communicated in the music.

The appearance of Williams's book on Dylan coincided with another epiphany for me. I wanted to locate a certain recording and picked up the telephone directory. The entry "Records-Retail" directed me to "Compact Discs, Tapes & Records-Retail." The reign of the vinyl record, one of the technological innovations fueling rock, was over. Digital technology, the wave of the future when I started writing, is today's commonplace. In some ways, the transition to compact discs has revitalized interest in rock's past, if only for the short term as record companies cash in on baby boomers who repurchase the music of their youth. A vast archival search is under way, as companies dig through tapes stored away for decades, looking for the best possible master for their digital reissue. The box set of digital remasters has become the historical record of musical careers, as everyone from Eric Clapton to Aerosmith to the Monkees releases a three- or four-CD retrospective just in time for Christmas shopping. I keep looking for the Village People box set. During the same period, of course, overall sales in rock music have declined.

This digital revolution highlights rock's struggle with the binary opposition of copy and original. Like film, rock recordings have many copies, yet some are privileged as "originals." I do not treat the categories of authenticity and originality as fixed universals dwelling in some Platonic heaven. The rock community adapts them to its own needs. Indeed, different communities within rock develop them differently. At the same time, these categories carry a certain amount of ideological baggage, inherited from the high-art tradition. Rock is largely unified by an intellectual framework in which "high art" categories have been appropriated and deployed in the creation and consumption of popular music. Not that there has been a conscious construction of such a framework. But it is present in the opinions of the musicians, critics, and fans struggling with the implications of mediation and technological reproducibility.

I want to make it clear that I never try to isolate features *unique* to rock. I never claim that any specific features are necessary or sufficient for a piece of music to be rock. I point to no essence of rock music, nor offer a strict definition of it. I have tried to identify and theorize about central features that are common to many of the instances that are taken to be paradigm cases of rock music.

I also want to be clear about the *level* of specificity appropriate to an aesthetics of rock. As a concept for grouping a diverse set of events, objects, and discursive practices, it is highly schematic and abstract. With any concept, the fewer its potential referents, the lower the level of abstraction. "Cow," for instance, is at a lower level than "mammal." But unless all cows are Holsteins, "Holstein" is lower yet. In viewing a large chunk of popular culture as rock, we operate at a relatively abstract level, more so than is typical in musicology, sociology, or cultural studies. As such, "rock" operates largely as an ideological abstraction, not as the label of an observable property of the phenomena it unifies.

I emphasize this point because many writers locate rock at a lower level. For instance, Philip Ennis proposes that rock represents the "maturation" of rock and roll. As such, he regards it as operating at the same level of abstraction as rock and roll. Ennis is not alone in this thought, but his version is explicit enough to bear discussion. He identifies four basic elements as essential to any artistic system. With rock, these began "functioning at a high level" beginning around 1965, so that the "art form" became self-reproducing, reaching "full maturity" in 1970.[10] First, the audience for various styles of rock and roll "blended into a single one," and as the teenagers of the initial rock-and-roll audience aged, they became interested in a broader range of musics, particularly folk and jazz. Second, musicians from various streams within American popular music came together to form "a new and different musical idiom," capable of a deeper expression of human experience. Third, traditional distribution and performance vehicles gave way to a new infrastructure. Fourth, a distinctively rock criticism emerged as its "self-conscious, self-proclaimed" voice. Upon reaching this critical mass, rock could "grow its own artists, audience, distribution systems, and critical apparatus."[11]

But the configuration of these four elements is not unique to artistic systems, high or low. Professional football and the fashion industry can be analyzed in terms of the matrix of producers, distributors, audience, and criticism. Ennis underplays the fact that a communicative relationship holds between producers and audience, and too little attention is paid to the *creative medium* through which artists reached their audience, distributed by the infrastructure and surveyed by the critics.

Maturation is a dubious metaphor here, but it is widely used, as when Deena Weinstein writes of the formation, crystallization, maturation, and decay of heavy-metal styles.[12] We are better off avoiding biological metaphors of growth and reproduction that presuppose a teleological interpretation. Or perhaps we should modify the metaphor to the language of epidemiology. Contrary to Ennis, it is not clear that rock developed a new infrastructure; rock metastasized gradually in existing institutions of clubs, radio, and record companies. Even the rock festival format was grafted to a tradition of jazz and folk festivals. Or we could confine ourselves to the differentiation, stabilization, and decadence of symbolic systems over time. Better to employ Pierre Bourdieu's concept of the "cultural field" surrounding each art form, an analytical framework that remains neutral about the health or maturation of the overall system.[13]

Ennis claims that a *single* audience and a *unified* musical idiom coincided in the years 1965 to 1970. It probably looked that way at Monterey and Woodstock, but having a common audience is no evidence of stylistic unity. When Jimi Hendrix toured as opening act for the Monkees, the audience hardly embraced Hendrix as a fellow traveler. The fragmentation that Ennis, Charles Hamm, and so many others link with Altamont (December 1969) and the early 1970s was already present. Rock, like rock and roll before it, has always embraced a range of musical styles, appealing to a range of distinct audiences and subcultures. Looking at Britain alone, Dick Hebdige points to the deep divisions between teds, hipsters, mods, skinheads, and rockers during the 1950s and then the 1960s.[14]

Calling rock the "most important *stylistic* development in American popular music" in the late twentieth century, Charles Hamm provides a valuable treatment of continuities and discontinuities between rock and earlier popular music.[15] But as Leonard B. Meyer emphasizes, style "is a replication of patterning . . . that results from a series of choices made within some set of constraints."[16] Emphasizing rock's eclecticism and stylistic diversity, Hamm never points to recurring stylistic choices characteristic of rock. While he does list five auditory characteristics typical of rock and roll in the 1950s, he does not have a parallel list for "rock." Instead, he directs us to rock's emphasis on flexibility of formal patterns, diversity of instruments, and an increased emphasis on electronic equipment and manipulation of sound.[17] Hamm even begs the question by proposing that when the San Francisco sound became popular, "the term 'rock' came into use for their music and other music drawing on elements of their style." But do Blue Cheer, Jefferson Airplane, Country Joe and the Fish, Moby Grape, the Beau Brummels, and the Grateful Dead share a style, with common ways of organizing and articulating sounds? Or, as with the more recent Seattle scene, are we dealing with a marketing hook that arises as much from geography as from style?

Less intent on essentialism is musicologist Allan F. Moore, who denies that rock has a "unified style." It is neither a genre nor style, but a set of musical practices and listening strategies identified with a particular history of musicians. But nothing reoccurs in every case. At best, argues Moore, we can pick out a set of musical features and audience responses that are *common* to much of rock music. As modes for articulating sound, stylistic characteristics are audible features that are grouped together by a musical community as "widely pertinent" across a range of particular "exemplars."[18] Despite the presence of a few common *patterns* across its exemplars, rock is not really a musical style.

It is not a coincidence if my approach echoes certain ideas of Ludwig Wittgenstein's later philosophy. Rock's identity emerges only at the level he calls a musical *tradition*. Wittgenstein observes that the cultural demands on interpretation and appreciation are unusually pronounced in the case of musical traditions. He describes it in this way:

> The words we call expressions of aesthetic judgment play a very complicated role . . . in what we call a culture of a period. To describe their use or to describe what you mean by a cultured taste, you have to describe a culture. . . . An entirely different game is played in different ages.[19]

While it is tempting to dismiss such remarks as ideologically loaded and largely irrelevant to rock, Wittgenstein is acutely aware that diverse language games coexist within the dominant culture. Each group "does something entirely different" with music, clothing, or architecture.[20]

The validity of one's responses to music are a function of what one does with it, which in turn is a function of what one's culture permits one to do with it. Gothic cathedrals and Beethoven symphonies demand radically different responses, and not simply because of their intrinsic qualities.

Nor does Wittgenstein limit "cultured taste" to high culture. High culture is merely one among many cultural games. He emphasizes the cultural conditioning that lies behind our ability to make nuanced distinctions in response to different traditions: "What belongs to a language game is a whole culture." How do children use music; how do women? Is it reserved for men only? To generate an account of what "appreciation" means for a musical tradition, "we would have to describe the whole environment."[21] That task is impossible. At best, theorizing produces a blueprint.

Rather than seek stylistic traits that unify the various musics identified as rock, some turn to literary theory in the hope that issues of genre will do the job. Indeed, a literary genre can be identified with a set of evolving conventions governing content development and audience response. We are reminded that individual musicians cannot assume sole "authorship" of the meanings of rock, for meaning arises through largely unconscious expectations of what may and may not be done. (Readers accept the intervention of the hand of God in Stephen King's *The Stand*, but would be troubled by a similar plot device in an Agatha Christie detective novel.) Rock has characteristic approaches to articulating rhythm and timbre. Still, we must not forget that genres involve cultural conventions and transpersonal rules. Ever evolving, they do not exist apart from the histories of production and use of specific artifacts. Here, we do well to remember rock's specifically American roots, as well as its close relationship to a capitalist entertainment industry. Too often, however, style or genre analysis ignores Wittgenstein's warnings and adopts the ahistoricism that mars too much in academic analysis.[22]

Unlike so many writers on rock, I do not analyze the lyrics of rock songs. My emphasis is on the music, not on the texts sung as part of the music. Rather than citing lyrics, I often quote from interviews with rock musicians and, less frequently, from rock criticism. Treating rock as a musical art, I assume that we have little chance of understanding what is going on unless we take account of the thinking of those who produce it. Given contradictory pronouncements by a rock musician and an academic theorist, I look for a scholarly position that squares with the views of the musicians. As George Berkeley proposed nearly three centuries ago, let us "think with the learned, and speak with the vulgar."

I am indebted to many people for their support, advice, encouragement, and critical comments; chief among them are Philip Alperson, Lee Brown, Noël Carroll, Sue Cataldi, Mark Chekola, Joe Fodor, Cheryl Foster, Timothy Gracyk, John W. Heintz, Arnold Johanson, Thomas Levin, Phyllis May-Machunda, Mara Miller, David Myers, Nikolas Pappas, Joel Rudinow, Crispin Sartwell, and the anonymous readers at Duke University Press. I am grateful to the administration at Moorhead State University for providing some release time and financial support for some parts of this project. Although they had no direct input into this work, I am indebted to Peter Kivy and Stephen Davies, whose work has been pivotal to the development of my thinking about music; Kivy's published work has continually reminded me that good theorizing is not incompatible with good writing. At Duke University Press, I am grateful to Reynolds Smith for believing in the project and seeing it through the writing process, and to Sharon Parks for fielding so many of my mundane questions. Parts of chapter 6 previously appeared as "Adorno, Jazz and the Aesthetics of Popular Music" in the *Musical Quarterly,* vol. 76, no. 4, pp. 526–42. Parts of chapter 7 previously appeared as "Romanticizing Rock Music" in the *Journal of Aesthetic Education,* vol. 27, no. 2, pp. 43–58. (Copyright 1993 by the Board of Trustees of the University of Illinois. Used with the permission of the University of Illinois Press.) I am grateful to those presses for permission to incorporate that material. Finally, to Athena, Thelonious, and Tatiana for being such a loving and supportive family.

I

That Wild, Thin Mercury Sound:

Ontology

The early Elvis records live on without Elvis being a beautiful male animal who swung his pelvis. . . . The basic thing, the basic energy, is on the records.
—John Lennon, 1980[1]

What distinguishes rock & roll from all the music that precedes it . . . is its elevation of the record to primary status. —Robert B. Ray[2]

Rock music is neither a style nor a genre of music. While this claim flies in the face of some ordinary usage, the obvious differences among styles of rock music supports it. Rock's most distinctive characteristic within popular music may lie in the realm of ontology, in *what* a musical work *is* in rock music as opposed to what it is, for instance, in jazz or country or folk. Rock is a tradition of popular music whose creation and dissemination centers on recording technology. This is not to deny that rock contributes to the long tradition of American popular song, as documented by Charles Hamm.[3] But we should be careful not to overemphasize the continuities between Stephen Foster, George Gershwin, Chuck Berry, and Patti Smith. In rock the musical work is less typically a song than an arrangement of recorded sounds. Rock music is both composed and received in light of musical qualities that are subject to mechanical reproduction but not notational specification. This thesis informs my subsequent decisions about what's central and what's peripheral in an aesthetics of rock.

Consider a simple case. Driving down the highway, I turn on the radio just as a commercial ends and a new piece of music begins. I hear a simple bass pattern, a single bar of music, and then my companion reaches out and punches a button, switching to her favorite station. She says, "I don't like Steely Dan." Now, we have heard either of two things. We either heard Walter Becker play the opening of "Rikki Don't

Lose That Number" (1974), in which case we heard rock music, or we heard Teddy Smith play the opening of Horace Silver's "Song for My Father" (1964), in which case we heard jazz. The snatch of music was objectively one or the other, but Becker was quoting Smith and there is no stylistic difference between the two. Why is it rock if Becker is playing it, but jazz if Smith is? The answer surely includes more than whatever we would have heard had the station remained unchanged. Part of the answer lies in what Becker and Smith were doing when they played that bass riff; much of the answer is that they belong to a specific artistic tradition. It is a mere contingency that Smith was in a recording studio with the tape rolling, but not that Becker was.

What's in a Name? Rock or Rock 'n' Roll?

In order to see that rock is not just a style of popular music, it can be useful to distinguish between rock and its direct progenitor, rock and roll. Although the commercial potency of rock and roll was responsible for the subsequent birth of rock, most recent rock music is not rock and roll. Discussions of popular music frequently blur the distinction. In his attack on "rock" music in *The Closing of the American Mind*, Allan Bloom complains that "rock has the beat of sexual intercourse" and characterizes it as "primitive" and "barbarous."[4] Yet it is clear that Bloom equates rock music with its pervasive reliance on a syncopated 4/4. A similar move is made by Kathleen Higgins. Rightly criticizing Bloom for confusing "rock ideology" with "rock music," she argues that "popular music" can be as positive an influence as classical music.[5] But in her treatment of the Dionysian dangers of popular music, Higgins begins with "rock 'n' roll" and then introduces "rock music" as a synonym, so that she appears to regard Roxy Music's "More Than This" as rock and roll. I do not think that I am idiosyncratic in thinking that "More Than This" is just not rock and roll.

It is not simply that rock or rock and roll are vague categories, with boundaries as subject to change as a map of the Balkans. As with most other concepts through which we organize experience, classification of a specific case depends upon the range of contrasting concepts available. Consider the task of classifying the color of a patch of paint. If I have only the most basic color terms in my vocabulary (e.g., "red," "blue"), I may have no problem in saying that the paint is red. But offer me more categories, such as light red versus red versus dark red, and I may well reclassify the same sample. Offer me a color wheel of the sort used by professionals for mixing paint, and I may well tell you that the color falls between "holly red" and "antique ruby."

In the 1950s, there were fewer categories for popular music. The phrase "rock and roll" was introduced to replace "rhythm and blues," largely to indicate that whites as well as blacks performed the music.[6] (In 1955, Buddy Holly was the opening act for a "rhythm and blues" show headlined by Bill Haley; by 1957, his promotion material always highlighted the phrase "rock 'n' roll.") There is something to the charge, leveled by a number of African American writers and musicians, that the phrase "rock and roll" was adopted so that whites could mimic rhythm and blues for their own purposes and profit. During Elvis Presley's first interview, on a Memphis radio station, the disc jockey made sure to ask Presley where he went to high school so that the local audience would understand that he was white. But the new phrase, dating back to the 1930s but now popularized by Alan Freed, served a function of indicating that a certain record was neither jazz nor classical nor standard pop music. Forty years later, the same phrase can function either as a generic label or to indicate a specific style of rock. Yelled by someone in the audience at a concert, it indicates a desire for up-tempo music, that is, as a specific mode of rock.

While there is only a loose consensus about the proper use of these labels, those who knew the music as it was in the late 1950s and early 1960s insist that most rock music is not "rock and roll." John Lennon said that his musical tastes were "rock and roll" and little else: "Wop bop a loo bop." But in the same interview he said that "I always liked simple rock."[7] Bob Dylan professes confusions about rock, but not rock and roll:

> What is [rock]? I don't like rock. Is that Twisted Sister? I like rock 'n' roll; now that's a different thing. Rock is hard . . . But rolling is smooth and easy. A lot of the roll is gone from the music I hear, sure it is.[8]

But was "Like a Rolling Stone" ever smooth and easy? Then there is Van Morrison, the rock musician's rock musician, who denies that "rock and roll" means anything anymore:

> The way I live my life from day to day is so far removed from what people think of when you say "rock and roll." I've got nothing to do with all that rock and roll stuff at all. When I started out, when I was a teenager, rock and roll to me was Little Richard, Jerry Lee

Lewis and Chuck Berry and people like that. But now, what is rock
and roll? Rock and roll is a mind trip. It's not music anymore.[9]

At the same time, Morrison denies that *Astral Weeks* (1968) is rock
music:

Of all the records I have ever made, [*Astral Weeks*] is definitely not
rock. You could throw that record at the wall, take it to music
colleges, analyze it to death. Nobody is going to tell me that it is a
rock album. Why they keep calling it one I have no idea.[10]

Of course, a quarter century after its release, the album is regularly
cited as one of the ten best rock albums.

If fans and musicians cannot agree on usage, consider the confusions
of a fifteen-year-old who gets into the music today. On its commemora-
tive stamp honoring Otis Redding, the United States Postal Service
identifies him as a "rhythm & blues singer," just like Clyde McPhatter.
But Redding identified himself as a *soul* musician. In 1995, the huge
Columbia House music "club" requires members to specify a prefer-
ence among hard rock, alternative (recently replacing "modern rock"),
Latin, soft rock, light sounds, dance/pop, easy listening, R&B/soul,
rap, jazz, country, heavy metal, and classical. All but four of the categories — jazz, country, classical, and easy listening — involve music that
would be called rock if that were the only other choice. (The jazz and
country divisions include some music that would be admitted as rock
and roll or jazz-rock fusion.) Columbia House classifies the 1970s music of Roxy Music, the Sex Pistols, and B-52's, and Elvis Costello as
alternative, whereas just plain "rock" includes U2, the Pretenders, ZZ
Top (elsewhere listed as "hard rock"), and Bonnie Raitt. And 1950s
rock and roll is covered within the broad heading of "Classic Rock."

In the long run, little would be gained in debating whether "rock" or
"rock and roll" — or, worse yet, "rock 'n' roll" — is the proper category
here. In speaking about the broadest possible category that contrasts
with jazz, country, and classical, common usage currently leans toward
"rock" as the general category. But if we want to make distinctions
within rock, the very same term denotes guitar-heavy music with a debt
to rock and roll. To paraphrase Nelson Goodman's view that art is not
a fixed set of objects, we ought to ask *when* something is rock and not
which things are (Nelson contrasts the two questions about the concept
of art itself).[11] Goodman's answer about art is that symbolic function is
the crucial factor. But this will not do to distinguish why one performance of a tune is rock and another is not; compare "Where or When"

as recorded by Ella Fitzgerald (jazz) and by Dion and the Belmonts (rock and roll). Crudely, my answer is that genealogy is decisive, but plotting genealogy is hardly an objectively neutral undertaking. Just as one can belong to one family by birth and a different family by marriage, one and the same musical *composition* can have both rock and nonrock performances. It is less clear that a single *recording* could be both rock and nonrock at the same time.

A glance at jazz will illustrate my point that musical category is a matter of genealogy as much as sound. The concept of rock, like that of jazz, is an umbrella for a wide range of musicians and performance styles with some common antecedents and influences. Jazz includes Louis Armstrong's recordings with the Hot Fives and Hot Sevens, Thelonious Monk's solo piano recordings, Charlie Parker's sessions with an orchestra, and John Coltrane's *Love Supreme.* Each is stylistically distinct, and not merely in the sense that each musician has a unique style; each played in a style that other musicians emulate. And some jazz musicians change styles. Consider Miles Davis on *Birth of the Cool, Kind of Blue,* and *Bitches Brew.* Each of these albums features a different style of jazz (cool, modal, and fusion, respectively). Just as we can highlight aesthetic features which are central to jazz without closing the door on further development of new styles, features now recognizable as central to rock do not close off the development of further rock styles.

In sum, auditory qualities alone are insufficient to classify a musical work. When Branford Marsalis releases an album, it is jazz. But when he appears on a Grateful Dead album (*Without a Net,* 1991), he's playing rock, even if he's playing exactly the same horn part that he might play on one of his own albums. When Grateful Dead guitarist Jerry Garcia appears on Ornette Coleman's *Virgin Beauty* (1988), he is performing jazz, even if he plays exactly the same guitar parts that he might have played during a Grateful Dead concert. When Frank Zappa puts an instrumental track on his albums, it's rock music even as we recognize its jazz or classical influences. But when Pierre Boulez records an album of Zappa's music, it's classical music. Steely Dan's "Rikki Don't Lose That Number" takes its bass line from Horace Silver's "Song for My Father," yet that sequence of notes is rock music in the first case and jazz in the second.

To continue the contrast of rock and jazz: while jazz may stem from the improvisational practices of New Orleans black music around the turn of the century, it is not restricted to music of the New Orleans style. Jazz is no truer, no more authentic, for sticking to its roots;

attempts to be "authentic" in that way can seem hollow re-creations rather than living jazz. In a similar way, rock may stem from the commercial blend of country with rhythm and blues together with some black gospel influences that became popular as rock and roll in the fifties, but rock is not limited to that stylistic mix. Any influence can be incorporated into rock — and usually is, we might quip — and it still remains rock.

Borders Between Traditions

As a musician, I just want to make some great records.
— Keith Richards, 1992[12]

As a strictly musical hybrid (as a distinct style of performing music), rock and roll predates its commercial success in the fifties. Nick Tosches argues for the early 1940s.[13] In one of his last interviews, Leonard Bernstein observed that "there was rock & roll in the late 1930s" and points to Ella Fitzgerald's work with drummer Chick Webb.[14] Count Basie advised his audience to "rock" as well as "jive." Bob Dylan maintains that Bessie Smith played rock and roll. Yet John Lennon, Bruce Springsteen, and a host of other rock musicians regularly point to Elvis Presley's earliest recordings as definitive rock and roll, as its defining rather than originating moment. Better still, the Sun sessions themselves demonstrate that rock and roll is a *performance* style. It cannot be identified with the songs, since the Sun sessions exclusively featured songs adapted from other styles, such as Bill Monroe's bluegrass hit "Blue Moon of Kentucky" and the rhythm and blues of both Junior Parker's "Mystery Train" and Wynonie Harris's version of "Good Rockin' Tonight" (1947). When Sam Phillips brought Elvis together with guitarist Scotty Moore and bass player Bill Black, Phillips consciously sought a merger of white and black styles. But we should not jump to the conclusion that only certain types of songs can be thus adapted. There have been excellent rock-and-roll adaptations of songs by the Gershwins, Hoagy Carmichael, Irving Berlin, Kurt Weill, Harold Arlen, Rodgers and Hart, and a score of lesser-knowns. Cole Porter, of course, supplied all the songs on the AIDS research benefit album *Red Hot & Blue* (1990).

Furthermore, songs conceived as rock and roll are often performed otherwise. That is, rock songs are routinely adapted in the other direction, into nonrock. Think of the music of Paul Simon or the Police as it is sometimes rescored as background music or as Muzak. These insipid renditions are not anyone's idea of rock and roll. Jazz trumpeter Freddie Hubbard performs a driving rendition of John Lennon's "Cold Turkey," easily recognizable as Lennon's song but also clearly jazz. And there are even "classical" treatments, of the sort "Baroque Beatles" or "Mozart Plays the Sex Pistols" (the former is genuine, the latter not). So rock and roll should not be identified with any body of songs so much as with a general performance style.

If rock and roll is the performing style most closely associated with rock, the more inclusive category of rock was not clearly differentiated until around 1965. The distinction is blurry, in part because so many early rock artists were also rock and rollers. A clear example is the Beatles, who started as rock-and-roll musicians but ended up as something quite different. I doubt that you could teach someone what rock and roll is by playing their recordings of "Julia," "Blackbird," "Here Comes the Sun," or "Yesterday," but you might be able to do so by playing their versions of "I Want to Hold Your Hand," "Long Tall Sally," "Bad Boy," "Helter Skelter," and a few others. As Phillip Ennis suggests, it is partly the incorporation of a broader spectrum of performing and arranging styles which led to recognition of the broader category, rock.

However, many rock musicians come to rock without any apprenticeship in rock and roll. Think here of Joni Mitchell, Pink Floyd, Kate Bush, Leonard Cohen, Tori Amos, Brian Eno, and any number of black vocalists, from Al Green to Prince. Despite their subsequent boast of "the greatest rock and roll band in the world," the Rolling Stones started as a *blues* band that played in jazz clubs: "we were so aware of being blues purists."[15] In 1962, Jagger said that he hoped that audiences would not regard the Stones "as a rock 'n' roll outfit." Of course, the Stones played their fair share of rock and roll once they overcame their "purist" attitude, but they were never *purely* rock and roll in the way that the Beatles were in their early years.[16]

Pulling this together, rock embraces a host of performance styles, but most have *some* basis in African American popular music, are rooted in song, and paradigmatically exist as *recorded* music. If I fail to offer a definition in the form of necessary and sufficient conditions, so be it. At best, such a definition would map the extension of the term. I think we must be willing to leave the border fuzzy.

Rock musicians can support careers in virtual absence of live performance, so that audiences know their work only through recordings. In classical music, Glenn Gould is notable as one of the few musicians who sustained a viable career after abandoning live performance. But in rock it is not all that unusual. Here, as is so often the case, the Beatles serve as an example. Not only did they cease touring in 1966 to concentrate on studio work, but subsequent generations have the same access to their music as anyone did during the late sixties, namely, the recordings. Even when musicians stage year-long world tours, only a fraction of their audience gets to see them; if the careers of successful rock musicians depended on live performance, audience size would be self-limiting, as it appears to be for classical and jazz.

Furthermore, rock reputations are made as much by recordings as by live performances, and thus it is possible for musicians to be a direct influence on others many years after the fact. Only a few thousand Americans saw the Sex Pistols on their sole tour in the United States, but thousands of kids are turned on to their music every year. Despite all the press devoted to their antics during their brief career, the Sex Pistols sold most of their records long after the band broke up. It took them a decade to earn a gold record for *Never Mind the Bollocks* (1977), and then another five years to go platinum. Alex Chilton's post-Box Tops group, Big Star, sold few records during their short existence in the early 1970s. But now their recordings are regularly cited as an influence by bands whose members were in diapers when Big Star recorded (e.g., the Replacements, Teenage Fan Club, the Loud Family). The Doors and Jimi Hendrix sell more records and probably have more influence now than when they made their music. The lion's share of popularity and critical acclaim might come to serious composers after death, as with Bach, but the crucial difference is that they are only known through the interpretations of performers. When my children dance to the Beatles, they don't respond to someone's interpretation of the music, but to the Beatles' music itself. The Beatles advised us to dance to songs that were hits before our mothers were born; when my children dance to Elvis Presley's rendition of "Blue Suede Shoes," they do just that.

1965: Dylan and the Beatles

The distinction between rock and rock 'n' roll was firmly established among rock fans, musicians, and critics by 1967 and was taken for granted in early issues of *Rolling Stone*. Rock is generally understood as popular music closest to, but superseding, rock and roll; it is sometimes contrasted with "pop," which is regarded as more commercial in its aims. Jon Landau reflects common wisdom when he says that "The

Beatles, the Stones and Dylan were the first inductees to rock's (as opposed to rock and roll's) pantheon."[17]

Yet critical efforts to delineate rock as a distinct musical genre have been few and have tended to emphasize its cultural impact. Just as Duke Ellington disdained the label "jazz" (he preferred the more inclusive phrase "Negro music"), critic Robert Christgau proposes "semi-popular music" as a better phrase than "rock." It acknowledges that genuine mass popularity, measured by record sales, often eludes influential and critically acclaimed musicians.[18] In 1973, Christgau proposed that rock was "all music derived primarily from the energy and influence of the Beatles — and maybe Bob Dylan, and maybe you should stick pretensions in there someplace."[19] But "influence" covers a multitude of sins. It may seem that their status as songwriters is foremost, but their position as *recording* artists has equal relevance to their status as the founders of rock.

Bob Dylan's supposedly commercial sellout of 1965, when he began recording and then playing concerts with an amplified band, is a key event in the break from rock and roll. His self-titled debut album (recorded 1961) features only two original compositions; the other eleven are blues and traditional folk tunes. Dylan was marketed as a "folk" musician, and subsequently as a protest singer. Critics and fans recognized that the folk and blues traditions predated rock and roll and so regarded them as purer and less commercial than rock and roll. (Muddy Waters, master of the electrified Chicago blues, was also marketed as a folk musician at this time; witness albums with such titles as *Folk Singer* and *The Real Folk Blues*.) The audience for this music typically disdained rock and roll and regarded Dylan's decision to electrify as an abandonment of "genuine" music. So they seem at a loss to comprehend the *aesthetic* motivation for his change of direction. At his second electric concert, at Forest Hills, one fan taunted him with the shouted question "Where's Ringo?" In the same vein, a reviewer remarked that fans who came for "protest songs . . . got the Beatles, instead."[20] The Beatles still represented rock and roll, although not for very much longer. Dylan represented something else, supposedly more artistic even if *musically* simpler. "Folk records" were not perceived as commercial and mass-marketed popular music. The irony here is that Dylan was aggressively marketed by Columbia Records, and "Blowin' in the Wind" had been a major hit for Peter, Paul and Mary in 1963.[21]

It is difficult, today, to grasp the anger that was directed against Dylan. His concerts throughout 1965 and 1966 were a nightly repeat of the turmoil that had greeted Stravinsky's *Le Sacre du Printemps* in 1913. Many critics began talking about a "new" and "old" Dylan, as though discussing two different people. One letter to *Sing Out!* took the form of an obituary: "His last illness, which may be termed an acute case of avarice, severely affected Mr. Dylan's sense of values, ultimately causing his untimely death."[22] And there is that sublime moment, preserved on the so-called Royal Albert Hall bootleg, when someone screams "Judas!" and Dylan drawls "I don't believe you. You're a liar!" before launching a majestic version of his current hit, "Like a Rolling Stone."[23] In retrospect, it seems that popular-music audiences were not yet prepared for the possibility of artists who were stylistically adept and willing to abandon genres as frequently as a snake sheds its skin. In short, while Dylan's songs were acknowledged to be lyrically complex and challenging, the audience was not prepared for any *musical* challenge or surprise. Hence, their sense of betrayal and ensuing anger.

So what has all of this to do with rock as distinct from rock and roll? Although Dylan never hid the fact, his musical inspirations were originally country, blues, and rock and roll; inspired by Little Richard, he had played rock-and-roll piano in a number of bands (even playing one or two professional gigs with Bobby Vee) *before* metamorphosing into a folkie about the time he went to the University of Minnesota. As implied by the title of his first genuinely electrified album, *Bringing It All Back Home* (1965), Dylan was returning to his formative influence, rock and roll. But the result *wasn't* rock and roll. Reviewing Dylan's electric debut at the Newport Folk Festival that year, Paul Nelson reacted by writing "Dylan doing his new R&R, R&B, R&? stuff knocked me out . . ."[24] Nelson's inability to pinpoint the style — the "R&?" is most telling — was soon resolved when Dylan's new style, as well as that of his many imitators, was dubbed "folk rock." (Dylan himself hated the label.) But within six months, Nelson characterized one Dylan recording as "pure joyous rock."[25] No hybrid term was sought; a more encompassing category was now recognized.

I do not know that Nelson's was the first print use of "rock" in the relevant sense, but surely it was one of the earliest. By April 1967, Paul Williams noted that "very few people have the balls to talk about 'rock and roll' anymore. . . . rock has *absorbed* mainstream music."[26] A few months later, a reviewer discussing the Monterey International Pop Festival insisted that it was mainly a rock festival, with minimal pop. But the distinction was still elusive: "I think creative pop is rock, just as creative pop thirty years ago was jazz (or swing)."[27] Robert Christgau soon observed that "a term like 'rock' is impossibly vague; it denotes, if anything, something historical rather than aesthetic. 'Mass art' and 'kitsch' are pretty vague as well."[28]

At the time, with rock styles proliferating in every direction, it must have seemed that there was no unifying aesthetic. Hence Christgau's subsequent "historical" stab at it as music influenced by the Beatles and Dylan (and today, their influence twice and thrice removed). Within a short time critics recognized a plethora of rock styles, including soul, Memphis soul, the blues revival, Motown, the San Francisco sound, acid, heavy metal, and then country rock, art rock, jazz rock, southern rock, swamp rock, and a myriad of others which proliferated in the decades since. These were distinct styles of *performing* the music. Critics often united them under the umbrella of rock on cultural grounds, treating them as manifestations of youth and leisure culture but seldom as a movement with a distinct aesthetic.[29]

But a crucial step was Dylan's melding of previously distinct categories through his return to rock and roll after mastering the craft of songwriting in other idioms. The result was not the rock and roll of his youth; the albums *Bringing It All Back Home, Highway 61 Revisited,* and *Blonde on Blonde* are steeped in blues more than rock and roll, and while "Like a Rolling Stone" may be based on the changes to "La Bamba," its six-minute length was itself a leap beyond earlier rock and roll. And while the 1965 Newport Folk Festival and subsequent tour publicized Dylan's new sound, Dylan "went public" only after becoming confident with it in the studio: *Bringing It All Back Home* and *Highway 61 Revisited* were already completed, and the recording sessions for the latter were instrumental in fixing the instrumentation that he subsequently adopted for live performances.

Dylan's trademark sixties sound was itself an accident of the recording studio, particularly the combination of piano and swirling electric organ so distinctive on *Highway 61*.[30] But it would be a mistake to suppose that Dylan conceived of the songs and then arranged them. In 1977 he said:

> The closest I ever got to the sound I hear in my mind was on individual bands in the *Blonde on Blonde* album. It's that thin, that wild mercury sound. It's metallic and bright gold . . . That's my particular sound. . . . It was in the album before that, too [*Highway 61*]. Also in *Bringing It All Back Home*. That's the sound I've always heard.[31]

Dylan suggests that he already heard this sound in his mind's ear, and that these recordings were his most successful approximations of it. He does not point to his live performances of that period, and he did not arrive at it by experimenting in live performance. Dylan and his contemporaries are sometimes disdained for their musical illiteracy; their musical sources were other records. As composers, they composed with sound, not in notation. The songs on *Blonde on Blonde* were composed at the recording sessions themselves, evidently to take advantage of the available resources. The cream of Nashville's studio musicians were paid to sit and play cards while Dylan composed. The resulting collision of blues, country, and rock and roll was a unique sound: "dandy's blues . . . the sound of a man trying to stand up in a drunken boat and, for the moment, succeeding."[32]

The Beatles were simultaneously erasing stylistic boundaries by moving in the opposite direction, from live rock and roll to studio craft. A disorderly group of rock and rollers, the Beatles bashed out dance music in Liverpool and then Hamburg from 1957 to 1962: "It was the coarsest, most brutal rockabilly, straight legacy of Presley, Perkins, Richard, and Vincent."[33] But after their astounding chart success and their frustration with the new constraints of touring, playing the same half-hour set every night to screaming fans who couldn't tell when they were out of tune, they learned to master the recording studio. By 1965, in part influenced by Dylan's songwriting, they produced what is arguably their first *rock* album, *Rubber Soul,* soon followed by *Revolver.* The albums were foreshadowed earlier that year by an individual album track on *Help!* There, among some very basic rock and roll, they placed Paul McCartney's ballad "Yesterday." Featuring only McCartney and a string quartet, there is no trace of rock and roll except, perhaps, in his vocal phrasing and heavy accent. (That very same afternoon, McCartney screamed the fierce rock and roll of "I'm Down.")[34] The stylistic flexibility achieved in 1965 meant that rock and roll was now only one of their many styles, no longer identical with the general aesthetic movement in popular music then under way.

Although 1965 was the crucial year for both Dylan and the Beatles, I do not mean to suggest that the rock aesthetic of creativity through recording was born that year. If we are to choose a year and place, the best candidate is 1954, with Elvis Presley at Sun studios in Memphis. But these recordings are so strongly identified with rock and roll that it is only in hindsight that the style, rock and roll (actually rockabilly), can be distinguished from the recording aesthetic which characterizes rock music generally. Sun studios refined and popularized the rockabilly *style* (so much so that Roy Orbison was forced to rehash "Ooby

Dooby" for years, instead of creating the ballads that he loved and which became his trademark). In contrast, the rock aesthetic invites stylistic flexibility and innovation that supersedes rock and roll. In short, rock is popular music of the second half of the twentieth century which is essentially dependent on recording technology for its inception and dissemination. Its major *musical* developments have almost always occurred in recording studios, as in the cases of Presley, Dylan, and the Beatles.

Elvis at Sun

At the height of his reign, [Phil] Spector's authority over a song was not unlike that of Frank Capra, Federico Fellini, or George Lucas's authority on celluloid.
— Mark Ribowsky, Spector's biographer[35]

The next stage in my analysis is to show that rock and roll, as personified by Elvis in the Sun sessions, employs recording as its primary medium. Records, not simply songs or performances, are the relevant object of critical attention. Elvis was the voice of rock and roll, but the achievement (and we must remember that it is not his alone) transcends the merger of styles identified with rock and roll. The merger also involved an aesthetic of recorded sound; the musical works do not exist apart from the recording process itself. Bill Haley's "Crazy Man Crazy" (1953) had already scored a national hit by merging elements of rhythm and blues with country and western. With the Sun sessions, the sound of the recordings was as relevant as any other aspect of the interpretation, something not evident about Haley's recordings. By gradually reconceptualizing the *process* of popular musical creation and of audience access, rock and roll pointed the way toward rock music as ontologically richer than traditionally allowed of music.[36]

It is likely that Presley would never have become a professional musician were it not for recording technology. As with Dylan's decision to tour with a band only after creating two rock albums, Presley quit his job as a truck driver only after public acceptance of several records. He then learned to perform live (to *re*-create) what had been created in the studio. When Presley left Sun for RCA, he added a drummer, D. J. Fontana. Fontana recalls Presley's instructions at early recording sessions to "play it simple because some of these guys in those club bands can't learn this stuff if it gets too complicated." Cover bands would need to play "exactly what we're playing."[37] In short, Presley understood that the records were the model for future performances, not just his own but those of club bands across the country.

Dave Marsh has written about the implications of the Sun sessions:

> Elvis, Scotty, Bill and Sam built their music in the recording studio, the first time anyone had ever created a major musical innovation except by working it out in front of a live audience or by laboriously composing it on paper first. Magnetic recording tape had only recently made it possible to do a take of a song, listen to a playback, analyze it, then try another rendition and repeat the process. . . . This approach was liberating in two ways — it freed them from the inhibiting effects of audience disapproval while their music developed, and it liberated them from a dependence on tyrannous songwriters since their new style would obliterate any previous version . . . none of the members was a skilled songwriter.[38]

Marsh rightly emphasizes that the trial-and-error process facilitated by the new technology was essential to Presley's development, just as it would be for the Beatles and so many others in the next decade. The Sun recordings were collaborative reinterpretations of familiar songs, which the three musicians performed over and over, altering the tempo here, the melody there, the phrasing elsewhere, surveying take after take until they arrived at a synthesis that was strikingly original.

On the second point, that the recording process freed them from "dependence on tyrannous songwriters," Marsh is less secure. If he means that the interpreters become co-composers with the songwriters, no longer revealing the musical work through their performance but generating a new musical work by transforming the song while fixing it on vinyl, Marsh makes an important point. Elvis, Scotty, and Bill were dependent on songwriters and took preexisting music as their basis. The best Sun recordings, particularly "Good Rockin' Tonight," "Mystery Train," and "Blue Moon," successfully "obliterate" previous interpretations by erasing any distinction between the performance and the musical work. This music unifies an interpretation with a specific sound medium as inseparable parts of a single work; each listener who learns these songs through these recordings grasps every aspect as properties of a *total musical work*. The timbre of Presley's voice, the phrasing, even the sound of his voice *on that particular day,* is as much a part of the musical work as the melody or the syncopation.[39] (Or consider the Beatles' recording of "Twist and Shout." The raw sound of

Lennon's voice at the end of a twelve-hour recording session is essential to its effect.)

As Peter Guralnick observes of Elvis's first single, "That's All Right,"

> It sounds easy, unforced, joyous, spontaneous. . . . There is a crisp authority to Scotty Moore's lead guitar, Elvis's rhythm is ringing and clear, the bass gallops along in slap-happy fashion. . . . The sound is clean, without affectation or clutter.[40]

Guralnick notes of the Sun sound generally,

> The sound was always clean, never cluttered, with a kind of thinness and manic energy . . . The sound was further bolstered by a generous use of echo, a homemade technique refined independently by Sam Phillips and Leonard Chess in Chicago with sewer pipes and bathroom acoustics.[41]

In short, these recordings epitomized rock and roll as a performance style, but they also embodied a new *sound* as an essential quality of the musical work.

The idea of a new "sound" is also present in Greil Marcus's analysis of the Sun sessions.

> Each song is clear, direct, uncluttered, and blended into something coherent. There is that famous echo, slapping back at the listener . . . The sound is all presence, as if Black and Moore each took a step straight off the record and Elvis was somehow squeezed right into the mike.[42]

It is not simply the rock-and-roll interpretations which are striking; interpretative originality would hardly impress us with such force, after some forty years. They capture great performances, but we can respond to them today only as great *recordings*. Sam Phillips forged a new sound that highlights Elvis's interpretative abilities, and it is hardly possible to separate the quality of immediacy, created by the recorded sound, from the purely "musical" aspects of these interpretations.

Finally, there is the testimony of Robert Ray, who likewise emphasizes that the Sun recordings were records first rather than recordings of musical performances:

> the performances that began rock & roll, Elvis's Sun recordings, could not be reproduced in any live situation except a very small and empty (to permit reverberation) room, since Elvis's acoustic

guitar and Bill Black's acoustic bass simply could not be heard. (Having grown up in Memphis, I know. I attended several early Elvis performances.)[43]

The Fender electric bass was not introduced until 1958, allowing adequate bass sound in live performance. But no amount of engineering has ever allowed a concert situation to recapture the intimacy that studio recordings offer the human voice.

This attention to the Sun sessions is offered to show that the attraction is not merely "a beautiful male animal who swung his pelvis." As John Lennon insists, the attraction is in the records themselves, including qualities generated by the very process of recording. As Lennon says in this chapter's epigraph, the basic energy is on the records. Recording technology allowed Sam Phillips and the three musicians to develop their ideas in private and over time, but it also shaped the result as a specifically recorded sound. They did not simply work out fresh arrangements of songs to be recreated in subsequent performances; their arrangement transforms "Mystery Train" into rock and roll, but the arrangement is merely one aspect of its aesthetic impact. *How* it sounds (e.g., the echo, the "presence"), how it sounds when we play the records, is due to decisions made in the recording process. These qualities are expressive elements and relevant features of the musical work. How else shall we understand, as praise, a critical evaluation of the Velvet Underground's *White Light/White Heat* which says "the basically crummy mix only highlighted the abrasiveness of the entire structure"?[44] And what are we to make of a review that criticizes Warren Zevon's self-titled 1976 album on the grounds that "the overall sound has the same somewhat flat, dull finish that is the chief flaw of [Jackson] Browne's own solo albums"?[45] The critical vocabulary could be that of a specialist in Renaissance painting, appraising the patina of an old master.

Even before the emergence of rock around 1965, producers like Ahmet Ertegun and Phil Spector self-consciously approached records as sculptured sound, and not merely as rock and roll that happened to be recorded. Spector's celebrated "wall of sound" is particularly noteworthy. The overall sound is so significant to the effect that their recent digital remix has been cause for complaint:

> longtime fans may have trouble acclimating themselves to the pristine digital sound. Spector remixed all the tracks in mono (naturally), and I can't imagine CD renderings sounding any better. What's missing, though, is the hot, groove-bursting *fullness* of the original vinyl 45s — a quality that digital technology tends only to

"correct." Thus there's an alien clarity to some of the early material, especially on headphones . . .[46]

Spector's monolithic sound was emulated, as noted in this description
of Bruce Springsteen's "epic" *Born to Run* (1975):

> all this talk of epic comes down to sound. . . . Jon Landau, Mike
> Appel, and Springsteen produced *Born to Run* in a style as close to
> mono as anyone can get these days; the result is a sound full of
> grandeur. For all it owes to Phil Spector, it can be compared only
> to the music of Bob Dylan & the Hawks made onstage in 1965 and
> '66. With that sound, Springsteen has achieved something very
> special.[47]

Anyone who has heard the songs from *Born to Run* performed live, or
in subsequent recordings of live performances, knows what the reviewer is stressing. The sound of the record is part of the musical work.
Live performances of the songs, particularly of the songs "Born to
Run" and "Backstreets," are looser and sound cruder; it can make for
fine rock and roll, but the "grandeur" is lacking.

The live performances of these songs stand to the recorded as the film
and Broadway adaptations of a novel stand to one another. More precisely, John Steinbeck's *The Grapes of Wrath,* its John Ford film adaptation (1940), and the recent adaptation of the novel as a theatrical play
are three distinct but related works. The *song* "Born to Run" is a
musical work with many performances, in the same sense that the play
has many performances. While the song appears as the fifth track on
Born to Run, that track (the *recording*) is a distinct musical work in its
own right, in the same way that Ford's film is a distinct artwork in its
own right. Others have made this point, of course, including Jim Curtis
and Stephen Davies. But where Curtis singles out the *Sgt. Pepper* album (1967) as the decisive move that "obsolesces live musical performance," I want to push this central element of the rock aesthetic back a
decade.[48] And where Davies says that "works of this type are not common or typical of musical works in general," one must remember that
what's typical depends on context. In rock, musical works with a status
"like that of a film" are perfectly common.[49]

Ontological Categories

I have been arguing that listeners immersed in the rock tradition regard
the sound of rock recordings as highly relevant to their impact and

meaning. Although the argument is based on selective examples, this is not a weakness. "Rock" is a vague term and is best understood by acquaintance with paradigm cases, and my examples are as central to rock as any claiming that label. Pushing the argument forward, we see that "performance" and "song" are often awkward categories for rock. Traditionally, critics and theorists have distinguished between the musical work and its performances. "The work" is assumed to be a composition and receives a disproportionate share of theoretical attention. The prevailing view is that characteristics of different performances do not belong to the composition. Furthermore, many of its properties will not be apparent in performances.[50]

Prior to our own century, musical works were usually known through performances that varied widely from one another in their interpretation of it. But not always. There were some mechanical devices for generating music, ranging from music boxes to player pianos, and some gifted souls could recover musical works solely by reading scores. In this tradition, the musical work is abstracted from the performances by determining which features are common to a range of different interpretations. (Knowledge of a score is often helpful in guiding the listener.) This extraction process requires some degree of familiarity with the relevant musical norms. Taking Bach's thirty *Goldberg Variations* as a single, multipart work, it is one musical work that has had thousands of performances. The performances are individuated by time and place (by when and where they are performed). They usually vary from one another in other ways, as when two performances are at different tempos and are played on different instruments. Suppose the *Goldberg Variations* are performed on a harpsichord and then a piano. Despite the very different timbres of the two performances, despite the presence of rubato in the piano rendition, and despite any differences in tempo, knowledgeable listeners will recognize them as performances of a single work. In Western musical tradition, the musical work has generally been identified with the sound-structure, not the sounds themselves. Here, the work is a melody and its variations.

Most rock criticism focuses on a different work: recordings are the primary link between the rock artist and the audience, and the primary object of critical attention. These musical works are *played* on appropriate machines, not performed. Consequently, rock cuts across the typical dichotomy of musical work versus its myriad performances. The relevant work (the recording) frequently manifests another work, usually a song, without being a performance of that song.

But no specific *sound* belongs to the *Goldberg Variations,* since the timbre of the harpsichord is not essential to it. The fact that Emerson, Lake, and Palmer play classical standards on rock instruments revolts many listeners from both the classical and rock camps, but insofar as they follow the score, their performances are genuine instantiations of the musical works. At most, we say that they offer new arrangements of the works.

This critical apparatus does not elucidate what's going on with music that is to be played, not on instruments in live performance, but on machines. When music is conceived *as* a recording and not merely as a performance that happens to be recorded, traditional ontology does not have a place for the musical work, except perhaps as manifesting an arrangement of a musical work. Roman Ingarden acknowledges the problem but brushes it off: "The duplication of a particular performance of a musical work by means of the phonograph or radio introduces special problems which we will not examine more closely here."[51] But few rock recordings consist of "duplication of a particular performance." Most of them collate features from many partial performances (a vocal track here, a guitar solo there), none of which are performances of the complete work.

Since two musical performances will differ in their auditory qualities while counting as performances of the same musical work, no musical work has all the properties of its various performances. Following Stephen Davies, we can say that the performances are "thicker" than compositions. But which properties belong essentially to musical works? According to Davies, musical works

> do not have any *single* ontological character. Some musical works are thick with properties, others are thinner — some works include the performance-means as part of their essential nature, and much more besides, while others are more or less pure sound structures.[52]

The *Goldberg Variations* is ontologically very thin: it can be grasped through performances on a wide variety of instruments. As long as the proper note relationships are present, widely different approaches are equally "accurate." But Davies proposes that some works, particularly more recent ones, have narrower parameters. They are ontologically thicker, in the sense that performers have fewer options with respect to performance means if the performance is to count as an instance of *that* work.

If baroque music offers a paradigm of the ontologically thin, the high classical era was already moving toward thicker works. Beethoven explicitly counseled against anyone else transcribing his works, yet Liszt made piano transcriptions of Beethoven's orchestral works. We make a distinction here that we do not make for Bach's *Goldberg Variations.* When Liszt played a Beethoven piano sonata, he was playing the very same work that had been played by Beethoven, but when Liszt played his own transcription of a Beethoven symphony, he was playing a new, derivative work. Only someone who was very well schooled in classical orchestral music *and* in the limits of the piano would be able to grasp Beethoven's symphony from the piano performance. Beethoven's melodic themes and variations are all present in the transcription, but we cannot reduce a symphony to its themes and variations.[53] Conversely, attempts to complete Mahler's sketches for his unfinished tenth symphony have generated several versions, each of which can be regarded as a distinct musical work derived from the same musical germ.

Consider a more radical case. Arranging Ravel's string quartet, let us say for high school marching band, would result in music with an entirely different timbre (not to mention a loss of dexterity). Although the musical line of each of the four instruments in the quartet could be played by different groups of instruments in the marching band, Ravel's work could not be "recovered" from the resulting performance. The musical work is insufficiently "disambiguated from other works" in the marching band performance. In both cases we have a new, albeit derivative, musical work.

As Davies observes, "transcriptions parasitize the identity of their models" and so "are not treated as interchangeable with the original. Instead, they are treated *and advertised* as works which stand in their own right."[54] Of course, the mere fact that they *are* treated as distinct does not prove that they *should* be, but the fact that they are *advertised* (in the broadest sense) as such is a reason to suppose that they should be. A strong reason to treat Duchamp's *Fountain* as a work of art is that he advertised it as one. A strong reason to treat John Cage's *4′33″* as a musical work is that he advertised it as such.

Applying this analysis to the distinction between rock music and the rock-and-roll performance style, the latter tends to favor songs that are ontologically thin. As with any popular song, the musical parameters have to be broad enough to provide wide latitude in performance options. You need a piano for a Beethoven piano concerto, but not for "Whole Lotta Shakin' Goin' On." Add a saxophone solo to a Mozart aria and it no longer counts as an accurate performance; do the same with a Cole Porter or Beatles song and it still counts as a performance of that song. Two very different rock-and-roll performances of the same song may both count as accurate, because songs are "disambiguated" or differentiated by little more than chord progression and basic melody. As Davies says, "in the absence of highly developed systems of notation, there is a tendency for musical works to become simpler and for improvisational and performance-skills to become more important for their own sake."[55] The performance-means characteristic of rock and roll can be applied to a wide range of songs, as can the general recording aesthetic of rock.

In contrast, as the objects of critical attention in rock, the *recordings* are ontologically thick. We generally know the music by playing tapes, albums, or compact discs. When rock music is discussed, the relevant musical work is not simply the song being performed. To employ terminology currently in vogue, we can say that recordings are the "primary texts" of this music. Consider Bruce Springsteen's *Born to Run* (1975). As a musical work, it is "recovered" by the audience by playing tapes, LPs, and compact discs (much as one "recovers" a film by watching a screening). If one listens to *Born to Run* in all three formats, one will notice slight differences in the sound quality, but what makes each count as an "authentic" presentation of *Born to Run* is that each is causally derived from a single master tape produced in 1975 by the team of Jon Landau, Mike Appel, and Bruce Springsteen. One can know *Born to Run* only by playing something derived from that master tape.

While one can have access to a song through a score (one can learn "Born to Run" and the other seven songs from sheet music), one cannot know the album in that way. If the master tape and all recordings derived from it become lost, it will be unrecoverable as a musical work. However detailed our score and however much we know about the production of the album, essential properties of *Born to Run* would not be recovered. The precise sound of the album is part of its impact, as is the timbre of Springsteen's voice at that point in his life, filtered through echo and buried in the mix; if we do not have these, we do not have the musical work that Springsteen wanted us to hear. And we have access to the musical work that Springsteen created *just in case* our copies are *appropriately* derived from that tape. Were Springsteen to rerecord the album and we were to hear the results, I suspect we would say, like Prufrock, that the result is not it at all.

Originals, Falsifications, Versions

The old picture in a new frame. — Jimmy Page describing
the digital remasters of Led Zeppelin[56]

If the "sound" of the recording is part of the musical work, there is a
temptation to say that adaptation of the recording to a new medium for
delivering that sound must be a falsification of that work. The argument runs as follows. When *Born to Run* and Phil Spector records are
recovered by the audience by way of a sound reproduction technology
other than the one intended, and where that adaptation changes aural
qualities of the music, we aren't listening to *Born to Run* or Phil Spector
anymore. The CD of *Born to Run* is derived from the original tape, but
not appropriately derived from it. Therefore, the CD version of a predigital recording is no longer the genuine item.[57] It is, like a forgery, a
separate work altogether. This view is not my own, but I will pause in
the larger argument to consider it.

Neil Young provides a pithy summary:

> My album *Everybody Knows This Is Nowhere* is now available on
> CD, but it's not as good as the original, which came out in 1969.
> Listening to a CD is like looking through a screen window. . . . It's
> an insult to the brain and the heart and feelings to have to listen to
> this and think it's music.[58]

Young never suggests that *recording* is inherently problematic or a
falsification of music, and he specifically refers to the vinyl incarnation
of the album as "the original." His complaint is that the digital remix
reduces his album to "what's dominant at each moment." The CD
stands to the album as a photographic reproduction of a painting
stands to the painting: a copy that should not be confused with the
genuine article. He implies that digital remastering is a forgery.

While declawing this proposal demands some hair-splitting, it is not
without a larger purpose. Different meanings accrue to different versions of cultural products, largely because they offer us different features or different emphases among features. This is particularly true of
popular culture, where many different versions of a work may circulate
simultaneously. You and I cannot belong to a common audience or
share thoughts about a work's meaning unless we are responding to
instantiations of the *same* work. If we are in the same audience at a
performance, or look at the same painting in a museum, no problem
arises. But in the age of mechanical reproduction and manipulation, we
are often on less secure ground.

The heart of Young's complaint is not simply that the digital remix is an *inferior* listening experience (although it may well be). In its current state, a view of the Parthenon is decidedly inferior compared to its appearance in the days of Socrates, but that does not mean that what we see on the Acropolis today is inauthentic or a fake. It is the original. But if Neil Young wants his audience to hear "the original" *Everybody Knows This Is Nowhere* — on vinyl — today, that will usually be a decidedly inferior listening experience. Some people keep vinyl in relatively pristine condition, but where will the new generation of Neil Young fans get their vinyl copy? At a garage sale or used record store or a Salvation Army thrift store? The average copy will sound pretty crummy.

There are many cases, Phil Spector and *Born to Run* among them, where the digital mastering is problematic. But in many cases, such as the Derek and the Dominos *Layla* remix and much of *The Story of the Clash, Vol. 1*, there are sonic improvements. Jimmy Page went back to the original preproduction tapes of the Led Zeppelin sessions to digitally remaster them, and he is right to be pleased with the resulting sound. At the same time, much of the rock audience listens to music on cassettes, with a marked deterioration of sound quality and loss of sonic detail, but no one is tempted to regard them as falsifications of the "original." Young seems to mean that even the best CD is a falsification of his album when compared with the results on good vinyl and that the remixed *Layla* or Led Zeppelin remasters, improved sound or not, are falsifications as well.

However, I am not sympathetic to the idea that these adaptations are forgeries, falsifications, or inauthentic means of knowing a recorded work. I have heard Carl Perkins on an original Sun Records 78, played with a thick stylus on a Victrola. The sound had a force and cutting edge that I have never heard elsewhere. Likewise, the *Metal Box* version of Public Image Ltd.'s second album (1980), at 45 rpm, has everything over the standard vinyl release, the American *Second Edition*. To hear Carl Perkins on a long player or *Second Edition* rather than *Metal Box* is an unfortunate concession to economics and prevailing technologies. Yet analogies with other media allowing multiple instantiations suggest that they are cases of the work.

Consider other areas where we have multiple instantiations of a work, yet where there are major differences in perceivable properties of those instantiations. The differences are not simply contingencies of the specific instantiation: different instantiations are often to be grouped as instantiating different versions of the same work. We find different translations of a single poem and revised versions of symphonies. Thomas Hardy's novel *Tess of the d'Urbervilles* was originally serialized in the *Graphic* newspaper; a longer version of the same novel was revised for publication in book form (1891), and then expanded again in its fifth edition (1912). Films are also known in many versions. Jean Renoir's film *The Rules of the Game* can no longer be seen in its longest commercial version (1939); its subsequent restoration (1959) was pieced together bit by bit from recovered rushes but about a minute is missing. Films have properties in some theaters that they lack in others. For instance, *Apocalypse Now* (1979) was initially released in selected theaters that could handle its special sound-track mix of three sound sources. How many seeing that film today — generally at home on video with a different screen ratio — experience the unnerving feel of helicopters roaring in from behind?

In the performing arts, performances are grouped according to interpretive strategies; there are "productions" in theater and "arrangements" in music. (Earlier, we saw that there are rock and nonrock arrangements of the same song.) We view Shakespeare in shortened versions and hear Beethoven's symphonies without all the repeats specified in the score. Thus, even the bowdlerized *Romeo and Juliet* read in American high schools instantiates that play rather than counting as a forgery or different work. The text of a play is akin to a musical score, notating a work rather than being the work. The score-copies of musical works and editions of a play often come to us in different versions, so that no single edition offers definitive criteria for counting performances as genuine.

In short, we allow for an extremely wide latitude of variation and interpretation in identifying works. In specific cases we may always remain vexed by the problem of deciding when variation or interpretation crosses the line and counts as a new but genealogically related work. Well-informed intuition may be all that we ever have to do the job. What must we be informed about? Mainly the practices of the tradition in which the performance/instantiation arises. In nonperforming arts that allow multiple genuine instantiations of works, we tolerate a considerable latitude of variation among versions.

I have been pushing the analogy between cinema and recorded rock music. The practice of releasing films in a range of versions or "cuts" has obvious parallels to releasing the digitalized *Born to Run* and Phil Spector records. And films are more like novels or poems than musical compositions or plays. In the performing arts, *each* specific instantiation — each performance — is treated as a new interpretation of it. In contrast, film is "shown" or "screened," never performed. We do not regard each showing as a fresh interpretation. For music meant to be known through recordings, we should look to the nonperforming arts to guide us to criteria of authenticity.

While Hardy rewrote some of *Tess,* Renoir did not reshoot any of *Rules of the Game.* He merely oversaw that process of editing it together from the pieces that could be found. But the physical source of the later version was the same as for the 1939 release, and for this reason we count it as the same film and not a "remake" (a new film based on an older one). In 1939, Renoir sanctioned the release of two shortened versions of *Rules of the Game* (cut to eighty and ninety minutes) that did violence to the plot and characterizations in the film. His own character, Octave, was all but eliminated. Nonetheless, even these truncated releases are instantiations of that film, just as anyone who read *Tess* in its original serialization read a shorter but no less authentic instantiation of that novel. The initial commercial version of *Blade Runner* contains narration by Harrison Ford and some extra footage at the end (a scene of a car driving through mountains, actually acquired from footage left from *The Shining*). These were removed from the "director's cut," and other footage was restored. So although an instantiation's causal history is central to its authenticity, the integrity of the physical source cannot be our sole criterion for counting something as a version of the same work. Causal history must be understood in a way that includes the intentions of those engaged in editing, restoration, adaptation, or other changes which produce new versions.

A further complication is that new versions often involve some sort of substitution in the presentational medium used for instantiating the work. The original readers of a serialized novel are faced with the brute fact that they cannot skip ahead to the end to find out "whodunnit" or to see who lives happily ever after. (When the first installment of Edith Wharton's *The House of Mirth* appeared in *Scribner's* in January of 1905, Wharton herself did not yet know that the main character would die in the closing chapters.) But today we can choose our own pace and can jump ahead, encountering any number of changes made when the author revised the text. Be that as it may, the conventions of reading literature say that both audiences have read the same novel. Similarly, unless we say that the English translation of a non-English text is a version of that very same work, we make hash out of the very idea of translation. And I have never seen a compelling argument that every interpretation is a new work. One might qualify having read Rimbaud or Tolstoy by saying "I've read it in translation," but certainly the translation rendered access to one work rather than another, and the reader intends to read that one rather than some other.

To know how literature and films are made and distributed is to know that there are versions and editions, and even the practice of canonizing some as more "definitive" than others does not make forgeries of the less definitive ones. In any medium allowing multiple instantiations (whether in the performing or nonperforming arts), the identity of specific cases cannot depend on any specific set of perceptual properties appearing in every one of them. With films, transfer to video is not thought to generate a forgery or different work even though the seemingly essential property of motion picture projection is lost. We must be prepared to tolerate considerable variance among them based on all sorts of contingencies in their causal histories. When Bob Dylan's "Like a Rolling Stone" was released as a single in 1965, the first three minutes were on the A side of the 45 and the remaining three minutes on the B side. The need to flip it over in midsong disrupts its flow and impact, but the 45 was hardly a "fake" or illegitimate instantiation for that reason.

In short, an instantiation can be quite corrupt or deficient and still count as an instantiation. The fact that some versions offer less desirable modes of recovering a work does not itself make them inauthentic. As John Passmore argues about the status of performances, "we cannot say that only good performances count as performances of *Swan Lake*." To do so would be to treat "poor performance" as an oxymoron, which is not our practice.[59] The very act of complaining about it presupposes that we are talking about *the same* work. Likewise, defective presentation (a flawed reel of a film or a misprinted page in a novel) are to be counted as instantiating the film or novel, not as separate works.

Passmore goes on to say that "it is only when the performance is so bad that it would be impossible to judge the work from it that we can refuse to name it" (that is, to say it instantiates *Swan Lake*). But this cannot be right; we must first know *which* work is instantiated in order to say that it is defective. If the performance is "so bad" that we cannot judge the work, it does not become some *other* work, does it? It is, after all, *as* a performance of some distinct work that we judge it to be defective; specifically, that of which we judge it to be a bad instantiation. (We could be mistaken and regard something as a bad instantiation because we misattribute it, as when a friend misread a title in a ballet program and it affected her judgment of the dance piece.) Appropriate evaluation depends on identity and not vice versa.

A second argument bolsters the preceding one. An incompetent remake of a film or an incompetent set of variations on another composer's theme does not devalue the earlier work. These are separate works. But an instantiation of the same work will sometimes devalue that work. This is most obvious in cases where an art form does not allow multiple instantiations: a botched cleaning of a painting can ruin it. Something similar can occur in arts that allow for multiple instantiations. The restoration of the twenty-first chapter to American editions of Anthony Burgess's *A Clockwork Orange* certainly changes its meaning, for the worse. Colorization of film is not loathsome because it replaces one work with a new work. The problem is that colorized versions (containing what amount to arbitrary changes in the film's look) squeeze the black-and-white prints out of circulation.[60] In saying that a digital remaster is a travesty of an older recording, one already implies that it instantiates that work. It is neither a fake nor a forgery (special cases of being a distinct work).

Just as Neil Young cannot mean the CD of *Everybody Knows* is a different work on the grounds that it is a bad version, we must take care to separate the issue of an instantiation's identity from the issue of its quality. Passmore heads toward firmer ground when he offers two criteria for establishing an instantiation's identity in nonperforming arts; he invites us to generalize from the case of literature:

> it must be a genealogical descendant of the copy-text [or analogue] of that work and must not differ from it in ways which would affect my judgment. The first criterion is the crucial one, but the second criterion rules out corrupt versions or bad translations . . .[61]

The first criterion focuses on the cause of the instantiation, while the second focuses on exhibited qualities of the result (the product or effect, one might say).

The first criterion, properly interpreted in light of the medium in question, is indeed the crucial one. But the second reintroduces the suggestion that we should evaluate how good the version or instantiation is in order to determine whether it instantiates the work at all. Furthermore, it is too loose to be helpful, since qualities that will affect "my" judgment may be lost upon "your" judgment. Worse, why is it only a deterioration that counts against its being an authentic instantiation? When Thomas Hardy rewrites *Tess* or a director reedits a film or a composer rescores a symphony, altering it in ways that *improve* it, why doesn't this count against the genuineness of the new instantiations, as well?

Older rock music's digital transfer is not the first time that issues of authenticity have arisen in terms of recording formats. A similar issue arose when mono gave way to stereo. However terrible "simulated stereo" sounds, the sixties vogue for it gave us botched restorations rather than forgeries. Likewise, as stereo caught on and producers created separate mono and stereo mixes of the same tracks, several albums were created on which distinctly different versions were generated from the same master tapes. *The Beatles* (1968, the so-called, "White Album") is a case in point. John Lennon's scream "I've got blisters on my fingers!" at the end of "Helter Skelter" is absent from the mono mix; the mono version of "Don't Pass Me By" is two seconds shorter than the stereo yet there is more of the fiddle at the end, a result of speeding up the tape so that the whole track is pitched higher; each version of "Piggies" has a different set of pig snorts at the end. On Bob Dylan's *Highway 61 Revisited* (1965), "It Takes a Lot to Laugh, It Takes a Train to Cry" has a harmonica track on the stereo mix that is absent from the rarer mono release. Since these differences do not make one version less authentic than another, I do not see why digital remixes are not genuine instantiations.

There are, however, many remixes that constitute distinct works. But in these cases there has been an intention to produce something that is to be treated as a distinct work, usually signaled by the fact that the remix is given a separate title. Paula Abdul's second album, *Shut Up and Dance (The Dance Mixes)* (1990), consisted entirely of remixes of tracks from her hit debut *Forever Your Girl* (1988); the same year, Fine Young Cannibals released *The Raw and the Remix,* again featuring radically revamped versions of earlier tracks. Brian Eno's most recent collection of songs, *Nerve Net* (1992), was released in tandem with a set of twelve remixes of two tracks; the set of remixes is longer than the "original" album. But each remix is assigned a separate title. Bruce Springsteen's biggest seller, *Born in the U.S.A.* (1984), was followed by four remixes of "Cover Me," two of "Dancing in the Dark," and three of the title track. All were done by Arthur Baker and specified that they were "special versions" that were "based on original production by" the team that assembled the album. Taken as a set, the remixes are as long as the album.

While each of these is genealogically linked to another recording (the "original"), each involves an attempt to create a distinct end-product from a common source. While they are audibly different from the originals, audible differences are insufficient to make them distinct works. It seems that both genealogy *and* intention are required to distinguish one work from another when we are dealing with nonperforming arts that have multiple genuine instantiations. The remixes just described are advertised as such, and the audience is invited to treat them as separate works. As limiting cases, they remind us of rock's collaborative urge. The remixes are usually the work of someone other than the original producer(s). So in appealing to intention as a criteria for deciding whether something counts as a different work, I do not appeal to some occult or inaccessible quality such as a mental state. The intentions of others are known by reference to their behaviors and statements, and in these cases we have clear evidence of an intention to generate a distinct work. In the case of digital remastering of older material, we do not.

Let us wind up by looking at some related and borderline cases. The first is the remake under the guise of someone's "greatest hits." These usually come about when an artist changes record companies; I once made the mistake of buying the Coasters' *Sixteen Greatest Hits* on the Trip label and received sixteen atrocious remakes. It was not the "Yakety Yak" I remembered. Similarly, after Roy Orbison's "In Dreams" was highlighted in David Lynch's *Blue Velvet* (1986), Orbison released *In Dreams: The Greatest Hits* on Virgin in 1987. How many record buyers knew that these were entirely new recordings of his 1960s hits, precipitated by the fact that Monument records owned the rights to the originals? Because these were new recordings by Orbison and by the Coasters, unrelated to the master tapes which yielded the "original" hits, genealogy tells us that they were new works. Because they were labeled in a manner that would tend to deceive record buyers, they are basically forgeries of earlier works.

However, the mere fact that different instantiations have the same title but distinct causal histories is not sufficient to make them forgeries. The initial stereo and mono pressings of *Highway 61 Revisited* featured a completely different take of "From a Buick Six," a difference corrected so that all subsequent pressings feature the take that was originally on the mono version. (There are therefore three different versions of the album on vinyl.) Because the stereo rarity was yanked immediately, it appears to have been an error, pure and simple. It is neither a forgery nor a version nor a work in its own right. It belongs to the distinct category of the outtake.

Finally, let us return to the idea that a single work with earlier and later versions is comparable to different editions of a novel or poem. The later versions are causally derived from the original tapes, but new elements are introduced. Here we must appeal to intention. For instance, Kate Bush stripped the vocal track from "Wuthering Heights"

(1977) and supplied a new vocal for her "best-of" *The Whole Story* (1986). These are revised versions of the same work, not new works. Because Bush made no other changes and followed the original lyric and melody, it seems appropriate to think of it as an artist's revision of an existing work, rather like painter Pierre Bonnard's practice of slipping into museums and putting a few daubs of paint on works he'd completed years earlier. Another obvious analogy is to retouching paintings of nudes in order to hide exposed genitalia. While these changes are intended as aesthetic improvements, similar cases have been generated by commercial realities. Bang Records stripped Van Morrison's line about making love in the grass from "Brown-Eyed Girl" (1967) for the single release (mono mix), replacing it with a repeat of the "laughing and a-running" line from the first verse. Pink Floyd similarly replaced the term "bullshit" with "bullblank" for copies of the single "Money" (1973) sent to radio stations.

A more radical case is the digital remastering of the Mothers of Invention's *We're Only in It for the Money* (1967) and *Cruisin' with Ruben and the Jets* (1968), to which Frank Zappa added new bass and drum parts. While Zappa regards the change as an aesthetic improvement, it was done because the original two-track master tapes had been improperly stored and had deteriorated badly. Zappa had to go back a generation to the session tapes and re-create a new master. (The situation is similar to that of restoring Renoir's *Rules of the Game*.) Since he was engaged in restoration anyway, Zappa felt it appropriate to remedy the inadequate job done with the original bass and drum parts. Except for bass and drums, there is an appropriate genealogy and the intention is to have it treated as the same work ("there was no way to leave it alone" if it was to appear on CD, Zappa says), so these seem to be new editions of the same work.[62] The same thing happened when Robert Fripp assembled the King Crimson retrospective *Frame by Frame* (1991); Fripp stripped Gordon Haskell's voice from "Cadence and Cascade" and his bass from "Bolero," replacing them with the work of more recent members of Crimson, Adrian Belew and Tony Levin. Other tracks were severely edited, generally removing improvisational segments (e.g., eight minutes of "Starless"). Fripp's justification for this tinkering is less utilitarian than Zappa's. Fripp regards these changes as aesthetic improvements consistent with providing an overview of several years' music in seventy-two minutes.

As with films and novels and poems, whether or not something counts as an authentic instantiation depends on the causal history of the copy in question. Causal history includes both the method of production of the instantiations and the intentions of those who bring them about. As a consequence, some of the properties which are peculiar to specific formats and versions may not be essential properties of the work. Those who own Led Zeppelin's fourth album and the Beatles' "White Album" on vinyl and who have a turntable with a neutral setting can play "Stairway to Heaven" and "Revolution 9" backward, hearing invocations to Satan (as well as a weather forecast) on the former and the supposed story of Paul's death in a car crash on the latter. Those who have the CD cannot. Those who have the vinyl have a work that is organized into distinct sides; those with the CD do not. By the same token, I have a copy of the Rolling Stones' *Between the Buttons* (1967) pressed on blue vinyl. The blue vinyl is a contingency of a specific pressing, and we must be prepared to acknowledge that many other properties of our versions are equally contingent, sound *quality* among them.

Autographic Musical Works

A major thrust of this analysis is its opposition to the background assumption of mainstream musicology, a discipline that posits "structural autonomy" as the ideal toward which all music — not to mention musical analysis — gravitates. Among musicologists, there is the whole tradition that Rose Subotnik calls "empiricists" and "positivists."[63] Among philosophers, there is Nelson Goodman's analysis of the ontological character of musical works. Embracing the traditional distinction between musical works and performances, Goodman identifies the work with the sound-structure specified in the score: the work that is performed is ontologically very thin.

Believing that the sound-structure *is* the work, Goodman regards music as an allographic rather than an autographic art form. The distinction concerns our criteria for determining the identity of specific objects and events as embodiments of artworks and texts. In the autographic arts, such as painting, "even the most exact duplication of it does not thereby count as genuine." Music and literature are therefore allographic, because every accurate duplication (e.g., copy or performance), by whatever means, is a genuine instantiation of that work. In music, "all correct performances are equally genuine instances of the work." For this reason, "in music, unlike painting, there is no such thing as a forgery of a known work."[64] If an art form allows forgeries of known works, it is autographic. Although some autographic arts, such as printmaking, allow multiple copies ("end-products") of a work, not every accurate duplication is a genuine instance. No matter how exactly it resembles legitimate prints, a print will be a forgery if not printed from the original plate. Photocopiers can do wonders, but a photocopy of one of Goya's etchings is not itself a Goya etching. *In the autographic arts, history of production rather than notational determination is the key to individuating the work.* It is, in the end, the decisive factor in determining authenticity.

Many have challenged the view that musical works have only those properties which are "amenable to notation." But there is little challenge to the position that music is always allographic.[65] It is assumed that any feature *not* amenable to notation (e.g., tempo specification) is not essential to the composition. Thus, a work specified for piano but played by kazoo orchestra counts as a performance of the work, provided the score's notation guides the playing. Musical works end up at the thinnest possible end of the spectrum.

Against Goodman and mainstream musicology, I think precise details of timbre and articulation can be essential properties of a musical work. Like printmaking and cinema, rock music is normally created and distributed through a multistage process in which end-products (through which the audience knows the work) are genuine only if derived causally from an appropriate first-stage entity. Printmaking is two-stage. The first stage results in the plate. Let us suppose it is etched. The end-products are the prints derived directly from that plate. Any print from that plate is genuine (an "original"). A print created by any other means, however perfect a likeness, is a forgery. Western art music is typically multistaged. As traditionally practiced, the first stage culminates in the score. Copies are then made, from which performances derive. Performances are the end-product. When end-products are produced by this process, music is allographic, since notational fidelity plays a necessary role in individuation.

The *Born to Run* album is a musical work, but it is autographic, because notational determination is entirely irrelevant to the genuineness of its instantiations. Furthermore, while I have argued that the CD version is not a forgery, *Born to Run* could be forged. (Just as a film is an autographic work even when derived from a novel, which is allographic, rock recordings are autographic works but are often derived from allographic ones.) If Springsteen or anyone else rerecords the songs on *Born to Run,* notational fidelity may occur (we may genuinely have the same eight songs in the same order), and it may resemble *Born to Run* as closely as two performances might. But it won't be *Born to Run,* the work that got Springsteen onto the covers of *Time* and *News-*

week in 1975. Notational accuracy is insufficient for access to the relevant piece of rock history.

Suppose further that it is the twenty-second century and all copies of *Born to Run* are lost, but its critical reputation survives and collectors are willing to pay huge sums to obtain a copy. So we construct a new album. We have an accurate score that notates every sound on the album, and we digitally re-create Springsteen's vocals by "sampling" his voice from other recordings that have survived. The result is not only notationally accurate, but it is "the most exact duplication" possible. To borrow Jerrold Levinson's phrase, we have a sonic *doppelgänger*. From a formalist perspective, we must have produced a genuine instance of the only relevant musical work. But the digital tape we sell to collectors as the rediscovered album will be a forgery; both the first-stage digital sequence and its audio products, the "end-products" bought by the collectors, are fakes. And this is despite the fact that we've produced a notationally accurate sequence of the eight songs, and that the *songs,* as allographic musical works, are accessible through the tapes. The tape does not provide access to the same work that Springsteen labored over for months in the studio, namely the record that he wanted his audience to hear.

The distinction between allographic and autographic has been criticized on the grounds that Goodman's explicit definition of "autographic" may not do its intended job.[66] He actually offers several slightly different formulations of the distinction. Worse, it is hard to swallow the idea that any time a musical work "duplicates" another by virtue of notational agreement, they must be the same work. The formalist credo that historical factors play *no role* in the identity of musical works is so stringent that he hardly seems to be talking about music as it exists in our world. Provided that two composers have different backgrounds "of interpretive and characterizing practices," it has been proposed that the two could produce two different musical works despite the fact that they produce identical sound structures.[67] Regarding this as a thought experiment, I agree. In actual practice, if a composer duplicates the music of a predecessor without acknowledging the influence, we suspect plagiarism (however unconscious).

But this much is clear: in order to regard paradigm cases of Western composition as allographic, we must deny that notation is the *only* factor relevant to the identity of a musical work. We should allow that historical factors must be brought to play to determine what aesthetic properties and meanings adhere to those sound structures. Adopting Levinson's alternative analysis of the distinction, that a work is allographic if a historically indicated structure is presented and autographic if notational determination plays *no* role in its genuineness, we again find that our fake *Born to Run* offers genuine instances of allographic works (the songs) while forging an autographic work.[68] So it is false that the only relevant musical works are allographic. Furthermore, musical works are not restricted to sound structures plus performance-means; that is, rock musicians compose works whose replication demands far more than structural accuracy plus various limitations on performance means.

Goodman could say the following in response: "There may indeed be forgeries of performances . . . but these, if in accordance with the score, are nevertheless genuine instances of the work."[69] What work? The eight songs, yes. *Born to Run*, no. *Born to Run* is not a performance of eight songs in a specific order. Nor is it, as Roman Ingarden assumes, mere "duplication of a particular performance." It is only accessible by playing, on machines, end-products derived from a montage of partial performances that Landau, Appel, and Springsteen combined on a strip of magnetic recording tape in 1975.[70] Consider the fifth track on the album, the title song. We hear several guitars playing simultaneously, all played by Springsteen and overdubbed one by one. As the next chapter shows, thinking that this track duplicates a particular performance is as naive as thinking that Stanley Kubrick's *2001: A Space Odyssey* visually records genuine interplanetary travel. "Born to Run" as it appears on the album *sounds* like a performance, but a genuine performance is a continuous event at a specific time and place.[71]

There is, of course, a serious limitation to thought experiments such as the fake *Born to Run* that sounds exactly like the genuine article. Presented with such a fake, we have little reason to care that it is a fake as long as it features every sonic quality of the original. An original is not always more rewarding than a fake.[72] However, the point of the example is not to establish criteria for artistic success; the point is to uncover our intuitions about distinguishing one work from another. We must not confuse the question of ontological status with value judgments. In the absence of knowledge about an object's causal history, forgeries often offer us satisfying aesthetic experiences. And even a genuine instance, such as a deteriorated painting or the tape of a Gear Daddies' album that someone dubbed for me on a cheap cassette player at low recording levels so a "ghost" of what was previously on the tape remained, may prove to be decidedly unsatisfying.

Since we live in a world where sonic doppelgängers are little more than a conceptual possibility, the thought experiment's only value is to test our basic intuitions about what counts as genuine and what counts as fake. Yet it calls attention to the distinction between an artist's musical activity and something more specific, namely the *works* that the artist *sanctions* as items for appreciation and critical evaluation. Musical activity includes everything from practicing scales to idle strumming of a guitar or trying out different chord sequences. Even if recorded, these snatches of musical activity are not performances in any usual sense; they are not put forth for appreciation. We distinguish finished from unfinished works. Bruce Springsteen put a lot of music on tape in the process of recording *Born to Run,* including a version of the title track that has a double-tracked vocal and a string section. But that completed track is not one of Springsteen's works, any more than Seurat's sketches and studies for *A Sunday Afternoon on the Island of La Grande Jatte* are further instances of that painting. Those sketches were not sanctioned by Seurat for critical appraisal, and when we look at them we understand them *as* products of his process in producing the sanctioned work. While the Derek and the Dominos *Layla* box set features unfinished tracks from the recording sessions, we are to understand that these additional tracks are not part of the work itself. (Some critics feel that this packaging does a disservice to the original album.)

If a twenty-second-century sonic doppelgänger is contrived, let us consider an actual case. Suppose you have never heard Bob Dylan's celebrated album *Blood on the Tracks* (1975). Impressed by its reputation, you give me a blank cassette and ask me for a copy. I can give you a forgery without much trouble, namely, a tape of an earlier, rejected version of the album. In this case, we will have genuine instances of the allographic works, the ten songs, but we'll have a fake *Blood on the Tracks* without having a sonic doppelgänger.[73] My tape would be the equivalent of showing you one of Seurat's preliminary studies for *La Grande Jatte* and claiming that *it* was the painting that everyone regards as his masterpiece.

Unhappy with the record shortly before its release, but after some "advance" copies were distributed, Dylan rerecorded half of the songs with a different set of musicians. These later tracks, recorded in Minnesota, sound very different from the earlier ones, recorded in New York. If I give you a tape of the earlier, rejected album, it will be consistent with the score (give or take some changes in the lyrics, but there are often discrepancies between his published lyrics and the recordings, and this is consistent with the latitude in performance of popular songs). In short, you will hear genuine instances of the ten songs. But you won't have access to the genuine work in question,

Blood on the Tracks, because you don't have a genuine end-product. It will be like looking at an artist's sketches and preliminary studies instead of the finished painting. Many of the album's aesthetic attributes will be different (most notably for "Idiot Wind").

Because rock is almost exclusively a tradition of popular song, and popular songs are allographic and ontologically very thin, there is a tendency to downplay the ontological "thickness" of recordings as the unit of critical attention. Many efforts to dismiss rock music as derivative, primitive, and musically simple will strike us as misguided attempts to grasp rock exclusively as an allographic art form. Those who disdain rock typically respond only to the songs and performances, ignoring relevant properties and values like instrumental mix, stereo placement of various elements, echo on the voice, and even how ragged or nasal the singer's voice was at the time of the recording. But since recordings can be fakes, forgeries, or otherwise inauthentic presentations while providing authentic performances of specific songs, they are autographic musical works. And such works are the standard end-products and signifiers in rock music, and have been as far back as Elvis Presley's Sun sessions.

2

I'll Be Your Mirror: Recording
and Representing

The Machine Age can affect music only in its distribution. Composers must compose in the same way the old composers did. No one has found a new method in which to write music. We still use the old signatures, the old symbols. . . . Handiwork can never be replaced in the composition of music. If music ever became machine-made in that sense, it would cease to be an art. — George Gershwin on the phonograph[1]

Recordings and Performances

The photographic image is produced instantaneously by the reflection of light; its figuration is *not* impregnated by experience or consciousness. — John Berger[2]

"Rock 'n' roll differed from previous forms of music in that records were its initial medium," declares Reebee Garofalo, because "technology exists as an element of the music itself."[3] But Carl Belz may have been the first to note that "rock has existed primarily on records." Live performance notwithstanding,

> Although jazz and other types of folk music exist on records, they did not originate in that medium. For the most part, they originated and developed through live performances. Rock, it seems to me, has generally done the opposite. *Records were the music's initial medium.*[4]

Another critic soon noted,

> with the advent of rock (and I think it's still very much a characteristic of rock), what was important was not the song. What is remembered in rock is a particular entity of music and technology,

all put together in a very specific way and infinitely repeatable on the record, and *only* on the record.[5]

Although it is absurd to say that the song is not important, all three agree that recordings have a special status in rock. But what can it mean to call it rock's medium?

The symbiotic relationship between rock and recording technology hastened the process by which music meets its audience as a commodity. As a new way of connecting music and audience, its history cannot be separated from the decline of Tin Pan Alley, the rapid expansion of the record industry, and the transformation of radio.[6] As such, rock and roll was not just a new sound. But these trends do not show that recording is being used as an "instrument" or a medium. For that, we must address further issues: does this link support a distinct creative and interpretative activity? If so, recording is not just the commodification of popular music. Does it influence the musical thinking of both the audience and the musicians? If not, it is a mere confusion to suppose that "records were [rock] music's initial medium" or that rock recordings are autographic works.

One complication is that in musical traditions predating rock, recordings are basically byproducts of performances. For many musics, performance remains the basic medium. In Simon Frith's blunt words, "Recording was, in its early days, simply that: the direct recording onto a cylinder or disc. What record buyers heard was the sound of the original performance."[7] Thus early Edison recordings said "Edison Re-Creation" on their labels, and their paper sleeves promised "Comparison with the living artist reveals no difference." Victor Red Seals were advertised as "a mirror" of the human voice.

For musical traditions in which works routinely circulate by means other than recording, performance retains ontological priority over recordings. (One can have performances without recordings, but not vice versa.) Robert Johnson's music was unknown beyond the juke joints of Mississippi and Tennessee before "Terraplane Blues" became a minor hit. Recording for Vocalion in 1936 and 1937, Johnson performed in a hotel room. Had we been in that room, we would have heard the music of which we now have but an aural snapshot. Here, recording technology functions as a transmitting material. Musicologist Jacques Chailley notes that preservation is still the main function in recording the music of oral traditions: "those [traditional] musics which we hear from the record player . . . are only photographs in sound."[8] In short, for some musics recording still mechanically reproduces musical performances. Recording is a pseudo-performance, not the primary medium.

The claim that recording is rock's primary medium implies that recordings of the Beatles or Nine Inch Nails have a fundamentally different status than those of Robert Johnson, a Beethoven symphony, and an Aboriginal song. I argue that this special status extends to rock recordings that derive directly from a single performance. The four Replacements may have been together in the studio performing "Tommy Gets His Tonsils Out," so the track on *Let It Be* (1984) is an aural snapshot of a specific performance. However, the liner notes to *Let It Be* make it clear that many of the tracks are overdubbed; Paul Westerberg evidently plays all the instruments on "Answering Machine" and later on "Here Comes a Regular" (1985). Whether or not the group performed any of it whole, my analysis circles back to the fact that they belong to a tradition that typically does otherwise, using recordings to submit new musical works to the public. Rock musicians as diverse as Prince, Roy Wood, Todd Rundgren, John Fogerty, and Bruce Springsteen have made records on which they alone appear, employing overdubbing to sound like a group. Robert Johnson belonged to a tradition of a very different sort.

But not everyone grants that recordings can be anything more than byproducts of performances. Needing a label for the position that performances *always* have ontological priority, let us call it recording realism. It is related to an established position concerning photography and cinema: the parent theme is that any mechanical recording is essentially the documentation of some independent reality.[9] Although not himself a realist, William Moylan summarizes its basic aesthetic: "The recording medium is often called upon to be *transparent*. In these contexts, it is the function of the recording to capture the sound as accurately as possible, to capture the live performance without distortion."[10] Ideally, recording is invisible and the audience should *ignore* contributions of the recording process.

Realism populates the writings of André Bazin, Roland Barthes, Susan Sontag, Allan Casebier, Roger Scruton, Stanley Cavell, and many others. Some concentrate on photography, some on cinema. According to Sontag, photography is radically different from other "image-systems." Largely paraphrasing Bazin's contrast of painting and photography, she stresses that photography "is *not* dependent on an image maker":

> However carefully the photographer intervenes in setting up and
> guiding the image-making process, the process itself remains an
> optical-chemical (or electronic) one, the workings of which are
> automatic . . . The mechanical genesis of these images, and the
> literalness of the powers they confer, amounts to a new relation-
> ship between image and reality.[11]

In denying that language is present, John Berger similarly denies that
photography and film are representational media. By extension, sound
recording is not one, either. So it is not really an artistic medium.

There is a temptation to brush this off with a parody: because a piano
is a machine which "mechanically" generates tones depending on the
careful "setting up" (via keys) of the pianist, playing piano cannot be a
genuine artistic performance. But this parody misses the core idea here,
an idea deserving serious discussion. It is that when an independent
reality is recorded with a machine, the information is stored and reproduced without notational encoding or symbolic transformation by
a human. In Bazin's terms, the artist's personality is suppressed in favor
of the machine's "essential objectivity." It seems that John Fogerty's
Centerfield (1985), a truly "solo" recording, is not impregnated by
Fogerty's thoughts about the music except as those were present in the
act of performing.

Roger Scruton offers a precise formulation of the central realist assumption of Sontag, Bazin, Hernadi, Wolterstorff, Ingarden, and the
rest. With visual art, he notes, "properties of the medium influence not
only what is seen . . . but also the way it is seen."[12] Film, however, resists
introduction of the artist's *thoughts* about its subject matter. Its recording technology can only "reproduce" the look or sound of things and
so cannot be regarded as representational (Sontag's "image-system").
Scruton takes recorded music to be such a clear case of this that it
grounds his realism about film, and not vice versa. "A cinematic record
of an occurrence is not a representation of it," he insists, "any more
than a recording of a concert is a representation of its sound."[13] However reconfigured, no process of human interpretation or semiotic
transformation takes place.

To a stubborn realist, overdubbing and multitrack recording are basically gimmicks or shortcuts. Jazz purists seem particularly disposed to
regard splices and overdubs as a cheat. While realism is most persuasive
for undoctored recordings of specific performances, it easily stretches
to fit doctored and spliced recordings. Pieced together to approximate
one ideal performance (as Glenn Gould spliced together multiple takes

of Bach's *Goldberg Variations* to constitute one seamless performance), each fragment nonetheless takes its identity from its generating performance. Such techniques do not alter the essentially "reproductive" nature of recording: recording as a one-man band, John Fogerty or Prince must play the different instruments and sing the vocal parts. Extrapolating from film theory, recording realism says that editing and over-dubbing techniques introduce no special "human intention" between the music and its appearance in the reproduction.[14]

Even those who participate in cut-and-paste recording are apt to adopt a realist interpretation of their activity. As he was working on *Tommy*, Pete Townshend expressed concern over the audience's failure to understand that rock records seldom reproduce specific performances:

> A lot of people, I'm convinced, that buy records don't realize what happens when a group records on an eight-track machine. They don't realize that they record half of it one time, and then another eighth of it another time. They record it in eighths at different locations and this ceases to become music to me.[15]

Complaining that a recording presents music "secondhand," Townshend endorses realism. Of course, this did not stop him from using the very practices that made it cease to be music to him; after the failure of the 1971 Young Vic Theatre sessions, the Who returned to playing against prerecorded synthesized backgrounds. Soon, *Quadrophenia* was constructed layer by layer.

The elaborate nature of some rock recordings makes their composite nature obvious to alert listeners, such as the chicken squawk that turns into a guitar note on the Beatles' *Sgt. Pepper* (1967). But the construction of recorded "performances" can be impossible to detect by listening. For instance, consider Townshend's realist interpretation of the power of the Sex Pistols on "Anarchy in the U.K." and "Bodies." Townshend remarks that "what immediately strikes you is that *this is actually happening*. This is a bloke . . . who is actually saying something he sincerely believes . . ."[16] But Townshend is simply wrong about the first claim. Whether Johnny Rotten was sincere or not is an open question. He certainly *sounds* as if he means it. But we know for a fact that these records are not recordings of a performance that "actually happened." The recordings were produced by Chris Thomas, fresh from his work with Roxy Music and Pink Floyd. The guitar and drums were recorded first, then more guitar was overdubbed in spots and bass guitar was added. The vocals were overdubbed later. In one take? Several? Listening to the recordings does not reveal what "actually happened" any more than watching Sergei Eisenstein's *The Battleship Potemkin* (1925) shows what actually happened in Odessa in 1905. In the case of the Sex Pistols, there isn't even any prior event to dramatize and re-create, unless it is the emotions which the recordings *convey* (even if they do not actually *record* them).

Before laying out my extended argument against realism, I must offer two disclaimers.

First, recording's status as a distinct medium is not unique to rock. "Serious" composers have exploited recording equipment for composition and "performance." Yet this mode of musical activity is typically treated as marginal, experimental, or a special case. *Musique concrète*, in which all sorts of previously recorded sounds are assembled into original compositions, was generally more appealing in theory than in practice until DJs in the Bronx reinvented it in the 1970s, improvising break segments from fragments of recorded music. Relocated to the studio with the commercialization of rap, a technique of high culture entered the vernacular of mass culture.

Even theorists who allow that recordings can be autographic works find it hard to shake realism. While Paul Hernadi allows that cinema and television generate works in their own right, "a phonograph record or a videotape is a *technological* device for *storing* a *single* performance, edition, or animation."[17] Whenever recorded music is based on live performance — from a performance by musicians on instruments — he classifies playbacks as "secondary" instances of the musical work. The performances providing the recorded sounds are, of course, the primary instances. Thus, when Chic's "Good Times" (1979) turns up in "Grandmaster Flash and the Wheels of Steel" (1981), Hernadi must regard both records as secondary instances of a common performance. The originating guitar and bass performances of Niles Rodgers and Bernard Edwards would be primary instances, interpreting a musical work they'd composed. Because studio musicians were used to re-create "Good Times" as the backing for "Rapper's Delight" by the Sugarhill Gang (1979), it offers a distinct secondary instance. But *none* of these recordings are to be counted as autographic works. In the thrall of traditional assumptions, Hernadi contends that only recordings generated by computers without involving actual performance can be privileged autographic prototypes.[18]

Second, Lydia Goehr observes that while music's "mechanical reproduction" has the potential to challenge the traditional model of musical works and performances, the challenge has been largely unsuccessful.[19]

And I am not suggesting that rock *repudiates* prevailing concepts of the musical work. Rock's use of recording as a medium does not require a wholesale rethinking of music. Why assume that rock is entirely untouched by our prevailing ideologies of artistic production? Instead, rock adapts existing norms so that when recording is the medium, recordings simultaneously exemplify two different sorts of musical works: the autographic recording and the allographic song. Rock does not fully reject the model of composers and their "works" that stabilized in European high culture about two centuries ago. It thus feeds the assumption that—other than the special case of compositions for tape—its recordings are a reproduction and mere commodification of a performance. In short, rock retains some allegiance to established dichotomies of song/performance and composer/performer. As conventions of European high culture often taken as normative for all musical activity, their ideological biases have only recently been dragged into the glare of critical challenges.[20]

Defending the basic work/performance dichotomy, Roman Ingarden opines that a satisfying recording is basically a matter of good luck. After all, composers aren't always the music's best interpreters. When a recording features a composer definitively performing his or her own work, the composer's input alters the theoretical situation only to the extent that we now know that "the composer was *lucky enough, on a particular occasion,* to succeed in performing his own work." Ingarden thus dismisses any special status for "authorial rendering" by way of recorded music.[21] In other words, Chris Thomas was lucky to get good performances from the Sex Pistols, the music's composers. It seems that Brian Wilson's presence at the sessions for "Good Vibrations" (1966) was important only because he could not communicate through a written score; had he known notation, the performing and recording could have been left to someone else.

In sum, realism contends that performance has ontological priority over recordings. But I suggest that "Good Vibrations" and "No Future" are prime counterexamples. Although *based* on earlier performances, these recordings are "privileged" autographic works, primary instances, the basic texts. To shake off realism, let us turn to rock recordings that present songs whose identities are original to the recordings: the identity of the musical work is not determined by reference to the recording's underlying performances. As such, the recordings *represent* performances (in a precise sense outlined below) rather than *transmit* them. Transparency does not make sense of them.

Recording and Representing

The Photograph does not call up the past . . . what I see is not a memory, an imagination, a reconstitution, a piece of Maya, such as art lavishes upon us, but reality in a past state: at once the past and the real. — Roland Barthes[22]

The crux of the distinction between representation and mere recording (reproduction) is alleged to lie in differences in the relationship between the work and its subject.[23] When recordings are understood as essentially mechanical reproductions of the look or sound of something else, two points become central.

First, the recording relationship requires that two independent physical things or events must stand in an appropriate *causal* relationship to one another. With music, one of them is a musical performance. It is only by mimicking the sound of performances that recordings feature songs and other musical works. But a fictitious subject can't cause anything and so cannot be the subject of a mechanical recording. Since dinosaurs have long been extinct, there simply cannot be a photographic record of a dinosaur attacking a human, for that state of affairs has never and will never occur. Hence the films *Jurassic Park* (1993) and *The Flintstones* (1994) do not *record* the interaction of the dinosaurs and humans.

A representational relationship is needed to present situations that are not actual or to refer to a fictitious subject. As Scruton observes, representation is a matter of describing or depicting a fictional world — the interaction of humans and dinosaurs, for instance. So representation is *intentional:* mere resemblance won't do the job. This is not to say that the artist's intentions are sufficient to establish it. Those intentions must be supplemented by a system of representation by which they become accessible to others: there must be a representational medium. But a snapshot of Aunt Matilda records Aunt Matilda apart from any such system, provided she caused the image on the photo.[24]

As Arthur Danto is keen to point out, artistic media provide transfigurations of commonplace reality. Even if its subject and materials are "real things" appropriated from "real life," new properties are always added. In a truly invisible medium, never allowing properties over and above those present in the represented subject, the results would not be independent works or texts. It would be reduced to its content. Understanding artistic activity involves understanding the interpretative contribution of the medium to our grasp of the content.[25] In Roland Barthes' formulation, there is no writing or music that directly reflects reality. From the perspective of the audience, it is opaque: "clarity is a purely rhetorical attribute."[26]

So what does this have to do with rock, particularly for its audience? Consider Aaron Copland's point that "the choice of the sound medium itself will almost certainly influence the nature of the composer's thought." Thus, the "principal concern of the composer is to seek out the expressive nature of any particular instrument and to write with that in mind."[27] While Copland may be accused of overemphasizing expression at the expense of other values, he reminds us that in listening to music we are confronting human thought, not just sound. If recording is rock's medium and the audience does *not* take account of the medium, they can only respond at an unsophisticated level, confined to its most basic features and obvious meanings. The work is reduced to its descriptive, narrative, or expressive elements.[28] More complex meanings arise only as one relates it to a larger class of associated works and to the range of choices available in the medium. Without denigrating the response of less sophisticated members of the audience, if they treat recordings as transparent transmissions of performances that happen to be recorded, there is that much less room for encoding and disseminating meanings.

The second important point is that a recording informs us about its source performance by replicating visual or auditory features of it. Since a mechanical recording is not *designed* to remind one of its subject, it cannot express a thought about it. While it is always "of" one subject rather than another, it cannot take a position "about" that subject. A mechanical reproduction is a mute witness of history. A photograph of George Bush vomiting at a Japanese banquet may make him look pathetic or ridiculous, but it cannot express the photographer's idea that Bush is pathetic or ridiculous. At best, we can be encouraged to draw false inferences about the source; in a film, perspective makes it look as if Harold Lloyd is dangling from a clock at the top of a tall building, when he is merely on the second floor of a building on top of a steep hill.

How, then, can photographs and films have fictional subjects? Must a realist concede that *Jurassic Park* represents dinosaurs attacking humans? Not at all.

Consider an actual case, Julia Margaret Cameron's "King Arthur" (1874) — one of her photographs portraying scenes and characters from Tennyson.[29] Realism simply denies that King Arthur is the subject of Cameron's photo. The subject must be whatever caused the photograph, so the subject must be someone portraying King Arthur. The person's act of portraying Arthur, not Margaret Cameron's act of taking the photo, does the representing. Echoing Ingarden's remarks about "luck" in recording music, Scruton contends that Ingmar Bergman's *Wild Strawberries* (1957) is only a cinematic masterpiece because it documents something that is independently a dramatic masterpiece.[30] The representation of a fiction occurs in selecting or labeling the subject and the recording documents that independent case of representing.

Under realism, Townshend's practice of assembling "eighths" is of a piece with Eisenstein's brilliant montage technique in *The Battleship Potemkin*, or the interaction of humans and dinosaurs in *Jurassic Park*. The cinematic artistry consists in juxtaposing and blending photographs of dramatic representations, not in representing.[31] The recording artistry similarly consists in assembling recordings of what is already music, but the realist sees musical artistry as something else altogether.

One way to see that recording is rock's primary medium is to show that recordings — not simply the performances that are recorded — are genuine *representations* in the ordinary sense of that term.

Realism Rejected

Other times I'll go into the studio and play riffs with other people and then later on listen to the tapes and see what that wants to be. — Bob Dylan on composing[32]

Nothing I've ever done with a tape recorder is brilliant . . . if you think of what the true function of what a tape recorder is — if you think of it as an automatic musical collage device. — Brian Eno[33]

The hit recordings of "Good Vibrations," "Good Times," or "Rapper's Delight" feature three distinct songs. However, *songs* are never the causal source of sound recording. Performances are. But sometimes the originating performances are of indeterminate identity when recorded. As such, the recording's identity — as featuring a specific song — cannot be settled by appeal to the identity of the independent "subject" which has been recorded. Scruton's "recording" relationship does not hold.

In the simplest cases, the identity of the originating sounds *differs* from the identity of the musical work featured on the finished recording. Elvis Costello composed the song "Beyond Belief" (1982) by adding his vocal to instrumental tracks previously recorded with the Attractions for a different song, "The Land of Give and Take." Placing a new melody and lyric over the existing track, Costello changed the identity of those instrumental tracks. On *PsychoDerelict* (1993), Pete Townshend used tracks that had been recorded for other purposes some twenty years earlier! The music's identity was not fixed until the final stages in the record-making process. Thus the performances may be "of" that work rather than another only *retrospectively*.[34]

A song is paradigmatically a specified combination of text, melody, and harmonic support.[35] A song is not composed until these elements are stipulated as combined in a manner normative for identifying subsequent instantiations. In prevailing parlance, a *type* must be specified (in the same sense that the dime in my pocket and the one in your pocket, or two occurrences of the word "goof," are two tokens of a common type). Yet rock songs are often composed by the very process of merging the vocal track with some previously recorded music: Roxy Music's "A Song for Europe" (1973); U2's "Gloria" (1981); Paul Simon's "El Condor Pasa" and "Cecilia" (1969) and "Graceland" (1986); and the Talking Heads' "Once in a Lifetime" (1980). Producer Glyn Johns complains that many of the Rolling Stones' most celebrated recordings were a bore to record, simply because Keith Richards liked to record take after take, "playing the groove . . . without any sort of top line at all."[36]

With such recordings, the identity of the featured song cannot be reduced to that of the documented performances. As distinct musical works, these songs were not fixed until the tape editing was regarded as completed.[37] Like any "serious" composition on tape, the sounds assembled as the finished work do not exemplify any one musical work (rather than another) when recorded. For any art form, we consult intention and institutional practices in order to determine what work is before us. Here, we want to know why the recording is "of" the song that it is. With rock music, the basic method for presenting a new song is through its appearance on a commercially released recording. I say more about this in the next section.

For now, I want to concentrate on the idea that the *music* performed to generate the basic tracks had an ambiguous identity at the time of its recording. World Party's Karl Wallinger employs a collage method, consciously modeled on the work practices of the Beatles and the Beach Boys. Discussing the origin of several songs on *Bang!* (1993), Wallinger explains his composing process:

they're being written *as* they're being recorded, and they come together mainly in bits. . . . They're all recorded, really, in the same way. You could call it "the X-song." I don't iron things out, organize them, cut a demo and then do the real thing. The demo *is* the real thing.[38]

To be more precise, the "demo" (demonstration recording) becomes an element of the finished recording. For the song "Is It Like Today?" Wallinger started with a five-note melodic phrase; he and bass player Dave Catlin-Birch improvised a chord sequence against a drum machine and then recorded the rhythm guitar and bass in one take. The original five-note phrase then became the basis for Wallinger's improvised vocals, which were recorded while he listened to the backing track already laid down. This combination of melody and lyric served as the basis for subsequent revision and rerecording. Finally, keyboards, lead guitar, and backing vocals were added. The drum machine was eventually replaced with a drum track played by Wallinger. The musical work, as a distinct combination of text, melody, and harmonic support, was constructed on top of a rhythmic and harmonic schema (the generic "X-song") that could support any number of different songs. The identifiable song did not emerge until well into the process of creating the recording.

Faith No More's breakthrough album, *The Real Thing* (1989), was composed by such a process. The backing tracks were recorded by the band while they were auditioning for a new vocalist. When the other band members settled on Mike Patton for the job, they played him the completed instrumental tracks and then gave him two weeks to write lyrics and add vocal parts, turning instrumentals into songs. Similarly, two songs by Jimmy Page and Robert Plant on *No Quarter* (1994) were constructed directly on top of tape loops of North African drumming. If a different vocal line had been overdubbed onto any of these backing tracks, those tracks would feature (retrospectively) some other musical work than they do. The musicians were making music at various times in the recording process, but their music making did not count as performance of any specific work at that time.

Brian Eno exemplifies the rock tradition of constructing backing tracks with no particular plans for their later use. Pulling a track from his collection of tapes, he overdubs melodic and rhythmic material to "finish" the composition. A notable example is the basic backing track of "Sky Saw," on *Another Green World* (1975). It also became "Patrolling Wire Borders" on *Music for Films* (1978) and yet a third piece which Eno produced for the British band Ultravox in 1977. "Listen to all three," advises Eno, "and you hear what kind of range of different usage is possible."[39] When Eno constructed the basic track, its identity was fundamentally ambiguous. It was unfinished, open ended, and could become one work or it could be another. The fact that the same sounds led to three distinct musical works demonstrates that, prior to completion, the recorded sounds had no fixed identity.

Producing U2's *Achtung Baby* (1991), Eno was one of a team of seven who assembled the finished album from various "strata." The individual songs emerged when the musicians, producers, and engineers reached consensus on how to assemble the recorded sounds into something worth regarding as a new song. Bits of recorded music-making were mixed and matched, spliced and altered, deleted and revived. On *My Life in the Bush of Ghosts* (1981), assembled with David Byrne as a combination of backing tracks and "found" vocals, one of the finished tracks was originally created for a recorded sermon by radio evangelist Kathryn Kuhlman. When her estate would not allow the use of her voice for the project, Eno and Byrne were forced to rework the tracks, thus ending up with quite a different composition. Acting as a producer for the Talking Heads, Eno encouraged the group to improvise rhythms collectively in the studio; these sessions were taped, and then songs were composed over the top of the rhythm tracks. They became *Remain in Light* (1980). Dissatisfied with the resulting songs, Eno reports that had *he* been given "carte blanche to write whatever I wanted, song-wise, over the top," the results would have been radically different.[40] Working with David Bowie on *Low* (1977), Eno took a rejected track of the two of them playing a melody together on piano and added further parts; when Bowie heard the results, they continued adding parts until the finished piece emerged.

New works are often composed by combining recordings that originated separately. Rock musicians have created a number of extended compositions through assemblage on tape, among them Neil Young's *Arc* (1993), Frank Zappa's *Lumpy Gravy* (completed in 1967), and the suites on the Grateful Dead's *Anthem of the Sun* (1968). The long instrumental coda of Derek and the Dominos's "Layla" (1972) was added after the body of the song was composed and recorded. The edit is subtle and blends two independently written segments of music, yet "Layla" was only half composed before the splicing was completed. Clapton's live performance of it on *Unplugged* (1992) omits the coda and abridges the musical work, rather like performances of Shakespeare's *Hamlet* edited to last sixty minutes.

In all these cases, much of the time the musicians were making music *without performing any specific musical work*.[41] Reworking previously recorded music, the originating performances became identified with specific works only in retrospect. As with serious electronic music, the same technology that allows "a" performance to be constructed out of several partial performances facilitates composition and stipulation of the musical work. The identity of the music on the finished recordings cannot be reduced to the identity of the music when it was being performed; performances may cause all of the sounds heard upon playing the recordings without settling the identity of the musical work. Songs are present, but not by virtue of the causal relationship between recording and performance posited in the realist "recording" relationship.

Stipulating and Composing

Offered these examples, it is tempting to conclude that some rock recordings fit the realist analysis but others do not. But that is not my point. I'm rejecting realism for all rock. As rock gradually came to use recording technologies to compose, disseminate, and represent musical thought, recordings became the primary medium for the rock tradition.

Let us consider an arbitrary example, say Booker T. and the MGs' hit recording of "Hip Hug-Her" (1967).[42] As a soul instrumental, it is autonomous in the sense of being free of any extramusical subject matter. We can concentrate on the relationships between the recording, the composition, and the originating performance(s).

As far as I know, "Hip Hug-Her" mechanically copies a single studio performance, without editing or splicing or overdubbing. If so, my compact disc mechanically replicates a performance that occurred thirty years ago. It seems to exemplify realism, featuring "Hip Hug-Her" because the originating performance was already an instance of that piece of music. But maybe not. Stax/Volt got a four-track machine in 1967. Trying it out, perhaps Booker T. Jones took a previously recorded rhythm track and overdubbed a new keyboard part, and Steve Cropper added guitar the next day. Even here, with "Hip Hug-Her" assembled from several performances, there is no problem for the realist as long as each musician intended to play that musical work on each occasion.

But it may have been more like Elvis Costello and "Beyond Belief." Suppose they recorded the bass and drum parts with quite a different work in mind, only to have Cropper later use that track as the inspiration for a new guitar part. Perhaps Jones added the keyboard part *last* (it is the most distinctive component). The other three musicians may have been recording parts for some *other* musical work, which Jones then used to generate the composition known as "Hip Hug-Her." If so, isn't the musical work *independently represented* by the recording, apart from any causal relationship to the actual performances which exemplify that work at the time of performance?

Robert Johnson's recording of "Terraplane Blues" stands in a causal relationship to a specific performance of that song on November 23, 1936. In 1936, engineering was pretty much microphone placement and selection of the best take. Yet even if "Hip Hug-Her" was similarly derived from a single performance, many other recordings from the time were not, *including recordings by those same musicians*. In 1967, recording on tape allowed alteration along both the horizontal and the vertical axis of sound. On the horizontal, one moment of sound could be followed by another that did not follow it in real time; on the vertical, any sound might be overdubbed with another that was recorded at a different time. The engineers at Stax/Volt were learning these techniques: some of the spirited interplay between Otis Redding and Carla Thomas on *King and Queen* was edited together from various takes. Redding's untimely death spurred the process at Stax as Cropper and others worked on the demo tapes left behind. Redding's vocals were given new backings.

Furthermore, these musicians had little or no expectation of notational specification for their music. The musicians at Stax often produced cover versions of songs by learning them from commercial releases. So did Otis Redding when he covered "My Girl" and "Satisfaction." In turn, their own compositions were made known through recordings. And rather obviously so, since that one recording is the basis for all subsequent performances counting as being of "Hip Hug-Her." Once it was released and became a hit, bar bands across the country were playing the piece, having learned it from the record. (It is even possible that the musical work was never really performed until after the record was released.)

So why does my recording count as an instance of "Hip Hug-Her"? (Why does a serious composer's composition for tape instantiate one work rather than another?) Intention, rooted in musical and cultural practice, is decisive. Let us return to Cameron's photograph of King Arthur, where the subject is fictional and nonphysical. King Arthur does not cause it to be a photo of King Arthur. Realism proposes that when Cameron's subject posed, he conformed to existing conventions governing the representation of King Arthur. So she could rely on a familiar type. Films draw on our conventions of theatrical representation. While this does not directly furnish an account of the way recordings generate new musical works via the recording process, it does direct us to the fact that the identity of a representational work always hinges on prevailing artistic conventions. In particular, it hinges on the ways in which artists *announce* and *stipulate* new works, for its status as a distinct work cannot be separated from the process by which it reaches and is recognized by its audience.[43] This includes the ways technology gets used.

We must look to the larger context of music making to determine which traditions embrace the subject/reproduction relationship posited by realism, and which do not. But the fact that rock musicians have embraced them has implications for "Hip Hug-Her" even if that particular track documents a specific performance without alteration. Given the ways that recording technology is used by rock musicians, *any* rock recording requires something more than a causal relationship to performances to establish the identity of the music "performed." Other musical traditions, including jazz and classical music, have remained conservative in their use of the same technologies. Producers will "punch in" passages on the music's horizontal axis, but there is little manipulation on the vertical axis.

Rock has long deployed an institutional framework in which new musical works are to be stipulated and disseminated by a process of recording, labeling, and releasing them. As with "Layla," *Lumpy Gravy,* or U2's "Gloria," the first instantiation accepted as such—recorded and disseminated as such—normally fixes the musical work. Indeed, plagiarism suits sometimes hinge on the question of whether the defendant had access to certain recordings of it. While commercial release is not the only way to stipulate compositions in rock, it is certainly the most common. So whichever way "Hip Hug-Her" came about, the recording should not be viewed under the realist interpretation. Even if a specific performance caused all the sounds on the recording, that fact still does not make it count as a secondary instance.

These two uses of recording technology, to compose and to announce new works, are found in every subgenre of rock. It is standard practice in rap, as when a producer constructs an instrumental backing from short fragments of sound sampled from existing recordings, then gives the backing track to someone else, who composes and adds the vocal track. Here, an additional layer of thought is generated by the practice of musical relocation. But even the predigital, presampling age provides many cases of instrumental tracks that were fully complete before anyone wrote a melody or lyrics.

I have said that recordings can have musical works as their subject, as do performances. I concede that this sounds odd. The musical work is certainly not the subject in the way that Gertrude Stein is the subject of a photograph taken of her, nor even in the way that Picasso's painting of Stein has her as its represented subject. The Booker T. and the MGs recording instantiates "Hip Hug-Her" by *representing a performance* of it. The recording creates a "virtual" space and time in which a performance is represented as taking place.[44] Thus, just as performances of a musical work can be a standard way to announce a new (non-notated) composition, rock recordings can "impregnate" the heard sounds with the musician's and composer's thoughts by presenting a "virtual" performance.

So whatever the origins of the sounds on the recording, it provides the primary instance of the musical work "Hip Hug-Her." Subsequent performances instantiate that musical work because of a rule-governed intention to do so. Even where there are performances of specific musical works, already written and arranged when brought to the studio, there did not have to be. Neither a causal relationship nor a recording of an independent representation (the "King Arthur" scenario) is required to explain how rock recordings instantiate the works that they do. Realism may prevail for classical, jazz, folk, country, and other musics where fidelity to performance is still the goal. Under the conventions of rock the realist relationship between musical work, performances, and recording is moot; in part, thanks to rock's ongoing exploitation of the recording process itself.

Rehearing Recorded Music

That leads to the whole question of what you are aiming to produce when you make a record. . . . one argument that is frequently leveled at me is: "You're not being very honest." I say, to hell with that. We have a different art form here.
—Beatles producer George Martin[45]

Realists see recordings as mirrors. Like mirrors, they involve a unique, objective relation between an image and its subject. But where mirrors reflect the present, recordings freeze their subject for posterity. Freed from time's winged chariot, the image alters the viewer's relationship to the subject. Returning to a mirror we see something new (ourselves older). Looking at a photo or listening to a recording, we encounter the past. Recordings encourage a relationship to music that seldom occurred before the invention of the phonograph.

Those who take live performance as the paradigm of musical presentation are often suspicious of this new relationship. For composer Roger Sessions, a recording holds our interest "just as long as it remains to a degree unfamiliar":

> It ceases to have interest for us, however, the instant we become aware of the fact of literal repetition, of mechanical reproduction, when we know and can anticipate exactly how a given phrase is going to be modelled, exactly how long a given fermata is to be held, exactly what quality of accent or articulation, of acceleration or retard, will occur at a given moment. When the music ceases to be fresh for us in this sense, it ceases to be alive, and we can say in the most real sense that it ceases to be music.[46]

What Sessions offers as a universal truth is the attitude of a composer who distinguishes between a composition and each of its live performances. It comes down to the proposal that once we cease to be surprised by nuances of tempo and dynamics, the sounds no longer embody music.

Sessions assumes that one is listening to a work that one already knows; hearing an unfamiliar work, one can have limited anticipation of the qualities mentioned. Like Eduard Hanslick, Sessions regards music's expressive qualities as largely due to those differences. He fastens onto precisely those qualities which cannot be specified in the score and which vary in performance. They are more a function of the performing than the work performed, so the interpretative artistry is that of the performer rather than the composer.

This largely ignores the importance of performing personae as a construct in mass culture and the degree that our response is shaped by a familiarity with the artists involved. Much of the pleasure of a new Clint Eastwood film derives from having seen him in other films; much of our pleasure in a new release by a favorite singer is in its relationship to the established personae of the performer. Even failed works, like David Byrne's *Rei Momo* (1989), Bob Dylan's *Dylan* (1973), Joe Strummer's *Earthquake Weather* (1989), or Arrested Development's *Zingalamaduni* (1994) demand our attention because of the performer's previous work, in a way that a bad Poco or Vanilla Ice album cannot. Not that we'd ever want to memorize the Rolling Stones' *Emotional Rescue* (1980). But we do listen to failures in light of other records, in relation to a personality constructed in that medium over time, less than in light of live performances.

More importantly, when recording is the primary medium, the audience no longer listens for such variance. Imagine Sessions' remark about recorded music paraphrased as a critical comment about a movie or a short story. Through recording, music approaches the status of literature: we may read and reread a story or poem to the point of memorization, and yet take pleasure in it all the more. With recorded music, we know that each playing will be the same. We do make allowances for minor variations due to material factors (e.g., changing the settings on our equipment or buying new speakers). Interpretive variation only arises when different artists record the same song, or when the same artist rerecords it, as on a live release. No longer attuned to the question of how long the guitar will hold a note, we are free to savor and anticipate qualities and details that are simply too ephemeral to be relevant in live performance. When records are the medium, every aspect is available for our discrimination and thus for its interpretative potential.

Consider John Fogerty's reaction to Duane Eddy's first record, "Movin' and Groovin'" (1958). Fogerty recalls that the first time he heard it on the radio, "the big sound got me more than the lick or the tune." Rather than the specifically musical values as we normally understand them, Fogerty's first impression was that there was "some sort of an extra edge to the sound of that record."[47] From a realist perspective, Fogerty wasn't responding to the music at all; as he later learned, he was responding to the tape saturation in the mastering of the recording itself. It is clear that Fogerty, one year before he formed the band that would become Creedence Clearwater Revival, responded to the record itself, and not to the record as a transparent medium for getting at the music. When Fogerty was in the studio mastering *Green River* (1969) at RCA studios, RCA was in the process of converting many of Elvis Presley's older recordings to simulated stereo. Observing the process, Fogerty was outraged at the loss of the slapback echo artificially achieved by Sam Phillips on the recording.[48] Again, an important element of the musical experience is specific to the recording, not what's recorded. Like every other aspiring rock musician, Fogerty studied his favorite recordings and "memorized every note." In doing so, the "edge" and "size" of the sound were absorbed along with the notes played.

According to realism, this opportunity to focus on any and every detail of a record, including tape saturation or echo, is a flaw rather than a virtue. Scruton argues that representation is characterized by the artist's control of the details of the representation, whereas mechanical recording introduces details beyond anyone's control. If they are not there because of artistic intention, the audience is subjected to irrelevant sounds. On Elvis Presley's "Blue Moon" (1954), we can hear a soda machine in the background; on the Beach Boys' "Wendy" (1964), someone coughs during the instrumental segment; on Bruce Springsteen's "New York City Serenade" (1973), the piano pedals squeak; on Bob Dylan's "Wedding Song" (1974), the buttons on his coat sleeve clatter against his acoustic guitar. Run-D.M.C. may have been the first to sample records that carried the unmistakable sound of damaged vinyl, with "Peter Piper" (1986); audible clicks and pops were soon in vogue on rap releases.

There is an important ambiguity in Scruton's complaint. The particular details were not beyond control. Those in charge of the recording process can monkey with the recording, or try again and release a different take. Engineer Bob Fraboni noticed the sound of the buttons and asked Dylan to take off his coat and do the song again, but Dylan declined. All music is heard in a context in which there will be *some* aesthetically irrelevant details (if not these, then some others). While Run-D.M.C. did not place each individual popping sound, they chose to feature the sounds. It is only within the context of knowing music by way of recordings that we can even point to such details as the squeak of the piano pedal or the clicking buttons and ask about their presence. It would be absurd to complain of these things in live performance, and for someone who regards fidelity to performance as the recording ideal, it is odd to claim that their presence on a recording is a flaw. Some of Van Gogh's paintings are full of cracks, a detail he did not control; is he any less a representational artist for the presence of such factors? Much as time alters the details of a painting, and yet painters control what they can in the choice of paints and their placement on the canvas, leaving any number of details to chance and the painting's aging process, the recording artist controls some factors, chooses among best takes, splices and edits, and leaves it to the listeners to note what details they will.

To the extent that details can be controlled, Scruton frets that the artist "become[s] a painter." The ideal appropriate to the materials is abandoned. Genuine representation can occur in this manner, rather than mere recording, but only by accepting a framework of "largely unnecessary constraints."[49] But this is less a criticism than a backhanded compliment. Surely Scruton is reduced to quibbling over a difference of degree, not a difference in kind. A Picasso etching is a representational work, but one cannot think that every detail of every line in a Picasso print is there by conscious decision. And with modern recording technology, recording artists have as much control over the resulting sound as a visual artist over a print or a painting. There is not much weight to Scruton's position when George Martin can take two separate tracks, recorded in different keys and at different tempos, and slow one down and speed the other up, then edit them together to get the Beatles' recording of "Strawberry Fields Forever" (1967). The American mix emphasizes the artificiality of the edit, as Martin brings the orchestral version across the stereo plane. It is largely a matter of knowing which details were under the artists' control.

George Martin never became "a painter" producing a representation in quite the way Scruton has it. That had to wait for digital sampling. And however much the details of their recorded sound were manipulated, filtered, edited, and altered, Martin alone does not deserve credit for the recordings of the Beatles. Theirs was a collaborative achievement, crafting detailed representations of musical performances. The resulting recordings are less like a painting from the hand of Van Gogh or Jackson Pollock than one from a Renaissance workshop where masters and assistants are responsible for different parts of a complex work. Yet like those painters who find expression more readily in a palette of colors than in an etched line, many rock musicians find as much expression in the qualities of sounds themselves as in musical structures.

Memory and Tone Color

Mechanical reproduction of art changes the reaction
of the masses toward art. — Walter Benjamin[50]

Understanding music — listening to it, not simply hearing it — always requires a social dimension of learned knowledge of the music's basic parameters and conventions. Attention to form, as the organizing element of the heard sounds, is central to understanding most Western art music. However, apprehension of formal composition is hardly the primary attraction when listening and relistening to most rock music. Most of the rock audience shuns compositional complexity, either horizontally or vertically. In terms of traditional (syntactical) musical analysis, most rock music is simple and repetitive and predictable.

While there is nothing wrong with being more like a painter than a traditional composer, I have danced around the proposal that we should be bored by sustained attention when rehearing recordings of such repetitive, predictable music. What's left to discover during the hundredth listening to the Kingsmen's "Louie Louie" (1963) or the Ramones' "I Wanna Sniff Some Glue" (1976)? Leonard B. Meyer, in a passage closely paraphrasing Hanslick's diatribe against passive or "pathological" listening, draws the typical conclusion: "rehearing may often be tolerated precisely because *listening* is not taking place — even though physiological responses are recorded and 'something' is felt introspectively." The music is "a fortuitous stimulus to pleasurable daydreams."[51]

Yet "I Wanna Sniff Some Glue" and "Louie Louie" pull me in when I *listen* attentively. And, as a member of the rock audience, I do not think that I am the oddball. (While I may wonder how Jane's Addiction can hold anyone's attention on rehearing after rehearing, I do not doubt that they do.) Yet it seems unlikely that the drama of the unfolding form and suspense about its articulation in performance is crucial. This is particularly true once we note how often rock fans listen again and again to the same records; I know a student who literally wore out a new Neil Young cassette in a month. These two features of our behavior, the enjoyment of very simple pieces of music and the tendency to listen to them over and over, have been a problem for theorists from Eduard Hanslick to Leonard Meyer.

What is needed is a plausible account of how "Louie Louie" can retain its impact when the record is played over and over. The answer must be that song structure is often an incidental framing device for something further; a "coathanger," as John Shepherd puts it, upon which other qualities and "significant personal statements" are hung.[52] Alan Durant proposes that recording shapes listening by locating the corresponding pleasure in "precise recollection and anticipation: knowing sounds, movements, and instrumental textures by memory and familiarity, rather than by extrapolation from perceived patterns, symmetries and learned musical structures."[53] But *why* should this anticipation please us? It is precisely what infuriates Sessions. Yet they suppose we *can* have a precise recollection of recorded music after we have heard it often enough. They rely on the dubious assumption that memory operates as a storage system from which items can be retrieved intact. I do not deny that we memorize many details of particular recordings, nor that these recollections supplement "extrapolation" from perceived structure. But there is overwhelming evidence that those memories are not preserved intact. Our memories always leave it "to a degree unfamiliar."

In *The Power of Sound* (1880), Edmund Gurney anticipates these points. I do not mean his actual conclusions; he regards music's "colour" as a dispensable "secondary quality of phenomena."[54] Gurney holds that timbre cannot be important, for it cannot belong to a musical work (a composition's melodic and harmonic combinations). If he thus adopts the prevailing ideology, including its ontology, at least he sees the need to defend it. Simplified, Gurney argues that the work must be equated with a structure because that is all that we can remember with accuracy. Timbre is "reproducible in memory with the very minimum of realization of any actual sound-quality."[55] Thus timbre must not be relevant to works except in performance, and then only to facilitate our grasp of musical structure.

Shepherd, among others, emphasizes and critiques the view's lingering effects on contemporary thinking about music.[56] While he has important things to say about the way different vocal timbres communicate and reinforce traditional gender distinctions, Shepherd's account only covers the significance of *kinds* of tone color. (And even there, only for voices.) In the face of *specific* timbres of specific recordings, he falls back on the vague idea that variety keeps the audience "interested." Aesthetic properties are reduced to a sort of packaging for the social meanings. Furthermore, he locates them with performances. Again, it seems we shouldn't care about their specificity once we memorize a recording.

Enter Gurney's proposal about memory. Now, on one level he is mistaken. We can certainly remember the basic differences between the timbre of a saxophone and trumpet, or identify the voice of a favorite singer, and we can summon them at will into "the mind's ear." Furthermore, we can recall which of these qualities was featured in specific recordings, much as we can recall the color of a car we used to own. Perhaps practice in the rehearing of recorded music makes us more prone to remember timbres than was customary in Gurney's day.

On another level, Gurney suggests something that was not documented until very recently: auditory memories seem to be restricted to *species* of timbre. We can *hear* minute differences between similar timbres while listening, but these nuances begin to be forgotten about a second after the sounds cease. It just seems to be a brute fact that human perception and memory of timbre are parallel to those for both musical pitch and visual color.[57] As with memories of pitch and color, memories of timbres "fade" after a moment, becoming more imprecise with the passage of time.

I mean, of course, in cases where a timbre is heard and retained in memory as an image heard "in the mind's ear." As such, it is a specifically *auditory* memory. Such memories differ from — and are more specific than — our ability to call up the generic clues for a certain sound (e.g., allowing one to say that a sound is from an acoustic guitar and not a piano). Auditory memories differ in kind from memories that involve an internal motor encoding, as is typical with melodies. And to the extent that a memory of musical timbre might depend on an unconscious linguistic encoding, our memories would again be limited, for they could be no more precise than a verbal description. Just try to give a precise verbal description of Morrissey's voice or the timbral shifts during Hendrix's Woodstock performance of "The Star-Spangled Banner."

The expert consensus on auditory memory dubs memory of timbre "a modest human ability, once it is separated from semantic connotations."[58] When we have a persisting mental image "recording" a timbre, the specifics of the auditory memory of timbre are not retained over time. Musical training improves the ability, but there are upper limits on it. And that is for the timbre of the human voice, where we expect the upper bounds of success. Even for vocal timbre, we seem to remember and reidentify idiosyncratic features rather than true storage of the timbre itself. When timbre is the basis for expressive qualities of a work — and it seems very important for recorded rock — it will have an expressive impact in direct experience that will be absent in our memories of it. Hence listening to it will be important in a way that remembering it is not.

In my mind's ear I recall "Louie Louie" as having a thin-sounding, metallic guitar solo. But cognitive psychology predicts that I cannot recall the *precise* timbre of that solo. Presented with brief samples of several metallic guitar tones separated from other clues about the source, I will be unreliable in identifying the "Louie Louie" timbre. I am likely to confuse it with that of Steve Cropper's guitar on "Green Onions" (1962), which is very similar. Our memories are simply not fine-tuned enough to "store" and recall the sensuous quality of the "Louie Louie" timbre, even though it can be distinguished from the "Green Onions" timbre when the two are heard one right after the other.

The relative crudity of our schemata for identifying perceptual qualities also explains the fact that we can identify a species of timbre with considerable accuracy even when it is reproduced with poor fidelity. While pitch identification is normally based on the fundamental harmonic in a sound, our schemata for pitch are flexible enough to identify pitch even when these harmonics are absent, as with the tinny reproduction of low notes on cheap speakers. There are also nuances of pitch that we can distinguish only when we actually hear them: a range of perceptually distinguishable tones are nonetheless grouped together and remembered simply as middle C or some other basic category. (In controlled experiments, even trained musicians tend to identify a very flat middle C as "in tune" when it is heard apart from a melody, and cannot distinguish between equal-temperament and perfect intervals of isolated instruments.)

The inherent imprecision of our schemata for identifying precise perceptual qualities carries over to the storing of timbre in memory. Our memories of the pitch or timbre of specific sounds cannot be more fine-grained than our schemata. Hence, we have a limited recollection of musical nuance. More significantly, no matter how well we know the structure of a musical work or recorded performance, the local qualities always promise "the thrill of the unexpected: you never know exactly what you will hear."[59] You do not know, because you do not remember them with precision. Their precise quality is only known perceptually, while perceiving them. If Sessions is not surprised by nuances of accent and timbre, perhaps he, like Gurney, simply regards them as irrelevant details and abstracts from them when listening.

Where the tone color of a recorded guitar contributes to the expressive character of the music, one can *only* experience the contribution of that tone by actually *hearing* it again in its total musical context. What has just been said about specific instrumental timbres extends to all sound quality on recordings, as well as to *overall* sound qualities emerging from decisions made in engineering and production. If "Sister Ray" is magnificent for the crudeness of its sound, its crummy sound makes its impact in the aural experience but never fully in the memory of it. Rock is a music of very specific sound qualities and their textural combination. *Specific* sounds are as central to the music as are specific colors in painting.

Sound and (Artistic) Vision

Can't you hear the sound of that record, can't you hear that?
— Phil Spector on "Da Doo Ron Ron"[60]

The dry, lightly echoed sound gives the record tremendous bite.
— Jon Landau on *Between the Buttons*[61]

We wrote sounds. We thought a lot about sounds.
—Booker T. Jones[62]

So far, I have been steering around roadblocks to treating recording as a true medium. Yet I do not want to endorse John Mowitt's claim that recording assigns a radical priority to "the moment of reception in cultural experience."[63] Drawing on the gap between "sound" and its recorded "reproduction," Mowitt speculates about the social significance of the digital bit (used for compact disc encoding) in transforming the structure of listening. Mowitt predicts that digital recordings will lead to a new experience of listening, deflating the privileges of "agency" at the point of production and dethroning authorship.

However, the audience has no access to "the peculiar logic of the bit." There is no *experiential* confirmation of its operation. Despite his emphasis on music's cultural context, Mowitt is too eager to place social significance in the technologies themselves. But I have argued that recording technologies do not fully determine the relationship between recordings, the "original" sounds, and their reception. These relationships also depend on patterns of use, including choices made by musicians among the many options provided by recording technologies. So I now turn to the musicians. Long before music's digital reproduction, rock musicians were using the studio as an instrument, emphasizing both specific timbres and the overall recorded sound, creating autographic works that cut across traditional categories of original and reproduction.

The Beach Boys are sometimes dismissed as "pop" or as a nostalgia trip, yet their initial popular success coincided with critical hosannas. There may be little reason to pay attention to anything they've done since the early 1970s, but they were among the first to employ the recording studio as an instrument in itself. Describing their time in the sun, leader Brian Wilson remembers: "I was unable to really think as a producer up until the time where I really got familiar with Phil Spector's work. . . . It's good to take a song and work with it. But it's the record that counts. It's the overall sound, what they're going to hear and experience in two and a half minutes that counts."[64] In retrospect, Wilson's songs may be less impressive than his ability to sculpt recorded sound. His songs are so closely wedded to specific voices and sounds that they have seldom worked as vehicles for other groups or singers.

Reflecting on the complex overdubbing and mixing for "Good Vibrations," Wilson said "It had a lot of movements . . . Building harmonies here, drop this voice out, this comes in, bring the echo chamber in, do this, put the Theremin there, bring the cello up a little louder here . . . I mean, it was a real production."[65] While Wilson arranged early songs in his head, the commercial release of outtakes on compact discs reveals that "Good Vibrations" was very much a process of trial and error. Going for the "overall sound," he worked with the actual sounds. Because the group's success was closely wedded to Brian Wilson's musical imagination and sense of detail, his absences due to psychosis and drugs have often led the rest of the group to simulate themselves by recycling familiar harmonies on new recordings while sticking to the old hits in concert.

If the Beach Boys are known for their distinctive arrangements and textures, other rock musicians are primarily recognized for their songwriting. Too often, this means their lyrics. Reviews of Sting and Lou Reed read more like literary than musical criticism, with nary a mention of the music. Reading enthusiastic raves about groups I've not yet heard, I generally have no clue to what the music actually sounds like.

Yet when rock musicians discuss their work, we find that their creative process centers around aural rather than textual values. Sinéad O'Connor has a confrontational, nonconformist image that leads interviewers to discuss her personal life, lyrics, and politics. When we do get a glimpse of her thoughts on *composing,* her own focus is strikingly aural:

> Texture is probably the most important aspect of my songwriting. I'm trying to achieve texture. . . . I know other writers think of it the same way. The way that you see music and songs is in shapes and textures and colors. You don't see them in terms of the words or the music. You see the shape of it, the texture of it, the color of it. The guitar with the keyboard, the notes each one plays, goes to weave the fabric.[66]

Not surprisingly, when O'Connor's next album concentrated on cover versions of songs she'd grown up singing, arranged by someone else, *Am I Not Your Girl?* (1992) proved both an aesthetic and commercial failure.

Bob Dylan, probably the most celebrated lyricist in rock, is often denigrated for both his voice and his musicianship. Yet many fans are attracted to *precisely* these qualities. Dylan is aware of this, saying, "When I do whatever it is I'm doing, . . . It's not in the lyrics."[67] John Lennon once said about Dylan:

> [Dylan] used to come with his acetate and say, "Listen to this,
> John, and did you hear the words?" I said that doesn't matter, the
> sound is what counts—the overall thing. . . . You don't have to
> hear what Bob Dylan's saying, you just have to hear the way he
> says it.[68]

Two things strike me as significant in this anecdote. The first is that by
the time Dylan knew the Beatles, he was no longer introducing new
songs by picking up his guitar and performing them. He was playing an
acetate of studio work. Lennon's focus seems to have rubbed off on
Dylan; in his notes for *Biograph* (1985), Dylan explains why some of
his best songs were never released, with a laconic "a lot of stuff I've left
off my records I just haven't felt has been good enough. Or maybe it
didn't sound like a *record* to me."

The second point, that the singing was more important than the
words sung, was reiterated by Jon Landau. Reviewing "All Along the
Watchtower" on *John Wesley Harding* (1968), Landau notes that a
particular line "is a great line to sing in the tone of voice Dylan uses, not
the other way around. . . . I think it more natural to respond first to the
music and then to the words when one is listening to a song, and I think
that is in fact what most people do."[69] The commercial release of such
outtakes as "Jet Pilot," "Santa Fe," and "Someone's Got a Hold of My
Heart" aurally demonstrate that Dylan often works out the music before the lyrics. (In live performance, Dylan frequently reverses the process, overhauling the melodies of his most famous songs in order to
take advantage of the musicians with him onstage.)

David Byrne makes similar points about his early attraction to rock:

> When I grew up and first started hearing rock music, pop, and
> soul, it was the *sound* that really struck me. The words were, for
> the most part, pretty stupid. But it was the sound, the texture of
> the guitar and drums, the way one song sounded so completely
> different than another. The texture a group of musicians arrives at,
> in support of melody or lyrics, can be at least as important as the
> melody line or lyrics or whatever. It can make a statement that
> supports or contradicts it.[70]

In another interview, he emphasizes the same point in accounting for
the sound of the early Talking Heads: "A lot of pop music with its guitar and drum solos seemed to be superfluous to the idea of what the music was about. So why not strip it down and deal with the idea, which

often seemed to be textural rather than narrative? A lot of pop music communicated by texture rather than what the words were saying."[71]

Empirical studies suggest that Byrne's reaction is typical of the rock audience. In one study, fewer than a third of rock listeners could provide plausible interpretations of current hits, and more than a third of the time teens could not explain the lyrics to one of their three favorite songs. Decades of research on the effects of rock lyrics on the audience support one position: "lyrics are not the primary reason that the young have for listening to popular music but rather the musical beat or overall *sound* of a recording is of greater interest to teenagers."[72] Metaphors and allusions are largely lost on the teen audience, including those of "Stairway to Heaven," a staple of FM radio and certainly one of *the* best-known rock songs.

If many listeners have no clue about the meaning of the lyrics to "Stairway to Heaven," their focus on the overall sound may be closer to Led Zeppelin's intent than is usually allowed. To be blunt, in rock music most lyrics don't matter very much. Or, to be more precise, they are of limited interest on the printed page, divorced from the music. We emphasize the wrong thing if we think that profound lyrics are in any way superior to "Wop Bop A Loo Bop" as something to sing. Except for the highly atypical arrangement between Elton John and lyricist Bernie Taupin, the lyrics usually arise late in the composing process of rock music. Typical of their creative process, the Rolling Stones collectively recorded the music that became *Exile on Main Street* (1972) under the title *Tropical Disease;* only then did Jagger write the bulk of the lyrics and complete the vocal tracks, at which point the American emphasis of the lyrics demanded a title change.

Returning to Led Zeppelin, both Robert Plant and John Paul Jones confirm that some of the group's most powerful recordings arose as vehicles for a certain recorded sound. Plant recalls that "Houses of the Holy" arose from their interest in recreating a very specific drum sound that they admired on an obscure R&B recording. Jones relates that "When the Levee Breaks" (1971), the closer for their fourth album, also arose from a very particular drum sound. Recording the album in an old mansion house, the drums were placed in a hall beside a stairwell to eliminate leakage from tracks recorded in the main room. They placed two M1160 microphones high *above* the drums rather than record them closely, then ran it through an echo unit. Jones says that the sound "wrote the song . . . that whole song just came from the drum sound."[73] The song exists because it suits that specific drum sound, rather than the drum sound being fitted to a song independently composed. Here, structure seems the servant of a nuance of timbre and not the other way around.

In a sense, then, Scruton is right. Employing recording as their primary medium, rock musicians have become painterly. But not neoclassical painters like Jean Ingres and Jacques-Louis David, who insisted that color is subordinate to line and drawing. They are painters in the tradition of Eugène Delacroix, for whom color is the essence of the art. In fixing specific sounds and their colors as essential properties of a musical work, recording technologies or some other "canvas" grounds the autographic musical works.

Actual practice undercuts the realist assumption that our interest in a photograph or film, and by extension a sound recording, is primarily an interest in its subject or in its mode of representation, but never both. I see no "prima facie contradiction" in being interested in both simultaneously.[74] When I look at a painting, my interest in the painting's subject does not exclude an equal interest in its artistic qualities in representing that subject. When I attend a concert and hear a performance of a musical work, I attend to both the musical work and to its interpretation in this particular performance. Likewise, when I listen to recorded music which I know to be constructed as such, I may be equally interested in both the musical work and its articulation in this recording. Just as Scruton acknowledges that an "appreciative spectator" understands that an artist introduces a "way of seeing" in the relationship between a painting and its subject matter,[75] an appreciative rock fan understands that the process of making records introduces its own "way of hearing" the music.

Coda

The most succinct demonstration of what I have been saying about sound's central role in rock music is XTC's "History of Rock 'n' Roll," from their *Rag & Bone Buffet* compilation (1990). In a mock lecture lasting twenty-two seconds, Andy Partridge summarizes four decades of rock. He simply names successive decades, illustrating each with one characteristic sound. For the fifties, an Elvis-like voice hiccups before swooping upward; the sound is heavily echoed. We are in Sun studios. The sixties are a frenetic lead guitar run filtered through a Rotovibe pedal; the sound is a bit muddy and heavily equalized, dampening the higher frequencies. It could be the solo from a Cream single. For the seventies, two fat, sustained, and reverberating power chords on a guitar recall the sound of Mick Ronson on David Bowie's "Suffragette City" (1972). The eighties are a squeal of synthesized sound; they could be the synthesizer parts on Cyndi Lauper's *She's So Unusual* (1983). One might quibble with Partridge's choices, but surely these sounds are as central to the musical thinking of their respective decades as was the piano for Liszt or Chopin. But these sounds serve as such telling markers for their respective decades only because they appeared when they did as *recorded* music.

3

Record Consciousness

When it's done on a record, it's in your face. —Ice-T[1]

Look at the records. They speak for themselves.
—Lou Reed, on the Velvet Underground[2]

Materials and Media

● Although sound recording has no single, essential use, there is a continuing temptation to regard recorded rock as a mere substitute for—a documentation of—performances we cannot attend. The commercial apparatus surrounding rock encourages us to conflate rock's materials and medium. Thus, *Rock 'n' Roll Is Here to Pay* makes no distinction between medium and materials:

> Unlike film or even video, music and rock are inherently a grass-roots medium. Anyone can pick up a guitar, play bass, drums, or organ—millions do. In this respect rock is a people's music.[3]

The book is a classic; Chapple and Garofalo provide a groundbreaking analysis of repressive tendencies of rock music as an industry, particularly with respect to women and blacks. But in constructing their argument that popular culture is "manhandled" in a corporate society, Chapple and Garofalo set up an opposition between rock music and its recordings, with the recording industry as a separate, repressive institution. In contrast, the present chapter argues that material objects like guitars and drums do not really constitute an artistic medium. An artistic medium is a mode of organizing perception and of unpacking meanings.

As Timothy Binkley puts it, the artist's "medium is not simply a physical material, but rather a network of . . . conventions which delimits a realm over which physical materials and aesthetic qualities are mediated."[4] Film and theater are different media because the conventions of film demand attention to features that would count as irrelevant in a live performance. To understand a medium is to know which qualities are relevant to something's counting as a specific work. For Binkley, a medium includes "the parameters within which to search for and experience its aesthetic qualities. . . . The medium tells you what to experience."[5] These parameters also include identity criteria — the largely unstated rules for identifying and distinguishing between distinct works or texts.

In plain English, one might stumble upon an artwork of another culture and have no idea how to go about viewing it *as* the artwork that it is. We hear feedback. Is it a technical error or part of the music? (Should we wince or cheer?) Does this pause divide one piece of music from another? (Do we applaud?) It could have been predicted that executives at Decca would reject the Who single "Anyway, Anyhow, Anywhere," interpreting the squeals of feedback as technical errors. According to the conventions of recording in 1965, they were. A medium arises from a set of human *practices* with some range of materials. As such, the parameters can be changed. By getting their record company to release the single, conjoined with similar moves by the Yardbirds and the Beatles, the Who helped change the rules concerning the status of feedback. In our culture, of course, changes often arise in the interaction of technology and commerce. (At what points can we get money to change hands, and for what?)

My point is that one can be in the presence of a work, in the sense of observing its material embodiment, without knowing what work is present or what statement it makes. To see a postcard showing the *Mona Lisa* is to see a reproduction; most people with a minimum of familiarity with Western art will understand the postcard's documentary function. We do not count it as a work in its own right. In fact, many of the painting's aesthetic qualities are absent from the postcard reproduction. But when Marcel Duchamp takes a postcard featuring the *Mona Lisa* and calls it *L.H.O.O.Q. Shaved,* referring us to his earlier work *L.H.O.O.Q.* (a *Mona Lisa* reproduction on which he'd drawn facial hair), he transforms the postcard into *his* work, a Duchamp. An ordinary postcard reproduction of the *Mona Lisa* is not funny, but *L.H.O.O.Q. Shaved* is certainly humorous, and you don't "get it" unless you grasp the gesture involved. The postcard has become the basis for a distinct work of art with properties in its own right.

Generalizing from *L.H.O.O.Q. Shaved*, Binkley observes that "what counts as a work of art must be discovered by examining the practice of art."[6] To be more precise, it is best determined by examining the practice of *artists*. Material that ordinarily functions in one way (e.g., as a transmitting material) might become a material element of quite a different art. Duchamp used an ordinary reproduction to make a self-reflective statement about art. He undercut its documentary function. Often, so do rock musicians. Where Duchamp drew upon dadaism, in the studio rock musicians draw on almost any material and idea they come across. (I return to Duchamp and the postcards at the end of this chapter, when discussing sampling.)

When a common subject matter or theme is handled in distinct media, as when a novel is the basis for a film, an informed audience shifts its expectations about what belongs and what does not. At the same time, filmgoers who already know the book can feel cheated when minor characters are eliminated in a film or when the plot is changed. Disappointed upon seeing *Anna Karenina* on the screen, Virginia Woolf criticized cinematic adaptations of literature. But she also recognized that fidelity to a novel can never be our criterion for cinematic success. Film demands a *visual* correlative for literary content, and some aspects translate better than others. While she grasped what it might become, we might say that Woolf never actually developed cinema consciousness.

For most music, the medium is a range of allowable sounds together with principles for structuring those sounds. To learn about an unfamiliar tradition, one often starts with the most common instruments and basic musical forms. An introduction to the music of northern India might begin with a sitar and the concepts of *raga* and *tala*. But this distinction between matter and form encourages an idealized division of musical labor, of the sort emphasized by R. G. Collingwood: a composer might compose entirely "in the head," without employing any instrument to try out and to amend ideas. Such a composer works imaginatively with the medium. She might then communicate the piece by writing out the score, leaving its performance entirely to others. In that case, only the music's communication to others — in the score and subsequent performances — involves any *materials*. Pen, ink, and paper seem to be the composer's materials. Instruments manipulated to generate the sounds specified in the score are the performing artist's materials.

This idealization, in which a composer creates a work and performers interpret it, downplays the connection between medium and materials in actual practice. Much of the pleasure of art derives from attending to what an artist does *with* the materials in order to embody meaning.[7] Even Collingwood recognized that the composer's ideas about the medium were influenced by thoughts of the available materials for embodying the artist's imaginative constructs.[8] Practical strategies for handling "raw" materials to achieve specific effects generate artistic techniques. Rather than mere accidents of embodiment, technique can be highly relevant to the identity of a work. Mediating between the work's matter and form, technique must be included in the evaluation of musical compositions (as abstract types and not just in performance).

The upshot is that the audience's reception of art—high or low—requires an understanding of how *aesthetic qualities* and *meanings* emerge from the *materials*. We read works against a horizon of potentialities and limitations that artists explore in materials. The recent controversy over film colorization stems from refusals to adapt to the demands of an older cinematic medium as shaped by the available materials; a modern bowdlerization, colorization creates a new work by adapting an old film to the expectations of modern audiences. While I may not care for Liszt, I should be willing to admire him for writing piano music that exploits the dynamics of that instrument. By the same token, I would be ignorant to criticize Bach for producing keyboard music but no distinctively piano music.

In chapter 2 I argued that with most music, recording technology stands *between* the audience and the music. Like the sheet of glass that protects a painting from the audience in the art museum, the ideal of such recordings is transparency. Consequently, I agree that we know the music of bluesman Robert Johnson secondhand. Johnson's primary materials were his acoustic guitar and unamplified voice. Contrast any of his recordings with the Raspberries's 1974 hit "Overnight Sensation (Hit Record)." With giddy delight it reminds us of its own status as an attempt to have a hit record. Eric Carmen's ode to pop radio takes an overtly self-reflective turn after three minutes, when the song's chorus reappears with both the high and low ends eliminated. Squeezed and pinched to replicate the tinny sound of AM radio, we suddenly hear the chorus from a new perspective; the recording seems to announce, "Here's what I sound like *as* a hit record." Then, when normal production values return, it seems to say, "And now here's the actual record that would be that hit." The effect comes across whether one is listening on high-fidelity equipment or a cheap transistor radio. Like Roy Lichtenstein's paintings of paint strokes, "Overnight Sensation" briefly takes as its subject the very materials and qualities whereby something else is normally represented.

Primary and Secondary Materials

We've always mixed our own album. Mixing is half the album. Any band who doesn't do that isn't serious about their album. — Doors guitarist Robbie Krieger[9]

Far from being idiot savants who express themselves "immediately" and "from the heart," rock musicians are acutely self-conscious about their materials and the competing media of recording and performance. This stems in part from the tendency of ideas to outstrip their materials, including their musical instruments. To produce the distinctive bass riff of the Who's "My Generation" (1966), John Entwhistle had to use a Danelectro bass, which had unusually thin and thus malleable strings. Because Entwhistle kept breaking strings and replacements were not available in England, recording an acceptable take of the song required the purchase of three new basses. If no rock song featured a virtuoso bass part like that before, there is no room to criticize the omission.

In interviews about his guitar-playing Eric Clapton takes great pains to articulate the special qualities of his instrument. He emphasizes that he favors the Fender Stratocaster for its "unique" sound and its relative lack of sustain. This is certainly worth knowing, for if a long sustained note occurs during one of Clapton's electric solos, we should understand that he went out of his way to produce that sustain. He has harsh words for the way that some rock musicians have used synthesizers, particularly as an economical substitute for strings and other instruments:

> I don't like things that are supposed to sound like other things. I remember years ago, when I was working out an approach to a solo, I often used to go for the sound of a harmonica or saxophone. I'd ask myself how would King Curtis or Little Walter play this? . . . but I never wanted it to come out *sounding* like a sax or harmonica solo. Indeed, I would have been very upset if people thought it had.[10]

If an instrument is merely aping the sound of another, how is the audience to respond? What are they to musically understand?

Jeff Beck also favors Fender Strats and makes the same point about understanding the instrument:

My main preoccupation . . . is flying the flag for the electric guitar. My total concern is for the instrument itself, rather than gadgets that go with it. It is quite alarming what can be got out of a synthesizer, for example; you can't deny they produce fascinating effects.[11]

Like Clapton, Beck is concerned that if audiences do not understand the materials used, they cannot appreciate his achievement as a composer or performer. In the middle and late 1970s, when synthesizers were becoming common in rock music, Queen albums proudly carried the label "no synthesizers" to assure listeners that none were used in the making of their records. If Brian May was going to wrench novel tones and effects from his guitar, he wanted the audience to appreciate it. It has also become a commonplace for rock recordings to list, track by track and often in exhaustive detail, every instrument that appears, crediting the appropriate musician.

To take account of recording equipment, let us follow Virgil Aldrich and distinguish between primary and secondary artistic materials. If a chunk of marble is a sculptor's material for creating a statue — the very stuff that the audience will eventually see in responding to the finished work — then it is the primary material. The sculptor's tools, the hammers and chisels, are secondary materials for working *on* the primary. Thus a painter manipulates a brush (secondary materials) in order to place paint on a canvas (the primary materials) in order to create a visual object with various shapes, colors, and textures (the artistic medium).[12]

In rock music, the musical instruments are almost always several steps removed from the audience. In live performance, speakers deliver a combination of amplified and electronic sounds. We almost never hear "original" sounds; when the electricity fails, the music stops. Even the nonelectric inputs, such as human voices and any acoustic instruments, are modified by the choice of microphones. And another layer of shaping occurs when the sound is *mixed* in the process of amplifying it, adjusting the levels of various inputs, shaping the sound in response to the room's acoustics. Following Aldrich's analysis of the piano strings as the primary material in a piano recital, amplification and other electronic equipment count as the primary materials generating the sounds actually heard by the audience at a rock concert. Yet much of the audience may be only dimly aware of these contributions.

In the presence of instruments (amplified or not), we can at least see the artist's materials. The vast majority of the time, the audience for rock music listens to *speakers* delivering *recordings*. Exploring the limitations and possibilities of the recording process, crafting music in those terms, rock's primary materials are often the available recording and playback equipment. Guitars, pianos, voices, and so on became secondary materials. Consequently, rock music is not essentially a performing art, however much time rock musicians spend practicing on their instruments or playing live. And while I do not say that it is essentially a recording art, I do contend that recording is the most characteristic medium of rock.

Picturing Rock

A major trap is to buy into the imagery of rock promotion. Wittgenstein warned that "A *picture* held us captive." He was warning philosophers against focusing on a specific model or picture of language use, but the warning not to get too attached to any one representation of a subject is always worth recalling. The sense of reality inherent in a photograph creates a particularly overwhelming aura of authenticity, inviting us to formulate and retain dubious assumptions. The pictures we have of rock musicians are highly selective and distorting. Pick up an illustrated history of rock music, such as *The Rolling Stone Illustrated History of Rock & Roll* or *Rock Archives*.[13] The latter contains 1,100 photographs. Thumbing through the book, you find that perhaps ten of these feature a musician actually working in a studio.

Again and again we see two sorts of images. First, the posed formal portrait of the musician holding a guitar or seated at the piano. Second, the performer on stage, usually in the throes of passion, in live performance. The first two Elvis Presley albums, both on RCA in 1956, neatly illustrate the basic dichotomy: *Elvis Presley* shows him onstage, eyes shut and mouth wide open, with his guitar thrust in the air, while *Elvis* has him seated in a staged pose, strumming his guitar. Here is the musician, they seem to say, and here are his musical instruments, *his primary materials:* his voice and his guitar.

Television reinforces such pictures and compounds the message. We see musicians onstage, performing. (The fact that we may be watching a recording is easily forgotten since the process of generating the medium which presents them is itself invisible to us.) If any single event can be credited with rock as we know it today, it may be the first appearance of the Beatles on the *Ed Sullivan Show* (February 9, 1964). But this was hardly the Beatles as they were in Hamburg's red-light district, screaming rock and roll for sailors and prostitutes. This was

American television. They were four nice lads in matching suits, seasoned by experience in a recording studio with a savvy producer and arranger, playing to a crowd of screaming adolescent girls. They had tied their fortunes to the mass media, and the media required something acceptable in middle-class living rooms.

Rock journalism perpetuates the stereotype. For example, in recent feature profiles of Nine Inch Nails and Smashing Pumpkins in major rock periodicals, a common format appears. There is a short history of the band, a description of a visit with the band's frontman in his home, and then an "on-the-road" segment emphasizing how good the band was in some particular live performance. Yet in the studio, Nine Inch Nails is Trent Reznor, guitars, and a pile of sampling equipment, augmented by the occasional hired hand. Five others join him on the road. For the most part, the studio Pumpkins are Billy Corgan and drummer Jimmy Chamberlin; producer Butch Vig contributed as much or more than members James Iha and D'Arcy Wretsky to *Siamese Dream* (1993). Headlining Lollapalooza 1994, they are a quartet. Given their record sales, these groups are currently reaching far more people via recordings than in live performance. Yet the rock press "profile" emphasizes rock as live spectacle.

Finally, there is MTV and the modern promotional video. When rock performers are not acting out some vignette suggested by the song's lyrics, they lip-synch the song in a simulated performance. Even performers who seldom appear live, like Kate Bush and Mariah Carey, release videos that portray them in "live" performance before enthusiastic crowds. Again, the viewing audience easily forgets that the music was recorded in a studio and that the video is also a recording, usually of a phony event and not even a recording of a genuine live performance. The pictures assure us that the musician makes music by singing into a microphone and by playing instruments before an adoring crowd.

What we seldom see, in photographs or videos, is the reality of the creative process. The images in which rock is packaged and promoted tend to deny the recording process. Consider the documentary *Jimi Hendrix* (1973), with its choice footage from the Monterey Pop, Woodstock, and Isle of Wight festivals. Unless you already knew otherwise, the film would provide no clue that Hendrix often toured to secure funds for his New York studio, Electric Lady. The *Electric Ladyland* album was undoubtedly a studio creation: dependent on multiple overdubs, tape effects, and montage techniques, it presented "the recording-studio-as-additional-instrument."[14] Eddie Kramer, Hendrix's engineer, says that it "was literally a performance at a console, Jimi and myself doing it, with all this music flowing around us."[15] Yet how many Hendrix fans have a mental image of Hendrix sitting at a console, twiddling dials and constructing overdubs, painstakingly constructing the music, edit by edit? How many think of Eddie Kramer as a contributing artist? He receives the same amount of credit on the album as Linda Eastman (later McCartney), whose photograph graces the back cover.

Occasionally we do get a glimpse of the studio. Although it had a tremendous impact on Patti Smith, Jean-Luc Godard's *One Plus One* (1968) is seldom seen.[16] Part of it documents the Rolling Stones in the studio, working out "Sympathy for the Devil" through a series of distinct arrangements. But even Godard's documentation is skewed; he only filmed two evenings. Mick Jagger noted at the time that the filming "happened to catch us on two very good nights. He might have come every night for two weeks and just seen us looking at each other . . . looking bored."[17] *The Kids Are Alright* (1979) offers a fabricated look at the Who's recording process for "Who Are You" plus a spontaneous rendition of "Barbara Ann." There are several studio sequences in U2's *Rattle and Hum* (1988), but only complete and polished performances. The film's real emphasis is stadiums, large crowds, and Bono's effect on them.

More revealing is the Beatles' *Let It Be* (1970), chronicling their miserable month at Twickenham Studios. Yet the documentary's highlight is their rooftop performance during lunch hour on London's Savile Row. It stands out because the bulk of the film reflects the tedium of arranging and recording new songs. There are many false starts, a lot of waiting around, some arguing (George explodes and stomps out when Paul criticizes a guitar solo), and, sometimes, a song played from beginning to end. If this is truer to the process in which most rock music is made, it is no wonder that we seldom get to see it. Small windowless rooms and sterile studios are not as visually compelling (nor as gratifying for a performer's ego) as a crowd of responsive fans.

Besides the poverty of images documenting the experience of musicians creating music in studios, rock's stylistic hallmarks provide a second obstacle to grasping the contribution of the recording medium. Obvious stylistic features are re-created in live performance, tempting us to regard them as the whole basis of rock's appeal. What most of the concert audience forgets (or never acknowledges in the first place) is that the musicians are usually re-creating music, not making it. What survives the transfer to live performance is the music's main *stylistic* features, supplemented by theatrics. Even then it is easy to overlook the technology supporting and guiding the creation of the music. Crossing back and forth between the worlds of studio and stage, what benefits fall to rock musicians by playing up their face-to-face interactions with an audience rather than their toils at the mixing board?

For the same reasons that live performance is unlikely to become obsolete, packaging rock in terms of "live" performance will persist. The concert experience cements the bond of audience to performer in a way that nothing else can; the structure and pacing of concerts is designed to "gradually heighten" it.[18] Concerts also bond the audience members to one another; if one cannot bond personally with someone a hundred rows away, then at least one is confirmed in one's taste by the presence of other fans. For a little while, at least, the individual is tangibly immersed in a social community with a shared sense of purpose, an experience that often eludes us in modern culture. As Deena Weinstein remarks, this "unity of shared identity" depends on "a recognition of oneself in others," a process that cannot take place through other channels of the mass media.[19] The musicians, for their part, are expected to engage in a ritual display of energy and effort, signaling allegiance to the fans. Some frontmen — U2's Bono, Nirvana's Kurt Cobain, and Pearl Jam's Eddie Vedder — have followed the lead of earlier punk performers and practiced stage diving into the audience, demonstrating to everyone that their fans will not let them down. In such displays, Weinstein emphasizes, both musicians and audience engage in behaviors that signify their solidarity, as well as their distance from the larger culture. The concert experience is choreographed to obscure the fact that the event is a commercial exchange. (Never mind that they aren't giving away those shirts and posters and programs in the lobby.)

Live performance is so prominent in rock videos and the images of rock promotion and packaging, then, for its totemic function. Images of live performance encourage fans to imagine that they can be in an immediate and thus genuine relationship with the musicians. In this respect, a continuing celebration and simulation of fan/star interaction dimly recalls the ideas that floated around action painting and abstract expressionism in its prime. Painter Robert Motherwell described his aim as a felt experience that was intense, immediate, and direct. The canvas was to be an otherwise unmediated act of communication, documenting the artist's emotional flow. Rock is similarly packaged as the sincere overflow of unfaked emotion.

As critics and art historians have noted, pop art was partly a reaction through which artists signaled that no such communication was possible. Messages are always mediated — on the one hand, by the process by which audience and artist make contact; on the other, by the creative medium itself. While Kit Lambert and Pete Townshend briefly and unconvincingly tried to package the Who as pop art, a more convincing parallel development may be found in the overt artifice of glam rock, Madonna, or the Pet Shop Boys. Where pop artists like Roy Lichtenstein and Robert Rauschenberg delighted in calling attention to the artist's materials and mediums (as if to say "Look at me! I'm a mediated act of communication!"), Todd Rundgren abruptly stops the flow of *Something/Anything?* (1972) to play a "sounds of the studio" game, alerting listeners to the presence of tape hiss and bad editing. Some rock musicians are only too happy to puncture the pretense that they communicate directly with each and every fan.

The Two Media

I like to write and record much more than I do to perform.
— Van Morrison[20]

I feel an added pressure with the record. With a record, you have every opportunity to do it right, and it will be treated as if everything about it is intentional. . . . If I have a night onstage when my voice isn't up to par, I can struggle through it and feel okay about the show. But if I spell someone's name wrong on the goddamn album, I could beat myself up forever. — Lyle Lovett[21]

While popular images downplay the studio, the musicians themselves emphasize that different aesthetics govern live performance and the recording studio. A different craft must be mastered for each, and not every group makes a successful transition from performance to the studio.

Lyle Lovett emphasizes that the recording process fixes "everything" for inspection. As I argued in the last chapter, every sound is now treated as deliberate and therefore relevant. If a performer coughs during a live performance, we dismiss it as an irrelevancy, but if someone coughs on a record, our knowledge that the cough could have been deleted (or another "take" released) invites us to regard it as part of what is communicated. Indeed, the cough may be retained precisely because it lends the recording an aura of transparency on a "real" event.

Eric Clapton sees the stage as a forum for playing that can be "uninhibited and completely without direction. That can't be put on record, there's no way." Such music "belongs to the concert hall and the audience and should remain that way. And for the gods." In the studio

Clapton is "very deliberate," guided by his knowledge that the music will have to withstand the scrutiny of repeated listenings.[22]

> I wouldn't be able to work on the premise that my records are exactly the same as my performances. It wouldn't work for me, and people would be very disappointed. . . . And when they buy the record they know it's going to be that way, too. . . . Not that one diminishes the beauty of the other, it's just that *they're two separate entities.*[23]

More precisely, they are two different media.

The primary difference, as Clapton sees it, is the degree of "deliberation" involved in recording. The range of options available to Clapton during a live improvisation are limited to the sounds he can make with the instrument in his hands at that moment. He says that he cannot be "carefree" in the studio. It's the existentialist insight that greater freedom carries the burden of greater responsibility. One's options at any point in a recording are virtually unlimited. The opportunity for retakes and editing generates different criteria for success; there's always the question of whether another take might improve a vocal or guitar solo, or whether backward echo on certain drumbeats or phasing on the vocal will enhance the music.

Robert Plant emphasizes other differences between a recording and the performance generating it. A weak performance may yield a great recording, as on the first Led Zeppelin album, which he regards as "super" while his own vocal performances "aren't that great."[24] He is also concerned that the conditions for a satisfactory audience experience in live performance are very different from those for a successful recording. When performing, he observes,

> I'm not really that keen on the idea of recording stuff for posterity and saying hey, now we can put out a *live* Robert Plant album and stuff. 'Cause, really, I think the whole thing about a live gig is to go there, be a part of it, enjoy it, get wild or do whatever . . .

Plant's veto accounts for Led Zeppelin's being so poorly represented in released live recordings. When an interviewer remarked that a live recording captures half of the live experience, Plant agreed:

> It's sterile. . . . I think when you make a record in the studio you're really try [*sic*] and create an atmosphere and a mood and whatever it is and actually to do it live, things get extended and they get a bit sort of, um, you tend to expand things when it's unnecessary. And

so when you're sitting at home listening to it, you're going "I'd much rather have the original." . . . I hate listening to my voice, live. I just like making the record in the first place.[25]

Most significantly here, Plant treats the studio recording as the "original."

Similar ideas are voiced by John Mellencamp, who took up oil painting during a three-year sabbatical from the music business between 1988 and 1991. He compares a composed song to a painter's sketches:

> I enjoy the process of painting. I don't care if the paintings turn out. Now when you're making records, it's the same way. I just come in with like a folk song, and then we add the colors of the band — other background vocals and sounds and instruments. But going onstage is not a creative process after you've done it three or four times. It's just repetitive work.[26]

Mellencamp sees rock creativity in the studio process, not in the performing art which translates the finished music to live presentation. Some rock musicians, like the Beatles and Steely Dan, eventually abandon the stage without harming their careers.

Their insights are reflected in the relative commercial and critical failure of live recordings. Apart from *Frampton Comes Alive!* (1976) and *Cheap Trick at Budokan* (1979), one is hard-pressed to think of a rock musician whose live recordings are better received by fans and critics than their studio confections. Because the Grateful Dead are the exception that proves the rule, I turn to them in a moment. In practice, live recordings are the one place where recorded rock has a significant documentary function. Critic Robert Christgau notes that fans regard live rock albums as souvenirs and samplers. Musicians often use them to tread water artistically or to satisfy a contractual obligation to deliver another album.

Given a choice between any band's best studio work and their live recordings, how often would we choose the live recording over the studio? Would anyone choose *The Beatles at the Hollywood Bowl* (1977) over any of their studio albums? Would any Led Zeppelin fan choose *The Song Remains the Same* (1976) over any of their first five studio albums? Would anyone choose Marvin Gaye's *Live* (1974) over *What's Going On* (1971), Arrested Development's *Unplugged* over *3 Years, 5 Months and 2 Days* (1992), or any live Kinks album over *Something Else* (1968)? When *Rolling Stone* invited selected critics to name the one hundred best rock albums since 1967, *only one* live recording was chosen, Neil Young's *Rust Never Sleeps*. Premiering all new material rather than live versions of his earlier studio work, only the "basic tracks" were intact from the concert performances.[27]

The Grateful Dead have the reputation of a band whose primary strength is live performance. They consistently rank as a top concert draw and their core audience trades and compares tapes of their live shows with the devotion of Charlie Parker fans comparing alternate takes of his improvisations. Reviewing *In the Dark* (1987), the Dead's return to the studio after a seven-year absence, *New York Times* critic Jon Pareles opines, "Whereas most rock bands get wrapped up making music in studios, building songs one layer at a time, the Dead are primarily improvisers who make music on the spot, as a group."[28] This is a half truth. The Dead are keenly aware of themselves as recording artists when they turn to making records.

Prior to recording their first album, guitarist Jerry Garcia said "We're not a recording band. We're a dance band."[29] But this attitude did not last. The group was unhappy with their first album. Documenting the band playing their standard material in a studio, it "was a regular company record." Garcia attributes its aesthetic failure to the fact that they "were completely naive about it. We had a producer whom we had chosen . . . because he'd been the engineer on a couple of Rolling Stones records that we like the sound of." The problem, Garcia believes, was that "at that time we had no real *record* consciousness."[30]

Their realist attitude vanished with their second album, *Anthem of the Sun* (1968). The group went to the opposite extreme of self-production, and two lengthy musical suites were painstakingly assembled over a period of months from a series of live and studio recordings. The transition between "The Other One" and "New Potato Caboose" even features portions of an electronic composition that pianist Tom Constanten had done with a ring modulator in 1962. According to Garcia,

> after an enormously complex period of time, we actually assembled the material that was on the master tape. Then we went through the mixing thing, which really became a performance, so *Anthem of the Sun* is really the performance of an eight-track tape; Phil [Lesh] and I performed it and it would be like four hands, and sometimes [Dan] Healy would have a hand in. . . . We were thinking more in terms of the whole record.[31]

For all their reputation as a free-flowing live ensemble, the group often adopts a calculated construction of music in the studio. Jerry Garcia's phrase is apt: rock musicians typically view their artistic careers from the standpoint of record consciousness.

This concern for "the whole record" is echoed by Jackson Browne. Originally pegged as a singer-songwriter, the 1970s category that replaced the earlier category of "folk" musician, implying that recordings have a documentary role in the musician's career, Browne nonetheless embraces an aesthetic of records as a distinct sphere of music making:

> Each of us — me and my closest friends — hopes to make a *record*. There are records I love that are not good songs but are great records. Bert Berns and Jerry Ragavoy and Phil Spector and the Beatles made *records*. Records that stay records. "Walk Away Renee" is a good song but it's not a good record. . . . People were making significant sounding records from the beginning of rock & roll. Elvis's records, all the Motown records. Motown made those records the way they made the '55 Chevrolet. It's still beautiful and it still drives. . . . I find I'm really attracted to record making.[32]

Knowing that recording is the medium, few rock musicians settle for realist documentation of a great performance of a song.

Realism Again

What people want from a concert is reasonable sound — basically the same as the album without being identical — and strong visual excitement. If the performance is good enough in its own right, the audience is going to be too excited to notice the difference. — Midge Ure on performing live[33]

In the face of the ways recording technologies are actually used, a stubborn realist will admit that the theory is not descriptive but normative, providing an ideal *standard* for evaluating recordings. Just as one looks at reproductions of paintings in art books as a substitute because one cannot go to see the originals, one only listens to a recording because Caruso and Miles Davis are dead and Salt-N-Pepa and Metallica do not perform in concert upon demand, much less in one's car or home. Using the analogy with sound recording to defend realism as a standard for cinematic success, some film theorists make it clear that fidelity is the standard for psychological reasons: "Ideally the sounds coming from the gramophone's loudspeaker are indistinguishable from the sounds which first went into the microphone." The causal relationship between recording and subject "lends its immediacy and conviction" to the recording, so the audience feels like witnesses to independent reality even when they understand that it is a "fiction."[34]

But if we shift to fidelity to the sound of performances as a normative theory, many of the most celebrated rock recordings are failures. In fact, studio recordings have become the standard for judging live performances. Recording facilitates a certain indifference as to whether the music can be re-created in live performance. Thus Keith Richards remarked at the start of the Stones' 1975 tour,

> You can never tell what will work onstage. "Honky Tonk Women" was like that for a long time. . . . Sometimes we fiddle around, like with "Wild Horses." We must've fiddled around with that for four or five years before putting it into a show.[35]

Today, many can only approximate their recorded sound in live performance by playing against recorded tracks. But when Milli Vanilli could *only* perform live by lip-synching prerecorded vocals, it ended their careers. So audiences do recognize different conventions for the studio and the stage, tolerating far more manipulation in the former than the latter. This reflects a nascent recognition that there are different primary materials in live and recorded music.

Consider several recordings of Buddy Holly, one of the first rock and rollers to take charge of both writing and producing of his material. After two disastrous trips to Nashville in 1956, where producer Owen Bradley applied standard "country" ideas about arrangements and recording, Holly began to work independently at Norman Petty's studio in Clovis, New Mexico. In April 1957, Petty recorded "Words of Love," notable for featuring an overdubbed lead guitar and a second vocal in which he harmonizes with himself. How would realism have us evaluate this recording? We could approach it like a classical recording, where a series of takes are spliced together to simulate one perfect, ideal performance. But this hardly seems to work for the second vocal on "Words of Love." It's obviously Holly. Is it a failed pastiche? Or are we to approach it hypothetically and to evaluate it as if it were a case of brothers singing together, a what-if-Buddy-were-the-Everly-brothers? To my ears, at least, Holly's overdubbed vocals sound better than the "real" backing vocals (also overdubbed) on such cuts as "Oh Boy," "Think It Over," and the other Holly tracks credited to the Crickets. When Holly harmonizes with himself, verisimilitude is neither achieved nor intended. While I only know Buddy Holly's voice from his recordings (a photographic or documenting function), I do not have any sense of immediacy by which I am fooled into thinking that the total sound of

"Words of Love" sounds like anything other than a record. Its sense of immediacy only comes from records.

Along realist lines we might then consider Natalie Cole's Grammy-winning recording "Unforgettable" (1991), in which she duets, via recording, with her deceased father. It demands a more extended "as if"; we would have to evaluate it in terms of what it would have sounded like if an adult Natalie Cole could have dueted with Nat "King" Cole. As a matter of fact, the emotional impact of the song does not rest in its constructed "subject" alone (how the duet sounds); its affective power turns on our knowledge that it *is* the product of studio wizardry, that Natalie Cole is singing to the memory of her father, not with him in the studio. Holly's overdubbing is free of such sentiment, instead suggesting a man playing Greek chorus to himself.

Holly's overdubbing technique reached a new sophistication — or unnaturalness, if one is a realist — with "Listen to Me" (1958). The fidelity loss inherent in the primitive overdubbing process gives the vocal an ethereal, haunted quality. What situation shall we imagine, against which we can judge the fidelity of the sound? The Everly Brothers harmonizing, but one singing from beyond the grave? Further complications arise from the fact that Holly died in February 1959, leaving behind eleven "demo" recordings done in his New York apartment the month before, featuring nothing but Holly's own voice and guitar. Among them was a brilliant but decidedly uncommercial recording of one of his favorite songs, Mickey and Sylvia's "Love Is Strange" (written by Bo Diddley and itself an early masterpiece of overdubbing). Fellow Cricket Jerry Allison suggests that the 1957 hit recording of this song was Holly's inspiration for the overdubbed "Words of Love."[36]

Holly's tapes were eventually turned over to Norman Petty, who released them gradually over the next decade. But Petty did not release any tracks as Holly left them. The best known of the enhanced tracks was a posthumous hit, "Peggy Sue Got Married" (1959), spliced and overdubbed so that Holly seems to be accompanied by a full group. For the 1963 release of "Wishing," Petty took Holly's vocal from a non-commercial demo prepared for the Everly Brothers; one reviewer at the time noted that it featured the current Liverpool sound. It is as if Holly, a major influence on the Beatles, had lived to emulate them. Holly's version of "Love Is Strange" finally appeared in 1969. Petty again aimed at a contemporary sound, that is, a 1969 sound. By realist standards it should be dismissed as bizarre, a recording whose putative subject must be a recording scenario in which Holly did not die and then in 1969 decided to update a song from his youth. Yet the result is regarded as one of the most successful of the doctored recordings. Another well-received track created by doctoring the 1959 demo is "Slippin' and Slidin'," the Little Richard standard. Greil Marcus quips that it is "one of the best things Buddy Holly never did."[37] Upon its release in 1969, Marcus was reminded of the Band.

Other major rock stars have been subjected to posthumous "doctoring," most notably Jimi Hendrix, whose backlog of taped studio improvisations became the basis for such albums as *Crash Landing* (1975) and *Midnight Lightning* (1976), and Elvis Presley, for whom producer Felton Jarvis overdubbed new instrumentation to existing tracks on the abysmal *Guitar Man* (1980) and *I Was the One* (1983). More successful was a posthumous release that went back to Presley's overproduced studio work and *removed* the excessive strings and backing vocals. The Doors regrouped to provide their distinctive sound for *An American Prayer* (1978), a record built around tapes of Jim Morrison reading his poetry. Critics have dismissed some of these records, particularly the Jim Morrison album, but never for the fact that overdubbing took place.[38] As with Buddy Holly, some of the Hendrix releases have been greeted with enthusiasm. Critics have *selectively* attacked individual tracks for obscuring Holly's rhythm guitar or providing wooden backing for Hendrix. The criterion for success or failure is not simple fidelity to some "original" performance; everyone agrees that releasing unfinished tapes of endless studio jamming does no favor to anyone. The undoctored outtakes from George Harrison's *All Things Must Pass* (1970) and Derek and the Dominos's *Layla* (1970) are regarded as of lesser quality than the overdubbed releases, despite the fact that they document the "truth" of the performance.

Some rock musicians continue to insist that music is a performing art and emphasize the importance of live performance. Shortly after the success of his heavily overdubbed solo album, I heard an interview in which Tom Petty insisted that he was basically a live performer, and only incidentally someone who made records. But the truth is in the grooves (or, these days, in the digital coding). *Full Moon Fever* (1989) features an amazing simulation of the Byrds' "Feel a Whole Lot Better," on which Petty and producer Jeff Lynne re-create the sound of the Byrds' 1964 recording. It is anything *but* a documentation of live performance, and Petty's homage to an influence is clearly his homage to a specific recording.

Neil Young similarly insists that "I don't really make records—I do performances and I record them." He also says that anyone who records bit by bit is a "wimp."[39] But Young is being disingenuous. While many of his recordings, particularly those with Crazy Horse, have more or less documented undoctored performances, he frequently overdubs or edits the tapes (the guitar solo on the *Freedom* version of "Don't Cry" [1989] is truncated, as evidenced by the release of the full version of the same performance on the New Zealand release *Eldorado*). Some of his strongest early work was not what it seemed to be. The Buffalo Springfield recordings of "Expecting to Fly" and "I Am a Child" do not feature that group; Young plays everything but drums and bass. "Broken Arrow" is embedded in a montage of sound effects and was edited together from over a hundred takes. Like most of his solo debut in 1969, "The Loner" was constructed by overdubbing multiple guitar and vocal parts over bass and drums. (Two other "constructed" performances on the debut, "Here We Are in the Years" and "I've Loved Her So Long," were actually recorded by Young as an on-again/off-again member of Buffalo Springfield.)

If Young regards documentation of a good performance as the ideal, he has never let it stand in the way of tinkering in the studio.[40] His recording of "Will to Love" appeared on a Neil Young album only because Crosby, Stills, Nash and Young could not replicate the power of the demo recording that he'd taken to them. He released the track, which he had constructed in about eight hours.

> I just walked from one instrument to another and did them all, mostly in the first take. . . . I think it might be one of the best records I've ever made. I think as a piece of music, and sound and lyric and spirit, it's one of the best.[41]

If constructing records by overdubbing makes one a wimp, Neil Young is one of the great wimps of rock and roll. Actually, he is simply very good at making records.

Live Recordings

At one point the sound was so distorted that all you could hear was John's vocals and Paul's drums — the mikes were completely off. — Eyewitness description of the Sex Pistols' last concert[42]

The Rolling Stones on stage . . . it's a load of noise. On record it can be quite musical but when you get to the stage it's no virtuoso performance. It's a rock and roll act, a very good one, and nothing more. — Mick Jagger, 1968[43]

Yet another factor suggests that rock music cannot be held to a standard of reproductive fidelity. Even when adopting a documentary function, live recordings do not sound much like the originating event. The exception may be the Rolling Stones' *Got Live If You Want It* (1966). Although heavily augmented with studio rerecording, it has been described as very muddy tapes of teenagers screaming. Striving for aural fidelity, the documentary mode adopts its own artfully constructed perspective. But this is no surprise. Consider Roman Ingarden's idea of musical performance as a profile.[44] At any given time, one cannot see more than one profile of another's face. In any given performance, a musical work offers one among its various profiles. Performance is an interpretative activity, one way of "seeing" the musical work among many alternatives. Let us take it another step. Adapting Ingarden, a recording can represent a performance (rather than documenting one) when the sounds emanating from our speakers offer a distinct profile on the source.

When a pianist performs, we get an interpretation or profile of a work. But as audience members, we also hear the performance from a vantage point, different from that of the assistant who turns the pages of the music. In choosing among performances, a live recording privileges a profile. But a live recording must also construct a *vantage point* on that profile. There is, consequently, a profile on the profile of the musical work.

For instance, I have a copy of an audience tape of the Los Angeles performance that furnished most of Bob Dylan's *Before the Flood* (1975). Judging from the audience tape, the official "live" album does not reproduce even an approximation of what anyone in that room actually heard during the event. With rare exception, such as the Velvet Underground's *Live at Max's Kansas City* (recorded 1970, released 1973) and the Beatles' Hamburg tapes, live recordings are engineered to sound like performances where the listener is the whole audience. These two recordings originated with members of the audience, made on simple equipment for private use (hence their lack of engineering). The typical "profile" adopted for recorded live performance is very different: an audience of one listens to the music but not as it sounds coming from the speakers in the concert hall or arena; it is as if one is wearing special headphones whose sound is carefully mixed for clarity and balance. Yet this profile on the musical performance (as opposed to the profile which is the performance) does not belong to any particular seat in the concert space.

When the audience appears on a live album, particularly singing along, we hear them in the distance as they would sound to the performers on the stage. We are offered two perspectives simultaneously; the instruments are an idealized audience perspective while the audience is an idealized performer perspective. Like an overhead dolly shot in film, most recordings of live performances adopt perspectives that nobody has in real life.

There are performance situations in which live rock music sounds as clean as it does on records, but they are pretty rare and depend on having very good seats in an acoustically balanced room (not common in rock music!) or being lucky enough to be in an uncrowded club, seeing a group before they become famous. I saw XTC, the Blasters, and Los Lobos in the same small coffee house on a college campus. They sounded great, primarily because they were not yet famous enough to fill a larger venue. I saw the Talking Heads, Tom Waits, the B-52s, X, John Lee Hooker, and Van Morrison in larger general-purpose facilities on the same campus; their live sound ranged from the passable (Tom Waits performing solo on acoustic instruments, Van Morrison heard from the second row) to the terrible (X). Listening to available live releases by Waits, Morrison, X, and Talking Heads, all recorded within a year or so of my seeing them, I am reminded that recordings offer distinct profiles of musical performances.

To focus on one, consider Joe Jackson's *Big World* (1986), digitally recorded "direct to two track digital master," in front of an audience but with no alterations in postconcert production. Jackson aimed at aural realism: "what you hear," claims Jackson, "is an exact reproduction of the performances which took place."[45] But from whose perspective? Each instrument and vocalist had separate microphones, and an ideal balance of sound was created by an engineer at a mixing board. The musicians did not hear what is on the record, because their monitors would not have received the same output that went to the digital master. The audience heard yet a third set of sounds; when I saw the same group perform some of these songs later that year, what I heard did not sound very much like that record. The instrumental balance was quite different and there was none of the clarity of sound on the vocals and individual instruments.

If live recordings construct a sound that no one hears during a performance, it is only fitting that so many bands go to such pains to make their live performance sound like their records. The Who had terrible problems trying to recreate *Quadrophenia* onstage in 1973, trying to synchronize Keith Moon's drumming to prerecorded tapes. (One of the several reasons that the Beatles stopped touring was their inability to present their recent music in live performance.) Preparing for their "Zoo TV" tour of 1992, U2 spent weeks in rehearsal trying to figure out how to replicate the music on *Achtung Baby*, even toying with the idea of hiring another musician to help them. R.E.M. did just that when touring after *Out of Time*, as did Nirvana on their final tour.

If it sounds as if only art-rockers and critic's favorites use a cut-and-paste recording method and then run into problems translating their music to live performance, consider Def Leppard. Despite the huge sales of such metal-pop albums as *Pyromania* (1983), *Hysteria* (1987), and *Adrenalize* (1992), the band only released five albums in their first fifteen years together. One reason for the slow pace of releases has been personal tragedy within the band (drummer Rick Allen lost an arm in a car accident; one guitarist was fired and another died of a drug overdose while albums were in progress). But the most significant reason is the deliberate method by which their music is created; guitarist Phil Collen recalls working fifteen hours to record a single guitar riff, and six months of recording yielded only two guitar solos that were regarded as good enough to put on *Adrenalize*. The group's live repertoire is pretty much limited to their own music, which they slavishly copy from their own recordings. Bass player Rick Savage notes, "We'd feel more comfortable playing our own songs than anyone else's, because we're so blinkered from making these records." Singer Joe Elliott concurs, "there's no point in us rehearsing if we don't have a record that's good enough to go out and try and emulate."[46] Their priorities are clear: the records are the standard by which they're to be judged, even in live performance.

Aside from a few television appearances, Buddy Holly's demo recordings are the nearest thing we have to a live Holly performance. The demos offer one perspective on "Love Is Strange," more introspective and ruminative than the Mickey and Sylvia version. Norman Petty's overdubbed release of Holly's demo is something quite different, exuberant and open. The sound and texture of the overdubbed accompaniment blunt the starkness of the vocal, surrounding it with a warmth and radiance that soften the pain. The demo and the Petty overdub take distinct points of view on the possibilities of the song, not merely as better and worse presentations of a specific performance the month before Holly died. Its commercial release puts it in a tradition where the record takes the song, not a specific performance, as its subject. In rock music, even recordings of live performances must be heard against such a background, rather than measure studio recordings by fidelity to live performance.

Originality: Songs and Samples

You make records for other people, not for yourself. That's what it's about. I'm making it for the marketplace. — Van Morrison[47]

The uniqueness of a work of art is inseparable from its being embedded in the fabric of tradition. — Walter Benjamin[48]

One of the most significant effects of distributing rock *as* recordings is a blurring of the line between performance, arrangement, and composition. (The conventions of jazz improvisation also blur these distinctions, but in performance itself.) These distinctions still hold for legal purposes, much to the consternation of the Beatles, who had to pay royalties for using a snatch of a Glenn Miller arrangement on "All You Need Is Love," and Paul Simon, whose "Bridge Over Troubled Water" earned a Grammy for someone who'd merely transposed it from Simon's singing range to Art Garfunkel's. When musicians see recording as a distinct medium and blur the traditional division of labor between composer, arranger, and performer, we should not be surprised that the criteria for originality blur as well. The conventions for delineating one work from another within a medium are not to be found in a metaphysical heaven.

Was it T. S. Eliot who said that inferior poets borrow but great poets steal? Leonard Bernstein recast the idea, saying that good composers are the ones who "steal great steals."[49] Given that all artistic creation takes place within a tradition, that intelligibility for an audience necessitates a reasonable fit with the conventions of one's peers, each tradition must also work out for itself what is allowable borrowing and what constitutes plagiarism. Thus Lydia Goehr traces the process by which European composers abandoned traditional methods of composing (recasting familiar melodies and rearranging existing works for new ensembles), turning to a system in which the thematic material was to be entirely original.[50] If not, the work was to be clearly identified as derivative, such as Brahms' "Variations on a Theme by Joseph Haydn" and Vaughan Williams' "Fantasia on a Theme by Thomas Tallis." However, if we are now to respond to the originality of the recording and not the composition, we should expect rock to abandon these norms.

In light of the conventions about originality prevailing for nearly two hundred years, consider the opinion of Andrew Oldham, the Rolling Stones' first manager. Oldham wanted Keith Richards and Mick Jagger to start writing their own material: "As far as I'm concerned, when

Keith sat in a corner and played those 'Not Fade Away' chords, that was the first song the Stones ever wrote."[51] On the face of it, this claim is absurd. Viewed in terms of traditional concepts of music making, Richards was merely providing a new arrangement to Buddy Holly's "Not Fade Away." But from a rock viewpoint like Oldham's, the aim was to come up with an original *sound* for their next single, and a new sound was equivalent to a new song. Ironically, Richards did it by pushing back to Holly's rhythmic inspiration, Bo Diddley, and by restoring a percussive R&B feel and sound. The Stones soon mastered the process, and when they rearranged the Staple Singers' "The Last Time" (1965), they gave themselves songwriting credit. We should not be too surprised when Jagger-Richards take credit for "The Last Time." Here we find a lead to the norms of originality in the rock tradition.

Consider the following range of cases. Neil Young's lyrics openly credit the Rolling Stones for "Borrowed Tune" (1975), yet his own name appears as sole songwriter on the record label. Phil Spector allegedly got the vibraphone hook of "Spanish Harlem" (1960) from sometime songwriting partner Beverly Ross, but assigned Ross no credit. (Mike Stoller, who also worked on the music, declined credit for his contribution.) Mike Bloomfield provided a brilliant guitar riff to Bob Dylan's "Like a Rolling Stone," which Richard Thompson lifts intact and employs at key moments in "Wall of Death" (1982), with no credit to Bloomfield or Dylan. Of course, the music for "Like a Rolling Stone" derives from Ritchie Valens' "La Bamba" (1958), who in turn got it by rearranging a traditional Mexican song. The defining riff played by Eric Clapton on "Layla" (1972) is from an Albert King record, but King gets no credit as co-composer. Elvis Costello acknowledges that "Temptation" (1980) lifts a riff from the Booker T. and the MGs' hit "Time Is Tight" (1969), and "Lipstick Vogue" (1978) derives from the Byrds' "I See You" (1966). Costello takes all songwriting credit. Bob Dylan adapts traditional melodies and takes songwriting credit, then keeps the music and rewrites the lyrics of Johnny Burnette and the Rock 'N' Roll Trio's "Bertha Lou" (1957) as "Rita May" (1975), sharing credit only with co-lyricist Jacques Levy.

Led Zeppelin's "Rock and Roll" (1971) supposedly grew from Robert Plant's vocal improvisations at the end of their live performances of Little Richard tunes, and critic Dave Marsh hears several tunes from the 1950s in Jimmy Page's guitar riffs on the recorded version. "Custard Pie" (1974) is cobbled together from bits of Bukka White, Big Joe Williams, Blind Boy Fuller, and Sonny Boy Fuller. But Page and Plant take full credit for both. Willie Dixon sued the two of them for lifting his lyrics for Led Zeppelin's "Whole Lotta Love" (1969), and while they settled out of court, Dixon is not credited to this day. Plant justifies this by saying that his vocal *style* was original and "Page's riff was Page's riff" and, besides, the lyrics are now "happily paid for."[52] In the case of "Dazed and Confused" (1969), Page denies the allegation that the song (credited to Page and Plant) was plagiarized from an obscure 1967 record of the same name by Jake Holmes.[53] Brian Wilson put new words to Chuck Berry's "Sweet Little Sixteen" (1957) and the Beach Boys scored a hit with "Surfin' USA" (1963); Berry now appears as composer. The Beatles slowed down another Berry tune, "You Can't Catch Me" (1955), rearranged it and added new lyrics, then regarded the changes as sufficient to justify taking full credit for "Come Together" (1969). Borrowing directly from the Beatles ("Oh! Darling"), the Replacements credit one 1983 song as "mostly stolen."

Hundreds, if not thousands, have tossed new lyrics atop "Bo Diddley," but since you can't copyright a beat, Bo Diddley gets no credit. Diddley (Ellas McDaniel) complains bitterly about the idea that it belongs in the public domain: "'Bo Diddley' is not just a beat; it's a melody *and* a rhythm pattern. The same as 'Harlem Nocturne' or anything else."[54] Bruce Springsteen's "She's the One" (1975) is a case in point, but at least he acknowledged his sources when it was a staple of his live shows, leading into "She's the One" by singing snatches of "Not Fade Away," "Mystic Eyes," "Who Do You Love" (also by Bo Diddley), and other variations over a long "Bo Diddley" vamp. Oddly enough, the Yardbirds gave full credit to Bo for "I'm a Man" (1965) despite their rearrangement. When the Count Five threw new lyrics atop that arrangement a year later and had a hit with "Psychotic Reaction" (1966), they took full credit.

My point is not to fault anyone, but to observe that the conventions of rock make it exceedingly difficult to determine which cases involve fraud, theft, or misattribution. Within any tradition, the constraints of originality are defined by the fabric of the musical culture. Current legal guidelines for fixing authorship, in the form of songwriting credits, are an anachronism. When the Band's "The Weight" is licensed for a cola commercial, only its nominal writer, Robbie Robertson, stands to see much profit. In a tradition allowing limited harmonic development within each musical work, originality more often lies in the details of the arrangement, in the alterations wrought by subtle rewriting, and in the cumulative impact of these changes as they come together in the finished recording. But such criteria of "authorship" are generally ignored because publishing royalties are the most lucrative slice of record sales.

Lennon and McCartney took advantage of the fact that melody and lyrics are subject to copyright law, but rhythm patterns are not. Ringo Starr's drum pattern is one of the most arresting and original elements of the Beatles' "Come Together" (1969), and both Aerosmith and Tina Turner preserve it on their remakes. Yet Starr gets no writing credit. The Beatles and the Rolling Stones assigned almost all songwriting credits to Lennon/McCartney and Jagger/Richards, respectively, but the contributions of the other musicians were crucial to the development of the songs. Television, one of the seminal groups of the punk/new wave explosion of the 1970s, broke up in part because Tom Verlaine took songwriting credit for music that the other members, particularly Richard Lloyd, believed they had cowritten. Nirvana felt similar frictions. Other groups may have learned a lesson: R.E.M. simply assigns equal writing credit to every member of the group for every song, no matter how it originates.

Despite the conventions employed for assigned authorship, rock recordings frustrate the expectation that each work features *an* artist's intentions. The Rolling Stones' version of "Not Fade Away" combines a song written by a Texan imitating an African American with an arrangement by English musicians and production influenced by Phil Spector. Operating under traditional aesthetic assumptions, French film theorists offered the auteur theory, focusing on the director as the single artist behind the cinematic work whose vision and consciousness impregnates it and makes it a proper artistic representation. If we want to assign "Not Fade Away" to one person, it might be producer Andrew Oldham, who brought the various elements together. (Phil Spector was present at the recording session and may have contributed to the arrangement.)

Such cases show that we should resist extending the assumption of a single auteur to every rock recording. Having noted that some rock recordings are the self-produced work of a single individual, they are rare and hardly the model. Indeed, U2 has been so dependent on letting their compositions emerge spontaneously in group jamming, only to be sorted out and "fixed" retrospectively on their recordings, that vocalist and lyricist Bono was unable to perform a single one of his songs on an acoustic guitar when asked to do so in 1985. Yet at that point he had "written" and released some forty songs. The incident inspired him to sit down and compose his first song by traditional means, resulting in

"Silver and Gold."[55] Despite its many flaws, the auteur theory thus makes another convert.[56]

Instead of assuming there is a single controlling vision, as there is in a novel or painting, we should now jettison the analogy and emphasize that making films and records is almost always a collaborative process. "Mr. Tambourine Man" (1965) is one of the most glorious recordings in rock, but to whom do we credit the achievement? The Byrds, of course, despite the fact that Jim Dickson found and helped them arrange the Bob Dylan song and Terry Melcher was responsible for the recording itself, creating the backing tracks with session musicians like Hal Blaine and Leon Russell before adding the actual group's vocal and Roger McGuinn's twelve-string guitar. (The record thus represented the ideal Byrds performance before the members of that group were capable of performing at that level.) The result is magic. It hardly matters that it was crafted in stages by a dozen different individuals with divergent artistic visions. Rock is collaborative to a degree rare since Western art embarked on its glorification of the individual artist in the Renaissance.

Elvis Presley's fortunes as a recording artist often fluctuated with the quality and commitment of those who were around him at a recording session. His interest in recording fell off once he got into films, and *From Elvis in Memphis* (1969) is the only album of his final decade to show signs of coherent design. It was recorded as part of his calculated comeback. Generally, he did not choose the material he was to record or who he would record with, so he was as likely to sing "Do the Clam" or "(There's) No Room to Rhumba in a Sports Car" as "Suspicious Minds" or Billy Swan's "I Can Help." Presley seems to have thought of himself as an entertainer rather than a recording artist, regarding recording as a transparent medium. Asked whether he ever listened to his Sun recordings, in 1970 he answered, "They sound funny. Boy, they've got a lot of echo on them, man, I tell you. But that's what I mean. I think the overall sound has improved."[57] Ironically, when musicians like John Fogerty and Dave Edmunds cover early Presley songs in tribute to his influence, they carefully reconstruct the famous echo that Presley regarded as a recording flaw. Carl Perkins was in the studio with the Beatles when they recorded his "Matchbox." He reports their concern to sound just like his "old Sun record" of it.[58]

If the line between originality and theft in songwriting and arranging is hazy in rock, the haze thickens with digital sampling. But not because "sampling raises new questions about 'public domain,'" as Simon Frith contends. Examining the practice of rapping over music

sampled from previously released recordings, Frith alludes to Duchamp's *L.H.O.O.Q.* and asks, "Is this the same gesture as sticking a
moustache on a reproduction Mona Lisa?"[59] Certainly not, as the nod
to "reproduction" makes clear. Frith sidesteps the fact that there are
two distinct modes of appropriating music, and neither maps neatly to
the copying of visual works. A digital sample of an autographic musical
work has a very different ontological status than a "reproduction" or
performance of an allographic work like a song.

In a series of famous paintings, René Magritte calls attention to the
gulf between representations and their subject matter. Writing "this is
not a pipe" on the canvas, Magritte reminds us that a painting of a pipe
is not a real pipe. Magritte's pipe (two-dimensional, in the medium of
painting) does not *contain* any pipe (a three-dimensional object). When
T. S. Eliot paraphrases John Donne's line "Teach me to hear mermaids
singing" in "Prufrock," it produces allusion; no identifiable chunk of
the source poem reappears in Eliot's poem. In contrast, when Eliot
quotes others in "The Wasteland," actual snippets of their works reoc-
cur. Looking to the conventions of Renaissance painting, we count the
Mona Lisa as a singular, autographic work. Creating *L.H.O.O.Q.*,
Duchamp's primary material was the postcard (a photographic representation) and not the actual *Mona Lisa*. Or consider Andy Warhol's
reproductions of Campbell's soup can labels. His works never utilized
real labels. They were representations of soup can labels, not new tokens or instances. But when a new recording "quotes" a source recording
by sampling it, the sampled track is a genuine — if brief — instance
of it.[60]

While recordings can represent performances, a sample does not
represent its source. Sampling instantiates by direct quotation, not allusion. For many types of autographic works that allow multiple genuine
instances (e.g., films and recordings), mechanical reproduction of a
genuine token produces another genuine case of the same work. A
pirate tape of a hit record or film is a token of it even if there's a de-
generation in quality. The key difference from a legitimate token is legal
or moral: one has no right to profit from it. So when unauthorized
sampling is found, far more than attribution and royalties are at stake.
As black musicians have long complained, appropriation can rip someone off even as it feeds into great music. A staple of rap production,
sampling has unleashed close scrutiny; but since the sources are specific
copyrighted recordings and not an oral heritage, corporations are eager
to police the action.

Suppose Aerosmith had sampled the Beatles' recording of "Come

Together" in order to get a drum part, rather than generating their own sounds in copying the drum part. Aerosmith's "Come Together" would *include,* as a genuine element, part of the Beatles' *Abbey Road.* There would be no shift in the medium. But because Aerosmith put together their own version at both the stages of primary and secondary materials, their hit version does not include any part of the work known as *Abbey Road.* Having sampled directly from *The Joshua Tree* (1987) without clearance, Negativland's "U2" (1990) outraged the members of U2. Negativland soon found themselves at the losing end of a lawsuit and court injunction. Their recording includes U2's work, just as Richard Hamilton's famous visual collage, "Just What Is It That Makes Today's Homes So Different, So Appealing?" (1956), includes actual bits of various magazines. Hamilton's snippets did not cease to be fragments of magazines by being incorporated into the collage. Negativland's "U2" instantiates U2's song *and* recording, appropriating in the strongest sense. When Duchamp's *L.H.O.O.Q.* defaces a reproduction of the *Mona Lisa,* underneath the ink it remains a postcard. Duchamp refers or alludes.

Yet from the audience's perspective, sampling may function as no more than allusion. When M/A/R/R/S had a British hit with "Pump Up the Volume" (1987), featuring some thirty samples, they were sued by producers who could identify their own work as sources. M/A/R/R/S recorded a new backing track from scratch, using session musicians to play the sampled parts, and promptly scored a U.S. hit that was impervious to lawsuit. Evidently the audience responds to indirect quotation as readily as to sampling. To succeed *as* appropriation, a new meaning must be layered atop or against a source. Recall Frith's comparison of sampling with Duchamp's *L.H.O.O.Q.* Duchamp's piece doesn't work if no one recognizes the *Mona Lisa.* For the music audience, a sample or quote that's too brief or otherwise impossible to recognize will function as an original sound. When existing recordings are simply an economical means of acquiring a desired timbre or as source material for a rhythm, no further layer of meaning is generated. When Afrika Bambaataa constructed rhythm breaks from obscure rock records during hip-hop's early years, he may have laughed when he got the crowd to dance to the Monkees at parties, but it was largely a private joke.[61]

Framed as questions about ownership, legal fights about money can mask underlying battles about whose meanings are going to be left in the audience's mind. Since current copyright laws set no standard fee for the practice, some publishers display naked greed in the price set for sample clearances. However, such avarice does not justify free, unchecked sampling. Nor does sampling's potential to give us increasingly sophisticated work. Artistic and aesthetic criteria cannot themselves justify free, unchecked appropriation: I shouldn't be allowed to make a film version of a novel for free simply because I can make a good film. James Brown is reputed to be the most sampled of all recording artists. His recordings may be the basis for new artistic gestures, but the direct quotation involved implies that Brown deserves both credit and payment in a way that is less obviously deserved when his style is copied without the use of sampling.[62] If infringement suits are routinely dismissed when samples are too brief to contain an identifiable rhythm or melody, it is largely because the law is antiquated, rooted in the paradigm of publishing and of allographic works.

Finally, the ethics of sampling are complicated by the collaborative nature of record making. When George Clinton makes it easy for samplers to gain clearance and pay him for snatches of "his" music, as on *Sample Some of Disc, Sample Some of D.A.T.* (1993), he enhances the creativity of other musicians. But why should he be the only one to profit? Isn't that bass sample or keyboard riff more likely to be the work of Bootsy Collins or Bernie Worrell than Clinton himself? But the courts have rejected the copyright infringement suit brought against samplers by former Parliament-Funkadelic members, and Clinton is free to shortchange his own collaborators. As the embodiment of assumptions about authorship, our antiquated copyright laws reinforce the distinction between primary and secondary materials of other media. Worse, anachronistic laws reward "auteurs" who compose or arrange. The musicians who made the originating sounds are relegated to the level of secondary materials.

4

Pump Up the Volume

So much of rock is sheer sound, even noise, which
often overwhelms the ears. — *Dancing in the Dark*[1]

Wherever we are, what we hear is mostly noise. When
we ignore it, it disturbs us. When we listen to it,
we find it fascinating. — John Cage[2]

Bring the Noise

⬤ No music has received the appellation "noise" more frequently
than rock. In *A Natural History of the Senses,* Diane Ackerman
singles out the "Armageddon of heavy-metal rock" in a boys' dormitory as her primary example of noise: she describes it as diabolical
torture, so loud that it ceases to be music.[3] When my brothers and I first
began to buy rock records, my father complained that we were wasting
our money on recordings of car crashes. Rather obviously, he thought
they were noise. (And this was years before Greil Marcus said that the
first Sex Pistols' records sounded like traffic accidents!) In contrast
to Ackerman and parents everywhere, rock critics frequently mention
noise as a positive contribution. Nirvana, for instance, is praised for
its "blend of catchy melodies and punk noise."[4] In 1993, both David
Bowie and Anthrax released albums whose titles invoke noise: *Black
Tie White Noise* and *Sound of White Noise.* Bands have adopted names
like Noiseaddict and The Art of Noise. There are hundreds of songs
featuring the term in their titles. How are we to make sense of this? In
particular, what can it mean to describe one's own music as noise?

It seems that the rock community has reworked the *concept* of noise
in a way that converts an epithet of disdain into one of achievement.
My focus, then, is not that of detractors like Ackerman. It is on the rock

community's celebration of noise. As such, "noise" is not used pejoratively, nor is it used in quite the way that recent nonrock composers often intend. For how many besides John Cage and exponents of *musique concrète* enjoy sheer sound or noise as elements of musical composition? Bands like Suicide and Throbbing Gristle may bear their influence, but their music is unknown to most rock fans. One of the few cases in rock music to sell in appreciable quantities is John Lennon's "Revolution 9," but only because of its presence on *The Beatles* (the "White Album," 1968). Placed on the album against the advice of George Martin and Paul McCartney, there are certainly few besides Karl Wallinger who claim to enjoy it as anything more than clues to Paul's "death." Lennon's other work in the same vein, with Yoko Ono, attracted few buyers.

Other cases include the Grateful Dead's *Live Dead* (1970), which offers nine minutes of feedback improvisation, and Jefferson Airplane's "Crushingura" (1968), courtesy of Spencer Dryden, a slice of genuine electronic composition released shortly before "Revolution 9." Lou Reed's *Metal Machine Music* (1975) consists of sixty minutes of random feedback, but may have been intended as a slap at his record company, RCA. However, these experiments are hardly typical rock music. While Sonic Youth is closely associated with the experiments of composer Glenn Branca, guitarist Thurston Moore is at pains to say "the music was never just about feedback."[5] In the sphere of popular music, even Moore recognizes that aural sculpting of sound without a beat or melody is not accepted as music.

A more interesting dimension is found in the fact that most of rock music is disseminated through recordings. Analyzing the music of Jimi Hendrix, Sheila Whitely says of "Purple Haze" that its "sheer volume of noise works towards the drowning of personal consciousness."[6] This should give us pause; Whitely is discussing a recording, and *any* recording can be turned up to a level where it might "drown" personal consciousness through sheer volume. Surely Whitely herself decided that high volume is particularly suitable for "Purple Haze," more so than for "Little Wing" or "Spanish Castle Music." Listening to recordings and the radio, the audience controls the volume level. Yet different musics seem to demand different volumes. Heavy metal and rap call for more decibels than, say, Les Paul or a Bach concerto. David Bowie's *The Rise and Fall of Ziggy Stardust* (1972) carries advice on the back COVER: TO BE PLAYED AT MAXIMUM VOLUME. We don't find this advice on New Age recordings. So what role or roles does high volume play in our experience of such music? Does it make an *aesthetic* contribution?

Without proposing any one overriding meaning for noise in rock, I will map out several varieties present in rock music (often simultaneously). With the exception of excessive volume, their presence or absence depends on shared expectations of listening. Indeed, it is the tension between rock expectations and more traditional ones that allows various sonic properties to be noise in the way most valued in rock.

Let us start with the most basic assumption, that noise is to sound as a disruptive brat is to children: "Noise is any sound which is treated as a nuisance."[7] Or, as Edgar Varèse put it, "Subjectively, *noise* is any sound one doesn't like."[8] But how subjective is it? To categorize sound as noise is to assign it a status relative to established norms for allowable and proscribed sounds. In "classical" music, noise is usually a sound that distracts because it does not contribute to pitch articulation. Unfamiliar rhythms and harmonies are similarly unwelcome when they disrupt cultural expectations. On the other hand, if one's aim is disruption, noise will be a positive characteristic, representing the subversive, the marginalized, and the repressed. Jacques Attali observes that we cannot separate issues of music and noise from those of political control.[9] To describe any feature of a musical performance as noise is to recommend its censorship or suppression.

Attali regards all musical organization as political organization. Music is the sublimation and channelization of noise. When an individual embraces the musical rules of the dominant society, it reflects sublimation of that individual to the body politic, for "the code of music simulates the accepted rules of society."[10] On the positive side, music is thus a condition for the creation and consolidation of community. On the negative side, musical standardization can be a mode of political totalitarianism.

Musicians and musicologists often employ a very narrow technical notion, under which a sound is a noise only if its originating frequency is nonperiodic and thus of no determinate pitch, or at least random relative to human perception. In such cases the sound wave is too irregular to offer a determinate pitch in relation to other sounds. Robin Maconie observes that both "action noises" like the clatter of keys and instruments whose sound decays rapidly are also noise in the context of a modern orchestra.[11] In declaring that these are noises, the dominant musical culture controls access to music by assigning priority to its harmonic dimension.

Some noises are permitted because they are characteristic of specific objects, like the typewriter and pistol shots of Erik Satie's "Parade"

(1915). In this vein, the Beach Boys employed the munching of vegetables and the pouring of juice on "Vegetables" (1967), and Jefferson Airplane unleashed scissors and snorting nostrils on "Lather" (1968). Jackson Browne uses the sound of a car engine on *Late for the Sky* (1974), the Shangri-Las' gloriously trashy "Leader of the Pack" (1964) includes a motorcycle, and the Beach Boys end *Pet Sounds* (1966) on a note of pathos with the sound of dogs barking at a passing train. Rock features thousands of such examples, but they are not really *musical* elements of the recording. The specific sound is often irrelevant. Consider the birds chirping at the end of "Blackbird" on *The Beatles*. Other bird sounds would work just as well. There is no question of their being in tune with the music; a higher or lower pitch might work just as well. While evocative, such sound effects remain marginal cases of noise in rock music. What they readily demonstrate is that the narrow technical sense of "noise" — as unpitched sound — is not *always* a negative criterion of value in musical contexts.

Percussion instruments are the only unpitched instruments tolerated in most Western music. Their relative importance in rock surely played some role in its being "noise" early on, when the sounds of rock and roll constituted violence to established decorum. This was *Billboard*'s underlying message in a review of Wild Bill Moore's "We're Gonna Rock" (1948), describing Paul Williams' saxophone work as "honks, shrieks and . . . unmusical noises." At the same time, the accusation of noise is an implicit recognition that the audience for such sounds is not satisfied with the status quo. But five decades later, it is difficult to imagine *Billboard* attacking any release as noise. The charge is more likely to be a partisan attack, as the fans of one genre dismiss another. Attempts to recapture that original threat by highlighting new ways to make noise often do nothing more than carve out new genres that delight a small audience, ignored by most listeners.

Attali believes that there must be a crisis in the prevailing social order before a way opens to alternative modes of musical organization. These subversive codes may or may not succeed.[12] Noises may be repressed or they may be defused by being co-opted and assimilated. When embraced as a new mode of organization, they can become a standard for new repression.[13] Unwilling to censure any sound as unmusical, rock's power to signify the marginal and the dispossessed depends on its position as an alternative music. After forty years, mass success, and the collapse of the Soviet Union, there are few places in the world where rock is automatically dangerous, threatening, and subversive.[14] Attali gloomily concludes that rock is now a tool of bureaucratic power, doing more to silence people than to empower them.[15] There are pockets of noise left, as evidenced by the furor over "Cop Killer" and the difficulty rap groups have in securing concert venues, but on the whole rock's noise hardly threatens the social order.[16]

Categories of Noise

I never grew out of liking noise, from Little Richard . . . to the Stooges, so I always liked rock and grabbed hungrily at the Yardbirds/Who development, expecting great things. — Lester Bangs, 1970[17]

This is where the party's at — where the vibration from the bass . . . is best felt. Booommm!!! Right in the chest. Yeahhh. — MC T-Love[18]

Tape hiss and "white" noise are common examples of sounds that even a rock fan regards as noise; the former involves random frequencies at the high end of our hearing range, while the latter involves a mixture of all or many audible frequencies presented with equal intensity, so there is no fundamental tone to provide a definite pitch. Committed to the ideology of recording transparency, tape hiss and static are precisely the sounds that rock fans do not want to hear. While electronic music often employs such sounds as a raw material, they are generally regarded as musical only when they have been shaped or filtered to some specific range.

Nonmusicians who study noise, usually as noise pollution or the "noise problem," uncouple noise from pitch altogether. They recognize three very different ways in which sounds are unwanted. The connotations are again pejorative and involve a loss of organization or control. But rock musicians happily incorporate all three into their music.

In the first and widest sense, noise is any sound in the environment that interferes with human communication; any competing information that masks desired information qualifies. Static on a telephone line is noise, but so is interference with the picture on my television when someone runs an appliance in the kitchen. Statisticians use the term for random fluctuations in data that they regard as meaningless: "The cycles of temperature we've recorded are nothing but noise." It also includes disruptions in the anticipated flow of a communication. Stray notes in a musical performance are noise in this sense. When the Who incorporated random, unpredictable bursts of feedback in place of guitar solos on their early singles, they exploited this category of noise.

Secondly, any sounds that disturb or distract us are noise. When a ringing telephone disrupts our sleep, it's a noise, even if it communicates in a perfectly clear way that someone is calling. Otherwise congenial sounds are noise when they interfere with concentration and work.

Third and finally, there is sound which threatens us with physical harm. What this usually means is sound at a volume that threatens our hearing. Live performances of rock music have been measured at levels exceeding those of jets on takeoff, above the normal threshold for pain. Among the loudest acts have been the Who, Blue Cheer, the MC5, and the Clash. Manowar's 1994 attempt to reach 160 decibels and set a new Guinness record as loudest rock act was stopped, ironically enough, by a local noise ordinance.

Rock exploits all three of these categories, but whether in a pejorative sense depends on one's expectations. Rock lyrics can be indecipherable, poorly articulated, or lost in the mix. The instrumental accompaniment might then count as noise to someone who wants to understand the words. Remembering the first time he heard the Velvet Underground's "Sister Ray," Lester Bangs recalls that the only thing he could make out distinctly was the organ. In other words, its production and engineering make for a noisy recording. On the other hand, a pejorative charge of noise would assume that the words or instrumental lines are meant to be readily heard and understood. Bangs had no such expectation. (From this perspective, opera involves a lot of noise, too. The vowels are distorted and stretched in the singer's quest for volume, and the words are masked by orchestration. The result can be impossible to follow even when one knows the language.)

Like opera fans, rock fans often consult the libretto when they want to know the words. In rock, vocals are often mixed as one element among many, rather than foregrounded with an instrumental background. Indeed, older recordings can seem quaint with their overemphasis on the vocals. One of the indicators used to distinguish rock from pop is that the latter emphasizes vocals and de-emphasizes the rhythm section. Clear enunciation is essential for pop, whereas rock singers are notorious for injecting a degree of incoherence into their vocals. In pop, the voice is thrust to the front and the lower tones which can mask it are kept to the back of the mix. Rock takes a more democratic approach and balances the voice against the other elements of the mix. There may be no attempt at clear articulation, and expression is conveyed by the tone and "gesture" of the voice rather than the words. Among major rock performers in recent years, R.E.M. is conspicuous for not supplying lyrics. Their early records are also notorious for

Michael Stipe's lack of articulation; with their return to that strategy for *Monster* (1994), the record was often described as noisy.

Nonetheless, the main reason that rock is noise, for both fans and detractors, is volume. Any music played at intrusive volumes (e.g., Charlie Parker records at full blast while someone else is on the telephone in the same room) gets called noise. So Brian Epstein, manager of the Beatles, titled his ghost-written autobiography *A Cellar Full of Noise*. The cellar refers to his first visit to see them, at Liverpool's underground Cavern Club. Epstein emphasizes the volume of their show as it reverberated through the three tunnels that made up the club, but nothing in his description of the event suggests that he regarded the performance as unmusical or incompetent. After all, it led him to become their manager. But if we return to the idea that sound is noise when it harms or disrupts, volume is noise only in a derivative sense. Volume does not have to be noise in the pejorative sense, and certainly not when high volume plays some further role in the music.

Again, one such role is political. Philosopher Herbert Marcuse, evidently a stranger to American humor, quotes one of Grace Slick's quips about Jefferson Airplane's desire for ever greater volume as serious evidence that rock is essentially "noisy aggression."[19] Surely it is the *intrusion* of high volume, and not the volume itself, that constitutes the noise and the aggression. Whether one is listening with the volume cranked as one drives along, windows down so that all the world gets a share of your musical taste, or lives in an apartment or dormitory so that one can't help but experience the neighbor's music, rock is frequently intrusive. Its heavy bass frequencies can travel a considerable distance while still retaining an impact.

However, rock is not unique in this tendency to intrude into public space. Two hundred years ago, Immanuel Kant complained that "music has a lack of urbanity about it." Unlike literature, it imposes itself on the neighbors and thus "impairs the freedom of those outside the musical party." He even complains about Lutheran hymns, believing that windows should be closed during their singing:

> Those who have recommended that the singing of hymns be included at family prayer have failed to consider that by such a *noisy* . . . worship they impose great hardship on the public, since they compel their neighbors to either join in the singing or put aside whatever they were thinking about.[20]

Kant notes the public and thus explosively political nature of music making; unlike literature, one's taste for music is an unusually public fact about oneself. And of course this factor is exploited, as when a defiant Radio Raheem blasts Public Enemy's "Fight the Power" on his boom box in the pizza parlor, turning music into a weapon of aggressive pride and triggering the confrontation that climaxes Spike Lee's *Do the Right Thing*.

So when Tricia Rose faults a music professor's open hostility to rap music, attributing his dismissal to sheer ignorance and prejudice, she may be downplaying what he correctly understands. The man complains that "they ride down the street at 2:00 A.M. with [rap] blasting from car speakers, and wake up my wife and kids."[21] Isn't this an intended effect? Surely one function of playing it at this volume, at this hour, is as a gesture of defiance toward the dominant culture. Here we come hard against Attali's proposal that all distinctions between music and noise, as allowable and taboo uses of music, have a political and ideological dimension. Intrusions are not just personal affronts, disruptions of one's solitude and privacy. Rereading Kant's complaint, note his emphasis on "the public." To drive along at 2:00 A.M. with a booming bass is to make a statement about one's relationship to the bourgeois public, a public in the habit of sleeping at that hour.

Volume may initiate other, more subtle subversions in lending weight and impact to music. For a receptive audience, volume bridges the sense of distance between the audience and the performers by erasing the gap between the self and the music. John Shepherd argues that reliance on vision stresses "separation at a distance," whereas touch is fundamental to a distinction "between us and non-us." In contrast, hearing "stresses the integrative and relational."[22] When not functioning as mere background, loud music can break us out of our sense of detached observation and replace it with a sense of immersion, for it is literally around us (or, with headphones, seemingly inside our head). Where traditional aesthetic theories have often offered an ideal of disinterested contemplation or "psychical distance," the presence of noise can overcome the respectful, reverential aspects of distancing.[23]

According to Roland Barthes, there are now "two musics." There is music to listen to, and then there is music for playing.[24] In bourgeois life, the former dominates, so music "is no longer manual, muscular, kneadingly physical." The control of volume and its physicality is a key reason. Barthes further observes the younger generation's use of voice and guitar are noteworthy for preserving played, "amateur" music. While this may have reached its apotheosis later in the do-it-yourself aesthetic of punk, it spills over into most rock, including punk's nemesis, classic rock. At sufficient volume, any rhythm section has a visceral punch, physical and felt. As Barthes notes, popular music can be "manual" and "in a way much more sensual" than typical concert-hall music. I recall a performance by the Dream Syndicate at which a group of deaf students gathered directly in front of the speakers and danced to the sound waves they felt.

Barthes' point was brought home to me on a recent airplane flight. Plugging in the headset provided by the airline, I found the volume too low even when set at the maximum. Switching between programs of Beethoven and Bonnie Raitt, the latter just didn't sound loud enough at that setting, but Beethoven was fine. Beethoven, not surprisingly, is Barthes' own example of music that cannot be mastered by the amateur. It is for hearing, not playing. In contrast, live rock encourages a range of participatory elements prohibited in the serious concert hall. With recorded rock, many fans drum and sing along, and there is always air guitar.

Does volume have the potential to do more than break down detachment? While it is seldom realized, Shepherd contends it does. Music — particularly its timbre, texture, or grain — threatens the visual basis of Western social codes. But then shouldn't Beethoven, played loud, do the same? For Shepherd, "classical" music is still dominated by the visual character of notation, but "popular" music has the potential to challenge visually grounded distinctions supporting male hegemony. Providing a world "fluid in its evanescence," such music "reminds men of the fragile and atrophied nature of their control over the world."

However, if touch is basic to maintaining a line between self and nonself, the typical volumes of rock music may only reinforce a passive and atomistic sense of the self. Too often, rock's volume functions as a filter on the world, fostering withdrawal rather than facilitating communication. As Evan Eisenberg paradoxically phrases it, we often listen to records "as shields against other people's sounds. . . . certain kinds of simple music, such as hard rock, are right for the city, being not so much a substitute for silence as a fulfillment of noise."[25] At high volume, rock creates a cocoon of sound that screens out other, unwanted sounds. While I have no hard evidence, I suspect that this may be one of the major uses of rock music in daily life. Some people use jazz for this purpose. Some use country. Some use classical. But nothing else functions as well as rock. Physical and sensual, felt and heard, rock invites us to crank the volume and overwhelm consciousness.

The Quest for Volume

The best thing you can do, brother, is turn it up
as loud as it'll go. — Advice to Billy Gibbons from Jimi Hendrix[26]

The Stooges' music, for all practical purposes, is
one big noise that throbs. — Early review by Mike Jahn[27]

Why else is rock music played so loud? And why the urge to play Jimi Hendrix louder than Simon and Garfunkel, and Patti Smith or Hole louder than the Indigo Girls or Cowboy Junkies? Are they simply more suitable as noisy aggression? If volume were primarily a matter of aggression and resistance, it would occur almost exclusively as a public gesture. Yet rock is often played at low volumes when practical demands intrude. When my secretary listens to the radio at her desk, she listens to rock at a low volume. When it serves as background music in the mall, it may be almost subliminal. But these are public spaces where the presence of the public demands it. In personal space, one is relatively free to set the volume higher. And rock fans do.

Walkman wearers do so constantly. Although the personal headphone alleviates noise in the form of other people's loud music, it is one of the most prevalent sources of noise as a direct threat to physical health. There is ample evidence that headphones are causing permanent ear damage to a whole generation of rock fans. Most people who wear headphones turn up the volume to levels that are relatively higher than for the same music without headphones, exacerbating the threat to themselves in the very act of freeing others from their tastes. Here, rock fans employ high volume even when there is no "practical" or political need for it, and we can hardly write this off as mere foolishness or even as desensitivity to sound.

Peter Townshend attributes his serious tinnitus (a constant ringing in the ears) to frequent use of headphones at high volumes, rather than the tremendous volumes generated by the Who onstage:

> It was not loud guitar onstage rock 'n' roll style. It's very important to make this point. It was *earphones!* . . . It was going home after gigs, to my own studio, and playing guitar through the earphones. . . . Obviously I couldn't have a Marshall stack in my living room and practice with the babies upstairs. I used earphones for 20 years.[28]

Discussing his early days emulating blues guitarists, Keith Richards reveals that he started on acoustic: "It took a while longer to get the electric bit together. At the time we thought, 'Oh, it just makes it louder,' but it ain't quite as simple as that."[29] For just this reason, Townshend practiced at home through earphones at high volumes: "My sound was an electric sound. You couldn't reproduce it on an acoustic guitar."[30]

What both guitarists emphasize is that amplification is not just a question of volume (and thus not just noisy aggression). High volume is employed to produce sound of a certain character, unique to electronically amplified music. There is a reciprocal relationship between volume and sound quality; increasing the amplitude of a sound wave alters its characteristic pattern and thus its timbre. This may not have been anyone's original intent. Microphones were initially adopted to make music louder, but musicians now exploit the microphone, amplification, and resultant technologies for musical effects besides volume.

The pre-electronic way to increase volume is to add more instruments. The volume difference between a chamber group and a symphony orchestra in the same room is illustration enough. (One of the early criticisms of recordings as a medium for music was that early machines did not reproduce orchestral music loud enough!) But adding more instruments also requires a different arrangement of the music, and ultimately a different sort of music. You can't reproduce the distinct and interweaving lines of a string quartet by quadrupling each instrument or with a marching band or symphony orchestra. When a mass of instruments functions as a single voice, as does a string or horn section of an orchestra or band, texture thickens while flexibility decreases. In fact, guitar was a relatively underutilized instrument for public performance before amplification. The acoustic was a portable instrument for "cowboy" music and blues singers, but its sound was easily lost in any popular music ensemble. The banjo was far better suited to ensemble music.

In popular music, particularly the country and blues traditions nurturing rock, electrified amplification was the obvious solution to the problem of playing to large audiences with a small group. It was partly a matter of economic expedience; how do you play to more people, many of whom are dancing and few of whom are listening with the respectful silence afforded "serious" music, without swelling the payroll? Muddy Waters played acoustic country blues until he migrated to Chicago, where he plugged in and turned up the volume. A funny thing happened to Waters, transforming him from a delta bluesman into a protorocker. The technology of urban music transformed the blues: "The difference, of course, was amplification: not just amplification but an ingenious way of recording voice and electric guitar and bass, and blending them together into *a new sound*."[31] Amplification of electric guitar produces a new sound, not just a louder sound. Volume brings out characteristics of sound that are exploited by rock musicians for expressive purposes, and the audience plays the music at high volume largely because it is necessary for bringing out that "new" sound.

Consider Jimi Hendrix's advice to a young Billy Gibbons, quoted above. Hendrix was talking, of course, about the electric guitar. And if any instrument typifies rock music, it is the electric guitar, and exploiting timbre through volume is the common element in almost every case where rock is described as "noise." Volume becomes noise because of the *way* that Nirvana and Neil Young employ electric guitar: the tone colors that are most characteristic of their sound include heavy distortion and barrages of feedback. As with Hendrix, one of the mainstays is timbre that only occurs at top volume. As Tricia Rose observes about rap musicians's similar quest for volume, "Boosting the bass is not merely a question of loudness — it is a question of the quality of lower-register sounds at high volumes."[32] For that very reason, however, these uses of volume play a compositional role, akin to the choice of a specific and perhaps signature color in the palette of a painter.

The quest for new sounds explains why certain groups are singled out for trading in noise even when they may not cross over the pain threshold or play louder than other groups. Nirvana surprised pundits who were busy writing obituaries for rock when they shot past Michael Jackson on the chart in late 1991 and early 1992; early descriptions pegged them as purveyors of "punk noise" and as one of the new breed of "noise bands."[33] Yet Nirvana were not particularly loud, and anyway the volume of the recording (as opposed to a concert) is up to the person playing it. Similarly, when Neil Young tours solo, his lone piano or guitar is amplified and he sings into a microphone so that the thousands of fans in the auditorium can hear him. When he tours with Crazy Horse and cranks the volume, as he did during the Gulf War in 1991, one critic remarked that it was a great show "for noise freaks."[34] But again, Young does not play at unusual volumes for arena rock. The term is being used to characterize timbre more than volume.

Here we find another analogy between rock and cinema: volume is analogous to the size of the screen at a cinema. Both have an aesthetic function beyond the practical goal of delivering the sounds or picture to many people at the same time. A film projected onto a screen in a theater delivers one film to many people in the same place. But the problem of mass delivery can be resolved in other ways. Television solves the problem by having many small screens delivering the same picture to many small audiences simultaneously. Yet as a result of the techno-logical solution, there are well-known aesthetic differences between films produced for cinema projection and for television. The changes were qualitative, not just quantitative. Is there any reason to be sur-prised, then, if music conceived for electronic amplification and electric instruments differs from music conceived for unamplified delivery?

Seeing a film on a television screen distorts the experience of the big screen, even if properly "boxed" so nothing is cut from the sides in presenting it on a screen with a shorter ratio of width to height. Even when the dimensions of the frame are preserved, smaller scale trans-lates to less impact. *Lawrence of Arabia* and *2001: A Space Odyssey* are not the same experience away from the big screen. You need its size to experience the vastness of the desert or of space. As Matisse said of painting and drawing, changing the shape and size of the canvas changes both the content and the form of the work. And just as dif-ferent screen dimensions introduce different problems and possibilities for film, different volume levels are appropriate for different styles of rock. Led Zeppelin and the Sex Pistols, not to mention their countless offspring, are just not the same at Muzak volume levels. The next section looks more closely at the shifts in aesthetic qualities that occur when volume increases.

Some Basics of Acoustics

Everyone viewed it as a bunch of noise.
— Reaction to "River Deep–Mountain High"[35]

I can make something loud, but how can I make it the loudest, most abrasive thing I've ever heard? — Trent Reznor of Nine Inch Nails[36]

As much as any other technology, the electric guitar and bass were pivotal in the emergence of a distinct rock tradition. As Townshend and Richards emphasize, an electric guitar is not merely an amplified guitar. Jazz had already featured electric guitar, but rock developed the instru-ment in its own ways. Elvis gyrated while holding an acoustic; Scotty Moore had the electric solos, even if he was pretty much in the back-ground during live performances. By the mid-1960s, the solid-body electric guitar was entrenched as the emblematic rock instrument, and Bob Dylan was attacked viciously as a sellout simply for using one. A barrage of other electric instruments are used in rock, but the electric guitar remains the primary case of rock's adherence to an aesthetic dominated by the possibilities of unorthodox timbres and techniques.

Electric guitars send their signal to the amplifier from a set of magnets called pickups. The amp does not amplify the sound of the struck and vibrating string. Any motion of the metal strings alters the electric current flowing through the pickups; registering this motion rather than the sound of the strings, the pickups generate the actual frequencies sent for amplification, including harmonic overtones that are not otherwise present. In other words, although rock musicians often use pickups to amplify acoustic guitars, the electric guitar is not just a microphone mounted in an acoustic guitar. An electric guitarist creates and controls an electric signal by means of the instrument. The sounds produced depend on the capacities and interactions of the preamplifier and the amplifier. The instrument in the musician's hands can be regarded as a mere means to generating and manipulating electronic sounds.

Furthermore, sonic events are extremely complex. Phenomenological or heard differences in the sounds we experience can be traced to the physical dimensions of amplitude, frequency, duration, and form of the sound waves. (I will simply ignore the further complications introduced by the physical space in which the sound waves travel.) Their perceptual correlatives are volume, pitch, length, and timbre (tone color), respectively. An electric guitar's amplifier boosts amplitude, of course, but *it thereby alters the timbre* of any note that is played. Increased amplitude brings out more partials (both harmonic and nonharmonic). When a complex sonic event is given more volume, elements that are masked within the experienced sound emerge as distinct elements within the heard sounds. As Robert Walser notes, heavy-metal power chords produce tones both above and below the main tones.[37]

Timbre is not strictly a matter of which harmonics are audible and their relative amplitudes, of course; the transient harmonics are equally important. In brief, the attack and decay phases of a sound are equally important characteristics in generating distinct timbres. Here, too, volume brings out new elements of the attack and decay phases and thus enriches timbre, particularly in light of the fact that the attack and decay phases are rich with nonharmonic overtones. (At low volumes we easily ignore them.) The most celebrated example in rock music is the final chord of the Beatles' "A Day in the Life," on *Sgt. Pepper* (1967). The chord was struck simultaneously on four pianos, and nine takes were needed before the pianists got the chord precisely synchronized. By steadily increasing the recording volume as the chord died away, the chord can be heard for nearly fifty-four seconds. The long, dying fall that puts the album to rest would be impossible but for mechanical control of amplitude. (Reversing sounds alters timbre by reversing attack and decay, but this effect is not directly tied to volume manipulation. Celebrated examples include the backward guitar line on Jimi Hendrix's "Are You Experienced?" and the backward *echo* on several Led Zeppelin tracks.)

The loudness or volume of the sound depends on amplitude, not frequency. Pitch identification is basically due to the frequency of the fundamental tone. Frequency, measured in hertz, is rate of the physical vibration of the sound waves. As sound waves shorten, more reach our ear per second, and pitch goes up. Suppose we are listening to Nico on the stereo and turn up the volume. Doing so increases the force of the sound waves (measured in decibels or "dB"). We then perceive it as louder, yet Nico's characteristically low voice does not sound any higher in pitch. So amplification increases volume without altering frequency. (The way to raise the frequency and thus the pitch is to speed up the machine, such as playing a 33 rpm record at 45 rpm. In an age where turntables are becoming obsolete, the same effect can be duplicated on a cassette player with a high speed dubbing capacity.)

Selective amplification also allows control over a sound's brightness. When a select band of higher-frequency partials is amplified, so that they are more prominent in relation to the fundamental, it results in a brighter tone without changing the perceived pitch of the tone, since the frequency of the fundamental is unchanged. Older stereo equipment allows some control of this through a "tone control," and newer equalization equipment provides selective adjustment of brightness at specific band widths. Brightness and dullness is regularly manipulated during the recording process.

The upshot of these facts about acoustics and hearing is that, when we regard musical *works* as a matter of pitch and harmonic relationships, volume and timbre become independent variables of *performance*. But it is seldom so simple. The presence of forte and diminuendo in a classical score has its expressive function; the "surprise" in the second movement of Haydn's *Surprise* Symphony (No. 94) would not have the same impact if played softly! The pianissimo instructions at the very end of Beethoven's *Coriolanus* Overture bring about a quietness that surely stands for Coriolanus' death.[38] Nonetheless, traditional music theory and composers have said relatively little about volume's role in the presentation and reception of music. Even in the realm of electronic music, where volume is explicitly recognized as a distinct variable in the design of the music, it is often treated as independent of timbre. But with modern amplification systems and recording processes, volume and timbre are not distinct variables. Rock musicians display a remarkable consistency in exploring the connection between volume, timbre, and musical expressiveness, so that volume is employed as a means to an expressive end.

Russolo on Noise

Anything that sounds good to your ear, a nice type of sound, is music.
— Thelonious Monk[39]

The waiter brings the only fresh egg he has, but the man at breakfast sends it back because it doesn't fit his eggcup. Why can't music go out in the same way it comes in to a man, without having to crawl over a fence of sounds, thoraxes, catguts, wire, wood, and brass? . . . The instrument! . . . there is the perennial difficulty — there is music's limitation. — Charles Ives[40]

To the extent that rock music is played at volumes that damage hearing, there is no question: noise is present. But when the characteristic sounds of rock music are loud but not at damage levels, the most obvious pejorative senses of "noise" do not obtain. Its status as noise depends on its opposition to the entrenched view that some tone colors are simply not musical. Like Charles Ives, I can see nothing but prejudice and repression in the doctrine that certain timbres are inappropriate for music making. Like Ives, I think that specific sounds are only right or wrong in relation to a specific piece of music, not just a type of music. But this willingness to experiment with new sounds and customize works is decidedly modernist. Looking at its early formulations, we come to our final sense of "noise," the one most often used in the rock tradition to acknowledge the presence of noise *approvingly.*

If Ives toys with the idea and John Cage gets the lion's share of attention, both are exploring distinct strands of a tradition anticipated by Luigi Russolo's *The Art of Noises.*[41] Influenced by Balilla Pratella's two manifestos on futurist music in 1910 and 1911, Russolo issued a "Futurist Manifesto" for composers in March 1913. In it, he calls for the multiplication of timbres available to composers. He staged the first concert demonstration of his principles later that year. By June 1914, he had advanced in the practical application of his ideas to the point of conducting twelve concerts for "new electric instruments" at the London Coliseum. The instruments included "noise spirals" and an "orchestra of 23 noise tuners."[42] The World War halted his experiments and they resumed only sporadically afterward, grinding to a halt after 1927 due to lack of funding. His essays were published as *L'Arte dei*

Rumori in 1916, when the available instruments were mechanical contraptions rather than true electronic instruments.

Russolo's principal theme, the one that makes him of relevance as something more than a historical curiosity, is that sounds are normally distinguished from noises according to the richness of timbre: "the real and fundamental difference between sound and noise can be reduced to this alone: Noise is generally much richer in harmonics than sound. And the harmonics of noise are usually more intense than those that accompany sound."[43] The distinction is a convention of Western art music. Intent on precise pitch articulation, such music affirms allegiance to the abstract sound structure as the primary musical work. Nonharmonic partials are positively shunned. (It is said that the saxophone never became a member of the orchestra because of the difficulty in standardizing the harmonics.)

Vocalists in the same tradition, particularly those who sing opera, are taught to project their "chest" voice over their accompaniment. In the middle of the nineteenth century, "good tone" was described in no uncertain terms: "avoid all nasal, labial, dental, and guttural peculiarities; . . . remove thinness, thickness, slenderness, reedy harshness, as well as other disagreeable qualities which are without a name."[44] This ideal vocal quality emphasizes purity in articulation, and most of the frequencies produced with a normal speaking voice have to be eliminated through practice. Any richness of the contributing overtones is unwelcome noise.

If one wants a restricted pitch articulation in musical performance, the instruments of the classical orchestra and the classically trained voice are perfect for the job. But there is no compelling reason why richness of overtones should not be valued and exploited as much as richness in harmony. When one is interested in exploring texture, timbre, and rhythmic values — hallmarks of rock — amplification and the electronic mixing of sounds allow far more "noise" into the mix. The result is *not* noise in the sense of unpitched sound, indeterminate pitch, or disruptive sound. As Russolo notes, "every noise has a pitch." Excluding white noise, he is more or less accurate. More important,

> we want to give pitches to these diverse noises, regulating them harmonically and rhythmically. Giving pitch to noises does not mean depriving them of all irregular movements and vibrations. . . . there may be imparted to a given noise not only a single pitch but even a variety of pitches without sacrificing its character, by which I mean the timbre that distinguishes it.[45]

Selective electronic amplification is, of course, our best means of bringing about enriched overtones while preserving determinate pitch. The resulting music can thus conform to expectations of melody and harmony while expanding in another dimension.

In bringing his theory to practice, Russolo designed and constructed a wide range of mechanical "noise instruments." Each had a specific timbre, cones for sound projection, and pitch ranges of one to two octaves. Percussion, pitched whistles, and scraping sounds were combined in the belief that exposure to sounds "new for the ear" would allow the audience to experience new emotions. Who, he wonders, can "hope to discover any new emotions" in the standard orchestra?[46] Performed in groups of twenty or thirty instruments, contemporaries report that Russolo's ensembles were poorly rehearsed but produced a ferocious din.

Russolo reasons that because the standard orchestral *timbres* are so well known that they can produce nothing but a yawn, the *music* must suffer the same fate; thus, there is no longer any point to writing for the same old instruments. This argument is spurious in two ways. First, the familiarity of the timbres may direct our attention to melodic and harmonic aspects of the music, and these can certainly yield novel results in the hands of new composers. We should not infer anything about composers from a contingent fact about the audience. Second, and more serious, Russolo reasons that because established timbres elicit the emotion of boredom, new emotions will only be expressed in the music by eliciting new reactions in the audience, and this in turn demands new sounds for presenting music. Through novelty, "their interest remains ever alive, the attention ever receptive." As an argument, this goes nowhere. Interesting timbres may or may not produce "new" emotions, but there is no reason to suppose that musical works ever "discover" new emotions.

However, there is no need to accept Russolo's opinion that novel means will result in novel subject matter. It is perfectly consistent with the goal of avoiding boredom and maintaining active interest in music to simply rediscover the same emotions in new timbres. (For the time being, let us pass over the dubious suggestion that emotions are present in music by virtue of the music's producing that emotion in the audience.) It is enough to give a new face to a basic range of human emotions, among them sadness, joy, anxiety, and love. Why suppose that twentieth-century guitarists have anything radically new to say with their enhanced timbres? It is enough that they have a new way of saying it, so that we want to listen to them. Enhanced timbres may also contribute to refinement in the expression of emotion. In combination with melody and rhythm, musical performance can delineate and explore emotions more forcefully, if not always more precisely.

Russolo is closer to the mark with a different line of argument. If we are looking for a broader palette of sounds, for whatever reason, we must turn to more complicated sounds: "noise-sound."[47] Our environment provides us with an infinite variety of noises which can be organized into legitimate musical compositions by virtue of their predominate pitch. We can listen to the trotting of horses, the rumble of thunder, and the electric motors and other machines which surround us in urban life. But Russolo is not calling for *musique concrète*, nor for the random techniques of John Cage. We must, Russolo proposes, "conquer" the noises, "regulating them harmonically and rhythmically" while preserving their timbral richness.[48] Russolo's interest in "natural" tuning and enharmonic composition as an alternative to standard temperament and "the diatonic system" illustrates his keen interest in subtleties of pitch. Many of his remarks about the employment of enharmonicism and natural intonation are an accurate description of how rock vocalists slide up to and then off of the desired pitch, or hit the same note at audibly distinct pitches when it is repeated while producing the desired note in the scale. Despite his interest in "noise," he seems to have had no interest in sound compositions of unpitched sounds. While he advises us to listen to nature and our surroundings as evidence that modern notions of pitch are artificial and needlessly limiting, Russolo opposes the practice of constructing music out of the actual sounds in our environment.

He worries, quite rightly, that environmental sounds are invariably identified as effects "bound to the causes that produce it." When we reproduce the noises "of life," we invite the audience to form an impressionistic narrative centered around the sources. The result may be an aural composition, but it is not music as Russolo understands it. For genuinely musical composition, "timbres [must] become abstract material for works of art to be formed from them." When noise-sounds are thus made abstract, attention turns to the sounds themselves; "We hear it suddenly become autonomous and malleable material, ready to be molded to the will of the artist, who transforms it into an element of emotion, into a work of art."[49] Central to this process is our ability to control pitch, volume, and "rhythm" or pulse. As we will see in the next two sections, the electric guitar fits Russolo's recipe, as do more advanced synthesizers.

Russolo's "manifesto" is a defense of noise, then, in just the sense that noise is central to rock music. Rock musicians exploit technology for new and richer timbres while still maintaining recognizable melodic contours. Constantly scrambling for financial backing, Russolo did not have the means available today to any teen with three hundred dollars and a trip to a pawn shop. But he had the theory. Rock musicians, having the means, rediscover his theory in their daily practice. Intolerant of volume and unfamiliar overtones, rock's detractors hear this richness as noise, too, but not the sort that Russolo celebrates as "noise-sound." The presence of such noise is neutral with respect to musical value; it may contribute to the music, or it may be employed to mask the fact that the musicians have no musical ideas to offer. But it is seldom an end in itself.

Electric Guitar

Suddenly four men with brutally cut hair come on stage, bark
into a microphone, start making an industrial noise.
— First impression of the Clash[50]

Collision of melody and noise. — A description of Hüsker Dü's sound[51]

Composers extracting hooks, harmonies, and micromelodies out
of the git's capacity for infernal din.
— Concert review of My Bloody Valentine[52]

Tangled thickets of noise. — Review of Babes in Toyland[53]

We wanted noise. — Michael Stipe on R.E.M.'s *Monster*[54]

In the 1950s and 1960s, rock's formative years, there were basically two means of exploring the harmonics and overtones of noise-sound. One was having access to an electronic studio like those in Paris, Cologne, Milan, and New York. The other was possession of an electric guitar. The latter had the great advantage of being inexpensive, with the added advantage of requiring high volumes. Rock did not wait until 1965 and after, when computers and synthesizers began to be used, to incorporate "electronic methods of creating sound," as Martha Bayles contends.[55] Chuck Berry and Buddy Holly already had amplifiers.

Consider the judgment of one of Russolo's contemporaries, Bernard Bosanquet, Fellow of the British Academy: "It is the qualities of the media which give them the capacity to serve as embodiments of feeling . . ."[56] The mark of a true artist, Bosanquet contends, is the ability "to create, in his own medium, an embodied feeling in which he can rest satisfied."[57] Artists must respond to the peculiarities and limitations of the medium, and the ideal of personal expression is to embody feeling in a way that is appropriate to that medium and no other. We may quibble with the details of Bosanquet's theory, but when new instruments provide new sonic qualities, we normally admire those who successfully explore and exploit their possibilities.

By traditional aesthetic standards, B. B. King, Keith Richards, and Pete Townshend (not to mention Les Paul, Jimi Hendrix, Eric Clapton, Jeff Beck, Jimmy Page, Eddie Van Halen, Thurston Moore, and a host of others) would be exemplary musical artists. Their musical ideas arise from the instruments they play, without prejudices about its proper role or capacities:

> Even most guitarists who matured before 1950 — from Django Reinhardt to Howlin' Wolf — made the switch from acoustic to electric. The generation that followed them grew up and learned to play with electric sound. They did not have known techniques to transfer or modify; their musical ideas were as uncharted as the sonic territory their fingers were eager to explore.[58]

This seems a major reason rock is not more welcome in music departments: the music arises from the materials, not from theory. Let us examine the material basis of the instrument in greater detail, then the guitarists' own understanding of their musical objectives. The musicians are using new sounds for expressive effect, a strategy that extends to bass and keyboards and, through microphone amplification, to the voice as well.

Crudely summarized, a pure frequency is only sounded by a synthesizer. These smoothly undulating sound waves of a single frequency move through space like a snake slithering across sand. But pure tones (sine waves) lack tone color. In the days before synthesizers, all instruments generated harmonic overtones, accompanying waves creating additional peaks and valleys in the flow of sound waves. (The overall pattern of these waves provides a sound wave's "form.") The wave has a dominant or characteristic frequency and thus pitch, but the "choppiness" of the wave's delivery of that frequency is heard and registered as a quality of the tone. Oboes, for instance, produce a set of characteristic overtones that allow knowledgeable listeners to *hear* the source of a given melody as an oboe without having to see that it is. Overtones vary at different pitches and volumes, and with the attack and release of the note. Thus, different instruments have distinctive timbres, and individual players have their own, as well. (Synthesizers can mimic other instruments by sending characteristic overtones and transients along with the pure pitch. The sterility that many listeners find in early synthesized music is largely due to the instruments' tonal purity.)

We have already seen that an electric guitar's circuitry and amplification determine both the timbre and duration of the sounds produced. Acoustics generate overtones through the sounding board and box construction; rock guitars are frequently solid-body — no sound box — and thus acoustically "dead." Because sound is produced by any signal emanating from the current in the pickups, an electric guitarist can audibly sustain the same note at the same pitch many times longer than on any acoustic. With a cutaway construction at the base of the neck, the solid-body electric provides easy access to more frets and thus more tones than a standard acoustic. Because different wiring and pickup designs yield "purer" signals than others, the frequencies sent to the amplifier are not a precise replication of the movements of the strings. Where frequency gives pitch and amplitude gives volume, impurities of sound waves determine an instrument's characteristic timbre or tone color. Thus, different makes of electric guitars have tone colors that are uniquely their own, and guitarists often customize them to make them even more singular in their sound.

As Keith Richards and Pete Townshend emphasize, electric guitars are very different instruments than acoustic guitars. Yet because they are related in genealogy, acoustic "folk" and "classical" guitar sounds serve as the reference point against which electrics sound "distorted." The combination of acoustic guitar and recorder at the beginning of "Stairway to Heaven" sets a pastoral mood, giving way to Page's biting Telecaster tone for the solo. And these points about electric guitars extend to bass, keyboards, and other instruments.

To complicate matters, *amplifiers* have characteristic tone qualities of their own. Frustrated while recording the guitar solo for "Since I've Been Loving You" (1971), Jimmy Page was in despair: "I couldn't get the right sound out of the amp." The solution was pure serendipity; he appropriated an unfamiliar make of amplifier from the hallway of the recording studio. Page thought it "sounded so good . . . Finding this amp right outside the door really saved the day."[59] Finally, overloading an amplifier will distort the signal received from the guitar; the same frequency delivered at a low amplifier setting will have a different timbre than at the amplifier's highest setting.

In fact, the massive and distorted guitar tones of many hard-rock records are produced by overdriving relatively small amplifiers so that the signal distorts. Page's guitar sound on *Led Zeppelin* (1969) was derived from a Supro amplifier with a twelve-inch speaker. The weighty guitar riff on "Whole Lotta Love" (1969) was also from a small amplifier: its natural distortion when overloaded was emphasized and fattened by recording it through a microphone across the room.[60] One of the most influential uses of distortion, the Kinks' "You Really Got Me" (1965), is often attributed to Page's services as a session guitarist. The account given by the brothers Davies is more interesting. Not satisfied with natural distortion, it seems that Dave Davies produced the sound by taking a razor blade to the paper cone in a cheap amplifier.[61] (This was in the days before effects pedals.)

In another interview, Page emphasizes "there's no formula" for matching guitars and amplifiers:

> as the song would progress, I would almost be in a trance. I'd be looking at the guitars and thinking about the amplifiers that should go with them, to get the sound together. . . . I used Gibson guitars, Gresch guitars, Fender guitars and Fender bass, Marshall amps, Peavey amps — everything and anything, old and new. Every guitar is a different piece of wood, and when it's strung up they all sound different. . . . we try and mix the guitars so it'll work out best for the song.[62]

Recording a new song, instrumental timbres are as essential an ingredient as the pitch relationships themselves. To keep things fresh, Keith Richards reports that "if I'm using a certain sound, a certain amp and guitar, on one track, I'll deliberately break that all down and set something else for the next track."[63]

So volume is only a means to an end. By increasing the amplitude, guitarists coax sounds from their electric instruments that are unique to that setting. Tone colors emerge which do not exist at softer volumes. Michael Bloomfield, best known for his lead work with Paul Butterfield and Bob Dylan, related his first impression of Jimi Hendrix, playing in a New York club in 1966:

> Hendrix knew who I was, and that day, in front of my eyes, going off, missiles were flying — I can't tell you the sounds he was getting out of his instrument. He was getting every sound I was ever to hear him get right there in the room with a Stratocaster, a Fender Twin Reverb amp, a Maestro Fuzz Tone, and that was all. He was doing it mainly through extreme volume. How he did this, I wish I understood.[64]

The point is clear: electric guitars are not just louder. But loud guitars are frequently interesting guitars. The process of amplification is essential to their expressive manipulation.

So when Neil Young straps on an electric guitar, it is because he has something to say that cannot be said with an acoustic. One of his guitar solos is described by a critic as "a piercing shriek, then a chaotic noise that is more buildings falling than guitar solo. Forget those pretty, ringing high tones of the past, this is the bottom, pure electric sludge."[65] Young himself observes,

> I do have technique, but it's very gross. There *are* nuances and fine things about what I do, but they're done in such a brash way they're disguised; you don't really recognize them as anything but noise. . . . one note, flat, and just grind on it, and then *slowly* bring it up into tune. To me that's an expression; it's like a knife going into you and being turned until it reaches the target.[66]

Young recognizes that his electric playing is the vehicle for his feelings of anger, violence, and frustration. Compare the acoustic and electric versions of "My My, Hey Hey/Hey Hey, My My" on *Rust Never Sleeps* (1979); "the first is sweet and quietly anguished; the second defiant."[67] Young exploits the same contrast of tonal color on two versions of "Rockin' in the Free World" on *Freedom* (1990).

The sound of the electric guitar is decisive for many — including Sam Phillips, its producer — in pointing to "Rocket 88" as the first genuine rock-and-roll recording. Although credited to Jackie Brenston and the Delta Cats when released by Chess Records, it was recorded at Sun in 1951 by Ike Turner's group, the Kings of Rhythm. Its remarkable fuzz guitar, predating the invention of the fuzz box, was the result of mishap. When the group traveled they had to lash their amplifier on the roof of the car. When it fell off shortly before their recording session, the speaker cone was damaged. With a recording session booked and no practical way to wait for repairs, Phillips jammed some paper into the torn cone: "it sounded good," he decided, so they recorded. The resulting texture was unlike any other R&B on the radio; the guitar held its own in competition with the pounding piano and honking sax, and its distortion was a good deal of its appeal. Ike Turner's piano boogie was transformed into something new, and saxophone player Raymond Hill suddenly had competition for the listener's attention. As Phillips remarks, "*expression* was the key. . . . I listened for the effect, the total effect."[68] The addition of a new timbre to the sonic mix changes the total effect of what can be done.

Producer Owen Bradley preserved a similar "dirty" sound on Paul Burlison's guitar on "Train Kept A-Rollin'," by Johnny Burnette and the Rock & Roll Trio. Burlison reports that the "fuzz" sound appeared when he plugged in for a live performance; examining his amplifier after the show, he found that one of the tubes had been loosened during transportation. He learned to control the level of distortion by adjusting the tube, and his trademark guitar tone became an important source for many bands during the next decade. The Yardbirds and Aerosmith both released cover versions of "Train Kept A-Rollin'."

The constraints and pressures of another recording session led to the startling metallic tone of Billy Strange's guitar solo on the 1962 hit "Zip-A-Dee Doo-Dah." Designed by producer Phil Spector as a showcase for Darlene Love's vocal, Spector's impatience to cut the track led him to override the warnings of engineer Larry Levine, who wasn't ready. After three hours of practicing and of setting recording levels, Levine and Spector got into a fight when Levine tried to reduce the distortion levels on the tape. As Levine reset the levels on each microphone, Spector suddenly decided to record the guitar without its own microphone: microphones on other instruments in the room would pick up Strange's amplifier. When the delayed and echoed reverberations of the guitar were picked up by the other microphones, its recorded tone was transformed by the contribution of selected, delayed overtones. The sharp and biting timbre contrasts with the sunny singalong, tearing into the listener like barbed wire into flesh: it was "a fuzzy, tinny coil of disembodied noise."[69] The effect is a mercurial flash of violence that balances the single's otherwise sunny amble.

There is also the history of one of rock's most celebrated singles, the Rolling Stones' 1965 breakthrough "(I Can't Get No) Satisfaction." The basic riff was apparently derived from Roy Orbison's "Pretty Woman," which Keith Richards had heard night after night as the Stones toured with Roy Orbison in 1965. Richards' version came to him in his sleep, and he awoke long enough to play it into a bedside tape recorder. In the light of day Richards decided it was trivial, but Jagger added lyrics and the group took two stabs at the song in May of 1965. The first version featured Richards on acoustic guitar, and he rejected it as sounding too much like the folk-rock that was becoming fashionable: "it sounded like a protest song." The Stones tried again on May 12 as Richards, bass player Bill Wyman, and drummer Charlie Watts were overdubbed on top of the existing acoustic track. Pleased with the way his new fuzz device "takes off all the treble," Richards remarks that "we achieved a very interesting sound."[70]

What they achieved was more than interesting. By flattening the top of the waveforms and fattening the sound with new harmonics, the guitar sound filled out the record. The group's most successful records to that point were covers of lesser R&B hits ("Little Red Rooster," "Not Fade Away," "The Last Time"), but they were now studying the soul singles that were just appearing by Otis Redding and Solomon Burke. Soul, particularly the Memphis variety, featured strong riffing from a horn section; the Stones would not make the transition to horns until they borrowed Bobby Keyes and Jim Price from Delaney and Bonnie in 1969. According to Wyman, "We wanted to get an American sound instead of a thin English sound — we wanted to have a big fat sound, like an R&B band."[71] Recording at Chess studios in 1964 was a step in the right direction, but the fuzz box and Dave Hassinger's engineering at RCA studios in Hollywood were the real breakthroughs. Dave Marsh describes the resulting guitar tone:

> its hornlike quality was Keith's way of overcompensating for the Stones' lack of the horn section so crucial to the soul bands the group emulated. . . . Blurting out those unforgettable chords for the first time, Keith's axe is as big and bold as anything the Memphis Horns had to offer. And that, before anybody else gets a lick in, make "Satisfaction" a great record.[72]

The song Richards had rejected as too folkie was now urban soul, and the weight of the guitar texture makes all the difference. Not that Richards had to read Russolo to figure it out.

Despite its power to disrupt, rock has always been a reactionary art. Rock musicians accept a very traditional artistic goal, the expression of emotion. To do so they employ newer and noisier instruments. "Serious" composers have, by and large, repudiated expression. Many have retreated into formal manipulation of sound media (e.g., much of the nonrock that is called "new music") or some mode of expression that is decidedly less accessible to anyone lacking a degree in music theory. Henry Pleasants was not far from the mark when he said that most modern composers have little desire to say anything that can be grasped by the majority of people: "it is against precisely the expressive character of the music of the nineteenth century that he rebels."[73] Popular music, including rock, maintains the tradition of Western tonality and song. The noise element of rock is found in volume, in less precision in the articulation of pitch, and in "noisy," richer timbres. Largely unaware of parallel developments in high culture, rock musicians have been left to bring electronic music to the masses.

5

Jungle Rhythms and the Big Beat

It would be a good idea to remember that not all
the old music is beautiful either. — Giuseppe Verdi[1]

Rhythm's the key, not drumming, not noise.
— Grateful Dead drummer Mickey Hart[2]

The Reactionary Backlash

In 1985, many rock fans were amused by the absurd congressional hearings on the possibility of warning labels on recordings of rock music. Established after Tipper Gore heard the lyrics of Prince's "Darling Nikki" on *Purple Rain* (1984), the hearings made national news when the politicians grilled several musicians in a superficial, media-friendly discussion of the effects of rock on public morality. The future vice president, Al Gore, conducted the hearings despite the fact that no federal legislation on the matter was pending. But the implication was clear: if the music industry would not police its product, the government might step in. Stealing the show, Frank Zappa read the First Amendment and then stood up for rock at the sacrificial altar of public decency: "The establishment of a rating system, voluntary or otherwise, opens the door to an endless parade of moral quality control programs based on things certain Christians do not like."[3] Zappa did not see that the Gores were tapping a reservoir of anxiety that extends well beyond evangelical Christians, opening the door to a new era of rock bashing.[4]

At first, it was tempting to make sport of the idea of warning labels ("Warning: Satanic Influences, Macho Posturing, and Drug References May Harm Young Listeners"). The music industry ultimately adopted the label "Parental Advisory Explicit Lyrics." It has become something of a sales pitch for records marketed at teenage males. When sixteen-year-olds buy a Red Hot Chili Peppers CD, they want one with a warning sticker. But on the darker side, there has been a genuine chilling effect on retailers. Many large chains and discount stores will not stock them. Unsure what local courts might do in the wake of the 2 Live Crews' 1990 obscenity trial and the conviction of a store clerk who sold one of their records, smaller retailers often segregate recordings with raw lyrics or warning stickers — particularly rap — and will not sell them to minors. In early 1992, the state of Washington passed legislation criminalizing the sale of records with "erotic" lyrics to minors, and Congress began to consider similar laws. Although the Washington law was struck down as unconstitutional in 1994, its supporters soon drafted a new version. Since the sale of any obscene materials to minors is already illegal, laws aimed at rock lyrics signal a special distrust of popular music.

As the presidential election of 1992 heated up, puritanism about sex gave way to indignation and posturing about political content directed against the dominant culture. Rappers Ice-T and Sister Souljah were the featured scapegoats. At Bill Clinton's inauguration festivities in January of 1993, Clinton signaled a truce of sorts by appearing with uncontroversial rock figures. Second Lady Tipper Gore stood on the same stage with Fleetwood Mac and Michael Jackson; one can only presume that the Parents' Music Resource Center (PMRC) had somehow missed Jackson's lewd crotch-grabbing in the long version of the "Black or White" video (1991). But aware of the positive vibes created among most voters in a year when "crime" tops the nation's list of hot-button issues, Congress undertook new hearings in early 1994, this time focusing on gangsta rap. Five states toyed with laws that would prohibit minors from buying recordings that carry warning labels.

In earlier decades, government's response to rock was less direct. In 1956 and 1960, Congress applied pressure with hearings on BMI (Broadcast Music Incorporated, which collected royalties for many of the independent labels that were home to rock and roll) and then payola.[5] Since the 1960s, prosecutors have made an example of musicians' lifestyles. Because of their outlaw image, the Rolling Stones were singled out by the British government as an example, occasioning Keith Richard's snide remarks about their "petty morals" during his drug possession trial in 1967.[6] The specific flashpoints vary with time, but all such scapegoating aims at discrediting and marginalizing rock generally. The fact that political mileage can still be had by doing so suggests the depth of suspicion still directed at rock. Let us focus on the idea so dear to rock's puritan foes, that rock is inherently sexual.

Bloom's Neoplatonism

There are others so continuously in the agitation of gross and merely sensual pleasures . . . that their minds, which had been used continuously to the storms of these violent and tempestuous passions, can hardly be put in motion by the delicate and refined play of the imagination. — Edmund Burke, 1756

Claims that rock undermines the morals and psychological well-being of its audience gained an intellectual veneer with Allan Bloom's 1987 best-seller, *The Closing of the American Mind.*[7] Devoting an entire chapter to rock music, Bloom's basic thesis is simple. Rock music stirs up sexual desire, and anyone with too much libidinal energy is not in control of their own life. Where both the 1985 hearings and warning labels focus on lyrics, Bloom puts the threat in the music itself. To that extent, his challenge raises important issues in the aesthetics of *music,* and not merely the broad issue of the social responsibility of art.

For Bloom, music of the Classical and Romantic eras serves a noble function in Western civilization. The music of Mozart and Beethoven are, in the most literal sense, a civilizing force. The music which makes us "whole" is that in which melody, harmony, and rhythm are a means to a higher end, so that a balance may be struck between passion and reason: the religious man, for instance, "is exalted in his prayer by the sound of the organ in the church."[8] The barbarous elements of our psyche are informed and thus tamed by art. Not coincidentally, Bloom translated Plato's *Republic,* wherein Plato sketches one of the earliest defenses of music censorship. Bloom ought to have quoted directly from his own translation of Plato:

> And as for sex, and spiritedness, too, and for all the desires, pains, and pleasures in the soul that we say follow all our action, poetic imitation produces similar results in us. For it fosters and waters them when they ought to be dried up . . . so that we may become better and happier instead of worse and more wretched.[9]

Music, rightly controlled, is essential to education, for Bloom agrees with Plato that education is "the training or domestication of the soul's raw passions" and a condition for human flourishing and happiness. But when the music is in control, barbarism and misery result.[10]

While Bloom is more liberal than Plato, not just any music will do the trick. Rock, it seems, insidiously destroys the psychological balance and health of young people who enjoy and regularly consume it, "ruining" their hopes for a genuine liberal education. Instead of guiding the passions and subordinating them to reason, rock celebrates and encourages the passions themselves. But not all of our passions. Rock, Bloom proposes, "has one appeal only, a barbaric appeal, to sexual desire."[11] So whereas Mozart wrote the ideal music for the educated person, the Rolling Stones and Michael Jackson (Bloom's major examples) methodically destroy the soul, encouraging us to remain ever in a barbaric state of immature sexual desire. Rock is thus the antithesis of civilization and education. The result?

> A pubescent child whose body throbs with orgasmic rhythms; whose feelings are made articulate in hymns to the joys of onanism or the killing of parents; whose ambition is to win fame and wealth in imitating the drag queen who makes the music. In short, life is made into a nonstop, commercially packaged masturbational fantasy.[12]

If not for their pedigree, many of Bloom's remarks could be dismissed as simplistic paranoia. However, Bloom adopts the mantle of Plato's doctrine of the just soul of the educated lover of wisdom, and brings in Shakespeare, Aristotle, Rousseau, and Nietzsche as his rear guard. If our appetites and passions are not controlled, they will "rule" the individual in place of the soul's proper, naturally superior element, namely reason.

As in Book III of the *Republic,* Bloom supposes that music itself, particularly its rhythm, is essential to control over our worst appetites. However, rock "has the beat of sexual intercourse . . . sexual desire undeveloped and untutored." Constant exposure to this rhythm encourages sexual desire, making one incapable of appreciating the life of higher, mainly intellectual, pleasures. (There seems to be an assumption here that music is not itself an inherently intellectual pleasure.) Bloom concludes that, as a cultural phenomenon, the current music industry is a greater threat than — but is otherwise similar to — drug trafficking. America's tolerance for this music will some day be seen to be the "greatest madness" of our age, akin to yesteryear's tolerance of racism and witch-burning. It seems that Tipper Gore should not have worried about Prince's lyrics; the threat was in that old devil rhythm.

If Bloom's argument sounds silly, it's because he spells it out in such detail. But many others have made the same argument. After eleven people died because of inept concert planning for a Who concert in Cincinnati in 1979, John Fuller's *Are the Kids All Right?* placed the blame on the audience and the music.[13] Like Bloom, Fuller believes that the beat of hard rock can alter behavior: "I'm talking about . . . the Rolling Stones, The Who, Led Zeppelin and others with a distinctive heavy beat and pulverizing decibels—up and beyond the pain level." Specifically, hard rock employs a "definite shamanistic beat, a tribal beat" that hypnotizes the audience, leaving them vulnerable to manipulation by the lyrics.[14] Other variations on the same position provide even fewer details to the argument. The following lines, from a scholarly look at the lyrics of the Rolling Stones, could have appeared in Bloom: "The aggressive nature of the music, i.e., Richard's guitar combined with a heavy beat, reinforces the often aggressive feelings set forth in the lyrics. It's music for the id and it is very danceable. And what is rock 'n' roll dancing if not symbolic sex?"[15]

In various guises, the thesis resonates in the culture at large. In a less explicit form, it is espoused by jazz musician Wynton Marsalis, who claims that pop music is geared to a "sexual thing."[16] Jazz, he contends, elevates its audience while "pop" panders to the child. Although they tend to waver between sex and satanism as the specific threat, many Christian groups preach against rock's erosion of youthful virtue as an article of faith. It is preached from the pulpit by at least one Roman Catholic cardinal.[17] U2 nearly broke up after their first album because many of their Christian friends insisted that rock music and Christianity are incompatible. Their guitarist, Edge, still says that the conflict "was reconciling two things that seemed for us at that moment to be mutually exclusive. We never did resolve the contradictions."[18] (Contrast this attitude to that of Buddy Holly and the Crickets, who tithed 40 percent of their earnings from "That'll Be the Day" to their respective churches back home in Lubbock, Texas.) Finally, the basic idea permeates the rock press, perhaps as an echo of the African American tradition that regarded the blues as the devil's music.

Since any position that gains such wide acceptance deserves analysis, particularly when it advocates personal if not public censorship, I will explore Bloom's claims. Unlike more common concerns about the lyrical content of popular music, the charge that the *style* of music is the harmful element takes us to the heart of our assumptions about rock music. What is the rock beat, and could it have the sort of power claimed for it?

Democratizing the Beat

In rock and roll, the strident, repetitive sounds
of city life were, in effect, reproduced as melody
and rhythm. — Charlie Gillett[19]

It's that jungle strain that gets 'em all worked up.
— Response to violence at a concert, 1956[20]

In contending that "rock has the beat of sexual intercourse," Allan
Bloom sidesteps the thorny question of which music does and does not
belong in the category of rock. He mentions Michael Jackson, the
Rolling Stones, Prince, and Boy George. But these seem to have been
chosen primarily because of their high profile *at that time;* who today
would mention Boy George? And while Bloom claims to be worried
about the beat, he seems to have chosen his examples based on their
video images more than their music. What picture emerges if we examine MTV's "Unplugged" program, which features rockers playing their
material on acoustic instruments, or the Grateful Dead's *Reckoning*
(1981), an entirely acoustic collection of mostly blues and traditional-
sounding versions of their own material, or Joni Mitchell's *Mingus,* her
1979 collaboration with jazz great Charles Mingus, or Van Morrison's
album with Irish traditionalists the Chieftains? It is hard to see how
these share the "beat" of Prince's "Darling Nikki." But rather than play
the game of finding easy counterexamples, let us suppose that Bloom
understands rock to be recent popular music with the rock-and-roll
beat, clearly central to rock but certainly not present in many instances.
Let us examine the proposal that music with the so-called "big beat" is
harmful in the way Bloom contends.

To be fair, let us avoid the impression that rock fans and musicians
have any special insight into the rock beat. John Lennon once said of
rock that "it is primitive enough and has no bullshit, really, the best
stuff, and it gets through to you its beat. Go to the jungle and they have
the rhythm . . . You get the rhythm going, everybody gets into it."[21] The
"jungle" label must have been widespread, particularly in England with
its colonial heritage. Mick Jagger has said "My father used to call it
'jungle music' and I used to say, 'Yeah, good description.' "[22] But the
jungle idea is not just a British perception. It dates back to the earliest
days of American rock: witness Warren Smith's 1956 rockabilly classic,
"Ubangi Stomp," and Hank Mizell's 1957 "Jungle Rock." Not that the
author of either song had the musicological evidence to support their
conceit. At about the same time, Bo Diddley was looking for a record

label in Chicago and was turned down by Vee Jay: "They said it didn't sound right — said it was 'jungle music.'"[23] Rap has recently been added to the melting pot. Richard Shusterman claims that its "jungle rhythms" were reappropriated from rock and disco by rap DJs, "the musical cannibals of the urban jungle."[24]

The line that traces the rock beat back to "the jungle" (West Africa, to be precise) is indirect but genuine, and it provides a useful reminder of rock's overwhelming debt to the music of African Americans. And African traditions endow rhythm with the same power over us that worries Bloom: "In most of Africa the proper rhythm and the proper life go hand in hand: A good person is one who is filled with the right rhythm."[25] Perhaps influenced by African attitudes, early jazz musicians voiced similar views. New Orleans drummer Baby Dodds said that "drumming is spirit. . . . If you're evil, you're going to drum evil, and . . . you're going to put evil in somebody else's mind."[26] So worries about the harmful effects of rhythm have an African source along with the music itself, even if Bloom looks to Plato for his support.

Bloom, no less than Lennon and Jagger, assumes that the beat is the key to rock, and furthermore that we know what it is. But we must scrutinize it more closely if we are to evaluate the idea that rhythm can be licentious and thus harmful. It will become apparent that Bloom has made a series of rash assumptions in his indictment of rock.

To begin with, beat and rhythm are two different but related structural qualities of music. Bloom talks about "beat" when he probably means something more specific. "Rhythm" is notoriously ambiguous, since it can cover almost anything involved in the time element of musical organization, sometimes covering beat and meter, not just rhythm in the narrower sense. Put crassly, Bloom is worried about strongly accented backbeat, a single element in the rhythmic accents of much rock music. After a discussion to make this point clear, I will go on to argue that this feature has no special "sexual" aspect. I wouldn't deny that a good backbeat is extremely sensual, but that is another matter entirely.

In its strictly technical sense, beat is music's most basic rhythmic pulse. Explaining the beat of popular music, Peter Van Der Merwe notes that when we "spontaneously move in time to the music, we are marking the beat. In an obvious and superficial way, the music produces the motion; but it can only do so because, in a deeper sense, the motion has produced the music."[27] In Western classical music, the beat is there but often so implicit that it must be counted by the conductor; in live performance one can at least see it, particularly its basic subdivisions, even if one cannot feel it. In waltz time there are three beats to a measure, and in common time there are four. But pulse cannot be the sense of "beat" that Bloom identifies as sexual, for virtually all music has a steady rhythmic pulse, and most of Mozart's music has the same pulse as that of Jerry Lee Lewis, Public Enemy, or Metallica.

Since it is implausible to choose rhythmic pulse as the villain, we must next consider meter (which is not quite the same thing as beat) as the corrupting element. Meter is present when beats are subdivided and experienced as grouping together into units of equal duration (measures, conveyed in scores as bars), where each of these units is perceived as containing a pattern of stronger and weaker accents. A recurring accent on the first beat of the measure signals the basic pulse. In waltz time, we have ONE-two-three, ONE-two-three; in common time, ONE-two-THREE-four, ONE-TWO-THREE-four, with a weaker accent on three than on one. Except for some special cases, such as Gregorian chant and recent electronic music, all Western music tames the pulse by fencing it with meter. Thus 4/4 is so basic as Occidental meter that we simply call it common time. (It took decades for ethnomusicologists to realize that African drumming does not reflect division into meter. The traditional African drummer is not thinking in bar lines.) When meter rather than pulse itself is regarded as beat, meter is usually associated with a steady tempo.

As pulse is the basis of meter, meter is the basis of Western rhythm, whether in rock or jazz or classical. Two pieces with the same meter usually employ different rhythms, because the musical phrases that accompany the meter determine the placement of specific accents through a combination of note lengths and rests. Whereas every waltz places the accented or strong beat as the first of the three beats in the measure, two different Chopin waltzes will have different rhythms. (We can generate a very different rhythm within the same meter-and-note choice if we accent the last beat of each measure.)

In most classical music, rhythm and melody are two aspects of the same flow of sound. That is, the instruments that play the melody thereby play the rhythm. In a performance of classical music, vertical relationships such as pitch take precedence over the rhythmic flow. Because these vertical relationships are the basis of Western composition, and composition occurs apart from performance, the beat is sometimes subliminal, sometimes ethereal. However hidden they may be in the current of sound, measures and bar lines guide the rhythm. In rock, the subdivision and accenting of measures are frequently distinct contributions to the musical performance.

With the subdivision inherent in meter we have our first real candidate for something that might have the beat of sexual intercourse. After all, the vast majority of rock songs share 4/4 meter, so the subdivision of pulse that is common time seems the prime candidate for the beat Bloom means. (To simplify matters, let's ignore all the rock songs in waltz time. We will likewise ignore the 6/8 of Bob Dylan's "Rainy Day Women #12 & 35," the 5/8 introduction to Cream's "White Room," the 7/4 and 5/4 on the Pretenders' debut album, and the complex eleven-beat rhythm of the Grateful Dead's "The Eleven." Rock can be played in any meter, but we recognize anything but 4/4 to be unusual.) Although it is close to being a defining characteristic of rock, common time *itself* cannot be the sexual element in rock. Bloom's beloved Mozart used it often enough, but Bloom does not mention finding a sexual beat in the Adagio of Mozart's *Hunting* Quartet (the String Quartet in B-flat Major, KV458). If common time had the pulse of sexual desire, classical music would be as corrupt as rock. While Plato might nod in approval at this implication, Bloom certainly does not.

But if we turn from meter to rhythm, we are again frustrated. After all, rock musicians have frequently borrowed melodies (and thus rhythms!) from classical composers; Beethoven, Mozart, Satie, Ravel, Holst, Varèse, Bizet, Rachmaninoff, Bach, and Saint-Saëns have provided melodies, some of them Top 40 hits, for rock musicians. A stolen melody carries its rhythm with it. I was once at a funeral and was surprised when someone began to play Paul Simon's "American Tune" on flute; the deceased was elderly and I could not imagine that she was a Paul Simon fan. But then I remembered that it was a Lutheran ceremony, and they were playing its melodic source, a Bach choral ("Scared Heart") from *St. Matthew Passion*. Or consider the Procol Harum hit "A Whiter Shade of Pale" (1967). The melody and organ part are adapted from Bach's Suite no. 3 in D Major. Their rhythm is Bach's. Either Bach employed a sexual rhythm, in which case Bloom should vilify this music as a corrupting influence, or rhythm is not what Bloom is talking about.

The beat that worries Bloom is really something other than meter or the rhythms of the music. He must be concerned with the way that rock musicians have *handled* meter and accented the rhythm. Here, at last, is what the kids on *American Bandstand* meant when they said "It has a good beat and you can dance to it." It's not so much the rhythm itself as the articulation and clear *presence* of the organizing pulse together with its metrical elaborations. The accents are clearly articulated and not merely implicit in the flow of melody.

Rock bears constant witness to the distinction between meter and rhythm. If each beat in each measure were assigned a single note, each of equal duration, and if each note were stressed with the normal accents of that meter, then rhythm would match meter. (Country music tends in this direction, with the musicians staying pretty much on the precise beats of the measure.) Taken to extreme, we'd have extremely boring melodies, such as the verse melodies of Bob Dylan's "It's Alright Ma (I'm Only Bleeding)" or the Beatles' "Strawberry Fields Forever," something that only works in exceptional cases. A melody's rhythm is distinct from its meter because this rarely occurs. For instance, subdividing beats — say, two eighth notes for each beat in common time — results in a different rhythm than quarter notes alone. (The use of an eighth-note pulse in the guitar and bass was one of the mainstays of punk and new wave, creating a good deal of its propulsion and thus aggression.) A distribution of shorter and longer notes yields further variation in rhythm, as does the displacement of expected accents which we know as syncopation. Furthermore, when a piece of music features several distinct instrumental parts (let's say the bass player is only providing quarter notes on the second and fourth beats, while the piano is beating out sixteenth notes and the guitar is playing eighth notes), each has its own rhythm. But when all these rhythms maintain a driving pulse at a steady tempo while coming together on specific accents, and when some instruments consistently displace these accents from the first and third beats to the second and fourth, we have typical rock and roll.

This syncopation of the beat is singled out by Langdon Winner:

> The most fundamental defining characteristic of rock and roll, of course, has always been a 4/4 time signature in which the second and fourth beats are heavily accented. In all rock lyrics and dances the ineluctable "one-TWO-three-FOUR" is the force which sustains the motion.[28]

Try counting "one-two-three-four" at a steady rate, over and over, while slapping your thigh on the two and four. Maintained at a steady tempo, the characteristic motion is more a feel of back-and-forth than jazz's forward propulsion or classical's martial downbeat. Thus Bruce Springsteen says that "Charlie Watt's laconic two and four . . . *is* the Rolling Stones."[29]

Yet once we differentiate meter and rhythm, we see that there is no *one* rhythm or meter which is characteristic of rock. Just contrast the

Bo Diddley rhythm of "Not Fade Away" with Prince's dance-rock on "Little Red Corvette," or the lazy Creole stroll of Fats Domino's "Blueberry Hill" (a shuffle, actually) with the seven-beat bass pattern of Pink Floyd's "Money" and of Devo's "Jocko Homo" (Devo further complicates it by shifting the accent in alternating measures). Buddy Holly's "Peggy Sue" is as rock and roll as you can get, yet its drums employ a sixteenth-note pattern without backbeat.[30] My point is that 4/4 with backbeat is extremely common in rock, as one of the characteristics adapted from earlier rhythm and blues, but it is not essential. What is typical, if anything is, is the way rock characteristically displaces accents. In this respect, rock is closely related to jazz, and we might then recall that "rock" and "jazz" are both euphemisms for sex.

In his monumental study of jazz, Gunther Schuller separates the "democratization" of beat from its swing. What both rock and jazz retain from their African ancestry is the former. Jazz alone provides swing on a regular basis, hence Duke Ellington's celebrated remark that it don't mean a thing without swing. Rock rhythms are characterized by Aretha Franklin's 1971 advice to "Rock Steady." The democratization of the beat is the tendency to ignore traditional downbeats. The "so-called" weak beats (weak under traditional Western assumptions) "are brought up to the level of strong beats, and very often emphasized *beyond* the strong beat."[31]

When Bloom warns against the beat of sexual intercourse, he probably means this democratized syncopation of meter, and neither the pulse nor the meter nor any particular rhythm. In other words, our perception of syncopation is the result of grafting African democratization onto Western expectations about the correct placement of strong and weak accents. (Democratization without syncopation of the basic meter, as in the "four-on-the-floor" bass drum of disco, is as congenial to most rock fans as sunlight to a vampire.) Seen from a musicological perspective, the rock beat preserves an African attitude toward basic accents, rejecting the standard Western assumption that the first beat of the measure is the strongest.

In addition to a characteristic afterbeat syncopation, rock celebrates it by singling it out and calling it to our attention. So it's not just what rock does with the rhythm, it's also how it's presented in the music's arrangement. Classical composers tend to subordinate rhythm by incorporating it into harmony and melody. The rhythms of Mozart's symphonies — even when syncopated — are no less driving, predictable, and insistent than those of the Rolling Stones. *The issue is thus one of arranging*, of "orchestration," not just syncopation of the meter. In rock, the syncopation is usually emphasized by the drummer, who hits the snare on the second and fourth beats. The backbeat is emphatic.

There is a temptation to suppose that the backbeat is simple and mechanical. Jim Keltner, one of rock's most widely used session drummers, gravitated to rock from jazz. But to succeed he had to relearn drumming: "I'd thought any idiot could be a rock drummer, that all you needed was a hammer and a two-by-four. Of course, I was totally wrong." He was advised by his fellow players to simplify and to bear down on the backbeat: "My snare drum was too tight, I played too light, like a little mouse running all over the drums. . . . Finally I'm thinking, 'Shit, this ain't easy, this is difficult!' "[32] Earl Palmer, drummer for Fats Domino, Little Richard, and countless others, defined and then redefined basic rock drumming when he shifted from jazz to a rhythm-and-blues shuffle and then to a rock backbeat.

Kenny Aronoff, drummer for John Mellencamp, emulated Keltner and faced many of the same problems. After earning a bachelor's degree in music and working with various symphony orchestras, he tried jazz-fusion for several years before auditioning for Mellencamp (then known as "John Cougar"). Aronoff was told to dump most of his drum kit and to unlearn his fusion habits. "It took me about two years to learn how to play rock 'n' roll the way it was proper for the John Cougar Mellencamp band. But I could make the transition because I went back to my roots. Back to that Charlie Watts, Keith Moon, Creedence Clearwater approach to rock 'n' roll."[33] The lesson, then, is that rock's beat is not just a rhythm that is played along with the music. Rock's beat, particularly as highlighted by the drummer, is a matter of strategically accenting and interacting with the beats present in the rest of the music. There is nothing mechanical about it. Indeed, the Linn drum machine and its various clones are despised by many in rock because its inhuman perfection is perceived as sterile and antithetical to rock.

But I must emphasize that neither a backbeat nor a drummer is essential to the presence of the democratized beat. Moe Tucker's drumming for the Velvet Underground is as integral as Lou Reed's rhythm guitar or John Cale's avant-garde contributions, but there's no backbeat on "Heroin." Van Morrison's *Astral Weeks* (1968) is widely regarded as a watershed in the transition from rock-and-roll singles to album-centered rock. What little drumming there is, courtesy of the Modern Jazz Quartet's Connie Kay, provides accents and color but avoids the backbeat. Elvis Presley's Sun sessions had no drummer, but "Good Rockin' Tonight" rocks plenty. Bruce Springsteen's stark *Nebraska* (1982) has no drummer, but "Johnny 99" and "Open All Night" are the purest Chuck Berry he'd produced to that point. Bob Dylan's solo performance of "Subterranean Homesick Blues" updated Chuck Berry's "Too Much Monkey Business." It's pure rock and roll on nothing more than an acoustic guitar (finally released on *The Bootleg Series, Vol. 2*). But why should this surprise anyone? How else did the studio musicians learn it in the first place? So even when the drummer is on the beat, emphasizing and highlighting it, the beat is not just in the drumming. We should think of the drummer's task as finding and emphasizing a central rhythm, rather than creating it.

Rhythm guitar alone is sufficient to create the basic accents. So is the left hand on piano. The best rock drummers hammer it home—only more so. Listen to the acoustic guitar riff that drives the Rolling Stones on "Street Fighting Man" (*Beggars Banquet, 1968*); Charlie Watts drums *to* the rhythm of the guitar. The basic democratized rhythm of numerous Beatles performances is set up with an acoustic guitar; John Lennon, not drummer Ringo Starr, leads the band. Ringo accents Lennon's rhythmic thrust. Just listen to "If I Fell," "I'll Cry Instead," and "When I Get Home" from *A Hard Day's Night* (1964). Led Zeppelin's bombastic drummer, John Bonham, followed guitarist Jimmy Page, and not vice versa. Check out side two of *Led Zeppelin III* (1970, tracks 6–10). Finally, anyone who's seen the Talking Heads' concert film, *Stop Making Sense* (1984), will recall singer David Byrne onstage, alone with an acoustic guitar, stomping out "Psycho Killer" to a prerecorded rhythm track. Antiphony, not the drum track, drives the performance.

In taking the democratized 4/4 and making it explicit, whether on drums or in other rhythm instruments, rock sets the stage for further articulations of the rhythm. Against a basic and explicit rhythmic bed, the vocalist and other players are free to introduce contrasting rhythms and further syncopations. Other rhythms with distinct accents, particularly those of the vocal melody and any accompanying riffs, interact with the beat of syncopated 4/4 while retaining the customary accents on the first and third beats. Winner, again:

> Given the overwhelming necessity of this [4/4] pattern and the fact that there is a relatively large amount of time between each "TWO" and "FOUR," the problem for rock musicians is to figure out rhythmic devices to fill the intervals in an interesting way.[34]

While early rockers employed "the afterbeat and its variations," he notes that "the first ten years of rock developed comparatively few means of handling the subpatterns within the basic Big Beat." But since the "rebirth" of rock in the mid-sixties (after its "death" at the hands of the teen idols and surf instrumentals), rock musicians have explored "a large number of ways of approaching the rhythmic structure." Winner notes that Aretha Franklin's titanic recording of "Respect" has a soul beat in which four hurried accents occur on the third beat of each measure; each measure has up to ten distinct accents and subaccents.

Having staked out the territory of the rock beat in its democratization of meter, it is now time to consider Bloom's interpretation of the presence of this element of rock music.

Resemblance and Arousal

The "rock 'n' roll" school in general concentrated on a minimum of melodic line and a maximum of rhythmic noise, deliberately competing with the artistic ideals of the jungle itself. — *Encyclopaedia Britannica,* 1955[35]

To suppose, with Allan Bloom, that the rock audience responds to the democratized beat, but *not* to the polyrhythmic interplay that it allows and supports, is to single out one aspect of rhythm as the only element that matters. In its way, it is as simplistic as the PMRC's focus on lyrics as rock's sole bearer of meaning.

Nor does it help when Bloom defends his analysis by claiming that most rock lyrics "implicitly and explicitly describe bodily acts that satisfy sexual desire and treat them as its only natural and routine culmination for children who do not yet have the slightest imagination of love, marriage or family."[36] I gather that Bloom is thinking of "Get It On (Bang a Gong)" or "Love to Love You Baby" or "Sexual Healing." He is unaware that Bob Dylan's "Lay Lady Lay" is balanced by "Tears of Rage" and the Pretenders' "Brass in Pocket" or "Night in My Veins" by "I'm a Mother" and "Thumbelina." As for the claim that rock invites "bodily contact," he seems to overlook the fact that at medium and fast tempos, rock dancers often avoid any bodily contact. In any event, if the lyrics generate the sexual element, or if it is some combination of lyrics and beat, Bloom has only made his thesis less plausible. For why is it the beat, and not the vocal melody, which is made sexual by the lyrics?

On close inspection, arguments like Bloom's often undermine themselves. Like many devotees of Western art music, his rhythmic sensibility is so dull that he cannot identify the beat he hears. In an attempt to demonstrate the link between rock and sex, Bloom says: "Young people know that rock has the beat of sexual intercourse. That is why Ravel's *Bolero* is the one piece of classical music that is commonly known and liked by them."[37] *Bolero* is indeed distinctive for its driving beat. The first four measures announce the rhythmic theme on snare drums, and its danceable beat is due to the fact that it is one of his two specifically choreographic works. But it does not have the democratized and syncopated 4/4 of rock. *Bolero* is in triple meter. Take a look at the score; the meter is clearly marked as 3/4. Anyone who sways to its beat will discover that it is not the beat of "Satisfaction," much less "Me So Horny." Its limited similarity to rock is its orchestration of a dance rhythm. (The rock song that comes closest to Ravel's quirky piece is Roy Orbison's "Running Scared," which was a number-one record in 1961. It is likewise one long crescendo.) We can only conclude that Bloom is complaining about music that highlights rhythm, not a specific rhythm.

Even if he could identify a rock beat, Bloom makes other assumptions that we must consider. First, we must grant that sexual intercourse has a basic beat. Second, that its beat matches that of rock music. (Though if we had to identify "the" rhythm of sexual intercourse, wouldn't it be 2/4 rather than a syncopated 4/4?) Finally, we must then explain why this match is representational, with the one rhythm *signifying* and not merely resembling the other. And there is no reason to grant any of this trio of assumptions.

Having challenged the first at length, the third demands some attention. Even if rock had a beat like that of sexual intercourse, nothing follows. Two things that resemble one another do not thereby represent one another. Two sisters might resemble one another, and while the younger might be said to "have the face of" the older, we do not conclude that her face represents or in any way signifies that of her older sister. We can take it another step. A photo of the younger sister may look like a photo of the older taken at the same age — it might even be indistinguishable — but nonetheless it remains a picture of the younger, *no matter how strongly it resembles the other.* Mere resemblance, however strong, does not create representation.

Another example will clarify the point. Suppose I set my coffee mug down near the center of a rectangular desk. The longer and shorter sides of the desk are more or less proportional to the respective borders of the state of North Dakota. My mug happens to sit at just about the spot where Bismarck is in North Dakota. Do I therefore have a crude map of North Dakota? Of course not. Just because I've created something that has a corresponding structure does not show that one signifies the other. What makes lines and dots on paper into a map of North Dakota is the combination of putting the markings on the map in the right places in the context of an existing practice of mapping. Usually, my intention to have mapped the state will be conveyed by labeling it as such. In the absence of some indication that I intend it to be North Dakota, it could just as well be South Dakota.

To consider a more famous example, Chuck Berry's "Johnny B. Goode" has Johnny learn rhythm by playing his guitar in time to the passing trains. So the pulse of rock is here the pulse of the freight trains that pass Johnny's shack. Does Bloom want us to think that living beside a train track will lead to the same disruption of psychological health that he attributes to rock? Of course not, because however much a freight train mimics the rhythm of sex, we do not ordinarily interpret it as such. And in the absence of something more than similarity of rhythm, rock does not "have" the beat of sex. To suppose that rock's beat always signifies, and that it usually signifies the same thing, is as absurd as supposing that any rectangle with objects placed about it must be a map, much less that they all map the same place.

Perhaps Bloom does not mean that rock "has" the beat of sex in a representational manner. The only plausible alternative, that it is sexual because it *arouses* us sexually, is suggested by two remarks in Bloom's chapter on rock. The first is that rock "elicits" undeveloped sexual desire, and the second is that rock is "arousing and cathartic music."[38] In other words, rock has the beat of sex because its beat stirs up sexual feelings in its audience. Whether or not the music *resembles* or symbolizes sex is irrelevant: it is simply a matter of cause and effect, with the music as cause and its regular effect as the basis for its identification with sex. If it caused something else on a regular basis, let us say anxiety, then it would be anxious rather than sexual. Sometimes known as the "arousal theory" of music, this theory assumes that the character of the music is *affective* rather than cognitive (felt rather than understood). The metaphor of drugs is frequently introduced. Like an opiate, the person need not be aware of its presence or composition in order to suffer its effects.[39] The charge that rock has an unhealthy "subliminal" effect on its audience thus makes it a variant of arousal theory.

I find that beginners in aesthetics are sympathetic to this theory, but back off from it as soon as it is formulated with any precision. They are also surprised that rock music is only the most recent flash point in an ongoing debate. An early version was proposed some 150 years ago by Thomas De Quincey in his attack on Joseph Addison, who had criticized Italian opera. The fine arts, De Quincey argues, are characterized by the ability "to reproduce in the mind some great effect through the agency of *idem in alio*. The *idem,* the same impression, is to be restored, but *in alio,* in a different material — by means of some different instrument."[40] Music succeeds, then, if sound has the same effect on the audience that something other than sound usually has. Tolstoy offers a variation in *What Is Art?,* explicitly proposing that music is to be evaluated according to the value of the emotions it transmits.

As so many bastardized variants of arousal theory, only the style of music to be castigated changes with the years. R. G. Collingwood said virtually the same thing about jazz over fifty years ago:

> Thus music, in order to be representational, need not copy the noises made by bleating sheep, an express locomotive at speed, or a rattle in the throat of a dying man. . . . The erotic music of the modern dance-band may or may not consist of noises like those made by persons in a state of sexual excitement, but it does most powerfully evoke feelings like those proper to such a state.[41]

If the music regularly evokes sexual excitement, it is sexual. If it does not, it isn't. Whether it *sounds like* sex is beside the point. For affective purposes, Prince tracks like "The Most Beautiful Girl in the World" and "When Doves Cry" may be as sexual as explicit (and thus *representationally* sexual) tracks like "Come" and "Pheromone."

So Bloom's thesis about rock and sex involves a purely empirical hypothesis, to be accepted or rejected by determining how people feel when they listen to rock music. The fact that the lyrics are sexual or that the accompanying videos are blatantly sexual is irrelevant if hearing the music does not arouse people. To my knowledge, there is no clear evidence supporting Bloom; any data he may have is anecdotal. By his own admission, anyone who regularly listens to rock has more evidence on the topic than Bloom. My own guess would be that if rock arouses any one response with regularity, it is a mild euphoria and a desire to celebrate by leaping about and behaving childishly. If it regresses us emotionally, it is to a stage prior to the emergence of adolescent sexuality. But of course my evidence is as anecdotal as Bloom's.

Furthermore, the arousal theory of musical expression has its own problems. There is plenty of empirical evidence available to us suggesting that music is *not* described according to its effects upon its audience. First, personal experience tells each of us that it's often the reverse. A very sad song, such as the blues at its bluest, tends to comfort us, not to sadden us. If we described music according to its emotional effects, we would actually describe most of the music that we know to be sad as cheerful. Second, we are probably all aware that different people are affected very differently by the very same music (largely for its associations with events to which we link it). Finally, if arousal is subliminal and does not depend on representational features, how do we account for the fact that people find it so difficult to determine the emotions present in the music of other cultures or in an unfamiliar style? When I played Ravi Shankar's performance of the *raga Gara* to thirty students, most of them music majors, none of them thought that it was "romantic" despite that description of it in the album's liner notes. When I played the same group a Burundi song expressing home-sickness, none of them felt homesick in response. The majority thought it was sexual.[42]

A third objection is even more compelling: there is the obvious ques-tion of why we would listen to music so often if it were true. And why would we choose *this* music? Most of those who grew up with rock continue to listen to it well into adulthood, often employing it as back-ground music during the day. But who wants to be sexually aroused at work, or while studying or driving or buying groceries? Just as we cannot make sense of normal people choosing to listen to sad music if its sadness lies in its depressing effect upon its audience, we could not make sense of rock as background music if it actually arouses its au-diences. Sustained sexual arousal without release is hardly pleasant; in fact, it produces intense frustration. As Peter Kivy notes in discussing arousal theories, "it seems absurd to suppose that one would willingly, indeed enthusiastically, inflict such painful or unpleasant experiences on oneself for no further purpose of pleasure or self-interest at all."[43] It is therefore no more likely that rock arouses us sexually than that sad music imparts genuine sadness.

There is only one viable reply that Bloom could launch at this stage: the music really does arouse the emotions but we listen anyway because there is a further pleasurable purpose. Indeed, Bloom suggests as much in his remark that rock has a cathartic effect that releases one from the sexual emotions it arouses. When sad music makes us sad, vividly experiencing the emotions offers some release from them. We take satisfaction in this release rather than (paradoxically) in the sadness itself. Similarly, the sexual nature of rock music might be welcomed if it offers a release from our sexual urges. Rock would repress teen sex-uality, not fuel it. But then, of course, Bloom ought to praise it, not damn it.

Clearly, Bloom is scapegoating. There can be music which is pure rhythm, but there is virtually no melody without rhythm. If the rhythms of rock feed our raw sexual appetites, the melodies of Bach and Beethoven are to be damned along with those of Prince and the Rolling Stones. To suppose that rock "has one appeal only," sexual in nature, is to propose that the rock audience responds to no stylistic feature beyond its basic backbeat.[44] Bloom is drawing on the stereotypes of rock that flourish in the absence of serious thought about stylistic and aesthetic qualities as bearers of meaning. Unfortunately, by endorsing many of the same superficial stereotypes, rock musicians and fans encourage the jingoism of the attacks repeatedly made against them.

Rhythmic Complexities

The masses go for the beat. — Neil Young[45]

I will conclude by returning to the idea that rock has a "jungle" beat, looking at developments that have arisen in rock because of its *distance* from its West African heritage. Finally, I want to consider the *uses* to which they are put (besides suggesting sex to critics with a prurient interest).

Even in their most complex handling of accents and subaccents of the beat, rock musicians almost never re-create anything like the beat of "the jungle," which I have charitably interpreted as an ignorant reference to West Africa. Just as there is nothing primitive about rock rhythms — one is tempted to say that emphasis on harmony and melody has led to simplistic rhythms in much Western music — as a rule there is no longer anything African about them. African drumming is characterized by polymeters. While rock music is normally polyrhythmic, it is almost never polymetric. Western musical language is so impoverished with respect to rhythm that this distinction does not even appear in many specialized dictionaries of music. It thus requires a brief explanation.

As Gunther Schuller points out, "when the European thinks of polyrhythm, he generally conceives of it as two or more rhythmic strands occurring simultaneously, retaining, however, vertical coincidence at phrase beginnings and endings, at bar lines, and at other focal points."[46] In *Don Giovanni*, Mozart introduces three vocal lines with different dance rhythms, yet these melodies have synchronized vertical coincidences. In another familiar situation, if a jazz drummer is playing 4/4, everyone else is normally in 4/4, even in a passage with simultaneous but independent horn improvisations.

Although the vocal melody of a rock song will have its own rhythm, it will coincide regularly with the distinct rhythms of the other parts, typically on the downbeat defining the start of each measure. At the same time, one or more contrasting instruments accent the weak beats while remaining synchronized with the basic beat and meter. Thus the backbeat stands out. Even when the drummer plays behind or in front of the beat, it is as a variation of the basic beat and not a separate one. Add a second drummer or percussionist and one is freed from the chore of holding down the basic accents, and the music becomes even more polyrhythmic. Classic examples include James Brown, Santana, Parliament/Funkadelic, and Sly and the Family Stone; all are unusually polyrhythmic for Western popular music.[47]

Most African drumming is polymetric, creating contrapuntal cross-rhythms, and not merely polyrhythmic. The difference is that each member of the musical ensemble will operate "in different metric patterns which are, moreover, staggered in such a way that the downbeats of these patterns rarely coincide."[48] In short, the distinct rhythms of a polyrhythm share the same meter. In a polymeter they do not. In African drumming, the basic pulse is not even played; the master drummer guides and signals the others without actually providing any beat as more basic than the rest. In rock, the drummer normally plays the beat and perhaps some polyrhythms, interacting with rhythms generated in the same meter by the rest of the group. The basic pulse is spelled out. But as drummer Mickey Hart observes, once you add genuine cross-rhythms, most of them "can't be married to the backbeat."[49] True polymeters dropped out of the music in the African journey to America. The democratized beat and its polyrhythms were retained.

We see that if there is any one thing that can be identified as the rock beat, it is the accentuation of the second and fourth beats in common time. It gives rock its roll. It also creates a framework which supports further rhythmic complexities, so that three or four or more rhythms are maintained simultaneously. While this rhythmic interplay is seldom as complicated as that found in jazz (although it can be, as with Carlos Santana, James Brown, Sly Stone, Sheila E., and George Clinton), it is certainly more advanced than almost anything we find in the standard classical repertoire. Furthermore, as rock musicians have explored different subpatterns and intersecting patterns, there has been a series of distinctive rock rhythms.

Even in the early rock-and-roll recordings of the 1950s, there was no one rock beat. While Chuck Berry and rockabilly musicians favored backbeat, the New Orleans style of Dave Bartholomew and Fats Domino involved shuffles with a "swing" accent.[50] As each subsequent decade has introduced new rock styles, each has also involved distinct rhythmic styles. British rockers, particularly the Rolling Stones and the Beatles, featured solid backbeat. Southern soul music, much of it featuring the drumming of Al Jackson Jr. at Stax and Roger Hawkins at Muscle Shoals, emphasized a laid-back (slightly delayed) backbeat and a minimum of embellishment. Surf music, on the other hand, emphasized all manner of drum fills and rolls (little wonder that it was the personal favorite of Keith Moon). Phil Spector tended to couple the drumming of Hal Blaine or Earl Palmer with Latin percussion; the drummers were expected to come down hardest on the fourth beat and to improvise ornate fills as the song peaked and at the point of fade-out. Subsequent session drummers are expected to know what is meant when a producer asks for Charlie Watts or Stax or Phil Spector.

Moving on to the 1970s, the rhythms of punk were explosive when they were fresh, but partly because they returned to a more deliberate and uncluttered attack. In light of Hüsker Dü and subsequent thrash bands, the rhythms of the Sex Pistols and early Clash can now feel plodding and simple. Derived from a merger of Caribbean and New Orleans rhythms, reggae once felt exotic; Paul Simon had to travel to Jamaica to get it played correctly on "Mother and Child Reunion" (1972). (Reggae sounds "inside out" to many Americans. A backbeat is contrasted with accents on subsidiary beats. The bass is mixed prominently and normally plays a distinct melody or "riddum," emphasizing strong beats, while the rhythm guitar scratches out choppy chords on the offbeat.) The Police were initially admired for their appropriation of reggae; returning to their first two albums now, they feel spartan, with little of the rhythmic richness of the genre. Genuine reggae has far more activity between the beats. Disco was greeted with shirts and bumper stickers reading "Disco Sucks," but its relentless four equal beats to the measure at a medium-fast tempo keeps resurfacing, each time with a new name. The first rap record appeared in 1979 (the Sugarhill Gang's "Rapper's Delight"), and rap and house music's reliance on sampling and layered electronic rhythms takes rock in yet another direction.

Evidence that a new beat has emerged is that a new mode of dance is adopted for each style; different beats are suited to different uses. The story is often told of how producer Jerry Wexler taught the Stax/Volt house band the delayed accent that became the trademark of Memphis soul by *dancing* the jerk. The thrashing and body surfing that accompanies hardcore is antithetical to the sensuous movement of reggae or the gymnastics of hip-hop. High school cheerleaders still choreograph routines to old James Brown recordings, but the same music is hardly welcome on prom night, where one is more likely to hear James Brown sampled for the basis of a hip-hop track. The twist craze of the early sixties had its own distinctive basic rhythm, as did disco more than a decade later. Punk had the pogo. Reggae and hip-hop rhythms change a bit every year, as do their choreography.

Not only are there many variants of the basic approaches to beat, different treatments of specific rhythms are as individual as different pianists attacking the same piano sonata. For whatever reason, drummers are seldom composers, yet as musicians they are almost always the "composer" of the song's percussion parts. Whether handed the sheet music to a new composition or learning it by hearing it, rock drummers are expected to come up with their own drum part, usually on the spot. While no small part of the challenge is to find the beat and to emphasize it, the best drummers *compose* rhythmic patterns, accents, and fills to fit a specific song or recording. Russ Kunkel comments on working with Jackson Browne, who tends to write songs incorporating hushed passages in which there's very limited percussion:

> It's either a backbeat on the hi-hat or a backbeat on the bass drum. Or it's quarter notes on the snare drum just clicking away. If he keeps writing the same way, I'll be in a bit of trouble, because I've almost used up all my ideas on how to play his songs right.[51]

While the song dictates what is needed from the drummer, drummers are musicians in their own right and seek ways to individualize their drum parts. So while there are basic patterns and styles of rock drumming, each drummer tends to have a distinctive feel for rhythm and the beat.

No drummer wants to be a mere metronome (computer-driven click tracks serve that function through earphones for the musicians) or to sound exactly like any other. Keith Moon is the extreme case, a drummer who so individualized his contribution that his fellow musicians had to keep time for themselves, trusting that Moon would come back to the beat at the crucial points. He usually did. Kenny Jones found himself incapable of playing some of Moon's drum parts when he replaced Moon in the Who, while some songs had such singular drum fills that Jones felt compelled to learn them. Producer Jimmy Miller plays on the Rolling Stones' "You Can't Always Get What You Want" (1969) because Charlie Watts could not get the proper feel for the song. (Based on the official live recordings of the song, Watts has *never* gotten the feel for it.) R.E.M. drummer Mike Mills does not appear on "Untitled" (1988) because he objected to the beat that the other members wanted on that song.

Above all, rock drummers try to bring out the expressive character and drama of the music. As with the dimensions of timbre and volume, rhythms are introduced and customized to expressive effect. Far from sticking to a predetermined beat, different patterns and accents are introduced for different sections of a song. Consider Will Calhoun, drummer for Living Colour. On the title track of *Time's Up*, he comes down on the snare on two and a half and four, not the traditional two and four. On "Memories Can't Wait," on *Vivid*, the song is in common time "but there's no 1-2-3-4 anywhere, the beat is constantly shifting."[52] Calhoun also stresses the need to play behind or in front of the actual beat, or even to complicate it further, but always, he says, with an ear for the emotions of the song's lyrics. Another example of a simple yet effective rhythmic coloration is Tracy Chapman's hit "Fast Car" (1988). Chapman's acoustic guitar sets up the basic rhythm, and drummer Denny Fongheisser plays directly on the standard beat for the declamatory verses. But he plays in front of the beat on the chorus, heightening the escapism of the narrator's sentiments with a sense of forward rush, matching her desire to drive away from her troubles.

I have elaborated upon varieties of rock rhythm in order to make it clear that "the beat" of rock is not any one thing, nor is it the only thing that matters in rock's rhythmic pleasures. It is neither primitive nor simple, nor primordial nor mechanical. The poverty of Western thinking about rhythm, coupled with common prejudices and stereotypes about popular culture, obscures the diversity and role of rhythm in rock music. We must resist crude judgments about the beat of rock music, even when those crudities are surrounded by references to Plato, Rousseau, and other intellectuals of the Western canon.

6

Adorno, Jazz, and the Reception

of Popular Music

You can't conform to the formula of always giving the audience what it wants, or you're killing yourself and you're killing the audience. Because they don't really want it either. Just because they respond to something doesn't mean they want it. — Bruce Springsteen[1]

OHistorically, rock was peculiarly American. But increasingly, its ablest practitioners and innovators live elsewhere. Only the staunchest formalists can respond to it in purely musical terms. "We all live in America," observes U2's Bono, "in the sense that you turn on the television and it's America. As is a lot of the music we listen to."[2] U2's overt response was *Rattle and Hum* (1988). But the Kinks had beaten them to it, particularly with *Muswell Hillbillies* (1971). Mixing resignation and tenderness, "Oklahoma U.S.A." portrays the Americanization of the British imagination. The song describes an English working-class girl, no doubt of the Davies brothers' own Muswell Hill. She imagines herself a character in the musical *Oklahoma!* as she walks home from a local shop. The Kinks have been equally divided through much of their career, crossbreeding American mass culture with the English music hall.

But rock is only the most recent American music to succeed as an export. Debates about rock have a habit of recapitulating earlier disputes about jazz. If it is now a commonplace that jazz is particularly rich as a mass culture art form, or that it is America's only indigenous art form, such status does not transfer so readily to rock music. Yet at one time the ideal of musical autonomy made jazz problematic for many intellectuals. If only, some critics still lament, Louis Armstrong had been less interested in *entertaining* audiences who wanted canned versions of his earlier triumphs. What might have been? Rock music, even more nakedly commercial and formulaic than jazz, is seen as having all of jazz's vices with few of its virtues.

It will be useful to remind ourselves of the concerns that arose early on about popular music in modern bourgeois culture. In particular, there is the "pessimistic analysis" of jazz and popular music offered by Theodor W. Adorno. An interdisciplinary cultural critique steeped in Hegel and Marx and tempered by firsthand experience of Nazi totalitarianism, it has been rehashed so often and in so many contexts that it seems "almost itself a cliché."[3] Roland Barthes, for one, can sound uncannily like Adorno when it comes to popular culture.[4] At the same time, the nastier edges of Adorno's hatchet job on popular music are too often explained away as "Eurocentrism and ill will," as though none of it really belongs to his aesthetics.[5] To give him credit, Adorno was one of the first to say that any appraisal of music must begin with its social history and cultural norms. If only he had stretched that insight to include popular music.

The Classic Dichotomy

Using black despair—carefully filtered—to express young white hopes: *rock*. . . . Thus a degraded, censored, artificial music took center stage. Mass music for an anesthetized market. —Jacques Attali[6]

While it may seem odd to turn to a critique of jazz in an aesthetics of rock, two points should be considered. First, rock did not spring full grown, like Athena from the head of Zeus, from the throat of Elvis Presley or any other candidate for ur-rocker. Rock, whether in early rock and roll or some derivation, is an offshoot of popular jazz. Jazz fans often dismiss it as a bastard son, but the Rolling Stones took their drummer, their name, and the songs of Robert Johnson from jazz, rhythm and blues, and rural blues respectively. If jazz has become the pedigreed bloodline of popular music by downplaying entertainment values and dance rhythms for instrumental prowess, rock has largely succeeded by seducing the audience that jazz left behind.

Second, if one believes that rock cannot or should not be approached as legitimate aesthetic activity, Adorno's critique of jazz provides a major blueprint for that dismissal. His legacy is found in ongoing attempts to separate artistry and commercial entertainment in order to deny the aesthetic merits of the latter; to distinguish taste cultures according to listening ability, based on a norm drawn from European high culture; to emphasize (and denigrate) the predigested and standardized elements of popular music; and to read the success of repetitive forms of popular music as passive consumption and thus a triumph of corporations over consumers.

In popular discourse, these oppositions are packaged as a choice between music as artistic expression and music controlled by the entertainment industry. Thus the supposed purity of the first Woodstock festival was often invoked to damn the greed of Woodstock '94. The whole genre of "indie rock," notes Eric Weisbard, turns on the idea that "one could be a consumer without the traditional associations of gross commodification, audience passivity, and massness."[7] John Rockwell, music critic for the *New York Times* and no stranger to aesthetic theory, implicitly endorses the same dichotomy when analyzing Neil Young:

> there is an extraordinary, violent power to some of Young's best hard-rock music — the reiterated dissonant guitar chords at the end of side two of the *Rust Never Sleeps* album must be called artistic, since they have left "entertainment" so far behind.[8]

But must we choose between commercial entertainment and personal expression, as Rockwell implies? "After the Gold Rush" (1970) is one of Young's sweetest melodies and best-known songs, still appearing regularly in his live performances. Yet its combination of personal confession and environmental pessimism is hardly "entertaining."

Entrenched in both the indie nation and the *New York Times,* the dichotomy tempts almost everyone who defends popular art. Viewing popular music from within a framework of Deweyan pragmatism, Richard Shusterman advises that it "deserves serious aesthetic attention, since to dismiss it as beneath aesthetic consideration is to consign its evaluation and future to the most mercenary pressures of the marketplace."[9] Shusterman trumpets the aesthetic merit of selected works of popular music, but warns that much of it has a "noxious" social effect and is "consumed in a passive, all-accepting way."[10] Its failures embody just the sort of shortcomings identified by Adorno. At the risk of buying into the sort of optimism that offends Shusterman, I think that "entertainment" and the "marketplace" function as bogeymen here. Shusterman's primary example of challenging and multilayered popular music, Stetsasonic's "Talking All That Jazz" (1988), is no less a creature of the marketplace than, say, a piece of junk like Linda Ronstadt's *Mad Love* (1980). Ronstadt's nod to new wave is probably the nadir of her uneven career, but its status as commercial product is exactly the same as for her masterpiece, *Heart Like a Wheel* (1974).

Personal expression presupposes a community that shares a common vocabulary. If that community consists of millions of one's contemporaries (and not the thousands of middle-class concertgoers who supported classical composers in their heyday), the basic vocabulary is going to be rooted in materials afforded by mass media. At the same time, personal expression requires a personal or signature style, which in turn exists only as an individual's variation on a more general style. At least Rockwell sees this: "Like any great composer, Young varies and extends an idiom that is a common language for him and his audience."[11] Neil Young isn't better because he's more expressive than his contemporaries. He's more expressive because he's mastered the idioms of rock in which he works. Ronstadt's *Mad Love* is flat, unexpressive, and "fake" because she hadn't mastered the stylistic idiosyncrasies of new wave.

So I recommend navigating between two positions that are often treated as mutually exclusive. First, we should avoid the superficial idea that the idiom employed for purposes of entertainment is distinct from that of artistic expression. But we should be just as wary of the idea that only one idiom is suitable for all musicians working at any given time (an appeal to a universal standard that is implicit in the common defensive maneuver that it's all just music and its kind doesn't matter).

Another element of Adorno's critique permeating most discussions of rock music is the idea that popularity must be at the expense of art. One can never underestimate the masses. To use Adorno's language, only the "predigested" will sell, and a limited set of stock elements is endlessly recycled, disguised with pseudo-individualization. Adorno's thesis is nowadays updated to take account of the fact that the mass audience is not really homogeneous, but more a collection of subcultures; most music is consciously targeted at a specific segment of the audience. We are never going to hear heavy metal playing at the supermarket, nor anything as idiosyncratic as Neil Young's *Time Fades Away* (1973) or Run-D.M.C.'s *King of Rock* (1985). But where I shop for groceries I regularly hear mainstream hits from those years, including "She's Gone" by Hall and Oates and "Walk Like an Egyptian" by the Bangles. Which is fine by me; I like both of them. But music with any edge, disruption, or surprise, or music that downplays melody for rhythm and texture, is kept away from non-aficionados.

Consider heavy metal. Its musical signatures offend a large segment of the general audience, yet the aspiring heavy-metal guitarist knows the need to tailor material to the expectations of the heavy-metal crowd. Although Deena Weinstein makes no secret of her allegiance to rock and dismisses Adorno as a cultural elitist, his spirit is often alive in her writing. Weinstein's lengthy sociological study, *Heavy Metal,* wavers between two positions. One, much like Adorno's, posits a Faustian bargain that metal bands make for the sake of commercial viability. Another, contradicting Adorno, argues that the entertainment industry neither created nor shapes the subsequent development of metal as a rock genre.[12]

Weinstein initially allows that, however specialized heavy metal is in comparison with genuinely "mass" entertainment, record companies operate more or less as Adorno claims:

> Record companies need to market products that are both differentiated enough from competing products to attract attention and thus consumers, yet close enough to known products to appeal to a reliable established market. On one level, the signature sound [of a successful band] is like the blue beads or the green flakes put into detergents to set off one brand from its all-but-equivalent competitors.[13]

Weinstein's remarks about heavy metal could be stretched to any commercially successful rock band. Each can be placed within a specific category. Each displays some "signature" distinguishing them from others within the same category. What would the Rolling Stones be if they got a new drummer and lead vocalist (hint: listen to Keith Richards' solo work)? Faced with the loss of a key player, rock bands usually face a choice between crafting a new sound (and then "selling" it to an audience who may resist it) or replicating the old sound, running the risk of endless self-parody. The Who illustrates the problem of a signature sound. When they resumed recording and touring after the death of drummer Keith Moon, the result was Who-lite. Led Zeppelin wisely threw in the towel when drummer John Bonham died.

Weinstein implies that, on another level, commercial considerations are not the whole story. Yet she does not follow through to make that case. She concludes that each band's signature sound is inevitably a "compromise" between self-expression and the predigested sonic, visual, and symbolic dimensions that distinguish metal from other types of rock.

The other level is, of course, aesthetic. Rather than a compromise which prevents rock bands from fully achieving self-expression, the "code" for success might be understood as *initial requirements* for meaningfulness. Self-expression cannot be the spontaneous outpouring of the sensitive genius. If it were, it would be an inarticulate outpouring. As Ernst Gombrich and Richard Wollheim remind us, meaningful self-expression requires creation "within a set of alternatives that could, to a greater or lesser degree of completeness, be enumerated."[14] Alternatives that are common to a community are a general style. Ones directly associated with an individual (in rock, often a band) are the individual's style, which may be adopted by others so as to become part of the general style. The upshot, Wollheim argues, is that "it is only when we are acquainted with these alternatives that we as spectators can understand what emotion the picture is intended to convey." Rather than *just* a commercial compromise limiting the individual, the process of generating a signature sound within a broader nexus of established alternatives is essential to self-expression. Calling it a compromise is like calling my children's adoption of English as their native language a career move. I call it a necessary step in their enculturation. Prior to that, their prattle and babble in the playpen was inarticulate. Music without identifiable stylistic features is equally inarticulate.

Without falling prey to the cynicism of "rock and roll is here to pay," I think it time to move past the dogma that some taint or fault follows from the admission that rock is inherently commercial. Rappers would not trumpet their records as the "newspapers" of the African American community if they weren't commercially promoted and distributed. The "alternative" musician who genuinely scorns and avoids commerce is the anomaly here. Even Fugazi has a national distributor that keeps their CDs in stock at the local outlet, and Nirvana eventually agreed to an alternative back cover for *In Utero* (1993) and a renaming of "Rape Me" in order to get it stocked by retail chains who'd censored it. We need to move beyond the prevailing idea that "mass market cultural products" *inevitably* "invite a passive, absent participation" of "prefabricated entertainments."[15]

The Filthy Tide

Mass production strips every image of its singularity, rendering it schematic and quickly identifiable, so that it resembles a sign. — Robert Hughes[16]

The hermetic work of art belongs to the bourgeois, the mechanical work belongs to fascism, and the fragmentary work, in its state of complete negativity, belongs to utopia. — Theodor W. Adorno[17]

Where Marx proposed that religion is the opiate of the masses, Adorno assigns the popular arts a similar honor in modern society, vilifying them as tools of fascist consciousness. His sustained *Kulturkritik* of popular music proposes that social context, including both the means of production and of access to music, is the major factor determining both the music's significance and the audience's response. The masses, it seems, do not respond to music as music.

Adorno wrote frequently on "jazz," treating it as the exemplar of all popular music. He formulated many of his views in relation to popular music of the 1930s and restated many of them in his later writings, particularly the *Introduction to the Sociology of Music.*[18] The analysis of popular music, including jazz, gained additional theoretical support in his comparison of Schoenberg and Stravinsky in the *Philosophy of Modern Music* (1948).[19] Although his jargon and style pose formidable difficulties, he offers the most systematic exploration of the various assumptions that lead us to denigrate the musical value of jazz and other types of popular music.

When we survey his scattered writings on music and art, it appears that Adorno critiques jazz on two distinct levels, one local (generated by specific cases) and one global (arising from his general aesthetic theory). Both are required to support his contention that jazz is always "bad," even if some of it is "good bad music." By exploring the relationship between the two levels, we are in a position to appreciate their problematic connection in Adorno's thought. Ironically, his theory contains features that suggest that jazz is a distinct art and as "true" as the music of the Schoenberg school.

From the outset, one must note Adorno's frequently unconventional and ambiguous use of the term "jazz." If we go into almost any record store, we will find the merchandise divided into several categories, just as a supermarket has the produce in one area and the dairy products in another. In the record store, we expect that the popular hits will be in one place, classical music in another, and jazz in yet another. (Radio programming is similarly segmented, as Adorno notes.) There may be further distinctions, but imagine our surprise if Miles Davis were to be filed in the same section as Debussy, and Charlie Parker with Puccini. Adorno rejects such a grouping of jazz and classical, but not because jazz deserves its very own category. For Adorno, Davis and Parker belong with all the *other* "jazz." In other words, Miles Davis should be filed between Mac Davis and Spencer Davis. Charlie Parker belongs beside British rocker Graham Parker in the popular, or "light," music section. Better yet, none of their recordings should be sold in the same store as Beethoven, because this sort of merchandising only creates the false illusion that, as music, it is all just different types of the same thing, reducing Beethoven to the same vulgar level of kitsch. "The differences in the reception of official 'classical' music and light music no longer have any real significance," Adorno complains. "They are only still manipulated for reasons of marketability."[20]

Adorno challenges the accepted view that jazz is fundamentally distinct from and aesthetically superior to other entertainment music and popular culture. He thinks that approval of jazz reflects a false consciousness created by the "totalitarianism" of a profit-oriented "culture industry." Tending toward rushed judgment, Adorno frequently classifies *all* nonclassical music as jazz, evidently based on the dubious belief that jazz was the dominant and paradigmatic form of popular music during his lifetime. (Perhaps he did not know that jazz was never synonymous with popular music. He simply seems unaware that with the emergence of bebop and then rock and roll, jazz became decidedly less popular.) In what follows, I use "jazz" in its normal sense: Louis Armstrong, Charlie Parker, Wynton Marsalis. I widen the discussion to entertainment and popular music when Adorno's position calls for it.

For Adorno, the assumption that there are qualitative differences within popular music, so that the audience for jazz has something over heavy-metal fans, or that Van Halen is better than Motorhead, is an allowable but ultimately pointless differentiation among levels of junk. Adorno is stingy with examples, but he seems to allow that Charlie Parker made better music than Elvis Presley. He grants that there is "some good bad music . . . along with all the bad good music," but this only shows that qualified musicians are willing to sell out to market forces.[21] Stepping back to get a broader perspective, he then dismisses all entertainment music as a "filthy tide," which has been that way for more than a century now.[22] Those who champion jazz as great art are busy making discriminations among "drivel" and so have "already capitulated to barbarism."[23] For Adorno, jazz is simply the exemplar of music debased as commercial commodity, and of music that fails utterly as art.

Viewing jazz itself, apart from a broader position on music as an aspect of culture, Adorno introduces several crucial premises that hold, by extension, to all popular culture. His primary assumption, restated in the 1960s, is that the music itself "has remained essentially unchanged" since its first commercial success in 1914. (He probably means 1917, when jazz was first recorded.) Although experts and even college courses trace the evolution of jazz from ragtime through swing through bebop and beyond, "none of this alters the fact that jazz has in its essence remained static."[24] Whether we focus on its rhythmic vitality, improvisation, or experiments in tonality, Adorno insists that "the most striking traits in jazz were all independently produced, developed and surpassed by serious music since Brahms."[25] Jazz and pop music are therefore "the dregs of musical history."[26] They feature no genuine musical innovation, so any educational program or theory that creates an appreciation of jazz masks its "prescribed ever-sameness" of "standard devices." Those who become "addicted" to the music are no different from alcohol or tobacco addicts.[27] Two recent books on the connection between sounds and psychological health sympathetically argue that rock rhythms are indeed addictive, not to mention psychologically destructive.[28]

Since it cannot be desired for its aesthetic value, what accounts for the explosive growth of jazz and other pop music in this century? Having posited a static and repetitive essence, Adorno turns to a non-aesthetic account of its enigmatic success.[29] In *Aesthetic Theory*, he argues that the structure of artworks — including entertainment — always mirrors that of "the social process surrounding them."[30] Having denied that jazz can be interesting as music, Adorno makes the crucial inference that only a sociological analysis can account for its mass appeal. But now his concern with social process does double duty, explaining both the work's structure and its appeal.

At times, Adorno offers a psychoanalytic explanation: the audience unconsciously responds to a "castration symbolism" within entertainment music.[31] I find this unpersuasive, bordering on the unintelligible. His other explanation fares better: "Jazz, however directed, would hardly be so appealing if it did not respond to some social need; but that in turn is created by technological progress."[32] Progress creates leisure time for the masses, but the emptiness of this free time must be masked by those who are in control. The masses are free, up to a point, but powerless. Modern society responds with a "culture industry" whose products are "the decoration of empty time." By its very monotony, the simple "beating" of time in popular music generates an "ersatz sphere of physical motion" to cover up the boredom and angst of people's purposeless existence.[33] And because hearing is so passive, music is the ideal background for all daily activity, and so has ample opportunity to train "the unconscious for conditioned reflex." The result, Adorno claims, is a false consciousness. We delight in the process of killing time, as a substitute for confrontation with our social reality.

The *content* of popular culture responds to fundamental human needs but not, as might be supposed, through simple wish fulfillment. We know that we cannot attain happiness or liberation, he suggests, but we compensate by taking pleasure in our acknowledgment of the fact as we look on images of happiness and liberation. Comparing popular songs to the escapist Hollywood films of the 1930s, Adorno proposes that "the actual function of sentimental music lies rather in the temporary release given to the awareness that one has missed fulfill-ment. . . . They consume music in order to be allowed to weep."[34] Rock, infused with the mythology of rebellion, would seem to attract an audience who cannot actually rebel and overthrow the system. We are to conclude that middle-class white teens are attracted to countercul-ture music, whether hippie utopianism in the late 1960s or the harder edge of recent hip-hop culture, because it openly speaks of an oppres-sive system that they dare not confront; the temporary release comes from its frank admission that contemporary life sucks. But behind the lyrics are stale musical standardizations, denying the radicalism of the message with its numbing predictability.

The same technological progress that controls our time and destroys our individuality is also at work in the directed production of popular music. Adorno contends that "the jazz monopoly rests on the exclu-siveness of the supply and the economic power behind it."[35] He intro-duces the phrase "culture industry" to indicate the monopoly of those who centralize and direct the production of entertainment music. His emphasis on the consequent passivity of the audience is mirrored in a recent text on the sociology of music:

> The interesting thing about this market response system is that the public has little control over the content of the music. Record producers select songs and artists which will succeed in appearing high in the charts; pluggers tell station managers and retail man-agers what will succeed; finally the charts measure the success which the pre-selected material has enjoyed. In short, the com-panies talk to themselves through this complex system. Thus the charts measure the success of a sales campaign rather than shifts in musical taste. Indeed, *the music seems almost beside the point* in this process.[36]

But Adorno sees that treating the audience as mere consumer, passive and manipulated, creates its own theoretical difficulty. On this assump-tion, the culture industry faces the problem that those who create pop music must appeal to a false consciousness. Since the audience cannot accept musical quality, the music "must not go beyond what audiences are used to, lest it repel them." Yet the goal is to sell a product, requiring an endless stream of music that is seemingly new and original. Adorno resolves this contradiction by postulating "pseudo-individualization," in which very minor tonal and rhythmical modifications entice the consumer.[37] He compares the calculated process of rearranging various "frills" and "ornaments" with the factory customizing of automobiles; consumers make purchases based on minor differences, but everyone drives away in essentially the same vehicle.[38] The production practices of Motown and disco may be cases in point.

In short, Adorno regards even the most improvisational and progressive jazz as prefabricated product:

> Pseudo-individualization is what fools us. . . . Extremes of it are the improvisations in commercial jazz, which jazz journalism feeds upon. They stress instantaneous invention even though the metric and harmonic schema keeps them in such narrow bounds that they in turn might be reduced to a minimum of basic forms. In fact, the chances are that most of what is served up as improvisation outside the innermost circles of jazz experts will have been rehearsed.[39]

Despite differences that allow people to distinguish swing from bebop, or rockabilly from heavy metal, Adorno contends that this is a mere reshuffling of musically stale and "predigested" elements onto the skeleton of the thirty-two bar popular song, which serves as the "standard schema" underlying all forms of entertainment music.[40] In Attali's version, "despecifying degradation is one of the conditions for the success of repetition."[41] Adorno notes that the process is so stale that there are books on how to write hit tunes. He would be delighted to learn that such books are being written today for rock music.

So while Adorno grants that jazz is less despicable than pop music, the achievement is entirely relative. Jazz fails when viewed from the perspective of a broader critique. It fails in the same way that all entertainment music fails: it does not fulfill the necessary social role of art in contemporary society. This shift to a broader, global perspective of social critique is crucial to Adorno's evaluation of jazz, because it underlies his sweeping dismissal of music that he may never even have heard. Actually, I am not satisfied that Adorno has a coherent theory. What I take up is one very prominent thread of his writings.

The key point for Adorno is that art's "spiritual essence" involves the illusion of its coherence and meaning.[42] Artworks are essentially dialectical, driven by the paradox that they "pretend" to achieve a total unity among their contributing elements, yet no such unity can be achieved.[43] Every work fails to some degree; the failure of jazz and popular music is simply more radical. In the case of music, the homophonic tradition that arose with the adoption of diatonic scales and equal temperament guaranteed conflict, because "harmony is never fully attainable. . . . Dissonance is the truth about harmony. Harmony is unattainable, given the strict criteria of what harmony is supposed to be."[44] Adorno believes that Western harmony is one of the restrictive basic elements of popular music; tonality is *imposed* on music. Yet the history of music reveals an ongoing attempt to break free of this imposed constraint. Dissonance is the core of "modernism," so only dissonant music can be true in the modern age.[45] Indeed, works of art are themselves sites of discord between the competing, irreconcilable elements of mimesis and rational construction. So only works that reveal their inherent discord are true to their own essence.

Having identified tonality as a major illusion of most Western music (particularly popular music), Adorno champions Schoenberg's Viennese school as the most progressive and successful music of our century. Atonal serialism succeeds not merely as progress for music, but for society, as well: "No music has the slightest aesthetic worth if it is not socially true, if only as a negation of untruth."[46] Adorno blurs any difference between aesthetic progress and social truth by insisting that the objective solution to internal conflict of artworks is the "truth content" of the successful work. Truth content must not be confused with mimesis or any intention of the artist, and remains negative unless completed by a philosophical critique of art.[47] We can now appreciate the relevance of Adorno's charge that jazz merely recycles established conventions. By responding only to tonal structures that were developed in earlier times and under different cultural conditions, the mass audience resists challenging its own current *social* condition. Imagine his response to a contemporary rock concert, as adolescents respond with wild enthusiasm to musical structures that originated in the Mississippi delta a century ago. Mass taste can only be exploited by avoiding and not confronting social truth, and thus popular music is of low aesthetic worth.

In contrast, Adorno proposes that the "highest productions actually *negate*" the prevailing social norms.[48] The barbarism of jazz and other entertainment music is accentuated by the success of an alternative. Schoenberg's best work follows no prior model and avoids adopting any structures or fixed method of composing to replace the discarded old ways. "Only from twelve-tone technique alone can music learn to remain responsible for itself; this can be done, however, only if music does not become victim of the technique."[49] Only twelve-tone music provides a dialectical resolution of the problems of Western music by its complete *negation* of prevailing conventions of production and consumption. Accepting Schoenberg means rejecting the social oppression of the culture industry and the conditions that make it possible.[50]

Returning to jazz, the magnitude of its failure becomes clear. It is boring and repetitive and can only appeal to passive listeners. At the same time, this passivity makes its very consumption "contradict the objective interest of those who consume it."[51] As a segment of the entertainment industry, jazz *cannot* reject all that has come before. It can only enact a charade of being avant-garde by pretending to be a constant agent of change. Unlike Schoenberg and his school, jazz cannot "assert itself against the ubiquity of commercialism." Only a complete rejection of music's hedonic appeal can provide the requisite "definitive negation" that provides the truth content to music in the twentieth century; music must oppose and thus reveal the oppressive standardization of the culture industry.[52] Those who accept atonality know that jazz is enjoyed only as a conditioned reflex.[53]

To summarize, Adorno's evaluation of popular music takes place on two levels. On a local level, focusing on jazz, Adorno identifies its essence or basic tendency. Because it is monotonous and static, a predigested product, he turns to its commodity character to account for its mass acceptance. Jazz is then critiqued from the perspective of his general theory of art, according to which the successful, autonomous work must be socially true. In modern capitalism, only a negative truth is possible. However, because the previous analysis reveals that jazz is a controlled commodity of the culture industry, it cannot achieve social truth, since it would then fail as a product for mass consumption. Finally, jazz is nonetheless the best popular music; having shown *its* failure, all the other "jazz" consumed by the masses (from heavy metal to New Age) is more "filthy" still. So Adorno's general dismissal of jazz and of any other entertainment music presupposes an adequate identification of its true character. Without that, he cannot claim that its sole appeal is its aggressive marketing by the entertainment monopoly.

Essences and Predigestion

What are we to make of Adorno's charges? We need not share his basic assumptions about dialectical critique to sympathize with his claims about popular music.[54] Ironically, his charges often find their way into the lyrics of rock music, including hit songs. Most notable are the Byrds' "So You Want to Be a Rock'N'Roll Star" (1967); Public Enemy's "Don't Believe the Hype" (1990); Rush's "Spirit of the Radio" (1976); and punk/new wave songs of the Sex Pistols, "EMI"; the Clash, "White Man in Hammersmith Palais" (1978); and Elvis Costello, "Radio Radio" (1978). But with or without Adorno's basic assumptions, I do not see why anyone should agree to key claims in his critique of popular music, nor to the claim that only "definitive negation" through atonality provides value to music today. After discussing some rather obvious examples drawn from jazz and rock, I turn to issues which are more strictly philosophical.

Adorno's critique holds that, "in its essence," popular music involves pseudo-individualization of its "sole material," the standard schema of the popular song. This sweeping claim can be rejected even if we restrict the examples drawn from popular music — jazz in particular — predating Adorno's death in 1969. First, jazz musicians often dispense with popular songs, or subvert them when they do employ them. Near the apex of his development, Louis Armstrong extended the New Orleans tradition with his Hot Five and Hot Seven recordings (1925–27). Yet at that time, Armstrong had little exposure to popular mainstream standards, and he did not write thirty-two measure tunes. In fact, the group's weakest recordings are frequently of tunes composed by others, and Armstrong's strongest originals are head arrangements employing blues progressions. Among these, the masterful "Potato Head Blues" is neither the standard twelve nor thirty-two bars, and the highly admired "Weather Bird" (1928) is based on King Oliver's sixteen-measure tune. In brief, Armstrong's breakthrough as a jazz soloist did not derive from the popular, standard tunes of his day.[55]

Next, there is jazz that is based on popular song, but not "predigested" as a result. Although Charlie Parker's "Warming Up a Riff" and "Ko Ko" are both based on the chord changes of "Cherokee," they hardly constitute a mere ornamentation of the original song. "Red Cross," "Thriving on a Riff," "Chasin' the Bird," "Ah-Leu-Cha," and "Constellation" are based on Gershwin's "I Got Rhythm," but here again, Parker's transformation cannot be regarded as mere frills on the original tune.[56] A bedrock of popular song supports many of Parker's improvisations, but those songs are no more restrictive of his art than use of the sonata-allegro form in Beethoven's symphonies. As critic Len Lyons observes about Parker's use of a handful of songs as source material, "Parker's compositions are like snowflakes — similar in structure outwardly but intricately unique within."[57] The effect is the very antithesis of entertainment; regarding Parker's assault on "Cherokee," another critic notes that " 'Ko Ko' is not the kind of music one wishes to hear often. It is disturbing, in the way that some of Schoenberg is disturbing."[58] Adorno's claims about jazz are equally inappropriate for improvisations that Sonny Rollins and John Coltrane subsequently built upon standard tunes like "Mack the Knife" (Rollins, 1956) and "My Favorite Things" (Coltrane, 1960).

Parker's achievement is alone sufficient to show that a basis in popular song is not inherently restrictive. Yet there are plenty of cases where jazz musicians consciously abandon both the conventions of popular song and its standard chord progressions. Lennie Tristano's "Intuition" and "Digression" (both 1949) are perhaps the earliest free collective improvisations preserved on recordings. Better known are Miles Davis's *Kind of Blue* (1959) and Ornette Coleman's *Free Jazz* (1960), both of which avoid the framework of popular song composition.[59] Both avoid standard tonality. *Kind of Blue* consists of five group improvisations on themes of varying lengths, employing modal sequences that allow melodic invention independent of the harmonic bases of preset chord changes and diatonic scales. Although Davis did not originate jazz improvisation on modes in lieu of chord progressions, these sessions were the first to exploit fully the increased improvisational freedom afforded by the modal approach. Free of the harmonic straitjacket that Adorno regards as a basic "illusion" of popular music, *Kind of Blue* avoids all the conventions of popular songs. Instead, Davis's musicians improvise on initial themes with little or no group practice; the first full run-through of each piece is its final take.

Coleman's *Free Jazz* also rejects all the predetermined chord progressions of popular songs and improvises on a few short original themes. But where Davis places trumpet, saxophone, and piano in the foreground as individual soloists, Coleman downplays the convention of the foreground solo and offers thirty-six minutes of collective improvisation among as many as eight players at once. Nor does jazz require diatonic tonality. Furthermore, in many pieces by Charles Mingus and several by Ornette Coleman, varying tempos and unpredictable rhythmic fluctuations replace a steady beat. With these and many other works available to him, Adorno could have known in 1960 that jazz has no essential reliance on composed songs. It is not always true that "the metric and harmonic schema keeps them in such narrow bounds" that improvisation is mere ornamentation. It is perfectly correct to emphasize that improvisation requires a stable structuring schema, but that does not show that these schemata ensure "regression" in music in consumer culture.

Adorno formulated his views on jazz and popular music between, roughly, 1933 and 1941. It was the heyday of swing, when the most popular bands relied on stock arrangements and downplayed genuine improvisation, and that fact is sometimes used to explain his bias.[60] Most of my examples are drawn from postswing jazz and emphasize the improvisational freedom that was downplayed by the commercial success of the big bands. But Armstrong's success predates Adorno's writings on jazz, and other relevant examples can be drawn from the swing era (e.g., Billie Holiday, Coleman Hawkins's 1939 "Body and Soul" improvisation, etc.). Nonetheless, Adorno's writings suggest that he was not interested in any empirical evidence that might be brought against him. He claims to have a "qualitative insight" into the real essence of Western music, and any counterexamples are really only more subtle cases of oppression by the commercial culture monopoly. He seals his case by claiming that we presently lack the "extraordinary subtlety" required to verify or refute his position empirically.[61] (Yet Adorno thinks the essence of jazz, its oppressive standardization, can be derived from "acquaintance with the text of a single hit song."[62]) Presumably, anyone who gives in to the barbarism of popular music lacks the requisite qualitative insight to discern the true ideological effect of such vulgar trash.

To avoid gross question-begging in claiming to have found the "static" essence of popular music, Adorno can only retreat to the idea that anything of value in popular music and jazz has been "independently produced, developed and surpassed by serious music since Brahms." For Adorno, when jazz avoids popular song forms, diatonic scales, and a monotonous beat, its "innovations" are merely a recycling of earlier innovations that are now safe, unchallenging conventions.[63] In this way, all popular music is "predigested" and so will not challenge its audience.

But not just popular music is faulted. Adorno is no less severe in disparaging the audience that embraced Stravinsky over Schoenberg. Like popular music, Stravinsky's neoclassicism reinforces rather than negates the conditions that oppress consciousness. Schoenberg's school is the definitive negation of the tonal tradition now that composers have exhausted its possibilities. Among other factors, Schoenberg's compositions are praised for their obscurity; they are not readily grasped in the sounds of a performance. Rock music is indeed regressive in comparison; as argued earlier, how it sounds has a great deal to do with its power. And where twelve-tone technique leaves little room for expression, rock is dedicated to expression.

In constructing his critique, Adorno introduces several further operative assumptions. Above all, he treats all music as belonging to a single history: "In the process of pursuing its own inner logic, music is transformed more and more from something significant into something obscure — even to itself."[64] He seems to think that only one "logic" governs music at a given time: Stravinsky and popular music are alike in failing to advance it. Adorno's Eurocentrism surely plays a role here. He never observes that since knowledge of *Western* music theory and social history is necessary to appreciate Schoenberg's music, its significance is relative to *that* musical tradition and its compositional techniques. If ethnomusicology teaches us anything, it is that some music has a different "logic."

Finally, Adorno's contrast between popular and serious music presupposes that all music is to be interpreted in terms of autonomous *composition*. His typology of listening contends that only a few professional musicians grasp all of the "formal components" of a piece and its architectonic interrelations; only they achieve a fully adequate appreciation of music.[65] Equating music with the masters since Bach, Schoenberg is praised for having "resisted *all* conventions within the sphere of music."[66] However, neither Schoenberg nor Adorno reject them all. Both buy into the central convention that the musical work, as a work, is a unique composition. Operating with the fine-art ideal of autonomy, all music is regarded as an allographic art. We come to believe that structure alone "can assert itself against the ubiquity of commercialism."[67] But such assumptions are no more appropriate for jazz and rock than is Aristotle's *Poetics* for the films of Buster Keaton. If Adorno is concerned that the mass audience vulgarizes great music with a fetishization of its parts at the expense of the larger whole, his own fetishism lies in focusing on structure at the expense of other musical values.

Culturally Emergent Meanings

Art has no real essence because art has a history.
— T. J. Diffey[68]

It is often observed that the most "American" features of American popular music derive from African and European oral traditions. So why construct a typology of listening that privileges knowledge of a more formal European tradition? How have we rejected the tyranny of universal norms if we judge Duke Ellington, much less Public Enemy, according to the conventions of Bach and Schoenberg?

One of Adorno's most important themes is the need to historicize aesthetic norms. Although norms are objective in their day, they change.[69] And while he would never put it in such direct terms, his overarching philosophy regards aesthetic properties and values as culturally emergent.[70] Although known through publicly accessible objects like performances and scores, musical properties and values are not brute givens, apparent to everyone. Many appear only to those who understand a work's social and historical milieu. Under Adorno's typology of listeners, only a minority recognize the architectonic structure of a Bach fugue, much less grasp Schoenberg. But by the same token, jazz only presents the dregs of the past — constructed of familiar structural elements and presented in an arbitrary sequence with no principle of integration — to those who can only listen in terms of European music theory and history.

Despite the fame and familiarity of Beethoven's symphonies, few people know enough to recognize their formal merits. As Adorno complains, most listeners today hear the Fifth as a set of quotations from the Fifth. Most hear it as they hear popular music, unaware that the themes and melodies are only the bare material for the development and complex integration that constitutes its true value.[71] However, the complex formal achievements of such compositions are largely irrelevant to the appreciation of jazz or rock. That mode of listening is a specialized skill, seldom demanded in modern life. Indeed, for a great deal of recent serious music, *listening* habits are all but irrelevant. Structural relationships are largely conceptual; the human ear cannot identify them.

When Allan Bloom relates his delight at introducing his undergraduate students to Mozart, their enthralled response is ahistorical and uninformed. For all they care, it could have been written five years ago, after and as a progression beyond Schoenberg. I readily concede to Adorno that few of us "adequately" grasp this musical heritage, subsuming both Beethoven and Schoenberg under inappropriate listening habits. In the late twentieth century it may be more difficult for someone to hear Beethoven with appropriate listening habits than for someone raised in Austria (much less Walla Walla) to do so with Javanese gamelan music. One can at least go to Java for immersion in that culture. Not so for Beethoven's Vienna. Historically authentic performances of Beethoven rely on conjecture and speculation about early nineteenth-century music practices. "Authentic" performances are educated guesses.

So it cuts both ways when we historicize aesthetic norms. Because *informed* judgment is a precondition of worthwhile interpretation and evaluation, popular music does not benefit from an ahistorical, decontextualized approach. Those traveling from "high" to "low" will find obstacles to perceiving the music's emergent qualities. And because the mass audience is less monolithic than Adorno supposes, such qualities often vanish in crossovers between subcultures within popular culture. (Or are we to suppose that there are no such qualities for popular art simply because their codes are less obscure?) Tricia Rose emphasizes that for rap the specifics of place — right down to particular street corners — and the identity of one's posse are both essential backgrounds to meanings. As such, a white teen on a Nebraska farm watching "Yo! MTV Raps" cannot give an adequate listening to the coded social messages of videos by N.W.A. and Ice Cube.[72] But of course that is a risk one takes in making music for mass reproduction. Every audience member "reads" within a complex social and historical context. *Intelligent* listening occurs when one makes appropriate intertextual links and responds in terms of both musical and social contexts.[73]

If meanings are obscured as music moves from its place of origin, time plays the same trick on recorded popular music. In an informal listening experiment repeated with two groups of forty students, I was not surprised to find that rock and roll of the 1950s is nearly as foreign to their taste and understanding as is most classical and jazz. For all the predigestion and repetition that Adorno scorns in popular music, any stylistic element that is not employed in popular music of the last five or so years caused consternation for many students. Most of them found Buddy Holly's original recording of "Not Fade Away" (1957) all but unlistenable because of its dated background vocals ("bop, bop!"), but most of them liked the Rolling Stones' version and were surprised to learn that it was more than twenty-five years old.

To this extent, Adorno is certainly correct: popular music is customized with sounds and arrangements designed to make it sound "new," and many of these trivial embellishments quickly sound dated. Later generations of listeners recognize trite formulas of the past as just that. If the background vocals bleed the sensuality and drive out of Holly's "Not Fade Away," it may be because those vocals were overdubbed later and were never an intrinsic element of Holly's arrangement. They *sound* like period embellishments. But some "customizations" endure.

The guitar and vocal are timeless; Holly did not "hiccup" his vocal as a mere gimmick, pseudo-individualization. (When Bobby Vee recorded "Buddy's Song" in tribute, Vee's imitation of Holly's vocal style *was* a gimmick.) Holly's dips and swoops embroider the beat and thus bind melody and rhythm together, dissolving the traditional division between vocal and rhythm section. (Listen to the opening of "Rave On.") Exploiting the peculiarities of his own voice, he shades the simple lyrics with suggestion and subtle emphases.

Observe how chronology is implicit in what I've just said. If the Rolling Stones' "Not Fade Away" predated Holly's, or if Vee had been Holly's model rather than the other way around, different judgments would emerge. Stylistic properties are interpreted in light of a chronology, and in Holly's case they take a special weight because his music is a pivotal causal fork, branching off to the Beatles, the Rolling Stones, and Bob Dylan; Phil Ochs and Fleetwood Mac would subsequently cover him, and years later, David Bowie's "Ashes to Ashes" (1980) confirmed that a young David Jones was listening closely. Ignorant of chronology, what my students thought about Buddy Holly does not count for much. Their evaluations are often as rash as Adorno's.

The next complication is that while the past is fixed, its *history* is not. History is the story we tell about that past and an interpretation we place on it. However grounded in facts, chronologies invite revision. What seemed to be highly relevant about popular culture in 1940, or even 1960, seems less central today. Early histories of rock took little notice of the Velvet Underground; looking back from the early 1990s, their records now stand as a major achievement. In Carl Belz's *The Story of Rock,* Sonny and Cher get slightly more space than Creedence Clearwater Revival. Each generation rewrites rock's history, emphasizing and reevaluating different features of the past in light of the present. Each fan similarly constructs a separate narrative.

If Adorno's history—the "masters since Bach"—emphasizes economic and social factors, it also prioritizes composers, the scores they left us, and the theories they developed. Music is only performed to reveal "all the characteristics and interrelations which have been recognized through intensive study of the score."[74] He selectively ignores interesting facts about the past: Bach, Beethoven, and Mozart were admired in their day as superlative improvisers. Adorno ignores improvisational skills when he appraises Schoenberg. This omission fits neatly with the way the "technology" of classical music provides musical scores: music is reduced to deliberative compositional activity, and the paradigm of musical creativity is the composition of the independent musical work.

Yet Adorno also dismisses the goal of historically accurate performances of Bach, contending that neither the performance nor the score is "the work." Modern arrangements by Schoenberg and Webern are superior to historically informed performances on period instruments, because only "the most advanced composition . . . corresponds to the stage of [Bach's] truth," revealing the otherwise "hidden" work to modern audiences.[75] Music's truth remains hidden in most musical performances, however accurate, because the psychologically "regressive" mass audience has not learned to grasp it. He even claims that their inadequacy can be measured objectively by analyzing the *score* of a Beethoven symphony; those who know only broadcast and recorded music can be evaluated by playing it for them and noting their failure to identify the formal relationships established by analyzing the score.[76]

Adorno elsewhere impugns scores for standing between music and audience. Recorded music has the potential to be a "true language," no longer mediated by another system of signs (contemporary notation). He saw the potential of recording for reversing the pernicious effects of notation, but he did not see that popular music was progressive in this respect.[77] A few years before his death, Adorno granted that radio is less the problem than is a lack of accompanying critique, as if the mass audience would become aware of music's hidden core by being *told* what to listen for.[78] But even if we granted that much, surely his position implies that those who are not at home with American popular music are hardly in a position to discover its culturally emergent properties and to pass judgment on its value as music. Let us glance at jazz one last time.

If anything, the relationship of Parker's "Chasin' the Bird" and "Constellation" to "I Got Rhythm" illustrates that most jazz musicians conceive of their music in terms of individual performances, inviting individualized development of musical motives, rather than being fixed compositions. When successful, each jazz performance, recorded or live, is an independent musical work. As Sonny Rollins observes, "Jazz is the only music that happens while you're hearing it. . . . We don't want to make jazz too written . . . because that is what can kill it."[79] Neither written scores nor improvisation count for much in rock, so the relevant emergent qualities are different yet again.

The ideal jazz performance is a distinct, original, individual exploration of some musical idea, whether a popular song or simple riff. Of course, for jazz even the loosest jam session or improvisation requires an organizing schema, but the performance is tailored to the players' individualities and their resulting interaction. It is seldom as improvisational as Davis's *Kind of Blue,* but some degree of freedom in individual performances is essential.[80] With rock music the organizing schema is seldom approached along these lines, yet there is far more freedom for personalization of the material than, for instance, in a performance of Schoenberg's song-cycle *Das Buch der hängenden Gärten* (1909). Much of rock's personalization comes in rhythmic accents, timbre, texture, and vocal inflections.

Rock is not a complete stranger to improvisation; we have the Allman Brothers' thirty-four-minute collective improvisation on the theme to Donovan's "There Is a Mountain," on *Eat a Peach* (1972). But it is not the norm for rock. Solos are often brief and largely planned out in advance. The Rolling Stones' approach to recording "Not Fade Away" (1964) is more typical, as Buddy Holly's song is tailored to the particular strengths of the ensemble. Rather than regarding rock as an opportunity for improvisation or a faithful manifestation of an independent musical work, rock interpretation stakes out a middle ground which fuses a song and the available performance means (including engineering) into a distinctive product of mass reproduction. This is why "cover" versions are always a risk in rock. Inviting comparison with the "original" version, cover versions must either play on audience ignorance (as in radio's early days), indicate homage to an influence, or recast the song altogether. Jimi Hendrix's "All Along the Watchtower" is notable for making us forget its source in a Dylan recording (both 1967). U2's stabs at "Watchtower" and "Helter Skelter" on *Rattle and Hum* are homages that otherwise tell us little; the Beatles' "Words of Love" (1964) conveys their love of Buddy Holly, but it is hardly definitive.

While there are exceptions, jazz and rock usually involve a balance between the autonomy and cooperative production of its performers and technical personnel. Bound to the idea that a performance is a mere token of some independent musical work that is really the locus of value, Adorno cannot see that jazz and rock both challenge the traditional division between the musical work and its performance.[81] His analysis makes no room for the idea that Miles Davis, Gil Evans, and Teo Macero collaborated in the studio, or that the appeal of R.E.M.'s *Murmur* (1988) is a function of both R.E.M. and producer Mitch Easter. Beginning with the New Orleans tradition that nurtured Louis Armstrong, jazz has challenged musical convention with its "defiance of Western music's traditional distinction between composition and performance, in fact, its persistent disdain for any musical division of labor, the jazz musician being both creator and interpreter, soloist and accompanist, artist and entertainer."[82] Rock has gone a step further, as many musicians display a disdain for the traditional distinctions between engineer, producer, and distributor.

In considering the emergent qualities of American popular music, one can hardly overstate the importance of race.[83] However much African musical traditions were filtered through European music, the legacy of slavery carries complex social implications for both jazz and rock. Looking at the importance of repetition in all African musics, we see that it is not reducible to a mere repressive mechanism of industrial standardization. So its presence in most black American popular music might constitute "collective resistance to that system," not a capitulation.[84] Given that Aretha Franklin's version of "Respect" (1967) roared to the top of the charts at the height of the civil rights movement, it would be folly to listen to it in light of the same categories that should be used to evaluate twelve-tone technique. As a blending of urban black gospel, southern soul, and Top 40 pop, it displays no interest in providing a definitive negation of two centuries of tonal composition. But as a genuine collaboration between black and white musicians, any truth content stems from its negation of the tensions that were to explode with the coming urban riots.

While Louis Armstrong and Charlie Parker and Miles Davis wrote music during the lives of both Adorno and Schoenberg, black America and the Jewish middle class of the Weimar Republic place them within distinct musical communities. The gulf is sadly demonstrated by Charlie Parker's desire to escape the confines of his background by studying *composition* with Edgar Varèse. Western tonality is *one* starting point among several for jazz and rock. Popular music's similar emphasis on tonality does not imply any corresponding emphasis on autonomous compositions, as such.

Instead, the jazz tradition emphasizes musical performance as precisely that, performance. In his later years, Ellington insisted that jazz cannot even be defined. He stopped using the term because too many styles were contained under a single heading.[85] Nonetheless, when pressed to explain jazz, Ellington historicized it: "the story of jazz is a long list of great names," a list "of highly influential musicians, each with popular imitators."[86] (He predominantly named instrumentalists, not composers.) Critics and musicologists tend to agree. John Norris and others have argued that jazz is so intimately connected to the process of mentoring by and imitation of specific working musicians, the recent shift to academic schooling and music training has effectively killed jazz. With the dissolution of the old "apprenticeship system," most of what passes for jazz today "sounds like jazz but really isn't it."[87] Much of what passes for jazz today is no more than a museum piece.

If rock seldom approaches the improvisational heights of jazz or the compositional perfection of the classical tradition, it does not follow that it is trivial music. In assigning greater priority to recording than live performance, rock gains a tremendous flexibility. As I argued in chapter 2, structure is largely a coat hanger for other values.

It may also be useful to turn to poststructuralist thought, which often emphasizes the iterability and polysemy of signifiers. Recorded music is particularly fertile in these respects. Iterability is a signifier's capacity for repetition in new contexts. (Derrida emphasizes this feature in order to show that complex texts escape authorial intention.) Thus a generation of kids born in the 1970s thinks of "Ob-La-Di, Ob-La-Da" as the theme of the television program *Life Goes On*. They are more likely to relate it to Down's syndrome than to Charles Manson.

When Wagner's "Ride of the Valkyries" is used in a Warner Bros. cartoon or *Apocalypse Now*, it conveys meanings that Wagner never intended to pack into that sound structure. Wagner's intentions are not the only ones it will bear. In the terminology of John Fiske, the success of popular art may have less to do with the monopoly of the culture industry and more to do with its high degree of "semiotic richness and polysemy." In short, the products of mass consumption "cannot have a single, defined meaning, but they are a resource bank of potential meanings."[88] If iterability facilitates semiotic richness, polysemy is the capacity to support reinterpretation across cultural relocations.

Fiske illustrates polysemy with a look at American television shows. When seen by different audiences, the same program invites radically different interpretations.[89] Because mechanical repetition encourages almost limitless recontextualization, bringing it to a variety of audiences, recorded popular music also invites constant reinterpretation. Wagner's music plays different roles in a cartoon spoofing opera than against the background of Vietnam. The Hendrix performance of "The Star-Spangled Banner" means one thing in the film *Woodstock*, another on U2's *Rattle and Hum*. Here, the familiarity of the musical sources enriches meaning. Yet another dimension of meaning arises when familiar materials are combined. A montage is not just the sum of its parts, as anyone can tell from Grandmaster Flash's appropriations of

Blondie, Chic, Queen, and the Sugar Hill Gang on "The Adventures of Grandmaster Flash on the Wheels of Steel" (1981). Popular music also extracts new meanings by recycling established musical conventions (not just direct quotation). So when popular music draws on "serious music" — when heavy-metal guitarists consciously appropriate classical forms and devices like so many car thieves stripping a sports car — their borrowings generate meanings that cannot be reduced to past uses.[90]

These observations remind us that all music is historically grounded in the practices of musical communities. Its assessment must be grounded in a community of musicians and listeners, not in a transcendental "essence." Rock would seem to be heard most adequately by those who have a sense of the story that stretches from Elvis Presley and Chuck Berry to Madonna and Nirvana. If Presley's original fans are unlikely to see much merit in Nirvana, and vice versa, we can look back to Elvis and see the germinal seeds of both Madonna and Nirvana in the tensions of his career. Further layers of meanings arise for those who push back to the traditions that fed early rock and roll.

For all of these reasons, we should be very selective in adopting Adorno's *Kulturkritik* as it applies to popular music. What is identified as a static essence is a caricature, so there is little reason to deny that popular music can challenge a broad range of social conventions.[91] Its commodity character does not exhaust its appeal. Reviving the primacy of music as something *heard,* both jazz and rock reject the tyranny of the composer's intentions and the autonomous musical composition as the focus of listening. Emphasizing individuality and individual performance, jazz negates conventions developed by the tradition of Bach to Schoenberg. Offering recordings as primary texts, rock emphasizes a multileveled collaboration and negates the same conventions. At the same time, Adorno's insistence that nonmusical factors must be considered in interpreting and evaluating musical works reminds us that music's core properties are always culturally emergent. Rather than explain its appeal, the "culture industry" may generate barriers to hearing rock and jazz, just as Adorno thinks it has for serious music.

7

Romanticizing Rock Music

If now we reflect that music at its greatest intensity must seek to attain also to its highest symbolization, we must deem it possible that it also knows how to find the symbolic expression for its unique Dionysian wisdom.
—Friedrich Nietzsche[1]

He's the epitome of the Romantic Hero, and if you're a middle-class girl and you've read your Byron, that's Keith Richards . . . he's really an injured, tortured, damned youth—which is really such fun, isn't it?—Marianne Faithfull[2]

People have come to buy the clichés in rock music. You know, like it's somehow more acceptable to be addicted to heroin than to, say, hang out with jet-setters.
—Bruce Springsteen[3]

O It is fashionable to praise rock as a manifestation of the aesthetics of Romanticism, the aesthetic movement that elevates the artist's originality, emotion, spontaneity, and invention as the measure of aesthetic success. Rock musicians are often held to Josiah Royce's creed of the Romantic artist: "Trust your genius; follow your noble heart; change your doctrine whenever your heart changes, and change your heart often."[4]

According to one biographer, Guns N' Roses feature "the raging sound of Dionysus resurfacing."[5] We are invited to assign them the same respect as poets Wordsworth and Byron and composers Chopin and Liszt. In Camille Paglia's controversial book, *Sexual Personae,* she contends that in spite of its commercialism, American radio proves that we "still live in the age of Romanticism." The Rolling Stones "are heirs of stormy Coleridge."[6] Their accomplishment is of the same type as these nineteenth-century precursors. On this account, the major obstacle to seeing rock's value is the common confusion of commercial product ("pop" music) with rock music.

Another manifestation of the aesthetics of Romanticism is the idea that if rock music is not fine art, it is modern urban folk music.[7] As one rock critic put it, "it is just because they didn't worry about art that many of the people who ground out the rock-and-roll of the fifties — not only the performers, but all the background people — were engaged (unconsciously, of course) in making still another kind of art, folk art."[8] As above, a distinction is to be made between pop, an unauthentic exploitation of the masses, and this modern folk art. A third variation, to be considered at length in this chapter, merges the two strands: rock possesses the virtues of Romantic art while drawing much of its power from its folk music roots. On either formulation, the dogmatic opposition of fine art and entertainment is upheld.

The Dionysian Mode

I liked the [Sex] Pistols as well. . . . It's dishonest to say, "Oh, yes, we were just *wild*"; they weren't just wild. It was *considered* and *calculated*. Very art. The Clash as well. — Elvis Costello[9]

The most uncompromising romanticizing of rock comes from Camille Paglia.[10] The Dionysian rhythms that scandalize Allan Bloom are, for Paglia, one of rock's great attractions. An even greater attraction is the personae of the rock musician, particularly the singer. She calls for a return to rock's past glories, when the music was rebellious, vital, and pulsating with "surging Dionysian rhythms." (Technically, Nietzsche regarded rhythms as Apollonian and melodies as Dionysian.) Like Nietzsche, she thinks the masses are incapable of appreciating greatness when they encounter it. But rock musicians are legitimate artists and should be treated like other artists, supported with government subsidies, private grants, and special college scholarships.

This view deserves analysis because it adopts, without criticism, the prevailing story of rock music. Except for the proposal to support budding rock musicians with subsidies, these are all such common assumptions that most rock fans would probably applaud her endorsement and ignore the distortions, half-truths, and stereotypes. The story is this: "the pioneers of rock were freaks, dreamers and malcontents" who drew on an authentic tradition of "white folk music and African American blues." The 1960s were rock's golden age, when rock musicians drew their inspiration from poetry and Eastern religions. (She doesn't point out that Jim Morrison admired Nietzsche and that groups like the Doors, Steppenwolf, Uriah Heep, Mott the Hoople, and Steely Dan got their names from literary works, but I assume that that's the sort of thing she has in mind.) Above all, rock musicians were outlaws, "storming from city to city on their lusty, groupie-dogged trail." Because they are sensitive artists, we are to brush over the fact that this means the sexual exploitation of women, many of them grossly underage. But hey: sex and drugs and rock 'n' roll!

But rock soon fell victim to capitalism. Market forces corrupted it; co-optation eviscerated it. Paglia offers three pieces of evidence. First, the authentic source is lost. Neither fans nor musicians have direct knowledge of folk music and blues, "the oral repository of centuries of love, hate, suffering and redemption." Second, live performance has atrophied, leaving no room for spontaneous musical expression or artist-audience interaction. Once it was a performing art, with the focus on the performance. Now it's a mere show — fully rehearsed and with no room for artistic spontaneity — and a backdrop for partying. Third, greedy and manipulative managers exploit innocent young artists, turning them from self-expression to pandering to crass commercial interests, "milking" them for profit in exchange for "wealth, fame and easy sex." Is it a coincidence that Paglia is paraphrasing Bob Geldof's remark that people join rock bands for "three very simple rock and roll reasons: to get laid, to get fame, and to get rich"?[11]

The charge that rock is corrupted by money is frequently made in the rock community itself, with some justification. Elvis Presley, the Beatles, and the Rolling Stones were all models of the shotgun wedding between musician and manager; it seems fair to say that young artists, facing the maze of the business side of the music industry, acquiesce in their own exploitation in exchange for a manager's expertise. Thus Colonel Parker handled Elvis Presley, the Beatles had Brian Epstein, and the early Rolling Stones had Andrew Oldham. Management often exploits or outright robs the musician, as in such notorious cases as John Fogerty, the Grateful Dead (drummer Mickey Hart's own father lifted huge sums of money from the group), and Bruce Springsteen (the long gap between *Born to Run* and *Darkness on the Edge of Town* was due to litigation with his manager). Sometimes the abuse is less overt: Colonel Parker padded his own pocket by making sure that Elvis covered material published by Hill & Range, a publishing company in which Parker had a substantial interest. The list of complaints goes on and on.[12]

Yet when management succeeds, it is to the mutual advantage of musician and manager. Reflecting on Colonel Parker, Nick Tosches compares the success of early rock and roll to the franchising of fast food:

> Rock 'n' roll flourished because it sold. The more it sold, the more it flourished. The heroes, unsung and sung alike, of rock 'n' roll all had one thing in common: they liked Cadillacs. If rock 'n' roll had not been sellable, they would not have been making it, or trying to make it.[13]

But to sell in any volume, a musician needs corporate backing. Parker negotiated Presley's departure from Sun, a regional company unable to break him into the mass market, to RCA Victor, a corporate giant that could push the nineteen-year-old "country" singer in all popular markets. The Beatles would never have met producer George Martin without Epstein's exhaustive pavement-pounding on their behalf; Epstein also put them into matching suits and sanitized their tough image. We can only speculate about Jimi Hendrix's career had he not been transplanted from New York to London in 1966 by manager Chas Chandler, who bankrolled and helped form the Jimi Hendrix Experience, then teamed him with engineer Eddie Kramer.

The Dionysian image identified with the early Rolling Stones was almost entirely the invention of Oldham, a former publicity man for the Beatles who recognized the value of setting them up as threatening alternatives to the Beatles. If anything, the Beatles were the true delinquents. The Stones were middle-class and better educated.

Among other things, Oldham got *Melody Maker* to run the headline "Would You Let Your Daughter Go with a Stone?" As Keith Richards has remarked about the path to success, "In the early 60s nobody took the music as serious. It was the image that counted . . . [The group was] very hip to image and how to manipulate the press. You know, a lot of PR went into it, consciously."[14] Oldham's liner notes for such albums as *The Rolling Stones No. 2* (1965) aped the prose of *A Clockwork Orange,* but a passage advising teens to rob to get the money for the album was deleted on the corresponding American release, *The Rolling Stones, Now!* London Records seems to have been less hip to the market value of the "droog" image than Decca. Oldham went so far as to remove pianist Ian Stewart from the group simply because he did not look the part, the very sort of marketing decision that, publicized, denied credibility to other groups.

The Sex Pistols were not merely marketed. Much like the prefabricated Monkees a decade earlier, they were *created* by management who saw an image that could be sold to audiences.[15] (Were the Pistols calling attention to this similarity when they covered the Monkees' hit "I'm Not Your Stepping Stone"?) Malcolm McLaren, having failed in his recent attempts to market the New York Dolls as Marxist revolutionaries, was running a London clothing boutique undergoing an image change. It had recently been renamed "Sex." His motive in forming the Pistols may have been little more than to drum up more business for his shop. Unlike Brian Epstein and Andrew Oldham, who took existing bands and refined their image, McLaren recruited actual delinquents to portray delinquents, a move that may have guaranteed their collapse the following year. The group's demise was sealed when they added a truly Dionysian element, the musically incompetent Sid Vicious. Born John Ritchie, Vicious did not even play on their studio recordings, and from the evidence of the available live recordings he spent more time taunting the audience and living up to his image than playing bass.

Unlike Oldham's pretense that Fleet Street was responsible for the Rolling Stones' reputation, McLaren flaunted the marketing process as itself part of their "swindle" of the corporations that had taken control of rock and roll. His idea seems to have been that the act of calling attention to the process made it less dishonest. But the fact that the Pistols were at the low-budget end of rock music, sleeping on other people's floors instead of trashing expensive hotel rooms, hardly makes them more genuine. But there were plenty of disaffected kids who responded to what they represented, just as there had been plenty who, ten years before, aligned with the Stones over the Beatles because of their PR. The question for Paglia, obviously, is whether she is suckered by any of these controlled and manufactured images, too. In a system of music making and distribution that has been commercial since its inception, the line between authentic and unauthentic music is hardly useful.

Furthermore, as a *marketing strategy* the Dionysian image succeeds only to the extent that there are successful and appealing groups against whom the product can be positioned as an alternative. McLaren positioned the Sex Pistols against the decadence and betrayal of older, wealthy rock stars: yesterday's rebels, whose success was taken as evidence that their music was too artsy or commercial. In short, the Sex Pistols were marketed as the *new* Dionysian alternative. (This anticommercial pose may be punk's truest legacy; a decade later, virtually any group that employed a less accessible style was called an "alternative" band, a trend that continues.) In *England's Dreaming,* Jon Savage relates that McLaren had a fit when Johnny Rotten cooperated with the media in shaping his own image. During an interview for Capital Radio,

Johnny Rotten/John Lydon revealed his admiration for Captain Beef-heart and Neil Young. McLaren's objection lay not with the goal of a high media profile but with Rotten's new persona of a "man of taste." It wasn't sufficiently barbaric.[16]

Are we to regard the Sex Pistols as exploited, or as sellouts? Their own early fans — a small group who had followed them from show to show for months — accused them of the latter when they signed with record giant EMI. Their self-destructive sabotage of their own career was later hailed by critic John Rockwell as proof of their authenticity: "The break-up almost had to be . . . if they had 'succeeded,' they would have had to betray everything they stood for."[17] Yet toward the end of their final concert (Winterland, San Francisco, January 14, 1978), Johnny Rotten taunted the crowd with "Ever get the feeling you've been cheated?" He may have meant by the culture at large, or perhaps by the inflated reputation of punk, which had drawn five thousand curious Americans to see them.

Selling Out

I know who Bowie's sold out to; I don't understand what he's sold out from. Where is this authentic rock tradition, pose-less and glamour-free?
— Simon Frith, 1973[18]

The distance between what a rock musician or band "stands for" and what they "are" generates a tension that consistently confuses our at-tempts to grasp rock as a form of musical expression. Given the premise that the true artist must genuinely *mean* whatever is said, and that anything else is commercial manipulation, the charge of sellout has been the most damning one that can be brought against a rock musi-cian. As Rockwell has it, the Sex Pistols redeemed themselves only by destroying themselves; because their message was nihilistic, they were true artists only when they became genuinely nihilistic. By this line of reasoning, and in line with the Romanticism of the nineteenth century, their ultimate vindication was Sid Vicious's stabbing of his girlfriend in late 1978, followed by his own death by heroin overdose about four months later. Equally satisfying, from this point of view, was the suicide of Joy Division's singer Ian Curtis in 1980. With the suicide of Kurt Cobain, a true believer, this no longer seems such a satisfying outcome.

Again and again, rock critics and fans congratulate themselves for escaping commercial manipulation through the unexpected success of bands on minor labels or whose style is not widely popular. There are even glossy commercial magazines for "alternative" bands: *Options, Reflex,* and *A.P.* (Alternative Press) in the United States. These magazines survive, of course, on advertising revenue from the music conglomerates.

Anyone in rock who becomes widely popular is immediately prone to backlash, as in this letter to *Rolling Stone* about the album *Out of Time* (1991): "R.E.M. sold out after *Document.* The older they grow, the more they sound like everybody else."[19] Literally, of course, they sound like nobody else, and it is difficult to imagine a group with less critical and commercial standing getting the song "Losing My Religion" onto the radio in 1991. In the very same issue of the magazine, Nirvana's Kurt Cobain remarked that "I don't blame the average seventeen-year-old of calling me a sellout." Cobain is thinking of the reaction of their core audience to their being on the magazine's cover![20] Cobain, long past seventeen, still thought of rock as speaking for adolescents who are most in sway to Romanticism. At the same time, their record producer announced that he despised the audience for being "brainwashed" consumers.

More experienced musicians have a more complicated message about the process. Riding the crest of England's "new wave" to success as a solo artist and producer in the late seventies after moderate success in the pub rock outfit Brinsley Schwarz, Nick Lowe constructed his debut album around a series of jokes about the process of the sellout. The cover of *Jesus of Cool* (1978) features six portraits of Lowe, each suggesting a distinct musical affiliation, from heavy metal to psychedelic hippie. The point, it seems, is that any photograph is a fabrication. The inner sleeve sports a large graph on which Lowe plots the "estimated work hours" spent on each recording he's been involved with since 1969; the steady increase of hours devoted to recording is contrasted with a plunging line that represents "negative sales potential allied to public avoidance factor." In case we still don't get the joke, Lowe opens the album with "Music for Money" and soon follows it with "Shake and Pop," two songs celebrating commercial sellout. Lowe's American label, Columbia, rejected the original title. Repackaging his jokes for the American audience, *Pure Pop for Now People* replaced the inner sleeve with a "teen idol" motif, rerecorded "Shake and Pop" as "They Called It Rock," and replaced one of the cover portraits with one of Lowe wearing an American flag necktie. Unfortunately, neither album included Lowe's delightful love song to his record company (Stiff), "I Love My Label" (1977).

On the contemporary scene many hardcore gangsta rappers, recognizing the extent to which their success with white teens depends on an "outlaw" and outsider stance, consciously fan the flames of racial tension. At the same time, their own social mores are often conservative and reactionary (e.g., antidrug, homophobic, and brutally sexist if not downright misogynist). The armed insurrection they demand is a call for social justice rather than anything Dionysian.[21] Furthermore, the hip-hop scene is hardly of one mind about the priorities of commerce and authenticity. While Ice-T boasts "I made personal attempts not to go pop . . . and get on the radio," Dr. Dre counters that "it's about who makes the best record . . . it ain't even about that, it's about who sells the most records."[22]

Richard Shusterman looks at the tensions within hip-hop and sees a postmodern rather than a Romantic aesthetic, arguing that the techniques of rap oppose Romanticism's emphasis on originality and uniqueness. He also calls attention to rap's frequent warnings against the "dominant technological-commercial complex." Rappers face the same paradox that tormented Kurt Cobain:

> self-declared "underground" rappers at once denigrate commercialism as an *artistic* and political sellout, but nonetheless glorify their own commercial success, often regarding it as indicative of their artistic power.[23]

Shusterman interprets their boasts of success as evidence of a tradition that traces back to Frederick Douglass and the idea that the legacy of slavery is best overcome through the acquisition of property. In a more detailed treatment of rap, Tricia Rose disparages the idea that it is a postmodern form; rap's contradictions reflect the particular condition of African American urban life, not a general postmodern condition.[24] Rap music and hip-hop culture reflect long-standing Afrodiasporic aesthetic practices, coupled with new technologies and responding to the impact of changes in the urban landscape in the 1970s and 1980s.

Yet the contradictions noted by Shusterman and Rose can also be read as a continuation of Romanticism's opposition of commerce and art. Perhaps no reconciliation is possible as long as nineteenth-century or Afrodiasporic assumptions are applied to twentieth-century commercial product. The fact that rappers call attention to noncommercial standards while also flaunting their commercial appeal may be no more than a frank admission of the rules of the game. As Rose emphasizes, there would be no rap music without advanced electronic technology, and from the outset Bronx rappers were motivated by profit, however limited.

The Who called attention to the same tensions with *The Who Sell Out* (1967), simultaneously ridiculing and flaunting the commercial sellout inherent in mass music. They created a fake radio program, sandwiching their songs between genuine and phony advertising, including the delightful "Odorono." No appeal to Frederick Douglass is needed to account for their self-critical amusement.

Pete Townshend, their principal songwriter, later outraged many Who fans by allowing some of their biggest hits to be adapted as jingles for television commercials and adopting Budweiser as corporate sponsor for part of their 1989 tour. His response to a journalist's criticism of it was blunt:

> The public are already in the vise-like grip of advertising agencies' reductive demographic practices, reducing my career down to eight songs as AOR radio reproduces it. If somebody offers me the right price and I think it's worth doing, I'll sell the song. . . . What's the difference? There's further damage to be done?[25]

Rejecting any role other than songwriter, Townshend contends that the very vehicle that criticizes his practice is impossible without commercial advertising. In short, he rejects the very category of "sellout" as a possibility for rock musicians, which may be interpreted as revealing greater sophistication (and cynicism?) than Neil Young's 1988 slam at the practice of corporate sponsors, "This Note's for You." Not surprisingly, MTV found a lame excuse not to air Young's video for the track.[26]

My primary point in reviewing some facts about various groups and the commercial process is to establish that rock musicians themselves use Dionysian authenticity as a standard for artistic success. But they also use it as a selling point, and many do so consciously. Once Romantic stereotypes are part of their marketing strategies, the line between the real and artificial is hopelessly muddled. Yet the distinction between more and less authentic rock has attained the status of commonsense truth for rock fans and musicians. They are imprisoned and perplexed by the distinction. But rock musicians do not make music in a context that provides them with many noncommercial sources of art (except, perhaps, the pure amateurism of a group like the Shaggs), and they have very few noncommercial avenues for reaching an audience.[27] So the identification of a more authentic mode of expression with the noncommercial makes even less sense today than it did in the nineteenth century.

Groups form in emulation of the rock musicians they hear on records and see on videos, then reach a level of local success where further

success demands managers (or, sometimes, self-management) and serious financial investment in order to make their music known to a
broader audience, and then they can attain reliable distribution of their
recordings as the primary showcase for their music. If they do not know
so already, they soon learn that recording is the major avenue of exposure for their music, and it becomes the sphere of music making itself.
The Doors, who received the appellation "Dionysian" more consistently than any other group, were unanimous in regarding the production expertise and commercial smarts that went into their first album as
a central factor in reaching an audience. Jim Morrison compared their
albums to books and movies. Ray Manzarek analyzes their first album
in terms that are quite at odds with Romanticism.

> It's four incredibly hungry young men striving and dying to make
> it, desperately wanting to get a record, a good record, out to the
> American public and wanting the public to like the record. I feel
> any artist wants the public to like his act, or his record: I think that
> any artist creates from a driving inner need, but there's an outer
> need that's important too, and that's acceptance by some people,
> somewhere, somehow.[28]

Romantic poets and musicians are supposed to have a driving inner
need, and it helps if they're hungry and young, but surely they are not
supposed to be driven by a desire to be *accepted* or *liked*. However,
given the cost of making and distributing records, one's ability to continue to make records, as opposed to simply playing live shows as a
source of revenue, depends primarily on publishing and recording royalties and thus on successful record sales. If nobody likes your first
record, there may not be a second.[29]

Once a group signs with a record company, even a small label like
Sub Pop or Twin Tone, they join a commercial as well as an artistic
enterprise. In such a system, self-management or independent distribution are poor solutions for any musician who hasn't taken a vow of
poverty.[30] Reflecting on his long career, David Bowie concludes that
corporate financing has kept him from "compromising" the stage productions of his live shows:

> You're gonna get corporate situations everywhere. Soon as you
> sign to a major label you become corporate. Any of us could have
> stuck with an independent label and still sold records — maybe not
> as many. . . . It's certainly not changing my style of songwriting or
> performing.[31]

However powerful as an ideology, it makes little sense to judge rock from the standpoint of noncommercial or anticommercial criteria. Jon Bon Jovi, no stranger to accusations of being a hack who simplifies Springsteen, voices the paradox of the system: "I never understood musicians who say you're a sellout if you're commercially successful. Didn't you write that song because you *wanted* a lot of people to like it? If you want it to be art, well then, hang it on the wall."[32] As Simon Frith asked about Bowie in 1973, what do rock stars have to sell out from? Whether we are dealing with Madonna's latest calculated outrage or the counterculture stance of rappers and thrash bands, music making takes place within a commercial system that undercuts the relevance of Romanticism to rock music.

Under capitalism, the artistic question of "what do I want to say?" is continuously balanced against the commercial problem of "how many people are going to pay money for this?"[33] As one among the popular arts, this pattern is hardly unique to rock. But it may be that, stung by a perception that "it's only rock and roll" (popular music for the masses), there is all the more need to trumpet one's credentials as a musician, that is, as an *artist*. Rock often tries to play it both ways simultaneously. I have no doubt that much of the audience looks to rock for a Dionysian authenticity that they cannot find in other music. Some rock musicians are equally gripped by the conflict between Romanticism and commercial entertainment. I do not deny that rock is often perceived through a lens tinted with Romanticism. But I question the degree to which these ideas enrich our thinking about the music and its meaning.

The Commercial Framework

[A]t its best, rock music is a folk art form when it comes directly from the people who may know how to play one or two songs on their instruments and those one or two songs mean something to the people who wrote and sing them. . . . I'm talking about Cannibal and the Headhunters, little one-shot groups . . . — Frank Zappa[34]

Paglia's remedy for the sad state of recent rock? Given the contradictions and problems inherent in applying Romanticism to commercial product, salvaging Romanticism means divorcing rock from commercial manipulation. Whether the golden age is a myth or not, Paglia insists that rock will be saved from itself by remaking it in the image of Romanticism. Paglia may or may not understand the extent to which rock has taken advantage of romanticist assumptions, but she is cer-

tainly correct that rock must be judged a disgrace by romanticist principles.[35] However, where I conclude that Romanticism is not appropriate
for judging rock, Paglia prefers to retain Romanticism and to remake
rock.

Paglia recommends providing an alternative to the star-making machinery that diverts rock artists from serious music making. Like classical musicians, rock musicians must relocate to colleges and universities.
(Was Bob Dylan ahead of his time when, on his debut, he introduced
a traditional song as having been acquired among the fair fields of
Harvard?) For rock musicians supported by government and private
grants, prestige and artistic freedom will follow, compensating the musicians for the lost wealth, fame, and sex. After all, Paglia notes, both
Keith Richards and John Lennon attended English "art schools." She
neglects to mention that they were barely able to obtain passing grades
and that the schools were as much trade schools as art institutes; perhaps we should instead be satisfied that Mick Jagger went to the London School of Economics and Lou Reed studied with poet Delmore
Schwartz. If rock musicians complement their musical studies with art
history and literature, a liberal arts education will guide their spiritual development and rock will recover as the "authentic voice of our
times."

Charming as this retreat to the ivory tower may be, how would rock
music remain rock music under such a system? If one is going to focus
on the behavior and characteristics of the musicians as the basis for
evaluating the authenticity of the music they produce, one needs more
than a caricature. Where formalism may be accused of having a fetish
for the objects that artists produce, Romanticism makes a cult object of
the artist. Methodologically, we shift from close analysis of the "work
of art" to involvement with the creative "genius" whose work it is. The
proverbial chimps in a room pounding on typewriters for infinity might
churn out grammatical prose; where formalism looks at the prose,
Romanticism looks at the chimps, separating the true artists from the
sellouts who type for the bananas we offer them. While this is itself a
caricature, it reminds us to dig up some facts about rock's development.

Paglia's story simply disintegrates when we go through it one claim
at a time. Operating on the assumption that rock music started with
rock and roll in the 1950s, I think it is fair to say that her knowledge of
rock music is limited, or at least so uncritical about rock's prevailing
image that she focuses on confirming evidence for the "romantic" nature of the rock musicians she admires. Among other things, her chronology is hopelessly muddled.

Let us start with the pioneers of rock as Romantic archetypes. Who would this be? Topping any list of rock's pioneers would be Bill Haley, Elvis Presley, Chuck Berry, Little Richard, Bo Diddley, Carl Perkins, Buddy Holly, Jerry Lee Lewis, Fats Domino, and Ray Charles.[36] While this may be a list of freaks and dreamers, their dreams were mostly about making hit records and a lot of money. They were hardly malcontents, unless being an African American or poor southern white in the 1950s automatically qualified one. If anything, they represent the American underclass of the period, seeking respectability in money and fame. Perhaps Paglia is thinking of the sixties and its political posturing, but at that point we're already far from the folk and blues roots that she identifies as the source of their authenticity and expressive power.

The rebellion of rock's pioneers was of the James Dean variety, largely adolescent. If we are to believe any of the prevailing *sociological* analysis of rock, it tells us this:

> What mattered about rock 'n' roll in the 1950s was its youth; its expression of a community of interest between performer and audience; and its account of a generation bound by age and taste in a gesture of self-celebration, in defiance against the nagging, adult routines of home and work and school. . . . rock 'n' roll stardom soon became a matter of the youth voice and the youth song, so that Elvis Presley became rock 'n' roll's superstar because he so clearly *represented* his listeners and Chuck Berry became the most successful R&B performer to adapt its loose limbed lyrics to the interests of the white, teenaged record-buyer.[37]

It was also rooted in a desire for a sharp wardrobe (blue suede shoes immediately come to mind) and a pink Cadillac. Paglia complains that rock's original rebellion has been reduced to "high school affectation." Yet search as we might through early rock, *social* protest comes mainly from Chuck Berry, and it was *very* high school: "School Days," "Too Much Monkey Business," and "No Particular Place to Go." The Coasters' "Yakety Yak" and Eddie Cochran's "Summertime Blues" likewise gave voice to teens railing against parental authority.[38] There is occasional social commentary, but fairly mild, as in the undercurrent of black pride in Chuck Berry's "Brown-Eyed Handsome Man" or the Coasters' "Shopping for Clothes" and "Framed" (both written by the white production team of Leiber and Stoller).

The complaint is also odd in light of analyses given by Nik Cohn, Carl Belz, and many others. Writing in the late sixties, Cohn reflected the prevalent British enthusiasm for rock and American "pop" *as* re-flections of American adolescent life. He praised rock because it voiced teen concerns; the best popular music, he wrote, "is all teenage prop-erty and it mirrors everything that happens to teenagers in this time, in this American 20th century. It is about clothes and cars and dancing, it's about parents and high school."[39] Carl Belz, defending a view of rock as modern folk music, praised Chuck Berry for "unconsciously" ex-pressing the "ordinary realities of their world: . . . cars, girls, growing up, school, or music."[40] Even more recently, Chuck Berry's worldview was described as "cars, music, dating, school, growing up," illustrating that rock and roll "strove to create a self-contained adolescent world of values, meanings, and connections" from the very start.[41]

For Cohn and Belz, rock's decline started when the Beatles and oth-ers turned to self-expression and musical experimentation for its own sake. In short, rock lost its special identity when the musicians began to speak for themselves instead of speaking for their audiences. Consider the furor within the least adolescent strain of popular music, the "folk" scene of the early 1960s, when fans felt that Dylan was speaking for himself rather than for them. He became the object of scorn. Belz regards the ensuing singer-songwriter boom as the decline of rock and roll. We might recall that thousands of American fans burned their Beatles albums after John Lennon seemed to slight America's Christian values by saying that the Beatles were "bigger than Jesus," again sug-gesting that most rock fans expect rock musicians to represent the audience, not to think for themselves.

For all its claim to antibourgeois politics, punk was significantly concerned with expressing the sentiments of young rock fans. Express-ing the classic punk disdain for older, established rock stars, Brian James of the Damned said

> It must be really difficult, after you've been playing for ten years and you're used to like lush limousines and anything you want at the click of your fingers, to keep your mind back on the streets . . . We're talking for the kids, you know. We're playing to the kids — that's what rock 'n' roll's all about.[42]

Live punk, whether in London or anywhere else, typically generated a sense of community between performer and audience, yet the bond was definitely between "the kids" and *their voice,* musicians who mirrored them as they saw themselves. This sense of community was (and, in many communities today, still is) hostile to the dominant artistic-genius-who-dispenses-art model of Romanticism. At the same time, the punk community quickly generated its own hierarchy. Early in the documentary *The Decline of Western Civilization* (1980), a fan boasts that punk has no "rock stars," then we see the drummer of the Germs wearing a Ramones T-shirt on stage. A few feet away, an audience member celebrates the Sex Pistols with an "Anarchy in the U.K." shirt. Then, like many a rock star, Black Flag's singer boasts of his sexual conquests (as "victims"). The ideal of community is routinely tainted by a combination of hero worship (by fans) and distancing from the audience (by musicians).

The issue here is not whether Cohn and Belz are right and Paglia is wrong; both approaches seem rather simplistic. The point is that to many insiders as well as outsiders, rock and roll has always been associated with teenagers. Only later did it develop affectations toward art. So Paglia's alternative story of rock's decline, as a shift from genuine rebellion to high school values, sounds like selective memory that focuses on the late 1960s rather than rock's first decade as the point for all comparisons. As such, it is hopelessly slanted as the basis for any argument that appeals to rock's special strengths. There is no more reason to single it out as the strain of rock that deserves our encouragement than the teen concerns of Chuck Berry and the early Beach Boys.

Let us now turn to the idea that only *subsequent* rock musicians were corrupted by money, fame, and sex. If rock's pioneers had any consistent message, it was a desire for sex. As critic Dave Marsh says of Buddy Holly's 1957 hit "Oh Boy," "Edgy and excited, he sings the opening way too fast . . . But as he jitters along, the cause of Buddy's nervousness becomes clear: He's about to get laid. Probably for the very first time."[43] Little Richard reports that Holly was a "wild boy for the women" and claims that he and Holly once shared the same woman backstage as Holly was being announced to the audience.[44] Listening to the music itself, there is Hank Ballard's widely banned "Work with Me, Annie," Elvis Presley's cover of "Good Rockin' Tonight," Chuck Berry's less overt "Carol," and countless others that rely on innuendo to make their point.

Anyone who's seen Martin Scorsese's *The Last Waltz* knows that easy sex could be a powerful incentive to becoming a rock musician. In one of the interview sequences, Robbie Robertson and the others who were to become The Band confess that they hit the road with Canadian rockabilly singer Ronnie Hawkins in the late 1950s because he promised they'd get more groupies ("pussy") than Frank Sinatra. David Crosby, a musician whose best work was with the Byrds prior to his fame with supergroup Crosby, Stills, and Nash, twice tells us in his autobiography that one of his motives for becoming a musician was that it was the quickest way to get sex.[45] While touring in the 1960s, the Beatles and Rolling Stones constantly contracted venereal diseases.

As for fame, when the musicians who became three-fourths of the Beatles were depressed and ready to throw in the towel, John Lennon rallied them with a chant. He would say "Where are we going, fellows?" and they answered "To the top, Johnny" in American accents, followed by "Where is that, fellows?" and "To the toppermost of the poppermost."[46] In other words, they were going to the top of the record (pop) charts. Why the faked American accents? Because, as Lennon said, "Elvis was the biggest. We wanted to be the biggest, doesn't everybody? . . . Elvis was the thing. Whatever people say, he was it."[47] I have already mentioned complaints about managers who take advantage of innocent young musicians. Yet it was with the Beatles' sudden popularity that this accusation gained currency; Britain's *Daily Worker* made the same criticisms in 1963.[48] (As a matter of fact, the Beatles' initial contract was dreadful, and they received little of the wealth that they generated at this early stage.)

Within a decade the general line of argument had become a staple in the establishment critique of rock. Similar complaints were hurled against punk from its very inception; Bill Grundy's infamous interview of the Sex Pistols on Thames Television's *Today* show starts with the accusation that they can't be genuine given their huge advance from EMI. The print media soon adopted the same line. When Frank Zappa testified before a congressional committee on "Contents of Music and the Lyrics of Records" in 1985, his arguments were disparaged with repetition of the question "do you make a profit from sales of rock records?"[49]

Yet from the viewpoint of many rock musicians, the hypocrisy is not in "selling out" to a corporation but rather in *denying* that one is engaged in an essentially commercial enterprise. Thus, Malcolm McLaren's strategy of boasting about the sums he'd "swindled" from EMI and A&M. Sting, who started within the punk/new wave orbit, ridiculed the Clash for espousing Marxism while they rode the system to success with the marketing slogan "The Only Band That Matters."[50] For himself, Sting freely admits "I like to have hit records." He merely resists the tendency to equate having several hits with having a formula for hit records.[51]

Keith Richards and Mick Jagger have made no secret about the degree to which their manager, Andrew Oldham, manipulated the press to achieve notoriety and fame for the Rolling Stones. They were willing participants in the manipulation, and Mick Jagger made no secret of his motives: "the fantasy is driving around in a big car, having all the chicks you want and being able to pay for it. . . . anyone who says it isn't is talking bullshit."[52] Speaking autobiographically, Pink Floyd's Roger Waters diagnosed the adolescent urge to become a rock star as "you feel you need all that applause and money to validate your life."[53]

Finally, even the sixties musicians that Paglia specifically singles out as purer and artistically truer than those of today, the Beatles and the Rolling Stones, were infiltrated by Philistines who worried as much about their bank accounts as their spiritual development. The Stones had difficulty recruiting drummer Charlie Watts because he refused to quit his day job and its steady paycheck, and bass player Bill Wyman was chosen as much because he had a spare amplifier as for his artistic potential. They were unwilling to fulfill the romantic stereotype of the starving artist. Stu Sutcliffe served as the Beatles' bass player before Paul McCartney; Lennon convinced his art school friend to buy a bass and join because he *looked* the part. A wretched musician, he played their first important audition with his back to the promoter in an effort to hide his ineptitude. Ringo Starr later joined as drummer, on a fixed salary, with the expectation of salting away enough money to open a hairdressing parlor when the group lost its popular appeal. Ray Manzarek, keyboardist for the Doors, admits that he teamed up with Jim Morrison to "make a million dollars."[54] Of course, Paglia might dismiss such anecdotes because they involve nonwriting or less conspicuous members of groups, whereas her focus is squarely on the singers and songwriters. But she thereby neglects the very players who give rock its Dionysian rhythms.

The greatest distortion in Paglia's argument may be the idea that early rockers had some "direct" connection with an authentic oral tradition that accounts for their expressive power. To begin with, there were few "white folk music" sources for rock. The primary noncommercial source was gospel music, as the spontaneous "Million Dollar Quartet" session of Elvis Presley, Carl Perkins, and Jerry Lee Lewis aptly demonstrates. Rock's pioneers knew hillbilly and country in a *commercial* form. Chuck Berry's first record, "Maybellene" (1955), was a simple rewrite of a country standard, "Ida Red." And most of what the early rockers knew of music — black or white — was obtained secondhand, from records.

Elvis Presley freely acknowledged that his musical sources were the radio, his phonograph, and religious "camp meetings."[55] When Presley walked into Sun Records in 1953 and taped two songs (purportedly as a birthday gift to his mother, although her birthday was months away), he covered the Ink Spots. When producer Sam Phillips invited Elvis to audition in January of 1954, Elvis chose two country tunes, also learned from records. At their next meeting, Elvis ran through a broader repertoire, "heavy on the Dean Martin stuff. Apparently he'd decided, if he was going to sound like anybody, it was gonna be Dean Martin."[56] So much for "direct contact" with rural traditions on the part of rock's first great popularizer.

The recordings of Buddy Holly are another case in point. Holly was immortalized by his death in an airplane crash; touring the Midwest in January and February of 1959, he and Ritchie Valens and the Big Bopper [J. P. Richardson] chartered a light plane and flew ahead after a gig in Clear Lake, Iowa, so that they could get some laundry done before the next night's show in Minnesota. Virtually everything that Holly ever put on tape has been released, most of it in a box set *The Complete Buddy Holly* (MCA Records, 1979). Holly was one of the first rockers to have some control over production and, like Chuck Berry but unlike Elvis Presley, founded his career on his own songs. Nonetheless, much of Holly's recorded legacy consists of cover versions of earlier songs. Many were rock-and-roll hits that had just been released by *other* rock pioneers: the Robins' (later the Coasters') "Smokey Joe's Cafe," Carl Perkins' "Blue Suede Shoes," Chuck Berry's "Brown-Eyed Handsome Man," Little Richard's "Slippin' and Slidin'," Fats Domino's "Blue Monday." He continued this practice right to the end. One of the very last things he recorded, on a tape recorder in his New York apartment, was a haunting version of Mickey and Sylvia's 1955 hit "Love Is Strange." His other sources were country; his first business card advertised "Western and Bop," and his early radio performances in Lubbock covered the music of Hank Williams, Flatt and Scruggs, and the Louvin Brothers.

Finally, consider the complaint that live performance has lost its spontaneity and communication and has become a rehearsed and meaningless show. Paglia points to the Beatles' stadium performances as the point of decline. How so? When the Beatles earlier played the cellars of Hamburg's red-light district, singing American hits in Liverpool accents to drunk Germans, was the setting really all that conducive to genuine artistic expression? By all accounts, including the one live recording made in Hamburg, they played brutal rock and roll for up to six hours a night. And the mix of beer and amphetamines that kept them going hardly made them sensitive to the audience or to their own development as "artists." Paul McCartney had it right when he described it as "noise and beat all the way."[57]

Paglia claims that the audience-artist bond is severed by the complexity and expense of ever larger sound systems and increasingly elaborate special effects. Yet these were the very things that first made rock concerts into something more than party music. The elaborate improvisations of Cream, the Grateful Dead and the rest of the San Francisco scene, Led Zeppelin, and Jimi Hendrix all came in the five years *after* the Beatles abandoned the stage for the studio. And their achievements depended on superior sound systems; improvisational rock was hardly possible when the musicians had no stage monitors and the cheap amplification system distorted the music into a dull roar, with a sound mix that put the tinny vocals far out in front. In the Beatles' early stadium performances, Ringo Starr's drums were not even amplified! Songs were truncated versions of the recorded performance; two verses and choruses might be played, with few instrumental solos.

Concerts as we understand them today, as extended performances by one or more artists, were rare events before the advent of the modern sound system. In rock's early days, the audience usually saw a specific singer or act as part of a "package" show featuring up to a dozen acts, each performing two or three songs and then making way for the next group and its performance of recent hits. At the height of their success the Beatles were onstage for about half an hour per show, and prior to their 1969 tour, Charlie Watts has said that the Rolling Stones never played more than "twenty minutes maximum" a night.[58] Watts credits "groups like Led Zeppelin" with changing the audience's attitude and making performances into genuine concerts.

Rather than modern counterparts of Wordsworth, Coleridge, Shelley, Keats, and Byron, rock musicians have always had crass commercial motives, playing dance music to mostly teen audiences. Their direct musical sources were usually commercial recordings by earlier musicians and their lyrics featured heavy doses of innuendo but little in the way of overt rebellion and, prior to 1965, almost nothing in the way of personal expression. None of this is offered with the intention of denigrating rock musicians. The genius of rock music has been to maintain musical creativity within a commercial framework. But if we are considering the claim that rock is either a folk or fine art, the available facts count heavily against such status.

Heirs of Coleridge?

If art is the church of the upper class and rock-and-roll is the church of the lower class, then what happens when they meet? Boom? . . . Are the crowds flooding the Met hoping for some kind of spiritual boon or blessing? Would they be better off at CBGB's? I don't know. — David Byrne[59]

Having outlined the historical distortions of Paglia's story, let us take up her most audacious proposal: "Rock music should not be left to the Darwinian laws of the marketplace. . . . For rock to move forward as an art form, our musicians must be given an opportunity for spiritual development." Steps must be taken to restore the lost individualism, spontaneity, energy, passion, and rebellion. Serious rock must focus on "dark" emotions, demonism, and spirituality. Purged of its economic dependence on a fickle and immature audience, "white suburban youth," rock will be recognized as the equal (or better) of current painting, sculpture, and serious music. She never explicitly says so, but her only standard of artistic achievement is rooted in her own acceptance of Romanticism's assumptions about the goals and value of art. But even by that standard, it is not clear that rock music and musicians belong in academia, as Paglia recommends.

Paglia might have quoted composer Roger Sessions for support: "the artist's values are not, and cannot be, those of the market. If one must think of him as writing *for* anyone, the answer is . . . he is writing for all who love music."[60] If modern composers have lost out to popular music, Sessions argues, it is mainly the fault of audiences who have become too lazy to listen with sympathy and understanding. In the same vein, Paglia recommends that rock artists write for posterity, not the commercial audience. Greil Marcus similarly argues that, if rock is only a commercial enterprise concerned with "profit and loss," it means nothing and "ought to be killed."[61] One is reminded of Monroe Beardsley's parody of the stereotypical Romantic hero: "shunning all contact with business, governmental, educational, and other institutions of society — or perhaps hidden in his lonely bohemian garret — he works away on his canvas, carves his stone," and so on. Commercial compromise comes later.[62] Paglia's twist is to free the artist from commerce by making artists dependent on *other* social institutions.

I would not devote such detailed attention to Paglia if others did not analyze rock in the same terms:

> In part because of its contradictions, the best way to understand rock and roll is to see it as a twentieth-century popular expression

of Western romanticism. In fact, rock may even be the last gasp of romanticism in this anxious materialistic and scientific age. More than any other contemporary cultural form, rock captures the central elements of the romantic spirit: its individuality, freedom, and rebellion, . . . its exultation of emotion, physicality, and imagination, and its relish of contradictions, extremes, and paradoxes.[63]

The most detailed of these attempts to link rock and Romanticism is Robert Pattison's *The Triumph of Vulgarity*, subtitled "Rock Music in the Mirror of Romanticism." Pattison contends that rock "is a unique integration of Romantic mythology and American blues."[64] Rock's aesthetic is "Romanticism vulgarized," so that it is less a clone than a "mutant variety."[65] Like Paglia, he identifies the Rolling Stones as the greatest rock band ever. (The Beatles, we are left to presume, are just not demonic enough.) Also like Paglia, he has almost nothing to say about the *musical* side of rock music.

Unlike Paglia, Pattison does not endorse Romanticism and he is sometimes condescending toward his subject. While he is aware that these myths are espoused by rock musicians, he does not regard them as anything *but* myths. Focusing on the prevailing idea of rock's "primitive" sources, he argues that rock artists themselves have adopted the doctrines of nineteenth-century Romanticism. He concludes that its "vulgar mode" is the cultural force behind rock, "and the Sex Pistols come to fulfill the prophecies of Shelley."[66]

Pattison's argument amounts to quoting extensively but selectively from rock lyrics. He puts rather too much weight on rock's supposed pantheism as the primary evidence of Romanticist influences. A serious weakness is the tendency to equate rock's mythology, as expressed in its lyrics, with the forces actually driving it; he likes to quote obscure groups like the Fall and then to assure us that in "describing themselves, they describe all rockers."[67] Yet I have already argued that rock musicians sometimes manipulate Romanticism for their own commercial gain. There is equal reason to believe that the attitudes of most rock lyrics are posturing and image-making for commercial purposes, and that many of the musicians are themselves perfectly aware of this. Thus Bruce Springsteen, both marketed and praised for his authenticity, now admits that his whole image in the 1980s "had been created." Although he helped to promote it, it was never fully under his control, so "it really always felt like 'Hey, that's not me.' "[68]

Pattison's argument also tends toward circularity. Anything that does not reflect Romanticism is written off as nonrock, so Pattison does not recognize soul and other black popular music as rock. Members of the Black Rock Coalition will be surprised to learn that African American music "has supplied the raw materials, but there is no reason to suppose that blacks share the Romantic preoccupations necessary for rock."[69] But it is absurd to think that such preoccupations are *necessary* for rock. When the Beatles covered black musicians like Chuck Berry and Little Richard, and when the Rolling Stones covered Chuck Berry and Otis Redding, did they take "raw materials" from black musicians and transform them? No, they took songs from musicians whom they admired as models of rock musicianship. On Pattison's thesis, what are we to make of Aretha Franklin's late-sixties work with producer Jerry Wexler (backed by several white musicians, including drummer Roger Hawkins), or such racially integrated groups as the Del-Vikings, Electric Flag, Sly and the Family Stone, Little Feat, Booker T. and the MGs, the Jimi Hendrix Experience, UB40, the Allman Brothers, the Doobie Brothers, Bruce Springsteen's various bands, the Dead Kennedys, the Revolution (with Prince), or the expanded version of Talking Heads? Do the white members supply the requisite romanticist mythology to transform the black musicians' contributions into rock?[70]

I do not deny that as an aesthetic program Romanticism enshrines many of the values that are popularly attributed to rock. As a reaction against Enlightenment classicism and its emphasis on "intellectual" values of order, structure, precision and technical polish, Romanticism first surfaced in serious music with the *Sturm und Drang*, flowered with program music and tone poems, and peaked with Wagner's music drama and chromatic explorations. The new values were "emotional" and were manifested overtly in change, excess, personal meanings, ambiguity, and idiosyncratic structures. But even if we can construct a case that the same conflict of values is present in any contrast of serious music with rock, parallels do not show causality. To the extent that there is any direct line between Romanticism and rock, it turns up more in British than American rock, no doubt due to the emphasis on the Romantic poets in British education.

The problem with the whole line of analysis is that *most* opinions about music sound like *some* aspect of Romanticism, if only because of the general presumption that music is preeminently concerned with the expression of emotion. These characteristics all fit jazz as easily as rock. In fact, with writers like Paglia and Pattison we may have a case of critical history repeating itself. Those who link Romanticism and rock sound like earlier writers on jazz, who found in jazz the same characteristics that are now attributed to rock, particularly the uncompromised

and spontaneous nature of the performance and the freedom and in-
stinctive self-expression of the performer.[71] And these values were often
espoused by jazz performers themselves.

Consider Billie Holiday. Not exactly known for her art school background or reading of Byron and Shelley, she denied having any influences except the records of Bessie Smith and Louis Armstrong:

> If you find a tune and it's got something to do with you, you don't
> have to evolve anything. You just feel it, and when you sing it other
> people can feel something too. With me, it's got nothing to do with
> working or arranging or rehearsing. . . . But singing songs like
> "The Man I Love" or "Porgy" . . . When I sing them I live them
> again and I love them.[72]

However much this sounds like Wordsworth's formula that poetry is a
spontaneous overflow of emotions "recollected in tranquility," we have
no reason to regard Lady Day as influenced by Wordsworth. Likewise,
we have no reason to regard rock as an expression of Western Romanticism. As Peter Kivy has so carefully documented, most of these ideas
about music were first advanced in the seventeenth and eighteenth
centuries.[73] It might be better to regard romanticist aesthetics as a
generalization to all the arts of assumptions that had long been held of
music, in which case rock has no special connection to Romanticism.

Furthermore, Paglia's account of rock is fraught with the same internal tensions that characterize the loose confederation of ideas con-
stituting Romanticism, particularly in relation to the folk tradition that
she praises as a source of power in early rock. To the extent that such
traditions have survived in Western culture in our century, oral folk
traditions are communal rather than individual artistic creations, and
they reflect the community rather than the personal self-expression of
the Romantic genius. Yet Paglia criticizes rock musicians who cater to
or reflect the values of the audience. The idea of a "folk" dimension in
rock is also present in her ideal of an authentic and spontaneous interaction between performer and audience, but this conflicts with the
reality that most rock fans are self-consciously aware that they are
members of a distinct subculture, and of distinct subcultures within
rock.[74]

Writers have been keen to link rock and folk music because it suggests a background that is not commercial pap for the masses. Romanticism provides a model, with its similar glorification of the rural "folk"
and their collective art as a less intellectual, more spontaneous, and
thus purer mode of expression. There is no reason to deny the fact that

there is some connection between rock and "white" folk music. But we must be careful about what this means. Rock musicians ranging from Bob Dylan and some members of the Grateful Dead, the Byrds, and other sixties groups came to rock from "folk" as it was then understood. But what this meant was that they played acoustic instruments and belonged to the alternative, politically leftist, and decidedly *urban* music scene centered around American universities and New York's Greenwich Village.

Dylan's debut album illustrates the result: it mixes country music, delta and country blues, and Appalachian music with several originals indebted to Woody Guthrie. When Dylan and the Rolling Stones imitated black American singers in a self-conscious blues purism, they were indeed behaving like many Romantic composers. Chopin and Dvořák borrowed musical materials from their native folk traditions, and Wagner and Mahler adopted folk poems and myths as texts. But the aesthetics of Romanticism were fraught with internal contradictions, among them the fact that the very process of seeking out and appropriating these sources contradicts the desired spontaneity and authenticity of expression. The contradiction holds no less for rock musicians than for nineteenth-century composers.[75]

According to Peter Wicke, the aesthetic values imparted to British rockers who attended art schools led to a calculated bohemianism and intellectual snobbery. Among those articulating their aesthetic principles, pop art and then situationism are prominent influences. (Punk has affinities with the brief dada movement, lending a name to the group Cabaret Voltaire.) However, Wicke suggests that their preoccupation with the authenticity of their self-expression precluded their participation in any sort of community with their audience, and they were often acutely aware of the distance between their own privileged status and the working-class lives of most of their audience.[76] These attitudes may even have worked against direct political activism on the part of British rockers. Prior to the Beatles single "Revolution" (1968), British rock lyrics stayed away from anything overtly political, whereas the American charts had featured political material since 1965.

As suggested in the previous section, rock re-creates Romanticism's contradictions in another way when the ideology of artistic freedom comes up against the reality that the musicians are engaged in a commercial enterprise. Within the actual context of the nineteenth century, Romanticism glorified the sensitivity and sensibility of the individual artist/genius, but the requisite artistic freedom had its price in the commercialization of music. When the Romantics celebrated individuality and folk tradition, it was in conscious opposition to the standardization and industrialization of the emerging bourgeois capitalism. Today, that means utter disdain for those who get their rock from MTV. A parallel is present within the rock audience; fans of hardcore express contempt for mainstream audiences who imitate their slam-dancing and thus strip it of its "underground" status, and many African Americans bristle at suburban whites who appropriate hip-hop style.

Yet it was bourgeois capitalism and the opportunity for self-promotion that provided the composer's freedom. When earlier composers like Bach or Handel supported themselves with pupils and commissioned works, their music was largely utilitarian, written for specific occasions: Bach's masses and chorales, Handel's oratorios with their religious texts and his *Water Music* and *Royal Fireworks Music*. Beethoven solidified the shift from the composer-for-hire to the composer-as-entrepreneur, with works sold to publishers rather than commissioned by royal patrons. Concerts became money-making ventures, designed to please the bourgeois crowd who could afford the fee. Beethoven was attuned to the need to please the audience, repeating movements of symphonies when the concert audience called for it and showing off with piano improvisations when challenged. He could also be sensitive to criticism, withdrawing and replacing the final movement of the String Quartet in B-flat Minor (the *Grosse Fugue*) at his publisher's suggestion after the audience reacted negatively at its premiere. Preparing the "Hammerklavier" sonata for English publication (op. 106), Beethoven suggested that the publisher might prefer it reduced to two movements, or with the movements in a different order. So much for pure art as the production of genius when you want to make a living from it.

This is not to say that Beethoven didn't chafe at the need to merge art and commerce. Responding to a question about writing on commission, one of Beethoven's conversation books records his ambivalence: "I do not write what I most desire to, but that which I need to because of money. But that is not saying that I write only for money."[77] He complained that he was "half a tradesman" and is reported to have insulted Walter Scott by saying "the fellow writes for money only."[78] Under the spell of the emerging aesthetics of Romanticism, Beethoven regarded artistic genius as the prerequisite of true art. He insisted that natural genius must be tempered by careful study of past composers, complaining that Weber and Rossini did not study enough to develop their natural talents.

At the other end of the spectrum, Wagner scraped together funding for his music dramas by a combination of self-promotion and spectacle. Wagner was keen to wrap himself in Beethoven's mantle, conducting the latter's Ninth Symphony at the 1872 dedication of Bayreuth. But Beethoven's willingness to meet the audience halfway had given way to Wagner's self-conscious Romanticism. Stubborn and uncompromising, his vision required absolute control of his creations, and he was vicious to anyone who criticized him. The result was precisely the opposite of Paglia's ideal performance as an audience-artist interaction that features improvisation and spontaneity. Ideally, the audience comes to the Bayreuth festival theater and listens to the *Ring* cycle in a hushed silence, broken only by the turning of pages as devoted Wagnerites follow the score. In short, there is no spontaneity of any kind; the Bach mass had found its secular parallel.

Which of these artists represents Paglia's ideal? Her advice to rock musicians, "don't become a slave to the audience" and "Don't tour" (study art instead), points to Wagner and not to Beethoven or to Romantics like Berlioz, Chopin, and Liszt, who more or less invented the modern promotional tour. More pointedly, she expects rock to combine two artistic goals that have been at odds ever since Romanticism cobbled them together. On the one hand there is the development of the individual artist, cushioned from and thus impervious to commercial demands. But this sort of autonomy is unlikely to foster energy, rebellion, and the emotional power of rock's pioneers. On the other hand there is the emotional power of the folk tradition, where the music emerges from the community in a way that blurs the line between creator and audience. But the communal nature of the folk process fits uncomfortably with the self-conscious artistry of the trained professional; training rock musicians at colleges and universities is not likely to connect rock with centuries of folk music.

Patronage and Ivory Towers

By its very nature, no rock and roll worth hearing ever came
from an institution of formal learning. — Langdon Winner[79]

I believe that if the university's fostering of art is
only kindly, is only altruistic, it may prove to be also
meaningless. — Ben Shahn[80]

Many critics of rock's commercialization are really recommending that it shouldn't remain popular music any longer, that is, a commodity designed for consumption by masses of listeners of varying degrees of musical knowledge. Putting aside their dubious folk ideology, such ideas fail to address how rock music would retain its identity apart from its popular base. Romanticism has a healthy strain of artistic elitism that is antithetical to rock, and any version of patronage is likely to produce that strain in rock. While I would not go as far as Nietzsche, he captures the problem involved when he attacks Romanticism: "the artist who began to understand himself would misunderstand himself: he ought not to look back, he ought not to look at all, he ought to give."[81]

Are the vicissitudes of commerce really an artistic kiss of death? Is it so bad to be "half a tradesman?" Paglia praises popular music and film as the two great art forms of our time, but film has fared quite well as a commercial enterprise. We should consider the likely consequences of treating rock like the other arts, trading the supposedly exploitive control by entertainment conglomerates for another set of institutional controls, operating with their own logic. When a show on "Corporeal Politics" was assembled at MIT, its National Endowment for the Arts (NEA) grant was killed by a Bush appointee. Aerosmith came forward with the vetoed $10,000. One can argue that Aerosmith was only doing their duty in supporting the arts. This duty is usually conceived as falling more heavily on the wealthy, as Paglia suggests when she says that successful rock musicians are "ethically obligated" to fund struggling musicians. However, even if there is some imperfect duty to support the arts, there is a big gap between this admission and the conclusion that *public* funds or institutions should be used.

Suppose that rock musicians emulate the rest of the art world. Funding through scholarships, grants, and other public funds is likely to remain severely limited. Patronage could cover only a fraction of the ten thousand or more artists who release rock recordings each year (many of these being groups of several members). The basic facts supporting this conclusion are well known. One percent of the budget on certain government buildings must be used for public art. Not counting this amount, in 1994 the federal government spent less than a dollar per citizen per year on arts funding. Corporations and private foundations generate a similar amount for the support of active artists. Beyond these measures, most citizens only contribute to the arts when they directly subsidize the events that interest them. As government funding for education is tightened, we often see that school districts are willing to gut their arts programs before touching sports programs. This decision raises little public outcry. In short, most art is a commodity, albeit of a special kind, and we adopt a pay-as-you-go attitude. Perhaps it is a blessing; do nations where per capita funding of art is many times higher than our own, such as Germany and France, have better art or a more appreciative art public? Has their support of fine art drained young talent from popular arts like rock music and film?

In practical terms, freeing artists from traditional commercial concerns means that *most* rock music will remain exactly what it is anyway: product for popular consumption. So the scheme divides rock into two camps. The larger camp will have to carry on as before. The smaller will consist of artists with grants, afforded the freedom to follow their own muse. (This would reverse the current process, where *mature* successful artists like Dire Straits, George Harrison, the Grateful Dead, Lionel Ritchie, Bruce Springsteen, and the Rolling Stones can wait five years between records and tours, producing what they like when they choose to do so.) But the select few singled out for support will face the same problems that occur in any patronage system, putting them on a collision course with freedom to explore Dionysian content.

Art patronage, particularly government or other "official" patronage, is often defended by pointing to art history. Patronage gave us the pyramids, Gothic cathedrals, and the Sistine Chapel ceiling. But history reveals few patrons who regard the artists they fund as free agents. Patrons usually have an agenda, and thus the city council that commissioned Auguste Rodin's sublime *The Burghers of Calais* refused to pay for the completed work when it did not glorify its subject in the manner they'd anticipated. One has difficulty imagining the Clash or rappers N.W.A. getting many grants under Paglia's scheme; she, after all, won't be making the administrative decision about who receives funding.

By operating within the sphere of mass entertainment, rock musicians have been relatively free of overt censorship. True, the Rolling Stones agreed to sing "Let's Spend the Night Together" as "Let's Spend Some Time Together" in order to appear on the *Ed Sullivan Show* in 1967, a form of self-censorship difficult to imagine in the 1990s. Ice-T faced the wrath of law enforcement officers across the country and subsequent economic boycotts by three major record-store chains before he agreed to pull "Cop Killer" off his album with Body Count. When his subsequent album met with resistance from Time Warner, he quickly relocated to Priority Records, releasing it intact.

Despite all the attention given to indirect censorship of rock and rap, recently highlighted by such cases as 2 Live Crew, Ice-T, and Sister Souljah, any teenager in America finds their recordings as easy to obtain as a copy of *Playboy*. As long as they do not run afoul of obscenity laws that restrict the speech of everyone in the United States, 2 Live

Crew are free to spew the most dreadful misogyny. Yet Stephen Sondheim rejected an NEA grant because of the restrictions involved, preferring the freedom of the commercial sphere. While the entertainment industry often balks and practices self-censorship when controversy erupts, the industry seems less subject to public or ideological pressures than are political appointees at the NEA.

Although those involved with the fine arts generally do not like to say so, there is something unfair about using public funds to support artists who are not interested in producing music that the general public wants to hear. I am sympathetic to Jeremy Bentham's argument that the arts "are useful only to those who take pleasure in them." The arts may have a general use, but specific works are of use only if they have an audience. If there were no privately supported art, public funding might be justified. But to the extent that public patronage is set up to further arts that lack widespread appeal, we are instituting a regressive tax "laying burdens on the comparatively indigent many, for the amusement of the comparatively opulent few."[82] Why tax the lower- and middle-class patrons of popular art, who expect no subsidy, to support opera?

This is done with the fine arts in the United States, with mixed success. Does opera flourish as a living art form, despite its heavy subsidization? Which has had a greater impact, the Who's *Tommy* or a modern opera like *Nixon in China*? I have enjoyed the latter on public television, a noncommercial forum subsidized by the federal government and grants from major corporations. But when "pledge week" rolls around, public television puts on Paul Simon and James Taylor concerts, not *Nixon in China,* Wagner's *Ring* cycle, or the BBC programming that dominates most of the time. I take these programming practices to be an open admission of the regressive nature of their funding in light of the public's true preferences.

Finally, training rock musicians at colleges and universities is likely to result in music that parallels the output of similarly trained jazz and classical musicians: highly accomplished, technically excellent, and intellectually challenging music that values extreme polish, individuality, experimentation, and novelty for its own sake, and continuous progressive change. As R. G. Collingwood complained more than a half-century ago, Romanticism tends to make artists into a segregated "special order or caste," with disastrous results. "If they form themselves into a special clique, the emotions they express will be the emotions of that clique; and the consequence will be that their work becomes intelligible only to their fellow artists."[83] Complaining that the artworld was tending to support "mystagogues" in an ivory tower who only communicated with one another, Collingwood did not see that mass art might be the remedy he sought.

It is not as though we are speculating without precedent here. In 1958, Milton Babbitt defended the modern composer's highly specialized art as something "progressive" and utterly divorced from the musical entertainment that pleases the mass audience. But further progress was only possible, Babbitt warned, if composers made a "voluntary withdrawal" from the public sphere and relocated to academia, where composers would be "free to pursue a private life of professional achievement as opposed to a public life of unprofessional compromise and exhibitionism."[84] It is "only proper," Babbitt argued, that the university become the home for serious composers, as it had for the mathematician and the theoretical physicist.

Twenty-five years later, Babbitt acknowledges that universities have indeed become havens for serious musical activity. But now he warns young composers of the price, complaining of the dreadful isolation and lack of support that awaits them in the university community. The retreat to the university has brought a "crisis" to serious composing: "It has splintered our musical society; it has in many ways isolated musical society from the rest of society with the academy." But a return to the world "out there" offers little hope, for the general public is "unheeding" and bound to be "uncomprehending." He ends on a note of despair. For composers "who dare to presume to attempt to make music as much as it can be rather than as little as one can get away with . . . and who've entered the university as our last hope, our only hope, and ergo our best hope, hope only that we're not about to be abandoned."[85] But what did he expect? It is instructive to contrast Babbitt's 1958 article with Ben Shahn's reservations about academic patronage, delivered the previous year at Harvard. Besides worrying that academic life is anathema to the individualism essential to artistic flourishing, Shahn warned of the isolation within the academic community that Babbitt would come to regret.[86]

Ezra Pound diagnosed the problem early on: "Music rots when it gets *too far* from the dance. Poetry atrophies when it gets too far from music."[87] While teachers and literature professors like to think that schools and colleges have some special ability to bring poetry and literature to the masses, we know that "good" literature is not what everyone wants. It is not even what most college students want: junk fiction and collections of cartoons top the sales lists of college bookstores. I am not putting down junk fiction and comics, but there is little reason to think that technically refined poetry means much to the majority of people. It has gotten too far from music, and most of the "serious" music composed in our century has gotten too far from the dance.

In cynical moments I agree with Babbitt: contemporary serious music is mainly produced by college professors for other college professors. Academics, however well-meaning, are the last group to keep rock rooted in the syncopated and danceable rhythms that have made it one of America's most successful exports. With typical hyperbole, Frank Zappa observed that when a composer "is a guy who owes his ass to a university, . . . to keep their pedigree or tenure or whatever," success requires a lot of compromise on substance ("ass-kissing"), with results "palatable" to "nincompoops" who run the institution.[88] If hip-hop culture has vitality, it may be because it isn't the province of college students who've immersed themselves in great literature under the direction of college professors. Lou Reed's study of poetry is the exception, not the rule.

If there is any element of Romanticism that we ought to keep out of art education, it is the notion of the artistic genius as a superior soul requiring the special nourishment of higher education, for the resulting chasm between artist and audience is probably one of the great obstacles to full enjoyment and participation in the arts by large numbers of our population. Why inject elitism into popular culture, where huge numbers of people willingly seek out at least one form of art without anxiety or feelings of inferiority? One of its attractions is that it is not regarded as "art," something one must work to appreciate. Romanticism is a poor model for *understanding* the achievements of rock music, and it is worse yet as a *justification* for treating rock music as we now treat the fine arts, as a "serious" enterprise.

Some fear that even if it is undesirable to apply Romanticism to rock music or to make a home for rock in academia along the lines of fine arts training, both are unavoidable.[89] The modern university is a great repository of culture; no ivory tower, it is open to the myriad influences of popular culture. Many rock musicians, like jazz musicians and film directors, will soon perfect their art in a professional, academic setting. If rock no longer seems very rebellious, it may be because its very familiarity has allowed us to assimilate it to the categories we normally employ for fine art. The concepts of genius, self-expression, sellout, and authenticity are firmly entrenched and are having an effect.

Perhaps it will happen. But of course that is no reason to support the process, and it is certainly no reason to suppose that rock music will be better as a result. More importantly, rock's arrival in academia may actually be a sign that, if not in a terminal stage, paralysis is setting in. As George Kubler documents in *The Shape of Time,* every artistic tradition seems to have its natural cycle of invention, change, and obsolescence.[90] The history of any creative tradition is a story built around the identification of singular inventions and singular achievements that cannot be predicted from their predecessors. They are only understood when viewed against that background. The cycle may spiral forward with new inventions and changes before final obsolescence; between the "prime" inventions (e.g., Picasso's *Les Demoiselles d'Avignon* or Elvis Presley's Sun sessions) we find a multiplicity of replicas and mutations. But at some point the tradition breaks down from aesthetic fatigue, and our needs are met in some radically new manner (often incorporating new technologies). In other words, there aren't always pressing social forces driving change, and the "problem" generating the creation of artifacts need not be replaced by a fresh problem. We simply tire of our minor variations of the same old thing. Rock may well be reaching the point of aesthetic fatigue, particularly for the baby boomers who have been its primary audience.

As new technologies supersede those grounding rock music, popular music will take new forms. If rock finds a place alongside jazz and classical music in the academies, the triumph of vulgarity will give way to the formal recital hall and a re-creation of that vulgarity. Those who today romanticize rock will begin the process of romanticizing the popular music that replaces it.

8

Sign O' the Times: Ideology
and Aesthetics

Hegemony?

The ideas of liberalism dominate Western thought: they shape societies and
they shape people's vision of themselves. And just as liberalism affects the social
and political world, so it penetrates popular music and art. — John Street[1]

I will conclude by examining the ideological dimensions of pairing
aesthetics and rock. First, there is a concern that philosophical aesthetics comes "burdened with the hidden ideological claptrap" of its
three centuries as handmaiden to high culture.[2] The complaint is that
aesthetic theory approaches its subject matter as autonomous objects,
to be judged by "immutable criteria."[3] Works of art are thought to
embody transcendent, universal, and timeless values. Everything that
matters about rock music is then obliterated, particularly the ideals of
truth and authenticity connecting fans to the music.

Second, the values of popular culture appear to be at odds with those
of the artworld and aesthetics. Because aesthetics opposes art against
commerce, any "aesthetics of rock" is undercut by my own argument
that rock is rooted in recording technology and inseparable from the
commercial operations of the modern music industry. Indeed, many
writers attempt to rescue rock from the twin threats of commercialism
and fine art by incorporating it into the cultural developments of postmodernism. Texts are seen to be infinitely reproducible, deeply mediated, and inherently intertextual. Issues of ontology — worries about
what a rock text *is* — are a straitjacket on rock. Existing primarily as a
social category, rock eludes or supersedes aesthetics. On this line of
analysis, Passmore was right: aesthetics is dreary.

Let us tackle these challenges in just that order. For our purposes, an
ideology is the system of concepts, attitudes, and values at the core of a

distinct worldview. (It is not restricted to Marxism's strict conception of false consciousness about economic and social realities.) Ideology is of particular concern when it structures social institutions and reinforces power arrangements by entrenching binary oppositions into our worldview. As Terry Eagleton sees the danger, "Ideologies like to draw rigid boundaries between what is acceptable and what is not, between self and non-self, truth and falsity, sense and nonsense, reason and madness, central and marginal, surface and depth."[4] Each pair, of course, carries a hierarchical ordering. Arising in contingent cultural arrangements, such systems become distinctly ideological and oppressive when they are treated as necessary or universal truths.

While granting that rock and aesthetics arrive freighted with ideology, I will argue that they are not necessarily at odds with one another. Specifically, I hesitate to embrace John Fiske's claim that "aesthetics is naked cultural hegemony, and popular discrimination properly rejects it."[5] Basically a politicized variant of Barnett Newman's quip that aesthetics is for art what ornithology is for birds, Fiske accuses aesthetics of promoting a dominant group's interests. Hegemony is present when the ideology of a dominant group seeps down to subordinate groups so that they accept and internalize it, displacing discourse representing their own interests. For example, in modern society the assumptions and interests of manufacturers and investors are favored in most discourse, whether the nominal topic is crime, education, or free trade. Largely unstated and even unconscious, the interests of the bourgeoisie are given priority in the culture, including aesthetic theory.

In his classic study of British music subcultures, Dick Hebdige explores the ideological warfare at the heart of popular culture. While he never quite denies that we possess an innate creative impulse and desire for beauty, he warns that traditional aesthetics cannot explain the subcultural appeal of certain musics. He directs us to the ideology that "saturates everyday discourse." Encoded in modes that come to seem natural or inevitable, social relations and processes are assimilated by individuals "only as forms in which they are represented." So most people absorb ideology at a level beneath consciousness. Hegemonic forms remain "shrouded in a [false] common sense that simultaneously validates and mystifies them."[6]

Discussing modern painting, Timothy Clark echoes Hebdige:

> The sign of an ideology is a kind of inertness in discourse: a fixed pattern of imagery and belief, a syntax which seems obligatory, a set of permitted modes of seeing and saying; each with its own

structure of closure and rendering others unthinkable, aberrant, or extreme. And these things are done . . . *surreptitiously.*[7]

Closing off alternative ways of framing issues, such domination can be more destructive than overt political repression. Is an aesthetics of rock prone to this? If aesthetic theory is more likely to celebrate the Beatles and Ice-T than the Carpenters and Three Dog Night, what patterns of closure are slipped in with the construction of a rock canon?

However, if ideology permeates rock as a hidden form, we cannot say what "aesthetic" is embraced in advance of looking at real cases. But even then the extent to which popular forms embrace or repudiate dominant culture, including doctrines of musical autonomy, is an open question. Disenfranchised groups struggle against hegemony while dominant groups struggle to legitimate their ideology. There may be temporary gains and losses for each, leading to mutual concessions and accommodations. Hebdige points to British working-class whites who appropriated elements from the culture of West Indian immigrants to signal alienation from their parent culture. Yet they did not thereby take on any of the philosophy of Rastafarianism. Popular modes representing the interests of the dominant class continued to seem "natural" depictions of how things are; the skinheads backed off from reggae when it started to overtly celebrate blackness.[8] Here we have a reminder that an aesthetics of rock cannot be constructed apart from concrete practices. We cannot presuppose that any particular ideology will be found in all facets of popular culture. After all, the Rasta philosophy maintains its identity in the face of the dominant culture. Or does it? John Storey argues that reggae supports rather than challenges the system it overtly condemns.[9]

Nor are specific instances clear cut. When "alternative" bands fashioned a tribute album to that king and queen of MOR kitsch, the Carpenters, it might be taken to embrace taste cultures that oppose rock's emerging canon, celebrating rock's heterogeneity. *If I Were a Carpenter* (1994) might also signal a resistive, ironic delight in "bad" taste. But for those suspicious of aesthetics, there would be no pleasure in reading it as an aestheticizing of rock music. Unlike paintings by René Magritte and Roy Lichtenstein that borrow liberally from familiar works in order to make art itself the subject of art, Sonic Youth are not supposed to be dabbling with aesthetics when they offer a heartfelt cover of "Superstar." Or if they *are* aestheticizing rock—as Shonen Knife seems to on the same collection, deliberately putting the audible cracks and pops of vinyl into a digital recording—they seem to cross the line into antipopular and hegemonic "art." Yet another interpretation would read the nostalgia overtones of these gestures as rock's move beyond modernism, into a postmodern repudiation of aesthetics. All of these readings have been floated in reviews.

To a pessimist like Adorno, participants in capitalism cannot avoid validating its monolithic control. Every expression of taste, including seemingly neutral acts like purchasing or reviewing a record, reinforces commodity mentality. More optimistic authors, including Fiske, Lawrence Grossberg, and Justin Lewis, believe that subordinated groups remain free to exploit the multiple meanings that can be drawn from commodities. Because meanings arise from their use in a host of contexts, the "author's" meaning — and power over the audience — can never be taken for granted. Fiske thus reads popular taste as a progressive reaction against oppression. Whether with blue jeans or Madonna videos, consumers retain a vestige of "popular force" that can counter prevailing ideologies with a progressive, oppositional ideology at the level of living out "everyday life."[10] John Lydon becomes Johnny Rotten by buying a Pink Floyd shirt and scrawling "I hate" above the band's name.

In an age when multinational corporations can get the American Congress to consider a new tax on blank cassette tapes to compensate them for copyright payments lost in home taping, home taping takes on a resistive air. Yet Fiske concurs with Sting that commodified pop culture cannot be radically oppositional.[11] Rock is often celebrated as a vehicle of sexual liberation. A closer look reveals an infestation of sexism. Most rock reinforces the most repressive gender roles. Even Madonna constructs personae that confirm dominant, patriarchal representations of women, simultaneously challenging gender restrictions and pandering to the male gaze.[12] When Chrysalis Records launched its "Blondie is a group" campaign in the late 1970s, Deborah Harry's image always dominated the visuals. Despite the high profile allowed female vocalists, rock remains structured as a largely male preserve — "guyville" is the apt phrase that Liz Phair lifts from Urge Overkill.[13]

In short, rock has not developed in isolation from the dominant culture. Perhaps it embodies a progressive reaction against the dominant culture and *at the same time* embraces traditional aesthetics, or at least some of it. As such, I will argue — if not directly, then in a flanking maneuver — that there is still some life left in the ideology of art. I do not simply mean that autonomous art still lumbers along in such institutions as art museums, multimillion-dollar auctions, and art institutes. These can be set aside as the enclaves of an elite class. There are other ways for its ideology to flourish. In the words of Roger Taylor, the world of art can stage a "raid into popular culture."[14] Like the imported water hyacinths that threaten to choke off the native plants in the Louisiana bayous, certain concepts of "high" art are imported into the waters of popular culture, take root, and threaten to drive out all other discourse. Perhaps it is happening with rock, as Taylor fears. To sort it out, let us turn to issues of art's autonomy.

Aesthetics and Autonomy

It is not a rock song or a pop song, bears little relation to their own early records and even less to the musical past . . . It simply exists in its own space.
— Description of U2's "Hawkmoon 269"[15]

Postmodernism is thus distinguished from modernism by the belief that artistic autonomy is neither possible nor desirable. — John McGowan[16]

Historically, philosophical aesthetics concentrated on fine art. It thus reinforced a narrow range of practices and values. It generally neglected art's social and historical context. Yet we would distort its history if we said that aesthetics imputes a uniform dogma of artistic autonomy to everything it touches. Many important writers, including Plato, Shaftesbury, Hume, and Tolstoy, have insisted that art always has a political or moral dimension. While critical of aesthetic's past claims, Janet Wolff points out that "the social coordinates of the aesthetic are becoming increasingly apparent" to those working in philosophy of art.[17] More attention is being paid to marginalized forms of art. As for those defending autonomy, different times and different schools of thought have promoted very different doctrines. A recent version, central to analytic aesthetics, is the institutional theory of art. It holds that art cannot exist apart from a specific supporting institution, a special "artworld." But when George Dickie thus joins Theodor Adorno, Allan Bloom, and Harold Bloom in defending autonomy while John Fiske and Rose R. Subotnik challenge it, we must wonder whether they are talking about the same thing.

In the last chapter I worried that if rock becomes too closely wed to the academic world, it will become sterile and empty. It would join what John McGowan calls "the modernist hope" and Peter Bürger calls bourgeois art, bounded by an institutional framework that minimizes links to the praxis of life.[18] Otherwise functionless, art is to be valued for its own sake, for its intrinsic excellence. As Lydia Goehr puts it, "Once created it should exhibit a permanence and self-sufficiency that would separate it from all worldly or historical contingency."[19] The avant-garde's symbolic attempts to disrupt its supporting social institutions have done little to reverse these tendencies. Wolff sees philosophical aesthetics as one of art's support institutions; as art's theorizing shadow, it comes across as the ideological attack dog of the bourgeois. Championing art's autonomy, aesthetics is accused of insulating art from life, stripping art of any positive social function.[20]

The fear is that in treating autonomy as ideologically neutral, traditional aesthetics and bourgeois art privilege one mode of pleasure: aesthetic pleasure in disinterested contemplation. As a result, Goehr notes, the audience for art enters a kind of false consciousness. Among other demands, the audience must pretend that its pleasure is not socially conditioned and that autonomy is not a historically contingent value. Above all, there is a tacit denial that such pleasure serves the interests of those who dominate the modern artworld. As Bürger argues, what is most bourgeois here is a claim to the *universality* of this mode of pleasure. Wolff concurs that such dogmas divert attention away from the social and economic factors in art. The dominant group furthers its interests with a pretense of neutral judgment. Either we try to validate rock by focusing on the small amount of it that lives up to traditional fine art values, or we fall prey to the prejudice that it has its own virtues, but is then a lesser music. Either way, we surrender to the hegemony of aesthetics.

But hardly any rock (and not a lot of other music) fits Bürger's description of bourgeois art or McGowan's criteria for modernism. First, rock's love affair with noise and visceral punch are contrary to disinterestedness. Second, where autonomous art is typically "the act of an individual," we have seen that rock is most often collaborative.[21] Third, in bourgeois society "the work of art becomes its own end," generating art that takes its own status as its primary content: aestheticist art. But as a commodity, rock is more like the pulp fiction that Bürger opposes to such art. Finally, the reception of bourgeois art is "by isolated individuals," reading a novel or viewing a painting. In contrast, early rock and roll was often heard from a jukebox, and much of the audience still uses the music for dancing or for other social gatherings, including concerts. On the other hand, in recent years the Walkman has reinforced isolated listening.

Studying taste preferences in France in the 1960s, Pierre Bourdieu concludes that "access to cultural works is the privilege of the cultivated class." He notes that some modern societies minimize the economic barriers to high art. Thus a Hmong immigrant living in Minneapolis can see original works by Edvard Munch and René Magritte any time she wishes, since the art institute charges no admission. None-theless, few people have a "real possibility" of accessing or understand-ing them. Although high-art objects are not rare, "the propensity to consume them is," because the ability to employ the appropriate "aes-thetic disposition" is largely determined by one's education.[22]

In sum, inequalities in education are linked to differences in tastes. While the strength of the association is subject to debate, Bourdieu recognizes that fine art is linked to praxis: its relative autonomy de-pends on very distinct social practices and the complexity of its codes. "The pure gaze" is neither a neutral stance of appreciation nor "a gift of nature," and Bourdieu rightly emphasizes the political significance of our current practices. Demanding an investment of cultural capital, fine art reinforces social distinctions and class barriers by encoding messages that alienate, confuse, or bore less-educated viewers. While France and New Jersey have their differences, Bruce Springsteen recalls his early encounters with art: "If you grow up in a home where the concept of art is like twenty minutes in school everyday that you *hate*, the lift of rock is just incredible. . . . Rock and roll reached down into all those homes where there was no music or books or anything. And it infiltrated that whole thing. That's what happened in my house."[23] He sought full engagement. Art demanded reverence.

Emphasizing such differences, Fiske contends that while the plea-sures of high art are hegemonic, those of popular culture are not. For members of the dominant classes (art history professors, for instance?), the real pleasure lies in controlling others who are made to feel inade-quate in their tastes. For members of a subordinate class, the pleasure lies "in exerting power over others . . . [and] in exerting power over oneself, in disciplining oneself." These pleasures of dominance and conformity, while real, are oppressive. Viewing autonomous art and popular culture as mutually exclusive categories organized around a series of opposing poles, Fiske invites us to celebrate "the more disrepu-table side of each antithesis."[24]

Rose Subotnik sees a similar polarization in the critical community itself. She criticizes the prevailing methodological ahistoricism and de-fends "Continentalists" like Adorno who are more explicit about their ideology.[25] But are these "antiautonomy" theorists any more likely to *question* their existing ideological commitments than those she accuses of positivism? In action, applied to rock, socially informed theorizing often forgets the music altogether. As Simon Frith notes, such analysis tends to reduce popular music to commercial function and other "utilitarian" social relationships. The operating assumption is that there is then no room left for aesthetic theorizing about the same subject matter. In short, having articulated why Hole and Sonic Youth are more progressive than Guns N' Roses, we are not allowed to suggest that the latter's higher record sales may have something to do with the quality of their songs, musicianship, and record production.[26]

I have noted Fiske's optimism about the progressive meanings that can be wrenched from popular culture. Unlike Subotnik or Goehr, he treats art for art's sake as an *adequate* description of what goes on in the world of high art, but never for popular art. (For then it would be hegemonic and antipopular.) Describing the two basic categories, he argues that popular culture sidesteps hegemonic pleasure by being "evanescent and ephemeral":

> Its constant, anxious search for the novel evidences the constantly changing formations of the people and the consequent need for an ever-changing resource bank from which popular cultures may be produced and reproduced.[27]

Where high-art meanings are singular and stable, those of pop are not. Where "good" art and high culture must stand the test of time, popular art is here today, gone tomorrow.

As a description of rock music, this doesn't quite wash. Year after year, Led Zeppelin's warhorse, "Stairway to Heaven," wins radio-station listener polls of favorite rock song. Kurt Cobain was inspired to play rock music by a Black Flag recording that was three years old when he first heard it; he was later drawn to the "sincerity" of Leadbelly.[28] I was recently walking through a public building and was pleased to hear the Rolling Stones's *Beggars Banquet* (1968) floating up a staircase. A paint crew was playing it on a boom box. All of them were younger than the music. The next day I passed a crew of workers siding a house; their boom box blared out Jackson Browne's *Running on Empty* (1977). Apparently nobody told them that they were transgressing the rules for popular culture. Yet as a backdrop to their work, the music did not receive the respectful attention characteristic of established cultural forms. It was neither bourgeois art nor the flavor of the month.

If Springsteen was not the sort to lap up the formal education that would unlock the artworld, there are ways to explain it other than by locating popular and high culture at opposite ends of a continuum. We need not conclude with Fiske and Bourdieu that popular taste is "the negative opposite" of disinterested or "legitimate" taste. In fact, their theorizing may be grounded less in the actual structure of taste cultures than in their mutual opposition to the classical formulation of the issues in Kant's *Critique of Aesthetic Judgment* (1790).[29] Both follow the tendency to read Kant as defending an extreme formalism, in which aesthetic value is restricted to formal relationships and art is to be appreciated apart from any connections to originating social processes. And Kant is often treated as a source of the *musicological* doctrine that Rose Subotnik attacks, that musical works are sui generis, ahistorical objects. Trained to concentrate on autonomous "internal" relationships or abstract structures, many theorists assume that all music is an allographic art.

As Kant is one of the founders of traditional aesthetics, jabs at him are to be expected. But he is too often the victim of selective reading. Kant certainly inspired such doctrines; it is less clear that he promoted them. For rather than defend art's autonomy, he defends the autonomy of certain aesthetic judgments.[30] Specifically, pure judgments of taste (of the form "This is beautiful") are autonomous when the viewer makes the judgment in a highly disinterested manner. Furthermore, Kant offers his analysis of such judgments only as a theory of beauty. He never treats it as a theory of *art.*

Looking beyond the best-known sections, Kant contends that artworks must be seen as purposefully produced, interpretable artifacts. Instead of defending art's autonomy, he attempts to steer between the extremes of structureless freedom and the blind rule-following of classicism. Art's limited autonomy lies in its underdetermination by historical and cultural factors. Both the vagueness of its rules and the human capacity for transcending those rules (in works of genius) ensure that art cannot be reduced to mere ideological encoding. Kant gets blamed for the dogmas of autonomy and formalism, but "art for art's sake" is far more the legacy of the nineteenth century. While many today bridle at the elitism of Kant's appeal to genius, it often makes its way into rock by way of the corollary ideas of unique expression and authenticity.

Although not their aim, a weaker sort of autonomy seems compatible with Bourdieu and Fiske. My response to Adorno emphasizes that all music carries culturally emergent properties and meanings. In Bourdieu's terms, rock's decoding demands possession of a certain cultural capital. In short, it is not plausible to contend that "aesthetic experience . . . cannot take account of any entity or fact which is not aesthetically perceivable in the work of art itself."[31] Even the formalist reception of music *as* radically "autonomous" depends on first acquiring specific conventions, taking account of certain facts. To the degree that high culture isolates art from everyday life, it remains a minority enterprise, "beyond" the reach of most people. While many people understand and enjoy both serious and popular musics, different practices are involved in making, disseminating, and listening to these musics. Rock's basic norms can be picked up with far less effort, but they are norms. And surely the practices of the musicians are central indicators of those norms. My frequent appeals to the intentions of individual musicians are not at odds with this. I have never used them to decipher individual works, but only to shed light on regulative assumptions of the rock tradition.

However, the fact that all reception demands cultural capital must be squared with the fact that works of art often survive cultural relocation. We need look no further than the African musical legacies shaping American popular music to see music's capacity to flourish outside its originating institutions. Setting aside doctrines about genius to which it is generally tied, autonomy comes in degrees. It is relative to a work's capacity to transcend its originating social processes. (This is not to say that specific musical properties are transcendent, universal, and timeless, or that we can construct a hierarchy of musics by appeal to such values.) Many impressionist and postimpressionist painters admired and learned from Japanese prints, most notably Vincent van Gogh, who made close copies of several prints by Ando Hiroshige. More recently, the National Resources Defense Council used a modification of Katsushika Hokusai's *The Great Wave off Kanagawa* as the main visual in its clean water campaign. Performance artist Adrian Piper likes to play with the fact that funk music is normally excluded from high-art contexts; bringing it into such contexts *as art,* she calls attention to the cultural barriers normally keeping it out.

Instead of looking for the line separating what is internal from what is external to a musical work, a line implicit in appeals to "art for art's sake" and positivistic musicology, we should examine musical works or practices as falling inside or outside of an established cultural framework. Autonomy can then be described as a work's capacity for survival outside the originating framework. As such, it is not reserved for fine art, and 1950s rock and roll comes off as far more autonomous than Chopin's piano music.

Put another way, music is autonomous if it sustains significance or meaning across cultural barriers. We find an echoing thought in Jameson's proposal that portability is the hallmark of autonomy.[32] Given Jameson's claim that popular songs are copies without originals, they are prime candidates for portability. But portability alone does not explain why rock is more popular than the electronic music of Babbitt or Stockhausen, for which the same claim can be made. Rock's portability is enhanced by its status as our culture's most accessible texts, requiring minimal cultural capital. Questions about a work's original meaning are relatively moot. Tracing meaning to a work's author is similarly frustrated by the collaborative nature of the rock enterprise. In portability we have a degree of musical autonomy that even Fiske must endorse.

Both stronger and weaker senses of autonomy are at work in Amiri Baraka's claim that the blues amounts to "an autonomous music" belonging exclusively to the poorest African Americans. He resents the fact that middle-class musicians, white or black, perform the blues even as its deeper significance is lost on them. Arguing that the music expresses emotions exclusive to "a black man in America" and that disinterested contemplation is at odds with its distinct cultural demands, Baraka challenges white appropriation (in short, both *Beggars Banquet* and the Beastie Boys) as a violent falsification of the music.[33] One sort of autonomy — meanings specific to the originating culture — prevents most whites from participating with full understanding. Aware of white jazz players like Bix Beiderbecke and Benny Goodman, Baraka distinguishes jazz from "legitimate" blues. He argues that jazz is fully "American" (fusing European and African materials). Jazz expresses the "socio-cultural continuum" of black society, including the emerging black middle class, making it "possible for the first time something of the legitimate feeling of Afro-American music to be imitated successfully."[34]

At the same time, Baraka's dismissal of white appropriations of blues makes no sense in the absence of a second kind of autonomy: the music attracts listeners who have little or no grasp of its originating context. Music's capacity to appeal to us in the absence of such information has led John Shepherd to concede that some significance is "purely intrinsic" to musical processes.[35] Music's impact cannot be reduced to other aspects of culture. We grasp central aspects of a culture *by* grasping its music, for musical practices partly constitute a culture. When the cultural demands are minimal, music can offer us a significant entry into at least some aspects of an unfamiliar culture. Baraka underestimates our capacity to respond to music when we know little or nothing of its sociological or historical origins. On his analysis, it should be a mystery that either jazz or rock has any appeal outside the United States.

Bourdieu recognizes this possibility, holding that popular art demands only "naive" mastery. Its basic codes require a minimum of cultural capital or competence, so it is readily consumed by those with minimal formal education. Yet it does not follow that rock *lacks* a distinct field of cultural production. Paradoxically, rock's relative autonomy lies in its hostility to the old ideology of autonomy. The categories and codes used in producing and listening to it reflect twentieth-century commodity culture rather than the drawing rooms, theaters, and salons that nurtured fine art, "pure" taste, and a "high" aesthetic. Because the rock audience rejects conventions of disinterested appreciation, the music avoids association with any *one* social institution. It crosses cultural, class, and even national boundaries with ease. Watching a huge anti-America rally in Baghdad on CNN recently, I noticed an adolescent male in the very front of the crowd sending mixed signals by wearing a Genesis T-shirt. To allow portability, consumer capitalism wears its own mask of ideological neutrality.

In sum, if an aesthetics of rock employs the ideology of art for art's sake, Fiske is correct to attack it as naked cultural hegemony. But the two do not have to go together, and not every appeal to musical autonomy is equally hegemonic. Once we recognize how elastic the concept of autonomy is, we should be surprised to find *no* traces of it in rock ideology and practice. I will conclude by arguing that such traces are particularly strong in rock's celebration of liberal individualism.

Rock Authenticity and Liberalism

The power of rock and roll lies in its ability to bring together and celebrate the production of difference and fun. — Lawrence Grossberg[36]

I think of liberalism as a political order dedicated to people's finding their own way; which is to say, a political order seriously concerned with the actualizing of consent. That is far from an empty idea. But it is not a program; and for that, thanks are due. — Leslie Dunbar[37]

Like the meanings of other concepts, those of philosophical aesthetics depend on their uses. Some years before the idea caught on in cultural studies, Wittgenstein put it this way: "Every sign *by itself* seems dead. *What* gives it life? — In use it is *alive*. Is life breathed into it there? — Or is the *use* its life?" The main source of our failure to understand is, after all, our lack of a clear view "of the use of our words."[38] These ideas are reflected in postmodern theory, particularly Jean-François Lyotard's *La Condition postmoderne* (1979).

In that spirit, let us look at cases where the concepts of art, artist, and authenticity are used to make sense of rock. As recently as 1976, Anita Silvers could plausibly observe that "we neither are sure nor care" whether "Rock Around the Clock" is art. Two decades later, *National Geographic* blandly tells its readers that the members of U2 are not only "artists," but are "in the vanguard of Ireland's artistic ferment."[39] I propose that this shift in attitude represents a vague recognition of rock's association with the project of liberalism. While largely implicit, this theme is particularly strong when these concepts are employed by the rock community.

Reflecting on how her music should be judged, Babes in Toyland's Kat Bjelland says, "Ultimately a record says how I'm feeling."[40] Rooted in the mediation of recording technology, how can a recording "say" how Kat Bjelland feels? It seems fundamentally at odds with the view, endorsed by the rock audience (fans and critics alike), that rock is immediate or "real" in a way that serious music is not. As an explanation of Nirvana's appeal, we are assured that "Cobain's anguished wail offered a refuge of authentic despair."[41] But Kurt Cobain was hardly the first rock musician to be celebrated for authenticity. Reviewing U2's 1983 live recording, *Under a Blood Red Sky*, Dave Marsh assures us that "The cheers are so loud, for once, because these guys are for real — and involved with the real world."[42] However it gets worded, appeals to authenticity are usually allied with appeals to truth and artistry; U2's "nakedness" and concern with truth, "in the sense of honesty," are supposed to be part of their striving "to realise their full artistic potential, that differentiated them from the rest."[43] For over a decade, Greil Marcus has published a "Real Life Rock Top Ten," most recently in *Artforum*. Real life, of course, is to be contrasted with the artificial, the fake, the plastic.

Bud Scoppa, penning liner notes to a CD compilation of Joe Cocker recordings, opines: "I defy anyone to listen to the final cracked syllables of 'You Are So Beautiful' or the gutted . . . shriek in 'Woman to Woman' without being moved by their *utter authenticity*. Joe Cocker wasn't kidding."[44] Yet Scoppa also notes that Cocker "had grown up listening to American blues and soul records," internalizing black American music until he "possessed it as fully as Al Green and Marvin Gaye." Whatever Scoppa's sincerity, this is posturing. As Baraka would be the first to insist, Cocker cannot possess it as fully as Green or Gaye. It remains a secondhand appropriation. But even if Cocker could, what has that to do with authenticity? If Joe Cocker had been "kidding," what would he have been kidding about? Surely his own emotions.

Even if we allow that his appropriations from American blues and soul function as a mere *sign* of authenticity, when his voice cracks it is to be taken as an outer expression of his own ravaged soul.

The unifying thread in these cases is an assumption that the unique individual is basic to authenticity. In a word, liberalism: there is no essential, common good beyond whatever autonomous individuals seek and choose as most worthy for themselves. I am not talking about liberalism in the narrow sense of support for "liberal" policies or giving priority to equality of opportunity over economic justice, but in the classical sense that underlies notions of artistic freedom. Nor do I mean the generally liberal slant of the political causes embraced by rock stars — Amnesty International tours, Live Aid, No Nukes, charity compilations like 1993's *Born to Choose* — so neatly skewered in *Buffy the Vampire Slayer* when Buffy recommends "the environment" as the senior dance theme because Sting wants to save the rain forest.[45] Rock's liberal humanism is of a broader sort, broad enough to encompass Neil Young's endorsement of Ronald Reagan. Today, rock is oppositional largely in its insistence that the music really does matter in an age when reactionary forces are allowed to dominate most public debate about the ideology of art.

If not outright libertarian, liberalism promotes attitudes and political structures that favor independent, self-determining, rational, unique persons. It minimizes constraints on what they think, do, and *feel*.[46] Largely indifferent to gender or economic class as a handle on making sense of life, priority is given to individual self-fulfillment. Such freedom is not without a cost. Terry Eagleton observes that "when the middle class was still an emergent political force, its revolutionary rallying cry of liberty was certainly, among other, finer things, a rationalization of the freedom to exploit."[47] From this perspective, rock's noxious commercial dimension seems a natural outgrowth of its overall ideology. But one of the "finer things" permeating rock is a promotion of individualism. John Street has traced successive versions of it in rock from the late 1960s. Focusing on lyrics and rhetorical gestures, his analysis opposes liberalism and conservatism.[48] He therefore overlooks the possibility that ideas about authenticity transcend those categories as the ideology of art invades rock.

An emphasis on "authentic subjectivity" is intimately associated with conventional or bourgeois musical reception.[49] Its continuing presence in rock conflicts with Jameson's analysis, according to which an important indicator of postmodernism — at least at its shallowest layer of ideology — is a "crisis in the belief in the possibility of authentic self-expression or objective representation."[50] The self-sufficient and centered inner self ("within which things felt are then expressed by projection outward") is now fragmented and dissolved. Jameson treats postmodernism as a residue of the failure of radical left of the 1960s, and as a historical rather than a stylistic category. Postmodernism is the era in which art casts off modernism's impossible demand for authenticity. It represents "the end of the autonomous bourgeois monad or ego or individual." In cultural forms such as music, we are left with pastiche: speech "in a dead language," the random play of the surface of styles.

But rock musicians and critics reveal little or no crisis of belief in the authenticity of self-expression. When Jameson singles out the Talking Heads, Gang of Four, and the Clash, he appears too eager to identify a brief trend as the culmination of an inevitable historical process, as a cog in his larger narrative.[51] Is the proliferation of pastiche something new, or something unrecognized (because its presence did not conform to the prevailing interpretative categories)? While it cannot be argued at length here, I suspect the latter. Rock has embraced pastiche since Elvis transformed a bluegrass tune with rhythm-and-blues stylings for the flip side of his first single, and the Marcells threw the Rodgers and Hart standard "Blue Moon" atop various "bomi-bomp-a-bomp" and "dip-dip-dip" combinations.

More recently, Whitney Houston took a lovely Dolly Parton country ballad and remade it as sheer bombast. While it is not to my taste, I suspect that her overblown take on "I Will Always Love You" dominated the charts in 1993 because the public accepted it as a powerful representation of strong feelings. As Andrew Goodwin points out, popular culture cannot reach a broad audience on the basis of pastiche. Much of the audience will have no idea about the sources and could care less.[52] And they respond to Whitney Houston more readily than to the minimalism, deconstructions of traditional music, and genderless persona that make Laurie Anderson the darling of postmodernism.

Lawrence Grossberg offers a converging argument for incorporating rock into postmodernism. He sees rock's belief in authenticity as nothing but ideology, reflecting "a particular sensibility which negotiated the relation between optimism and cynicism."[53] It was a mode of coping with the alienation and social tensions accompanying the radical changes in Western societies following the Second World War; fans "negotiated real life" by investing in rock. During rock's formative period, rock mattered by providing the measure of its difference from other cultural forms — rock differed absolutely from mere entertainment . . . "Inauthentic rock" is "establishment culture," rock that is dominated by economic interest . . . "Authentic rock" depends on its ability to articulate private but common desires, feelings and experiences into a shared public language.[54]

But Grossberg thinks these oppositions no longer dominate. He sees authenticity as an increasingly irrelevant value in the rock community. It has given way to the postmodern sensibility, dominated by a new cynicism that leaves no room for anything more than an "authentic inauthenticity."

Like Jameson, Grossberg regards postmodernism as a context in which "meaning and affect" are so divided from one another that we cannot see a way to reintegrate them. The affective is now unrepresentable. Terry Eagleton similarly announces that the "dream of authenticity" is now unintelligible. The postmodern sensibility values a "cynical, infinitely regressive self-ironizing."[55] Grossberg thinks "style is celebrated over authenticity" and enjoyment of a style is not taken to imply any investment in its significance.[56] Thus, a musician may create or appropriate a particular musical style (think of Neil Young's style-hopping in the 1980s, or Madonna's yearly reinventions) without commitment to any larger significance. Each change is a temporary investment; style for style's sake? The audience goes along for the semiotic ride, unable to take it seriously as anything that really matters.

Having rejected any sharp divide between entertainment and rock, I do not deny that rock fits many of the broad indicators associated with postmodernism. I am attracted to a good deal of Grossberg's analysis. But we part company on its central point. The ideology of authenticity is not on the wane in the rock community. As long as rock is catholic enough to embrace both Whitney Houston and Courtney Love, we should not assume that either is a truer indication of the current state of rock.

Consider Grossberg's claim that rock's principal strategy for dealing with the postmodernist age is an investment in "youth." Not in chronological age, but in the way the audience "defined themselves by their investment in their affective life" and "by their celebration of their own fantasies and pleasures as a way, if not of giving meaning to life, at least of rebelling against the artificial attempts to impose meaning and order on them."[57] The ability to have fun is rock's primary antidote — escape, not transcendence — to "the terrifying omnipresence of boredom." Daniel Bell similarly argues that hedonism is the primary cultural justification of capitalism and modernism.[58] But these categories are too narrow; intensity of feeling, not mere fun or pleasure, is rock's badge of honor. When the Sex Pistols declared rock dead and bragged of "No Feelings," they did so with all the intensity they could muster. When Courtney Love screams that her baby has been taken away, the grain of her voice signifies raw anguish. Where's the fun?

Little has changed since the 1960s, when rock first became identified with the discovery, revelation, and development of a "real" self. Although he does not link them, Simon Frith's contrast of rock with folk and pop locates rock squarely within liberal ideology: "Rock performance came to mean not pleasing an audience (pop style) nor representing it (folk style) but, rather, displaying desires and feelings rawly, as if to a lover or friend." This only makes sense on the assumption of a true self that warrants special protections:

> there is the sphere of what is called personal liberty — a sphere most difficult to define, but *the arena of the fiercest strife of passion and the deepest feelings* of mankind. At the basis lies liberty of thought — freedom from inquisition into opinions that a man forms in his own mind — the inner citadel where, if anywhere, the individual must rule.[59]

In short, liberalism posits a "unified, coherent individual who is constituted prior to all experience."[60] Literally beyond society's reach, the individual takes priority over politics, for its reality is prior to political and social life. Justifying the change in his writing in 1964, Bob Dylan thus attacked fellow troubadour Phil Ochs with the challenge, "The stuff you're writing is bullshit, because politics is bullshit. It's all unreal. The only thing that's real is inside you."[61]

Frith cites Janis Joplin as a prime example of rock performance for her ability to tap into her emotions ("which touched on self-loathing"), convincing the audience that "she was holding nothing back."[62] The same theme surfaces in Jim Morrison's division of the world into friends and everyone else: "If I had an axe I'd kill everyone . . . except my friends." A friend, however, "is someone who lets you have total freedom to be yourself."[63] Appeals to freedom run through Morrison's interviews; he regularly invokes the true self that must be found and let loose. Anyone who inhibits or restricts this true self is a tyrant, a "puritan," or emotionally dead.

However, such ideas did not die with Joplin and Morrison. Despite open disdain for her hippie upbringing, Courtney Love is not far removed from the rock practices and ideology informing their careers. Love certainly regards her personal identity or core self as a brute fact, fundamentally private unless revealed in the music. Neither socially embedded nor constructed, it is prior to gender politics, fundamentally at odds with her baby-doll dresses and Lolita image. While she thus justifies this visual play as feminist irony, the only trace of irony in her music is her cover version of Joni Mitchell's "Both Sides Now." Explaining her musical aims, she implicitly appeals to artistic autonomy: she will not release recordings made with husband Kurt Cobain because music is something "I have to do . . . on my own."[64] She sounds very much like the Victorian aesthete Walter Pater when she summarizes her relationship with Cobain, observing that there is no point to life "if you don't have heights of passion, moments of intensity and beauty." Her main criticism of Hole's *Live Through This* (1994)? "The purity was not completely there."[65]

Although Sonic Youth has a sterling pedigree in indie and alternative rock, Thurston Moore still dreams of emotional authenticity: "We want to be more conscious of the [music's] emotive value. We've always wanted to come across as pure in that way. Most of the times I see reviews, especially by younger writers, and they'll think we're being cynical. That scares me. That's one artistic temperament that I don't feel has any real place in music." When Moore says the four members of Sonic Youth "want this music to be poetic," it is with no trace of regressive self-ironizing.[66]

Moore may be caught up in a web of conflicting cultural norms, but what interests me is his identification of the *aspect* of the music that is authentic or inauthentic. The taint of inauthenticity appears when musicians present emotions that do not arise from their own lives. In previous chapters I argued that rock is inauthentic in several other ways: it celebrates live performance over studio work, its Romantic mythology disdains rock's commercial side, and its myth of primitivism (the "jungle") denies the importance of craft. But Moore's concern is with feelings. I have argued that many of rock's central features — its use of technology and its handling of rhythm, noise, timbre, texture — are primarily directed at the expression of emotion. No emotion seems to be beyond the pale. But faked emotion is. We are back to Scoppa's analysis of Joe Cocker.

Me'Shell NdegéOcello knows that her identity as a black female bisexual presents three strong obstacles to popular success. And while her lyrics insightfully address issues of hegemony, she falls back on the rhetoric of fine art when fans take her to hold antiwhite views: "I just made a record. I expressed myself. It's just like a painting. *It's a work of art* that deals with a certain period of my life. Some of the view on that album I don't even have anymore."[67] Pressed about his sexual orientation, Bob Mould denies that he has any duty to "come out and represent the gay community."[68] Appealing to the public/private dichotomy, he ties his music to the former, telling gays: "I'm not your spokesperson, because I don't know what you're about. I'm a person, a human being. I'm an artist. I write songs. . . . I've got nothing to hide, but there are some things that are mine and only mine." Mould insists that he should be viewed simply as "a human being" and that "some things belong *just to me.*"

When Mould repudiates gay activism by insisting "I'm an artist," or NdegéOcello protects herself by saying "it's a work of art," the underlying logic is thoroughly bourgeois. There is no indication that either has any specific doctrine in mind; they are not, so far as I can tell, burdened with Romanticism or formalism. What is most striking is their matter-of-fact manner, as if nothing could be more natural than to suppose that rock musicians are artists. Whatever Mould or Ndegé-Ocello thinks it means to be an artist, or Thurston Moore means by "artistic temperament," they certainly include the pursuit of authentic expression, and protection to do so with complete freedom.

So I mistrust any view that says "the" postmodern sensibility has replaced the ideology of authenticity. I cannot get the former to square with recent events. Kurt Cobain pens a note, loads a shotgun, and takes his life. I was traveling when the news of his suicide broke. I hadn't heard about it yet and entered a Tower Records store in San Jose, immediately sensing that something was going on. They were playing *In Utero* and the mood was grim. Nobody had told them that they didn't feel the music anymore. Here, the postmodern sensibility looked like a pose used to hide how much was really invested in the music. Nobody wanted to take "Rape Me" or "All Apologies" as a constructed fantasy any longer. By the same token, Cobain himself never seemed to take rock in the postmodern spirit. He was serious when he dismissed Pearl Jam as "false music."[69] Shortly before his suicide, Nirvana's biographer commented, "People talk about Kurt Cobain's wonderful sense of irony. There isn't any irony."[70]

Still, rock remains at enough remove from high culture to invite charges of pretension when rock musicians are called artists. Praising Paul Simon, Lorne Michaels observes, "There's something about him that demands that his work be truthful . . . I hate to use the 'A' word about him but it's why he's an artist."[71] Michaels wants to have it both ways, conferring the honorific mantle of artist on a rock musician while avoiding the elitism of the high-art tradition. As the Replacements unwound, Paul Westerberg reflected on the problem of his cultural location in rock: "It's been hard for me to do, but I've come to grips with the fact that I'm an artist. For years I pretended I wasn't. I pretended I was a punk, . . . a rocker, . . . a drunk, and a hoodlum."[72] Perversely, the career postmortem by critics and groundswell of grief following Kurt Cobain's suicide is saturated with claims that he was an artist: *Spin* praised his "artistic courage" in the same issue that named Smashing Pumpkins as "artist of the year."[73]

In conclusion, several very unfashionable themes cluster at the heart of an aesthetics of rock. As a cultural space in which the concept of "art" burrows into popular culture, rock seems to be a bastion of Enlightenment assumptions about the self. *Artistic* activity is offered as a strategy for surviving in commodified culture. When rock songs proclaim that rock will never die, this now looks less like a claim about the enduring attraction of the music and more like an expression of commitment to a liberal ideology at odds with the main themes of postmodernism. Rock authenticity posits an absolute dichotomy between the inner and the outer, between the true self and the socially constructed mask. If rock sets itself an impossible task, the resulting tensions supply a large part of rock's power.

These observations are not offered as a vindication of either philosophical aesthetics or rock music. They are offered as an observation that the two share a common ideological commitment. Recognizing liberalism as an ideology regulating rock, we are no longer impelled to search for some real dividing line between rock and pop, entertainment and art, authenticity and insincerity, and the marginal and the commercial. The *idea* that rock matters more than traditional culture is enough to empower many fans. Twenty-five years ago the protagonist of Lou Reed's "Rock and Roll" rejected her parent's material comforts and felt that her life was saved by rock and roll. It does not follow that she abandoned bourgeois attitudes. Instead, she was moved by the freshness with which rock gives public expression to their underlying values. Rock's continued vitality depends on the continuing power of an ideological abstraction. In its turn, the project of liberalism is refreshed with new modes of expression.

Notes

Preface

1 John A. Passmore, "The Dreariness of Aesthetics," *Mind* 60 (1951), pp. 318–35.

2 Paul Williams, *Bob Dylan: Performing Artist, The Middle Years 1974–1986* (Novato, Calif.: Underwood-Miller, 1992), p. 295.

3 Paul Williams, *Performing Artist: The Music of Bob Dylan*, vol. 1: 1960–1973 (Novato, Calif.: Underwood-Miller, 1990), p. 125.

4 Ibid., p. 174.

5 George Lipsitz, *Time Passages: Collective Memory and American Popular Music* (Minneapolis: University of Minnesota Press, 1990), p. 99. Another treatment of this theme is Jeremy J. Beadle, *Will Pop Eat Itself?* (London and Boston: Faber and Faber, 1993).

6 Ibid., pp. 109–110 (emphasis added).

7 Ibid., pp. 261–62.

8 Ibid., p. 14.

9 Similarly, Philip Ennis refers to the Tornadoes' instrumental single "Telstar" as a song, and says that the Dominoes' "Sixty Minute Man" was significant because "the song was a direct crossover to pop" and not a "cover record." In both cases he means the recording. Philip H. Ennis, *The Seventh Stream: The Emergence of Rocknroll in American Popular Music* (Hanover and London: Wesleyan University Press, 1992), pp. 216 and 418.

10 Ennis, *The Seventh Stream*, pp. 313 and 362.

11 Ibid., p. 315.

12 Deena Weinstein, *Heavy Metal: A Cultural Sociology* (New York: Lexington Books, 1991), pp. 6–7.

13 Pierre Bourdieu, *The Field of Cultural Production: Essays on Art and Literature*, ed. Randal Johnson (New York: Columbia University Press, 1993).

14 Dick Hebdige, *Subculture: The Meaning of Style* (London and New York: Methuen, 1979).

15 Charles Hamm, *Music in the New World* (New York and London: W. W. Norton, 1983), p. 645 (emphasis added).

16 Leonard B. Meyer, "Toward a Theory of Style," in *The Concept of Style*, ed.

Berel Lang, expanded ed. (Ithaca and London: Cornell University Press, 1987), p. 21.

17 Charles Hamm, *Yesterdays: Popular Song in America* (New York and London: W. W. Norton, 1979), pp. 441–42.

18 Allan F. Moore, *Rock: The Primary Text* (Buckingham and Philadelphia: Open University Press, 1993), p. 3.

19 Ludwig Wittgenstein, *Lectures and Conversations on Aesthetics, Psychology and Religious Belief* (Berkeley and Los Angeles: University of California Press, 1967), p. 8.

20 Ibid., p. 9.

21 Ibid., p. 7.

22 The perils of ahistorical analyses of popular music are emphasized by Lipsitz, *Time Passages,* chapter 5.

1   *That Wild, Thin Mercury Sound: Ontology*

1 Quoted by David Sheff, *The Playboy Interviews with John Lennon & Yoko Ono* (New York: Berkley Books, 1981), p. 141.

2 Robert B. Ray, "Tracking," *South Atlantic Quarterly* 90 (Winter 1991), p. 781; reprinted in Anthony DeCurtis, ed., *Present Tense* (Durham: Duke University Press, 1992).

3 Charles Hamm, *Yesterdays: Popular Song in America* (New York and London: W. W. Norton, 1979).

4 Allan Bloom, *The Closing of the American Mind* (New York: Simon and Schuster, 1987), pp. 68–81.

5 Kathleen Marie Higgins, *The Music of Our Lives* (Philadelphia: Temple University Press, 1990), pp. 187–88.

6 For an overview of various uses of "rock" and "rock and roll" between 1922 and 1955, see Nick Tosches, *Unsung Heroes of Rock 'n' Roll* (New York: Harmony Books, 1991), pp. 6–9.

7 Jann Wenner, *Lennon Remembers* (San Francisco: Straight Arrow Books, 1971), pp. 42 and 30, respectively; interview conducted in December 1970 and January 1971.

8 Bob Dylan quoted in Denise Worrell, "It's All Right in Front," *Time,* November 25, 1985, p. 123.

9 Quoted in Paul Vincent, "Van Morrison: The Mystic & His Music," *BAM,* 12 February 1982, p. 20.

10 Quoted in Joe Smith, "Van Morrison," in *Off The Record* (New York: Warner Books, 1988), p. 272.

11 Nelson Goodman, *Ways of Worldmaking* (Indianapolis: Hackett, 1978), pp. 57–70.

12 Quoted by Jenny Boyd with Holly George-Warren, *Musicians in Tune* (New York: Fireside/Simon & Schuster, 1992), p. 114. Richards calls it "pompous" to take credit for *writing* music: "Music is everywhere; all you've got to do is pick it up."

13 Tosches, *Unsung Heroes of Rock 'n' Roll,* pp. 2–5.

14 Jonathan Cott, "Leonard Bernstein," *Rolling Stone,* 29 November 1990, p. 79.

15 Mick Jagger, quoted in Jonathan Cott and Sue Clark, "Mick Jagger," *The Rolling Stone Interviews,* ed. the Editors of Rolling Stone (New York: Straight Arrow, 1971), p. 160; interview originally published 1968.

16 David Hatch and Stephen Millward, *From Blues to Rock* (Manchester and New York: Manchester University Press, 1987), pp. 99–100; Jagger quotation originally from an interview in *Jazz News.*

17 Jon Landau, "Rock and Roll Music," *Rolling Stone,* 1 April 1971, p. 44.

18 An illustration of Christgau's point is the rock cliché that the Velvet Underground's debut album, *Velvet Underground* (1967), initially sold around 10,000 copies, but that every person who bought a copy was inspired to start a band.

19 Quoted by Geoffrey Stokes, *The Beatles* (New York: Rolling Stone Press, 1980), p. 151.

20 Joseph Gelmis, "Show Sold Out; But Did Dylan?" in *Bob Dylan: A Retrospective,* ed. Craig McGregor (New York: William Morrow, 1972), pp. 80–81.

21 For an overview of the folk movement and its mystique, see Geoffrey Stokes, "Roll Over, Frankie Avalon," in *Rock of Ages: The Rolling Stone History of Rock & Roll,* Ed Ward, Geoffrey Stokes, Ken Tucker (New York: Summit Books/Rolling Stone Press, 1986), pp. 249–76.

22 "Letters to *Sing Out!*" *Bob Dylan: A Retrospective,* p. 117.

23 The show was actually at the Free Trade Hall, Manchester, England, 17 May 1966; there are published rumors that this famous bootleg will be released by Columbia/Sony as part of the Dylan *Bootleg Series.*

24 Paul Nelson, "Newport Folk Festival," *Bob Dylan: A Retrospective,* p. 73.

25 Paul Nelson, "Bob Dylan: Another View," *Bob Dylan: A Retrospective,* p. 106. Nelson's review of *Highway 61 Revisited* was written for *Sing Out!* February 1966. In March 1966, the *Berkeley Barb* was using "rock" retroactively, to cover 1950s rock and roll; see Hamm, *Yesterdays,* p. 425.

26 Paul Williams, *Outlaw Blues* (New York: E. P. Dutton, 1969), p. 93. The use of "rock" had its precedents, but what is important here is that its early uses referred to sex or dancing, while the years 1965–67 shifted the meaning to a type of music which was not always offered as dance music. In 1949, Roy Brown recorded "Good Rockin' Tonight," and in 1951, Gunther Carr dropped a syllable and recorded "We're Gonna Rock." Bill Haley's Comets split off to become the Jodimars and recorded "Let's All Rock Together" in 1956; in 1957, Elvis Presley had a hit with "Jailhouse Rock"; and in 1959, Johnny and the Hurricanes had a number-five hit with "Red River Rock," an instrumental version of the traditional "Red River Valley." All of these uses can be understood as referring to dancing; the sexual connotation is indirect.

27 Two paragraphs of the review are quoted in Derek Taylor, *It Was Twenty Years Ago Today* (New York: Fireside Books, 1987), p. 80. The original review ran in *Jazz and Pop* (August 1967).

28 Robert Christgau, "Rock Lyrics Are Poetry (Maybe)," in *The Age of Rock,* ed. Jonathan Eisen (New York: Vintage Books, 1969), p. 231.

29 One of the better analyses of rock as recent music of youth culture is Simon Frith, *Sound Effects* (New York: Pantheon, 1981).

30 See Geoffrey Stokes, "Roll Over, Frankie Avalon," pp. 309–10. Al Kooper's claim that his first attempt on organ is "the one they used on the record" is called into doubt by the subsequent release of a practice fragment of that song on Dylan's *The Bootleg Series, Vol. 2*.

31 Quoted by various sources, including Paul Williams, *Performing Artist: The Music of Bob Dylan*, vol. 1 (Novato, Calif.: Underwood-Miller, 1990), pp. 137–38; original source is Ron Rosenbaum's *Playboy* interview, January 1978.

32 Greil Marcus, "Treasure Island," *Stranded* (New York: Alfred A. Knopf, 1979), p. 267.

33 Marcus, *Stranded*, p. 257. George Harrison has said of the Beatles: "our peak for playing live was in Hamburg. . . . [we] still played mainly old rock 'n' roll tunes." Quoted in Geoffrey Giuliano, *Dark Horse* (New York: Plume/Penguin, 1990), p. 30.

34 See Mark Lewisohn, *The Beatles: Recording Sessions* (New York: Harmony Books, 1988), p. 59.

35 Mark Ribowsky, *He's a Rebel* (New York: E. P. Dutton, 1989), p. 4.

36 Experiments in *musique concrète* and electronic music composed on magnetic tape were a precedent for (and sometimes an influence on) the new recording aesthetic, and so rock might be considered the popular form of a broader category.

37 Recollection of D. J. Fontana in Max Weinberg with Robert Santelli, *The Big Beat* (New York: Billboard Books, 1984), p. 113. Preparing for their 1994–95 tour, the Rolling Stones rehearsed by playing over their earlier recordings.

38 Dave Marsh, *Elvis* (New York: Rolling Stone Press, 1982), p. 28. There's some hyperbole here. In popular music, Les Paul had already made significant use of multitrack recording and had altered the speed of the recording tape to create guitar solos that were too fast to actually perform.

39 John Lennon says of Presley's later years: "Even if he *wasn't* fat and drugged, he couldn't have been that guy who sang 'That's All Right' again. A friend of mine . . . went to see him. I wouldn't go, because I knew it wasn't him." In other words, the vocalist of the Sun sessions was fixed on the Sun tapes, unique to a time and place, and Presley's live appearances counted as an entirely different artist ("it wasn't him"). Quoted in Sheff, *Playboy Interviews*, p. 98.

40 Peter Guralnick, "Elvis Presley," *The Rolling Stone Illustrated History of Rock & Roll*, ed. Jim Miller (New York: Random House/Rolling Stone Press, 1980), p. 28.

41 Peter Guralnick, "Rockabilly," *Rolling Stone Illustrated History of Rock & Roll*, p. 62. Phillips actually used a tape delay.

42 Greil Marcus, *Mystery Train* (New York: E. P. Dutton, 1976), p. 168.

43 Robert B. Ray, "Tracking," p. 781.

44 Diana Clapton, *Lou Reed and the Velvet Underground* (New York: Proteus Books, 1982), p. 30.

45 Stephen Holden, "Surrealistic Jokes for L.A. Cowpokes" (Review of *Warren Zevon*), *Rolling Stone*, 15 July 1976, p. 63.

46 Kurt Loder, "Songs Lasting Three Minutes — and Forever," *Rolling Stone*, 28 November 1991, p. 94. Those who know the vinyl format of the Rolling

Stones' *Beggars Banquet* often find the clarity and enhanced separation of the instruments in the digital remix to be a defect.

47 Greil Marcus, "Springsteen's Thousand & One American Nights," *Rolling Stone,* 9 October 1975, p. 77. The Dylan comparison is insightful. Springsteen has said that Dylan's sound on *Highway 61* was its primary appeal: "The main thing I dug . . . was the *sound*" (quoted by Williams, *Performing Artist,* p. 159).

48 Jim Curtis, *Rock Eras* (Bowling Green: Bowling Green State University Popular Press, 1987), p. 186.

49 Stephen Davies, "I have finished today another new concerto . . . ," *Journal of Aesthetic Education* 25 (1991), p. 139.

50 See Roman Ingarden, "Untersuchungen zur Ontologie der Kunst (The Musical Work)," in Edward A. Lippman, ed., *Musical Aesthetics: A Historical Reader,* vol. 3: The Twentieth Century (New York: Pendragon Press, 1985), p. 371.

51 Ibid., p. 372. See also Nicholas Wolterstorff, *Works and Worlds of Art* (Oxford: Clarendon Press, 1980), p. 79. This proposal is challenged in chapter 2.

52 Stephen Davies, "The Ontology of Musical Works and the Authenticity of Their Performances," *Noûs* 25 (1991), p. 37. Following Jerrold Levinson, it seems more appropriate to say that they are regarded as pure tonal structures.

53 See Stephen Davies, "I have finished today . . . ," p. 140.

54 Stephen Davies, "Violins or Viols? — A Reason to Fret," *Journal of Aesthetics and Art Criticism* 48 (1990), p. 148, emphasis added.

55 Davies, "The Ontology of Musical Works," p. 31; he notes exceptions to this rule of thumb.

56 "Profiled," on Led Zeppelin, *Remasters,* disc 3 (Atlantic Records, 1992).

57 This objection was brought to my attention by Nikolas Pappas.

58 Neil Young, "The CD and the Damage Done," *Harper's Magazine,* July 1992, p. 23. Reprint of an editorial that originally appeared in *Guitar Player,* May 1992. Young's diatribe seems premature in light of his subsequent decision to record digitally; e.g., *Weld* (1991) and *Harvest Moon* (1992). Yet in 1993 he continued to dismiss digital sound; see Mark Rowland, "Neil Young Meets Peter Buck," *Musician* 174 (April 1993), p. 52.

59 John Passmore, *Serious Art* (La Salle, Ill.: Open Court, 1991), p. 65.

60 See Jerrold Levinson, "Colourization Ill-Defended," *British Journal of Aesthetics* 30 (1990), pp. 62–67. Levinson argues that, however badly done, colorized films are not forgeries of the work.

61 Passmore, *Serious Art,* p. 59.

62 See Zappa's explanation in Josef Woodard, "Frank Zappa," *Musician* 96 (October 1986), p. 28.

63 Rose R. Subotnik, "On Grounding Chopin," in Richard Leppert and Susan McClary, eds., *Music and Society: The Politics of Composition, Performance and Reception* (Cambridge: Cambridge University Press, 1987), pp. 105–113, and *Developing Variations: Style and Ideology in Western Music* (Minneapolis: University of Minnesota Press, 1992), chapter 1.

64 Nelson Goodman, *Languages of Art* (Indianapolis: Hackett, 1976), pp. 112–13. Goodman allows that musical performances (but not works) can be fakes through misattribution.

65 Jerrold Levinson disputes Goodman's analysis of autographic/allographic: musical works are autographic "by Goodman's yardstick," but allographic on Levinson's revised analysis. See Levinson, *Music, Art, & Metaphysics* (Ithaca: Cornell University Press, 1990), chapters 5 and 10, pp. 101 and 250.

66 Levinson, *Music, Art, & Metaphysics*, pp. 89–106.

67 Ibid., p. 101.

68 Ibid., p. 101.

69 Goodman, *Languages of Art*, p. 113 n.

70 As discussed in chapter 2, the jazz tradition retains an expectation that recordings will function as transparent windows on specific performances.

71 In rock music, many "live" recordings are anything but the duplication of particular performances. Crosby, Stills, Nash and Young retouched vocal tracks of their Woodstock performance. Grateful Dead fans report that "live" Dead albums sometimes falsify the originating performances; again, comparison of the albums with tapes from radio broadcasts reveal that instruments and solos are mixed out and replaced. Tapes of Bruce Springsteen's local radio broadcast from the Roxy in Los Angeles in 1978 demonstrate that at least one track on his *Live/1975–85*, "Backstreets," receives a drastic edit.

72 Goodman, *Languages of Art*, p. 119.

73 Such a tape will be a referential forgery; see Levinson, *Music, Art, & Metaphysics*, p. 103.

2 *I'll Be Your Mirror: Recording and Representing*

1 Sam Morgenstern, *Composers on Music* (New York: Pantheon, 1956), p. 513.

2 John Berger, "Appearances," in John Berger and Jean Mohr, *Another Way of Telling* (New York: Pantheon, 1982), p. 95.

3 Reebee Garofalo, "Understanding Mega-Events," in Reebee Garofalo, ed., *Rockin' the Boat: Mass Music & Mass Movements* (Boston: South End Press, 1992), p. 24.

4 Carl Belz, *The Story of Rock*, 2d ed. (Oxford and New York: Oxford University Press, 1972), p. viii, emphasis added. I disagree with Belz's thesis that rock is a form of folk art; see chapter 7.

5 James Goodfriend, quoted in *The Phonograph and Our Musical Life*, Proceedings of a Centennial Conference 7–10 December 1977, ed. H. Wiley Hitchcock (New York: Institute for Studies in American Music, 1980), p. 12.

6 See Phillip H. Ennis, *The Seventh Stream: The Emergence of Rocknroll in American Popular Music* (Hanover and London: Wesleyan University Press, 1992); Steve Chapple and Reebee Garofalo, *Rock 'n' Roll Is Here to Pay: The History and Politics of the Music Industry* (Chicago: Nelson-Hall, 1977); and Russell Sanjek and David Sanjek, *American Popular Music Business in the 20th Century* (New York: Oxford University Press, 1991).

7 Simon Frith, "Popular Music 1950–1980," *Making Music*, ed. George Martin (New York: William Morrow, 1983), p. 47. As Jacques Attali observes, "emphasis was placed on *preservation*, not mass *replication*." Attali, *Noise: The Political Economy of Music* (Minneapolis: University of Minnesota Press, 1985), p. 91.

8 Quoted in Ivo Supicic, *Music in Society: A Guide to the Sociology of Music,* Sociology of Music, no. 4 (Stuyvesant, N.Y.: Pendragon Press, 1987), p. 186.

9 See, for instance, André Bazin, *What Is Cinema?*, vol. 1, trans. H. Gray (Berkeley: University of California Press, 1967), and an analysis of Bazin in Noël Carroll, *Philosophical Problems of Classical Film Theory* (Princeton: Princeton University Press, 1988), pp. 93–171. This is not John Fiske's sense of the term, where "the essence of realism is that it reproduces reality in such a form as to make it easily understandable" (John Fiske, *Television Culture* [London and New York: Methuen, 1987], p. 24).

10 William Moylan, *The Art of Recording: The Creative Resources of Music Production and Audio* (New York: Van Nostrand Reinhold, 1992), p. 81 (emphasis added).

11 Susan Sontag, *On Photography* (New York: Farrar, Straus and Giroux, 1978), p. 158. The same position is advanced by Stanley Cavell, *The World Viewed* (New York: Viking, 1971), pp. 23–24. Cavell, in turn, acknowledges Bazin.

12 Roger Scruton, "Photography and Representation," *The Aesthetic Understanding* (London and New York: Methuen, 1983), p. 105. See William L. King, "Scruton and Reasons for Looking at Photographs," *British Journal of Aesthetics* 23 (1992), pp. 258–65.

13 Scruton, *The Aesthetic Understanding*, p. 122.

14 Ibid., p. 118, see also pp. 119–26. Later, I take issue with his view that interest in a recording is due to interest in its subject while interest in a representation is due to interest in how it represents its subject.

15 Quoted in Jann Wenner, "Peter Townshend," in *The Rolling Stone Interviews* (New York: Paperback Library, 1971), p. 97; original interview conducted 1968.

16 Quoted in Greil Marcus, *Lipstick Traces* (Cambridge, Mass.: Harvard University Press, 1989), p. 1, emphasis added; no source provided by Marcus.

17 Paul Hernadi, "Reconceiving Notation and Performance," *Journal of Aesthetic Education* 25 (1991), p. 53, emphasis deleted. See also Nicholas Wolterstorff, *Works and Worlds of Art* (Oxford: Clarendon Press, 1980), p. 79.

18 Hernadi, pp. 54–55.

19 Lydia Goehr, *The Imaginary Museum of Musical Works* (Oxford: Oxford University Press, 1992), pp. 266–67.

20 Ibid., pp. 245–57. The ideological dimension of this issue is treated at greater length in my closing chapter.

21 Roman Ingarden, *The Work of Music and the Problem of Its Identity*, trans. Adam Czerniawski (Berkeley and Los Angeles: University of California Press, 1986), p. 157, emphasis added.

22 Roland Barthes, *Camera Lucida*, trans. Richard Howard (New York: Hill and Wang, 1981), p. 82.

23 Ibid., pp. 104–14. Page 112 is particularly germane. See William Moylan, *The Art of Recording*, chapter 4. Moylan contends that "the recording process can capture reality" and "can be transparent in documenting a performance" (pp. 77 and 82); Moylan agrees that "the recording aesthetic is determined by the relationship of the recording to the live listening experience" (p. 88). Recordings

typically aim at fixing "perfect" or "definitive" performances "of a work," so many people have unrealistic expectations about live performance.

24 This assumption is challenged by John Tagg, *The Burden of Representation* (Amherst: University of Massachusetts Press, 1988).

25 Arthur Danto, *The Transfiguration of the Commonplace* (Cambridge, Mass.: Harvard University Press, 1981), pp. 149–60.

26 Roland Barthes, *Writing Degree Zero*, trans. Annette Lavers and Colin Smith (New York: Hill & Wang, 1968), p. 64.

27 Aaron Copland, *Music and Imagination* (Cambridge, Mass.: Harvard University Press, 1952), pp. 25 and 29.

28 According to Pierre Bourdieu, one then responds with the "codes from everyday life." Pierre Bourdieu, "A Sociological Theory of Art Perception," *The Field of Cultural Production* (New York: Columbia University Press, 1993); see also P. Bourdieu and Alain Darbel with Dominique Schnapper, *The Love of Art: European Museums and Their Public* (Stanford: Stanford University Press, 1990), and P. Bourdieu, *Distinction: A Social Critique of the Judgement of Taste* (Cambridge, Mass.: Harvard University Press, 1984).

29 See Mike Weaver, *Julia Margaret Cameron: 1815–1879* (Boston: Little, Brown and Company, 1984), p. 97; six photos are reproduced in *The Camera*, ed. Time-Life Books (New York: Time-Life, 1970), pp. 192–93.

30 Scruton, *The Aesthetic Understanding*, p. 102; see also pp. 112–13.

31 Ibid., pp. 124–25.

32 Quoted by Denise Worrell, "It's All Right in Front," *Time*, 25 November 1985, p. 123.

33 Quoted in Geoff Brown, "Eno Where It's At," *Melody Maker* 48 (10 November 1973), p. 41.

34 John Lennon criticized George Harrison for the latter's copyright problems with "My Sweet Lord," which was ruled to unknowingly plagiarize the earlier song "He's So Fine." Lennon revealed that he often wrote new songs by recording old songs, then changing the words and melody in the process sufficiently to count as a new song. The boxes of work tapes left behind after his assassination reveal that his music making would begin with a familiar song, only to become a different song by a slow transformation. Yet it was only by reference to the "new" song, at the end of the process, that the intermediate music making can be regarded as instantiations of that song rather than the one which started the process. Ironically, this is what Harrison did in plagiarizing "He's So Fine." Harrison had taken a different song and was in the process of rewriting it by trial and error when he inadvertently lapsed into copying "He's So Fine."

35 See Jerrold Levinson, "Song and Music Drama," in *What Is Music?* ed. Philip Alperson (New York: Haven, 1988), pp. 283–301.

36 Quoted in Mark Rowland, "Glyn Johns Meets Don Was," *Musician* 190 (August 1994), p. 52.

37 A stubborn Platonist who holds that composers only discover preexisting norm-kinds can interpret these cases accordingly, but the consequence is the same; tape editing replaces notational stipulation as the composition act by which the composer deserves credit for composing one work rather than another.

38 Quoted in Tony Scherman, "World Party: Greatness or Bust," *Musician* 175 (May 1993), p. 68.

39 Brian Eno, excerpted by Howard Mandel, "Pro Session: The Studio as Compositional Tool — Part II," *Down Beat* 50 (August 1983), p. 51. Similarly, Eno's "No One Receiving" and "M386" share a common instrumental track.

40 Quoted in Kurt Loder, *Bat Chain Puller* (New York: St. Martin's Press, 1990), p. 206; Eno interviewed in 1981. For a description of the process involved in the making of *Achtung Baby*, see Brian Eno, "Bringing Up Baby," *Rolling Stone*, 28 November 1991, pp. 42–50 and 116.

41 For arguments that the presence of a musical work is not essential in musical performance, see Nicholas Wolterstorff, "The Work of Making a Work of Music," in *What Is Music?*, ed. Philip Alperson (New York: Haven, 1988), p. 118, and Paul Thom, *For an Audience: A Philosophy of the Performing Arts* (Philadelphia: Temple University Press, 1993).

42 I choose this example because it is an instrumental, so there is no complicating issue of lyrics introducing an additional subject matter.

43 I agree with T. J. Diffey that any pieces "that have not been submitted to public scrutiny are not works of art." At least not yet; they may be later, through submission for scrutiny. Works not yet submitted are essentially unfinished, if only because the artist may yet change important features, in which case a *different* work may emerge. See Diffey, *The Republic of Art and Other Essays,* New Studies in Aesthetics, vol. 6 (New York: Peter Lang, 1991), p. 41. This squares with Mikhail Bakhtin's idea that a work of art is fundamentally *addressed;* see Bakhtin, "The Problem of the Text in Linguistics, Philology and the Human Sciences," in *Speech Genres and Other Late Essays,* ed. Caryl Emerson and Michael Holquist (Austin: University of Texas Press, 1986).

44 See Moylan, *The Art of Recording,* chapter 4, and Allan F. Moore, *Rock: The Primary Text,* Popular Music in Britain (Buckingham and Philadelphia: Open University Press, 1993), pp. 105–110. This interpretation is at odds with that of William Webster, "A Theory of the Compositional Work of Music," *Journal of Aesthetics and Art Criticism* 33 (1974), pp. 59–66. Webster believes that such recordings directly instantiate musical works, whereas I believe that they do so indirectly, by representing performances.

45 George Martin, *All You Need Is Ears* (New York: St. Martin's Press, 1979), pp. 76–77.

46 Roger Sessions, *The Musical Experience of Composer, Performer and Listener* (Princeton: Princeton University Press, 1950), p. 70. See also Roger Sessions, *Questions About Music* (New York: W. W. Norton, 1970), pp. 51–52.

47 Quoted in James Hunter, "John Fogerty Meets Duane Eddy," *Musician* 157 (November 1991), p. 52.

48 Ibid., p. 59. To ensure that the sound will be right, both Fogerty and Dr. Dre test work in progress by playing tapes of different mixes in their cars. Where Fogerty uses ordinary car speakers, Dr. Dre uses a bass-heavy system.

49 Scruton, *The Aesthetic Understanding,* p. 117.

50 Walter Benjamin, "The Work of Art in the Age of Mechanical Reproduction," in *Illuminations,* ed. Hannah Arendt (New York: Harcourt Brace, 1968), p. 236.

51 Leonard B. Meyer, "On Rehearing Music," *Music, the Arts, and Ideas* (Chicago and London: University of Chicago Press, 1967), p. 49. I deal with other versions of this accusation, by Adorno and Attali, in chapter 6.

52 See John Shepherd, *Music as Social Text* (Cambridge: Polity Press, 1991), p. 164. Originally "Music and Male Hegemony," in Richard Leppert and Susan McClary, eds., *Music and Society: The Politics of Composition, Performance and Reception* (Cambridge: Cambridge University Press, 1987), p. 163.

53 Alan Durant, *Conditions of Music* (Albany: State University of New York Press, 1984), p. 113.

54 Edmund Gurney, *The Power of Sound* (New York: Basic Books, 1966, reprint of London: 1880), p. 307. For a summary and critique of Gurney, see Malcolm Budd, *Music and the Emotions* (London and Boston: Routledge & Kegan Paul, 1985), chapter 4.

55 Gurney, *The Power of Sound*, pp. 296–97.

56 Shepherd, *Music as Social Text*, pp. 159–64.

57 See Diana Raffman, *Language, Music, and Mind* (Cambridge, Mass. and London: MIT Press, 1993), chapters 4 and 5. Raffman emphasizes the perception of ineffable nuances of pitch, timing, and speed "around the structural frame of the piece" (p. 91). She occasionally mentions nuance of timbre, but assigns it no particular communicative role. There may be individuals with unusually acute memories of musical nuance, but such individuals do not challenge my argument, since their abilities are hardly normative for the rest of us.

58 Robert G. Crowder, "Auditory Memory," in *Thinking in Sound: The Cognitive Psychology of Human Audition,* ed. S. McAdams and E. Bigand (Oxford University Press, 1993), p. 138; see pp. 134–40.

59 Raffman, *Language, Music, and Mind*, p. 96.

60 Quoted by Greil Marcus, "Who Put the Bomp in the Bomp-De-Bomp De-Bomp?" in *Rock and Roll Will Stand*, ed. Greil Marcus (Boston: Beacon Press, 1969), pp. 11–12.

61 Jon Landau, *It's Too Late to Stop Now* (San Francisco: Straight Arrow Books, 1972), p. 68.

62 Quoted in Rob Bowman, booklet notes for *The Complete Stax/Volt Singles: 1959–1968* (Atlantic Recording Corporation, 1991), p. 31.

63 John Mowitt, "The Sound of Music in the Era of Its Electronic Reproducibility," in Leppert and McClary, eds., *Music and Society: The Politics of Composition, Performance and Reception,* p. 173.

64 Quoted in David Leaf's liner notes to the compact disc reissue of the Beach Boys *Today/Summer Days and Summer Nights* (Capitol, 1990).

65 Quoted in David Leaf's liner notes to the compact disc reissue of the Beach Boys, *Smiley Smile/Wild Honey* (Capitol, 1990).

66 Quoted in Bill Flanagan, "Sinéad O'Connor," *Musician* 142 (August 1990), p. 46.

67 Quoted in Paul Williams, *Performing Artist: The Music of Bob Dylan*, vol. 1, 1960–1973 (Novato, Calif. and Lancaster, Pa.: Underwood-Miller, 1990), p. 261; original source is a 1984 radio interview.

68 Quoted in Jann Wenner, *Lennon Remembers* (San Francisco: Straight Arrow Books, 1971), p. 188.

69 Jon Landau, "John Wesley Harding," in *Bob Dylan: A Retrospective,* ed. Craig McGregor (New York: William Morrow, 1972), p. 262; review originally in *Crawdaddy!* 1968.

70 Quoted in Bill Flanagan, *Written in My Soul* (Chicago and New York: Contemporary Books, 1987), p. 343.

71 Quoted in John Howell, *David Byrne* (New York: Thunder's Mouth Press, 1992), pp. 47–48.

72 Jill Rosenbaum and Lorraine Prinsky, "Sex, Violence and Rock 'n' Roll: Youths' Perceptions of Popular Music," *Popular Music and Society* 11 (1987), p. 85, emphasis added. Further details of their research with teenagers are included in L. E. Prinsky and J. L. Rosenbaum, " 'Leer-ics' or Lyrics: Teenage Impressions of Rock 'n' Roll," *Youth & Society* 18 (1987), pp. 384–97. Their findings are consistent with those conducted two decades earlier, when two independent studies supported the conclusion that about 70 percent of listeners regard "sound" as more important than lyrics in rock music; see Graham Murdock and Guy Phelps, "Responding to Popular Music: Criteria of Classification and Choice Among English Teenagers," *Popular Music & Society* 1 (1971), pp. 146–47.

73 Robert Plant and John Paul Jones interviews on Led Zeppelin, *Remasters* (Atlantic Records, 1992), disc 3.

74 Scruton, *The Aesthetic Understanding,* p. 115.

75 Ibid., p. 107.

3 *Record Consciousness*

1 Quoted in Alan Light, "Ice-T," *Rolling Stone,* 20 August 1992, p. 30. Ice-T's given name is Tracy Marrow.

2 Quoted in David Fricke, "Waiting for the Band," *Rolling Stone,* 24 June 1993, p. 18.

3 Steve Chapple and Reebee Garofalo, *Rock 'n' Roll Is Here to Pay: The History and Politics of the Music Industry* (Chicago: Nelson-Hall, 1977), p. 315.

4 Timothy Binkley, "Piece: Contra Aesthetics," *Journal of Aesthetics and Art Criticism* 35 (1970), p. 269. The Duchamp example later in this section is taken from Binkley.

5 Ibid., p. 270.

6 Ibid., p. 271.

7 My influences on this topic include Monroe C. Beardsley, *Aesthetics: Problems in the Philosophy of Criticism,* 2d ed. (Indianapolis: Hackett Publishing, 1981); Bernard Bosanquet, *Three Lectures on Aesthetic* (London: Macmillan, 1931), pp. 58–75; and Aaron Copland, *Music and Imagination* (Cambridge, Mass.: Harvard University Press, 1952), chapter 2.

8 R. G. Collingwood, *The Principles of Art* (Oxford: Oxford University Press, 1958); see chapter 11, particularly p. 245.

9 Quoted in Andrew Doe and John Tobler, *The Doors in Their Own Words* (New York: Perigee Books, 1991), p. 19. Quotation dated as 1980 but no other information provided.

10 Interview in George Martin, *Making Music* (New York: William Morrow, 1983), pp. 139 and 141, emphasis added.

11 Jeff Beck, "Playing Guitar," in George Martin, *Making Music,* p. 143.

12 Virgil C. Aldrich, *Philosophy of Art* (Englewood Cliffs, N.J.: Prentice-Hall, 1963), pp. 36–40.

13 Jim Miller, ed., *The Rolling Stone Illustrated History of Rock & Roll,* 2d ed. (New York: Random House, 1980), and Michael Ochs, *Rock Archives* (New York: Dolphin/Doubleday, 1984).

14 John Morthland, "Jimi Hendrix," *The Rolling Stone Illustrated History of Rock & Roll,* p. 298.

15 Quoted in David Browne et al., "The Top 100 of the Last Twenty Years," *Rolling Stone,* 27 August 1987, p. 127.

16 A brief fragment is included in the film *25 X 5: The Continuing Adventures of the Rolling Stone* (CBS Home Video, 1989); Godard's film is now available on video as *Sympathy for the Devil.* Godard's technique in the film mirrors the studio process that we observe with the Stones; several distinct films have been spliced together on both the horizontal and vertical axis of organization. The tedium of many of the scenes reflects the tedium of the studio recording process, as if Godard is merely using footage of the Stones making a recording to clue us to the filmmaking process that he himself employs.

17 Quoted in "Mick Jagger," *Rolling Stone Interviews,* Jann Wenner et al., eds. (New York: Straight Arrow/Paperback Library, 1971), p. 169.

18 Susan P. Montague and Robert Marais, "Football Games and Rock Concerts: The Ritual Enactment of American Success Models," in W. Arens and Susan P. Montague, eds., *The American Dimension: Cultural Myths and Social Realities* (New York: Alfred Publishing, 1976), p. 47.

19 Deena Weinstein, *Heavy Metal: A Cultural Sociology* (New York: Lexington Books, 1991), p. 232. See also Kathleen Marie Higgins, *The Music of Our Lives* (Philadelphia: Temple University Press, 1991), pp. 145–56.

20 Quoted in Bill Flanagan, *Written in My Soul* (Chicago and New York: Contemporary Books, 1987), p. 420.

21 Lyle Lovett quoted in George Kalogerakis, "Lyle Lovett: Deep in the Heart," *Musician* 163 (May 1992), pp. 34 and 36.

22 Peter Guralnick, "Eric Clapton," *Musician* 155 (September 1991), p. 7.

23 Ibid., emphasis added.

24 Robert Plant interviewed on Led Zeppelin, *Remasters* (Atlantic Records, 1992), disc 3.

25 Robert Plant quotations transcribed from a syndicated radio interview, "Rock Line," 1990.

26 John Mellencamp quoted in Jon Bream, "Renaissance Rocker," Minneapolis–St. Paul *Star Tribune,* Friday, March 6, 1992, p. 6E. Robert Wyatt, whose confinement to a wheelchair following a fall from a third floor window has altered

his working conditions, also compares his music making with painting; Mac Randall, "Tough Guys Don't Dance," *Musician* 166 (August 1992), p. 38.

27 David Browne, "The Top 100," pp. 45–174. Big Brother and the Holding Company's *Cheap Thrills* (1968, with Janis Joplin) includes *simulated* live tracks.

28 Reprinted in Jerilyn Lee Brandelius, *Grateful Dead Family Album* (New York: Warner Books, 1989), p. 240; original publication in the *New York Times*, July 26, 1987.

29 Quoted in Brandelius, *Grateful Dead Family Album*, p. 42. From an interview for *The San Francisco Chronicle*, 1966.

30 Quoted in Jann Wenner and Charles Reich, "Jerry Garcia," *The Rolling Stone Interviews* (New York: St. Martin's Press/Rolling Stone Press, 1981), p. 195.

31 Ibid., p. 196.

32 Quoted in Bill Flanagan, *Written in My Soul*, pp. 377–78; interview conducted 1983. Browne is referring to a 1966 hit by the Left Banke.

33 Midge Ure, "Performing Live," in George Martin, *Making Music*, p. 220.

34 V. F. Perkins, "Form and Discipline," in *Film Theory and Criticism*, ed. Gerald Mast and Marshall Cohen (New York: Oxford University Press, 1979), 2d ed., pp. 52–53.

35 Quoted in Chet Flippo, *On the Road with the Rolling Stones* (New York: Doubleday/Dolphin, 1985), p. 35.

36 John Goldrosen, *The Buddy Holly Story* (New York: Quick Fox/Bowling Green University Popular Press, 1975), p. 85.

37 Greil Marcus, "Buddy Holly and Ritchie Valens," *The Rolling Stone Record Review* (New York: Pocket Books, 1971), p. 63.

38 Contrast this situation with that in the jazz community, where such editing invites anger or indignation; witness the reception to the new backing tracks for Charlie Parker on *Bird*. A year after Miles Davis died, the hip-hop album *Doo-bop* was constructed around unfinished tapes of his playing. Chet Baker's trumpet was given new surroundings on a Jim Hall album. Critic Kevin Whitehead attacked these presentations of jazz performances out of their original setting as "depressing" and "unscrupulous" ("Fresh Air," Minnesota Public Radio, September 3, 1992).

39 Quoted in Jimmy McDonough, "Too Far Gone," *Village Voice Rock & Roll Quarterly* (Winter 1989), p. 24, and Fred Shruers, "Neil Young and Crazy Horse Ride Again," *Musician* 148 (February 1991), p. 56.

40 As discussed in chapter 1, Young seems to regard recording on tape as a transparent medium, but digital recording as a falsification of the sound. For digital recordings, he thinks one must ask "what the music really sounded like." In saying that the vinyl release of *Everybody Knows This Is Nowhere* (1969) is the "original," and *not* the original live performance, he ignores the degree that equalization and mixing altered the sound on the master tape. See Neil Young, "The CD and the Damage Done," *Harper's Magazine*, July 1992, pp. 23–24.

41 Quoted in Bill Flanagan, *Written in My Soul*, p. 127.

42 John Helstrom, "The Harder They Fall," in Clinton Heylin, ed. *The Penguin Book of Rock & Roll Writing* (New York: Viking, 1992), p. 347. How did he hear vocals if the mikes were off?

43 Cott and Clark, "Mick Jagger," p. 168.

44 Roman Ingarden, *The Work of Music and the Problem of Its Identity* (Berkeley and Los Angeles: University of California Press, 1986).

45 Liner notes to Joe Jackson, *Big World* (A&M Records, 1986).

46 David Fricke, "Def Leppard," *Rolling Stone,* 30 April 1992, p. 42.

47 Quoted in David Wild, "Van Morrison," *Rolling Stone,* 15 October 1992, p. 152; interview conducted 1990.

48 Walter Benjamin, *Illuminations,* ed. Hannah Arendt (New York: Harcourt Brace, 1968), p. 225.

49 Quoted in Jonathan Cott, "Leonard Bernstein," *Rolling Stone,* 29 November 1990, p. 76.

50 Lydia Goehr, *The Imaginary Museum of Musical Works* (Oxford: Oxford University Press, 1992), chapter 8.

51 Quoted in Philip Norman, *The Life and Good Times of the Rolling Stones* (New York: Harmony Books, 1989), p. 30. Original source of quotation not given.

52 Robert Plant quoted in Charles M. Young, "Robert Plant's Manic Persona," *Musician* 140 (June 1990), p. 47. Page subsequently remarks, "They couldn't get us on the guitar parts or the music, but they nailed us on the lyrics. . . . Robert was supposed to change the lyrics." Quoted in Brad Tolinski with Greg Di Benedetto, "Days of Heaven: Jimmy Page," *Guitar World,* December 1993, p. 50.

53 See Matt Resnicoff, "Jimmy Page: My Life in Led Zeppelin," *Musician* 145 (November 1990), p. 62; Resnicoff remarks that Holmes' recording is "very, very close . . . musically and lyrically."

54 Bo Diddley quoted in Kurt Loder, "Bo Diddley," in *The Rolling Stone Interviews: The 1980s,* ed. Sid Holt (New York: St. Martin's/Rolling Stone Press, 1989), p. 184; interview conducted 1987.

55 Eamon Dunphy, *Unforgettable Fire* (New York: Warner Books, 1987), p. 261.

56 While Jerrold Levinson aims to offer a theory that covers notated classical compositions in Western culture, it is weakened by the idea that a specific individual must compose a new work.

57 Interview at the Houston Astrodome, 1970, in the film *Elvis: The Great Performances — Center Stage,* vol. 1 (Buena Vista Video). Contrast Presley's realist attitude with Brian Eno's judgment that the echo on "Heartbreak Hotel" is "better than the song itself, by far." See Mark Howell, "From a Stranger's Evening with Brian Eno," *Another Room* (June/July 1981), n.p.

58 Related by Carl Perkins in Bill Flanagan, *Written in My Soul,* p. 17.

59 Simon Frith, "Video/Pop: Picking Up the Pieces," in *Facing the Music,* A Pantheon Guide to Popular Culture, ed. Simon Frith (New York: Pantheon Books, 1988), p. 123.

60 My ideas about allusion and quotation are informed by Nelson Goodman, *Ways of Worldmaking* (Indianapolis: Hackett Publishing, 1978), and Stephanie Ross, "Art and Allusion," *The Journal of Aesthetics and Art Criticism* 40 (1981), pp. 59–70.

61 Reported in David Toop, *Rap Attack 2: African Rap to Global Hip Hop* (Boston: Consortium Press, 1992), pp. 65–66.

62   This also seems the position of Tricia Rose, *Black Noise: Rap Music and Black Culture in Contemporary America* (Hanover and London: Wesleyan University Press, 1994), pp. 88–93. Rose is particularly concerned about earlier contracts that shortchanged black artists.

4   *Pump Up the Volume*

1   Quentin J. Schultze, Roy M. Anker et al., *Dancing in the Dark* (Grand Rapids, Mich.: William B. Eerdmans Publishing, 1991), p. 290.

2   John Cage, "The Future of Music: Credo," in his *Silence* (Middleton, Conn.: Wesleyan University Press, 1967), p. 3.

3   Diane Ackerman, *A Natural History of the Senses* (New York: Random House, 1990), pp. 186–87.

4   Gary Susman, quoted in Dick Dahl, "Is It Only Rock 'N' Roll?" *Utne Reader* (May/June 1992), p. 42. Susman was writing for the *Boston Phoenix*.

5   Quoted in David Fricke, "Thurston Moore," *Rolling Stone,* 22 September 1994, p. 115.

6   Sheila Whitely, "Progressive Rock and Psychedelic Coding in the Work of Jimi Hendrix," *Popular Music* 9 (1990), p. 46.

7   F. C. Bartlett, *The Problem of Noise* (Cambridge: The University Press, 1934), p. 2.

8   Elliot Schwartz and Barney Childs, eds., *Contemporary Composers on Contemporary Music* (New York: Holt, Rinehart & Winston, 1967), p. 207.

9   For Jacques Attali, "A noise is a resonance that interferes with the audition of a message in the process of emission" (*Noise: The Political Economy of Music,* trans. Brian Massumi [Minneapolis: University of Minnesota Press, 1985], p. 26). See also George Lipsitz, *Time Passages,* pp. 109–16.

10   Ibid., p. 29, emphasis deleted.

11   Robin Maconie, *The Concept of Music* (Oxford: Clarendon Press, 1990), p. 36.

12   Attali, *Noise,* pp. 33–34.

13   See John Shepherd, *Music as Social Text* (Cambridge: Polity Press, 1991), pp. 163–64, and Dick Hebdige, *Subculture: The Meaning of Style* (London and New York: Methuen, 1979).

14   See Peter Wicke, "The Times They Are A-Changin': Rock Music and Political Change in East Germany," and Anna Szemere, "The Politics of Marginality: A Rock Musical Subculture in Socialist Hungary in the Early 1980s," both in Reebee Garofalo, ed., *Rockin' the Boat: Mass Music & Mass Movements* (Boston: South End Press, 1992), pp. 81–114.

15   Attali, *Noise,* chapter 4.

16   For a contrasting reading, see Tricia Rose, *Black Noise: Rap Music and Black Culture in Contemporary America* (Hanover and London: Wesleyan University Press, 1994), chapter 4.

17   Lester Bangs, "Of Pop and Pies and Fun," *Psychotic Reactions and Carburetor Dung,* ed. Greil Marcus (New York: Alfred A. Knopf, 1987), p. 41.

18   Brian Cross, *It's Not About A Salary: Rap, Race and Resistance in Los Angeles* (London and New York: Verso, 1994), p. 305.

19   Herbert Marcuse, *Counterrevolution and Revolt* (Boston: Beacon Press, 1972), p. 115.

20   Immanuel Kant, *Critique of Judgment,* trans. Werner S. Pluhar (Indianapolis: Hackett Publishing, 1987), p. 200.

21   Rose, *Black Noise,* p. 62.

22   John Shepherd, *Music as Social Text,* chapter 8, particularly pp. 154–64.

23   Pierre Bourdieu and Alain Darbel with Dominique Schnapper, *The Love of Art,* trans. Caroline Beattie and Nick Merriamn (Stanford: Stanford University Press, 1990), pp. 50–51.

24   Roland Barthes, "Musica Practica," *Image-Music-Text,* trans. Stephen Heath (New York: Hill and Wang, 1977), pp. 149–50.

25   Evan Eisenberg, *The Recording Angel* (New York: Penguin Books, 1988), p. 44.

26   Billy Gibbons quoted in Kurt Loder, *Bat Chain Puller* (New York: St. Martin's Press, 1990), p. 129.

27   Mike Jahn, *The Story of Rock from Elvis Presley to the Rolling Stones* (New York: Quadrangle, 1975), p. 274.

28   Townshend quoted by Charles M. Young, "Who's Back," *Musician* 129 (July 1989), p. 68. Bass player John Entwhistle has tinnitus, as well.

29   Richards interview by Robert Greenfield, "Got to Keep It Growing," *The Rolling Stone Interviews,* vol. 2 (New York: Warner Paperback, 1973), p. 225. Interview conducted 1971.

30   Charles M. Young, "Who's Back," p. 68.

31   Robert Palmer, "Church of the Sonic Guitar," *South Atlantic Quarterly* 90 (Winter 1991), p. 657, emphasis added.

32   Rose, *Black Noise,* p. 75.

33   Critic Gary Susman, quoted in Dick Dahl, "Is It Only Rock 'n' Roll?" *Utne Reader* (May/June 1992), p. 42, and Michael Goldberg, "Red-Hot Lollapalooza," *Rolling Stone,* 30 April 1992, p. 23, respectively.

34   Jim Farber, "New Ragged Glories," *Rolling Stone,* 9 January 1992, p. 56.

35   Danny Davis, in charge of promoting the record to radio stations, quoted in Mark Ribowsky, *He's a Rebel* (New York: E. P. Dutton, 1989), p. 223.

36   Quoted in Jonathan Gold, "Nine Inch Nails," *Rolling Stone,* 8 September 1994, p. 53.

37   Robert Walser, *Running with the Devil: Power, Gender, and Madness in Heavy Metal Music* (Hanover and London: Wesleyan University Press, 1993), pp. 41–45.

38   I borrow this example from Peter Kivy.

39   Quoted in Gerald Early, *Tuxedo Junction* (New York: Ecco Press, 1989), p. 260.

40   Ives, "Essays Before a Sonata," in Claude Debussy, Charles Ives, and Ferruccio Busoni, *Three Classics in the Aesthetics of Music* (New York: Dover Publications, 1962), p. 168.

41   Luigi Russolo, *The Art of Noises,* trans. Barclay Brown, Monographs in Musicology, no. 6 (New York: Pendragon Press, 1986).

42   A poster advertising the concert is reproduced in Andy Mackay, *Electronic Music* (Minneapolis, Minn.: Control Data Publishing, 1981), p. 15.

43 Russolo, p. 39.

44 Thomas Hastings, *Dissertation on Musical Taste* (New York: Mason Brothers, 1853; reprint New York: Johnson Reprint Company, 1968), p. 34.

45 Russolo, p. 27 (emphasis deleted).

46 Ibid., pp. 82–83.

47 Ibid., p. 28.

48 Ibid., pp. 25 and 27.

49 Ibid., pp. 86–87, emphasis deleted.

50 Jon Savage, *England's Dreaming* (New York: St. Martin's Press, 1992), p. 234; describing his first Clash show, October 1976.

51 J. D. Considine, "Hüsker Dü," *Rolling Stone Album Guide,* eds. Anthony DeCurtis and James Henke with Holly George-Warren (New York: Random House, 1992), p. 337.

52 Greg Tate, "The Blackhole Surfers," *Village Voice,* 17 March 1992, p. 69.

53 Simon Reynolds, "Belting Out the Most Unfeminine Emotion," *New York Times,* Sunday, 9 February 1992, p. H27.

54 Quoted in Christopher John Farley, "Monster Music," *Time,* 26 September 1994, p. 72.

55 Martha Bayles, *A Hole in Our Soul: The Loss of Beauty and Meaning in American Popular Music* (New York: The Free Press, 1994), p. 219.

56 Bernard Bosanquet, *Three Lectures on Aesthetic* (London: Macmillan, 1931), p. 67.

57 Ibid., pp. 63–64.

58 Michael Lydon, "The Electric Guitar," *Boogie Lightning: How Music Became Electric* (New York: Da Capo, 1974; reprint 1980), p. 149.

59 Jimmy Page quoted in Joe Bosso and Greg Di Benedetto, "Glory Days," *Guitar Legends* (Fall 1993), p. 40; interview originally published in *Guitar World,* January 1991.

60 Ibid., p. 42.

61 For a discussion of similar uses and abuses of technology by rap musicians, see Rose, *Black Noise,* pp. 74–80.

62 Quoted in Mauro Salvatori, "Frontman: Jimmy Page," *Musician* 178 (August 1993), p. 7.

63 Quoted in Scott E. Kutina, "An' I Know I Play a Bad Guitar," in David Dalton, ed., *The Rolling Stones: The First Twenty Years* (New York: Alfred A. Knopf, 1981), p. 163.

64 Hendrix routinely set his equipment at its highest volume settings. Bloomfield quoted in David Henderson, *'Scuse Me While I Kiss the Sky: The Life of Jimi Hendrix* (New York: Bantam Books, 1981), p. 184.

65 Jimmy McDonough, "Too Far Gone," *Village Voice Rock and Roll Quarterly* (Winter 1989), p. 22. The description is of the solo on Young's *Eldorado* EP.

66 Tony Sherman, "Neil Young," *Musician* 158 (December 1991), p. 7.

67 John Rockwell, "Neil Young," *All American Music* (New York: Vintage, 1983), p. 227.

68 Quoted in Robert Palmer, *Deep Blues* (New York: Penguin Books, 1982), p. 222.

69   Mark Ribowsky, *He's a Rebel* (New York: E. P. Dutton, 1989), p. 126.

70   Quoted in Dalton, *The Rolling Stones,* p. 53. As Dalton notes, the original acoustic track can be heard at various points on the recording, particularly six seconds into it.

71   Quoted in Dorothy Wade and Justine Picardie, *Music Man: Ahmet Ertegun, Atlantic Records, and the Triumph of Rock 'n' Roll* (New York and London: W. W. Norton & Company, 1990), p. 207.

72   Dave Marsh, *The Heart of Rock and Soul* (New York: Plume Books, 1989), p. 8.

73   Henry Pleasants, *The Agony of Modern Music* (New York: Simon and Schuster, 1955), p. 133.

5   Jungle Rhythms and the Big Beat

1   Quoted from Verdi's *Letters* in Jacques Barzun, ed., *Pleasures of Music* (Chicago: University of Chicago Press, 1977), p. 352.

2   Mickey Hart with Jay Stevens and Frederic Lieberman, *Drumming at the Edge of Magic* (San Francisco: Harper Collins, 1990), p. 118.

3   Frank Zappa as quoted in the published transcript, "Hearing Before the Committee on Commerce, Science, and Transportation, United States Senate," Senate Hearing 99–529 (Washington: U.S. Government Printing, 1985), p. 54.

4   For a careful analysis of some of these critiques, see Robert Walser, *Running with the Devil: Power, Gender, and Madness in Heavy Metal Music* (Hanover and London: Wesleyan University Press, 1993), chapter 5. Walser concentrates on the supposed link between heavy metal and satanism.

5   These crackdowns were supported by elements in the entertainment industry threatened by rock and roll; see Steve Chapple and Reebee Garofalo, *Rock 'n' Roll Is Here to Pay: The History and Politics of the Music Industry* (Chicago: Nelson-Hall, 1977), chapter 2.

6   Transcript of court testimony in David Dalton, ed., *The Rolling Stones: The First Twenty Years* (New York: Knopf, 1981), p. 100.

7   Allan Bloom, *The Closing of the American Mind* (New York: Simon and Schuster, 1987). See analyses of Bloom in George Lipsitz, "Precious and Communicable: History in an Age of Popular Culture," in *Time Passages: Collective Memory and American Popular Culture* (Minneapolis: University of Minnesota Press, 1990), pp. 21–36, and Lawrence Grossberg, *We Gotta Get Out of This Place: Popular Conservatism and Postmodern Culture* (New York and London: Routledge, 1992), particularly chapter 7.

8   Bloom, p. 72.

9   Plato, *The Republic of Plato,* trans. Allan Bloom (New York: Basic Books, 1968), 606d, p. 290.

10   Bloom, p. 71. The same basic argument is retraced by Alberto Boixados, *Myths of Modern Art* (New York: University Press of America, 1990). Boixados damns *The Beatles* (the "White Album") for its effect on Charles Manson and points to Gregorian chant as ideal music for turning the soul in the proper direction.

11   Bloom, p. 73.

12   Ibid., p. 75. The reference to killing parents is no doubt to the Doors' "The End." For more on the masturbation theme, see Dave Marsh, "Onan's Greatest Hits," *Stranded,* ed. Greil Marcus (New York: Knopf, 1979).

13   His title is a play on the Who's "The Kids Are Alright." See John G. Fuller, *Are the Kids All Right? The Rock Generation and Its Hidden Death Wish* (New York: Times Books, 1981).

14   See "Interview with John G. Fuller," *Popular Music & Society* 9 (1983), pp. 77–78.

15   Michael Powers, "The Rolling Stones: Danceable Mythic Satire," *Popular Music & Society* 10 (1985), p. 47.

16   Quoted in Rafi Zabor and Vic Garbarini, "Wynton vs. Herbie," *Musician* 77 (March 1985), p. 56.

17   In 1990, New York's Cardinal O'Connor publicly denounced Ozzy Osbourne, implying that heavy metal can lead to genuine demonic possession of its listeners; see Richard N. Ostling, "No Sympathy for the Devil," *Time,* 19 March 1990, pp. 55–56. For an overview of Christian objections, see Steve Lawhead, *Rock Reconsidered: A Christian Looks at Contemporary Music* (Downers Grove, Ill.: Inter-Varsity, 1981).

18   Bill Flanagan, "The View from the Edge," *Musician* 161 (March 1992), p. 60. See also Eamon Dunphy, *Unforgettable Fire* (New York: Warner Books, 1987), pp. 167–70.

19   Charlie Gillett, *The Sound of the City: The Rise of Rock and Roll* (New York: Outerbridge & Dienstfrey/Dutton, 1970), p. i.

20   "Youth: Rocking and Rolling." *Newsweek,* 18 June 1956, p. 42. Bill Haley and the Comets were performing when fights broke out.

21   *Lennon Remembers,* p. 100.

22   Quoted in "Mick Jagger and the Future of Rock," *Newsweek,* 4 January 1971, p. 45.

23   Quoted in Kurt Loder, "Bo Diddley," in *The Rolling Stone Interviews: The 1980s,* ed. Sid Holt (New York: St. Martin's/Rolling Stone Press, 1989), p. 185.

24   Richard Shusterman, "The Fine Art of Rap," *Pragmatist Aesthetics* (Oxford and Cambridge, Mass.: Blackwell, 1992), p. 203.

25   Mickey Hart with Jay Stevens and Frederic Lieberman, *Drumming at the Edge of Magic,* p. 195.

26   Quoted by Wilfrid Mellers, *Music in a New Found Land* (New York: Oxford University Press, 1987), p. 302.

27   Peter Van Der Merwe, *Origins of the Popular Style* (Oxford: Clarendon Press, 1989), p. 110.

28   Langdon Winner, "The Strange Death of Rock and Roll," in *Rock and Roll Will Stand,* ed. Greil Marcus (Boston: Beacon Press, 1969), p. 46. The emphasis on the second and fourth beats is so basic that James Brown's "Papa's Got a Brand New Bag" (1965) created a new sound by emphasizing the accents back on the one and three.

29   Bruce Springsteen, "Foreword," in Max Weinberg with Robert Santelli, *The Big Beat* (New York: Billboard Books, 1991), p. vii.

30   Analyses of these last three are provided in Katherine Charlton, *Rock Music Styles: A History* (Dubuque, Iowa: Wm. C. Brown Publishers, 1990), pp. 56, 216, 242.

31   Gunther Schuller, *Early Jazz* (Oxford: Oxford University Press, 1968), p. 8.

32   Tony Scherman, "Jim Keltner's Beatnik Beat," *Musician* 128 (June 1989), p. 78.

33   Quoted in Alan di Perna, "Kenny Aronoff," *Musician* 128 (June 1989), p. 104.

34   Winner, "Strange Death of Rock and Roll," p. 47.

35   Sigmund Spaeth, "Music, popular," *Britannica Book of the Year, 1955* (Chicago: Encyclopaedia Britannica, Inc., 1955), p. 470.

36   Bloom, p. 74.

37   Ibid., p. 73.

38   Ibid., pp. 73 and 74. This conjunction of arousal and catharsis suggests another confusion in Bloom's argument. If the music is cathartic, it purges or releases the feelings (e.g., angry music is cathartic if it resolves and removes our anger). If so, Bloom should praise rather than damn it.

39   See Peter Kivy, *Sound Sentiment* (Philadelphia: Temple University Press, 1989), pp. 21 ff.

40   Thomas De Quincey, "The Antigone of Sophocles," in *The Collected Writings of De Quincey,* ed. David Masson (Edinburgh: Adam and Charles Black, 1890), vol. 10, p. 368. Originally published 1846.

41   R. G. Collingwood, *The Principles of Art* (Oxford: Oxford University Press, 1958), p. 56.

42   Ravi Shankar, *Ragas Hameer & Gara,* Deutsche Grammophon 2531 216 (1979) and "Take Me Back to Mabayi," *Burundi: Music From the Heart of Africa,* Nonesuch Explorer Series 0298 (1974).

43   Kivy, *Sound Sentiment,* p. 236. See also chapter 13. Kivy discusses Jerrold Levinson's reply to these objections; like Kivy, I believe that Levinson has a weak case.

44   Bloom, p. 73.

45   Quoted in Tony Scherman, "Front Man: Neil Young," *Musician* 158 (December 1991), p. 7.

46   Schuller, *Early Jazz,* p. 11.

47   Notated examples are available in Katherine Charlton, *Rock Music Styles,* pp. 83 and 98.

48   Schuller, pp. 11–12.

49   Mickey Hart, *Drumming at the Edge of Magic,* p. 144. I do not want to create the impression that rock is devoid of polymetric playing. "Toads of the Short Forest" on Frank Zappa's *Weasels Ripped My Flesh* (1970) has one drummer in 7/8, the bass and two other percussionists in 3/4, and the organ in 5/8. But many rock fans find Zappa inaccessible.

50   See the interview with Earl Palmer in Weinberg, *The Big Beat,* pp. 91–92.

51   Interview in Max Weinberg, *The Big Beat,* p. 104.

52   Will Calhoun, quoted in Tony Sherman, "Will Calhoun on Creative R&R Timekeeping," *Musician* 152 (June 1991), p. 70.

6   *Adorno, Jazz, and the Reception of Popular Music*

1   Quoted in Dave Marsh, *Born to Run* (New York: Dell Books, 1981), p. 125.

2   Quoted by Liam Mackey, "I Still Haven't Found What I'm Looking For," in Niall Stokes with Liam Mackey, eds., *Three Chords and the Truth* (New York: Harmony Books, 1989), p. 134.

3   Susan Rubin Suleiman, *Subversive Intent: Gender, Politics and the Avant-Garde* (Cambridge, Mass.: Harvard University Press, 1990), p. 198. Similarly, "Rock music is strikingly devoid of critical concepts, apart from the elitist arguments of Adorno . . ." (David Buxton, "Rock Music, The Star System, and the Rise of Consumerism," in Simon Frith and Andrew Goodwin, eds., *On Record: Rock, Pop, & the Written Word* [New York: Pantheon, 1990], p. 435).

4   Roland Barthes, *The Pleasure of the Text,* trans. Richard Miller (New York: Hill and Wang, 1975), pp. 41–42.

5   Joseph Horowitz, *Understanding Toscanini* (Minneapolis: University of Minnesota Press, 1987), p. 239.

6   Jacques Attali, *Noise: The Political Economy of Music* (Minneapolis: University of Minnesota Press, 1985), p. 105.

7   Eric Weisbard, "Over and Out: Indie Rock Values in the Age of Alternative Million Sellers," *Village Voice: Rock & Roll Quarterly* (Summer 1994), p. 15.

8   John Rockwell, *All American Music* (New York: Vintage Books, 1983), p. 231.

9   Richard Shusterman, *Pragmatist Aesthetics: Living Beauty, Rethinking Art* (Oxford and Cambridge, Mass.: Blackwell, 1992), p. 177.

10 Ibid., pp. 183 and 176, respectively.

11 Rockwell, p. 228.

12 Deena Weinstein, *Heavy Metal* (New York: Lexington Books, 1991), chapters 3 and 5, and Robert Walser, *Running with the Devil: Power, Gender, and Madness in Heavy Metal Music* (Hanover, N.H.: Wesleyan University Press, 1993), chapter 1.

13 Weinstein, *Heavy Metal,* p. 78.

14 Richard Wollheim, "On Expression and Expressionism," *Revue Internationale de Philosophie* 18 (1964), p. 275. See also E. H. Gombrich, "Expression and Communication," *Meditations on a Hobby Horse,* 2d ed. (London and New York: Phaidon, 1971), pp. 56–69, and *Art and Illusion,* 2d ed. (Princeton: Princeton University Press, 1961), chapter 11.

15 Pierre Bourdieu, *Distinction: A Social Critique of the Judgment of Taste* (Cambridge, Mass.: Harvard University Press, 1984), p. 386.

16 Robert Hughes, *The Shock of the New* (New York: Alfred A. Knopf, 1981), p. 325.

17 Theodor W. Adorno, *Philosophy of Modern Music,* trans. Anne G. Mitchell and Wesley V. Blomster (New York: Seabury Press, 1973), p. 126. My other primary sources are Adorno's *Introduction to the Sociology of Music,* trans. E. B. Ashton (New York: Seabury Press, 1976); *Aesthetic Theory,* trans. C. Lenhardt (New York: Routledge & Kegan Paul, 1982); *Prisms,* trans. Samuel and Shierry

Weber (Cambridge, Mass.: MIT Press, 1981); "On the Fetish-Character in Music and the Regression of Listening," Andrew Arato and Eike Gebhardt, eds., *The Essential Frankfurt School Reader* (New York: Continuum, 1982), pp. 270–99; "On Popular Music" (1941) in Simon Frith and Andrew Goodwin, eds., *On Record* (New York: Pantheon, 1990), pp. 301–14; "On the Social Situation of Music," in Edward A. Lippman, ed., *Musical Aesthetics: A Historical Reader,* vol. 3, The Twentieth Century (Stuyvesant, N.Y.: Pendragon Press, 1985), pp. 221–70.

18 Its first two chapters draw extensively from material written in 1932–41, particularly "On the Social Situation of Music" and "On the Fetish-Character in Music," both originally in *Zeitschrift für Sozialforschung,* 1932 and 1938, respectively. "Perennial Fashion — Jazz" (in *Prisms,* pp. 121–32) recycles some material from "Über Jazz," *Zeitschrift für Sozialforschung* (1936), which originally carried the pseudonym "Hektor Rottweiler."

19 Key ideas reappear in *Aesthetic Theory* (1970). Summaries include Anthony Savile, "Beauty and Truth: the Apotheosis of an Idea," in Richard Shusterman, ed., *Analytic Aesthetics* (Oxford: Basil Blackwell, 1989), pp. 123–46; Martin Jay, *The Dialectical Imagination* (Boston: Little, Brown, 1973), pp. 185–93; and Andrew Edgar, "An Introduction to Adorno's Aesthetics," *British Journal of Aesthetics* 30 (1990), pp. 46–56. The best study, albeit nearly as lengthy as Adorno's own, is Lambert Zuidervaart, *Adorno's Aesthetic Theory: The Redemption of Illusion* (Cambridge, Mass.: MIT Press, 1991).

20 Adorno, "Fetish-Character in Music," p. 276. He compares Beethoven and jazz in *Aesthetic Theory,* p. 170.

21 Adorno, *Sociology of Music,* p. 32.

22 Ibid., p. 22.

23 Adorno, "Perennial Fashion," p. 127. The language in such passages is *evaluative* and not a neutral cultural critique.

24 Ibid., p. 121.

25 Ibid., p. 123. Adorno includes syncopation; see "Fetish Character in Music," p. 296.

26 Adorno, *Sociology of Music,* p. 29.

27 Ibid., p. 15.

28 Steven Halpern with Louis Savary, *Sound Health: The Music and Sounds That Make Us Whole* (San Francisco: Harper & Row, 1985), pp. 138–39; John Diamond, *BK: Behavioral Kinesiology* (San Francisco: Harper & Row, 1979), pp. 100–105. The evidence is entirely anecdotal.

29 Adorno, *Sociology of Music,* p. 29, and "Perennial Fashion," pp. 121–22.

30 Adorno, *Aesthetic Theory,* pp. 335–37.

31 Adorno, "Perennial Fashion," p. 129.

32 Adorno, *Sociology of Music,* p. 203.

33 Music for entertainment "inhabits the pockets of silence that develop between people molded by anxiety, work and undemanding docility" (Adorno, "Fetish-Character in Music," p. 271). See also "On Popular Music," pp. 309–11.

34 Adorno, "On Popular Music," p. 313.

35 Adorno, "Perennial Fashion," p. 129. See Attali, *Noise,* pp. 105–9.

36 Fabio Dasilva, Anthony Blasi, and David Dees, *The Sociology of Music* (Notre Dame, Ind.: University of Notre Dame Press, 1984), p. 87 (emphasis added).

37 Adorno, *Sociology of Music*, p. 31. See also "On Popular Music," p. 311.

38 Adorno, *Sociology of Music*, p. 25. See also "Fetish-Character in Music," pp. 279–80.

39 Adorno, *Sociology of Music*, p. 31. See also "Perennial Fashion," p. 123, and "On Popular Music," p. 308.

40 Adorno, *Sociology of Music*, p. 25. Adorno repeats his claim that popular songs are the basis of all jazz in "Perennial Fashion," p. 123. Adorno never acknowledges the importance of the twelve-bar blues form for jazz and rock, but of course a standard progression of I-IV-I-V-I is exactly the sort of standard schema that he regards as restrictive.

41 Attali, *Noise*, p. 109. Where Adorno regards mass culture as a reflection of social organization, Attali interprets it as a prophetic precursor.

42 Adorno, *Aesthetic Theory*, pp. 148–72. See also Thomas Huhn, "Adorno's Aesthetics of Illusion," *Journal of Aesthetics and Art Criticism* 44 (1985), pp. 181–83.

43 Adorno, *Aesthetic Theory*, p. 154.

44 Ibid., pp. 160–61. In this passage, Adorno seems to mean harmony in all arts, not merely music, but the contrast of "harmony" and "dissonance" suggests that he is generalizing from his views about music.

45 Ibid. See also *Sociology of Music*, p. 221.

46 Adorno, *Aesthetic Theory*, p. 197. Notice that aesthetic worth is totally distinct from beauty. See also "Cultural Criticism and Society," *Prisms*, p. 32.

47 Adorno, *Aesthetic Theory*, p. 186; see also pp. 191–93. At the end of *Sociology of Music* (p. 215): "The esthetic quality of works, their truth content, has little to do with any truth that can be empirically pictured, not even with the life of the soul. But it converges with social truth."

48 Adorno, *Sociology of Music*, p. 215.

49 Adorno, *Philosophy of Modern Music*, p. 115.

50 Ibid., p. 9.

51 Adorno, "Fetish-Character in Music," p. 275.

52 Adorno, *Philosophy of Modern Music*, pp. 17–18.

53 Adorno claims that rejecting atonal music requires some grasp of its significance ("Fetish Character," p. 298).

54 Many of Adorno's complaints are repeated by Ernst Krenek, "On the Ageing and Obsolescence of Music," *Exploring Music*, trans. Margaret Shenfield and Geoffrey Skelton (New York: October House, 1966), pp. 221–29 (originally published 1956). Adorno's influence is also strong in Alan Durant, *Conditions of Music* (Albany: State University of New York Press, 1984), and Joseph Horowitz, *Understanding Toscanini*.

55 For more details about the Hot Five and Hot Seven material, see Gunther Schuller, *Early Jazz* (Oxford: Oxford University Press, 1968), pp. 89–127.

56 All recordings 1945–48, on *Bird/The Savoy Recordings* (Savoy LP 2201). See also Gary Giddins, *Riding on a Blue Note* (New York: Oxford University Press, 1981), p. 116.

57   Len Lyons, *The 101 Best Jazz Albums* (New York: William Morrow and Co., Inc., 1980), p. 174.

58   Ross Russell, as quoted by Ira Gitler, liner notes to *Bird/The Savoy Recordings*. See also Simon Frith, *Music for Pleasure* (New York: Routledge, 1988), p. 59.

59   These recordings receive a lengthier discussion in Lyons, *The 101 Best Jazz Albums*, pp. 258–63, 376–79, 387–91. A detailed analysis of Davis's *Kind of Blue* is provided in Mark C. Gridley, *Jazz Styles: History and Analysis*, 2d ed. (Englewood Cliffs, N.J.: Prentice-Hall, 1985), pp. 216–23.

60   Fredric Jameson, *Late Marxism: Adorno, or the Persistence of Music* (Minneapolis: University of Minnesota Press, 1990), p. 141. See also Carol V. Hamilton, "All That Jazz Again: Adorno's Sociology of Music," *Popular Music & Society* 15 (Fall 1991), pp. 31–40.

61   Adorno, *Gesammelte Schriften*, vol. 8 (Frankfurt am Main: Suhrkamp Verlag, 1972), p. 324, and *Sociology of Music*, p. 27.

62   Adorno, "Fetish-Character in Music," p. 275.

63   Adorno, *Aesthetic Theory*, p. 309.

64   Adorno, *Philosophy of Modern Music*, p. 19.

65   Adorno, *Sociology of Music*, pp. 4–5. See also "Bach Defended Against His Devotees," *Prisms*, pp. 142–46.

66   Adorno, "Arnold Schoenberg, 1874–1951," *Prisms*, p. 170 (emphasis added).

67   Ibid. See also Zuidervaart, *Adorno's Aesthetic Theory*, pp. 234–37.

68   T. J. Diffey, "Essentialism and the Definition of 'Art,'" *British Journal of Aesthetics*, vol. 13 (1973), p. 117.

69   Zuidervaart, *Adorno's Aesthetic Theory*, p. 57.

70   The phrase and idea are from Joseph Margolis, *Art and Philosophy: Conceptual Issues in Aesthetics* (Atlantic Heights, N.J.: Humanities Press, 1980), pp. 27–49.

71   Adorno, "Social Critique of Radio Music," pp. 213–14.

72   Tricia Rose, *Black Noise: Rap Music and Black Culture in Contemporary America* (Hanover and London: Wesleyan University Press, 1994), pp. 9–12.

73   Adorno says that Schoenberg's and Webern's rescorings of Bach are "truer" in today's world than are supposedly "objective" performances ("Bach Defended," p. 146).

74   Adorno, "Bach Defended," p. 144. Here, Adorno echoes views which Schoenberg directed against Ferruccio Busoni; see Andy Hamilton, "The Aesthetics of Imperfection," *Philosophy* 65 (1990), pp. 323–31.

75   Adorno, "Bach Defended," p. 146.

76   Adorno, "A Social Critique of Radio Music," *Kenyon Review* 7 (1945), p. 217. His discussions of performance are mainly in the context of attacking Toscanini as a conductor whose radio performances of Beethoven reduce the music to the level of commodity. See Horowitz, *Understanding Toscanini*, pp. 229–43.

77   Theodor Adorno [as "Hektor Rottweiler"], "Die Form der Schallplatte," in *Gesammelte Schriften* 19 (Frankfurt: Suhrkamp Verlag, 1984), pp. 530–34; available as "The Form of the Phonograph Record," trans. Thomas Y. Levin, *October* 55 (1990), pp. 56–61.

78   Theodor W. Adorno, "Ueber die musikalische Verwendung des Radios," *Ge-*

sammelte Schriften 15 (Frankfurt: Suhrkamp Verlag, 1976), pp. 369–401. The essay was first published in 1963.

79   Quoted in Scott Spencer, "The Titan of Jazz," *Rolling Stone,* 13–27 December 1990, p. 230.

80   See Ted Gioia, *The Imperfect Art* (Oxford: Oxford University Press, 1988). As a result, recording still functions in a realist manner with jazz.

81   See Hamilton, "Aesthetics of Imperfection," pp. 323–40.

82   Gioia, *The Imperfect Art,* pp. 15–16.

83   See Reebee Garofalo, "Popular Music and the Civil Rights Movement," and Kristal Brent Zook, "Reconstructions of Nationalist Thought in Black Music and Culture," both in Reebee Garofalo, ed., *Rockin' the Boat: Mass Music & Mass Movements* (Boston: South End Press, 1992), pp. 231–40 and pp. 255–66.

84   Rose, *Black Noise,* p. 72.

85   Duke Ellington, *Music Is My Mistress* (New York: Doubleday, 1973), pp. 452–53.

86   Ibid., p. 415. In 1962, critic Nat Hentoff could name only Jelly Roll Morton, Duke Ellington, and Thelonious Monk as "major indigenous jazz composers." See Hentoff, *The Jazz Life* (London: Peter Davies, 1962), p. 224.

87   John Norris, "The Aesthetic Values of Jazz," *Coda Magazine* 199 (1 December 1984), p. 9. Norris contends that jazz "was created and nurtured by several hundred performers . . . They *alone* made it great—unlike classical music where the composition is the most important ingredient." Sonny Rollins expresses similar sentiments in Spencer, "The Titan of Jazz," p. 230.

88   John Fiske, *Understanding Popular Culture* (Boston: Unwin Hyman, 1989), p. 5.

89   Ibid., p. 30, and John Fiske, *Television Culture* (New York: Methuen, 1987), chapter 6.

90   Walser, *Running with the Devil,* chapter 3.

91   Herbert Marcuse was considerably more open than Adorno to the possibilities for popular music, proposing that blues, jazz, and rock and roll were capable of negating "affirmative" culture. See Marcuse, *An Essay on Liberation* (Boston: Beacon Press, 1969), pp. 36–38.

7   Romanticizing Rock Music

1   Friedrich Nietzsche, *The Birth of Tragedy,* trans. Clifton P. Fadiman, in *The Philosophy of Nietzsche* (New York: Random House, 1927), p. 1038 (section 16).

2   Quoted in Geoffrey Stokes et al., *Rock of Ages: The Rolling Stone History of Rock & Roll* (New York: Summit Books/Rolling Stone Press, 1986), p. 284.

3   Quoted in James Henke, "Bruce Springsteen," *Rolling Stone,* 6 August 1992, p. 44.

4   Quoted in Frederick B. Artz, *From Renaissance to Romanticism: Trends in Art, Literature, and Music, 1300–1930* (Chicago: University of Chicago Press, 1962), p. 227.

5   Danny Sugerman, *Appetite for Destruction: The Days of Guns N' Roses* (New

York: St. Martin's Press, 1991), p. 47; Dionysus and the Romantic tradition are linked to the band throughout chapter 2. See the critique by Robert Walser, *Running with the Devil,* pp. 167–71.

6 Camille Paglia, *Sexual Personae* (New York: Vintage Books, 1990), p. 358.

7 An interesting variation of this thesis is defended in Richard Shusterman, *Pragmatist Aesthetics* (Oxford and Cambridge, Mass.: Blackwell, 1992), pp. 201–35. Arguing that rap is the form of popular music that best exemplifies a postmodern aesthetic, Shusterman avoids endorsing rap as folk music.

8 Robert Christgau, "Rock Lyrics Are Poetry (Maybe)," in Jonathan Eisen, *The Age of Rock* (New York: Random House, 1969), p. 232.

9 Quoted in Greil Marcus, *Ranters & Crowd Pleasers: Punk in Pop Music, 1977–92* (New York: Doubleday, 1993), p. 224; interview with Elvis Costello originally published in *Rolling Stone,* 2 September 1982.

10 Camille Paglia, "Endangered Rock," *New York Times,* Thursday, 16 April 1992, p. A23; reprinted in Camille Paglia, *Sex, Art, and American Culture* (New York: Vintage, 1992), pp. 19–21. Unless otherwise credited, all further quotations from Paglia are to this piece.

11 Quoted in *Melody Maker,* 27 August 1977; quotation disseminated in Tony Augarde, *The Oxford Dictionary of Modern Quotations* (Oxford and New York: Oxford University Press, 1991), p. 89.

12 See Steve Chapple and Reebee Garofalo, *Rock 'n' Roll Is Here To Pay* (Chicago: Nelson-Hall, 1977).

13 Nick Tosches, *Unsung Heroes of Rock 'n' Roll* (New York: Harmony Books, 1991), p. 2.

14 Keith Richards in *25 × 5: The Continuing Adventures of the Rolling Stones* (CBS Music Video, 1989).

15 The definitive work is Jon Savage, *England's Dreaming: Anarchy, Sex Pistols, Punk Rock and Beyond* (New York: St. Martin's Press, 1992). See also Greil Marcus, *Lipstick Traces* (Cambridge, Mass.: Harvard University Press, 1989); Tricia Henry, *Break All Rules!* (Ann Arbor: UMI Research Press, 1989); Curt Loder, *Bat Chain Puller* (New York: St. Martin's Press, 1990), pp. 345–48; Craig Bromberg, *The Wicked Ways of Malcolm McLaren* (New York: Harper and Row, 1989); and Mary Harron, "McRock: Pop as a Commodity," in Simon Frith, ed., *Facing the Music* (New York: Pantheon, 1988), pp. 173–220.

16 Savage, *England's Dreaming,* p. 381.

17 John Rockwell, "The Paradox of the Sex Pistols," *New York Times,* 5 February 1978, p. D5.

18 Simon Frith, "Zowie Bowie," in *The Penguin Book of Rock & Roll Writing,* ed. Clinton Heylin (New York and London: Viking, 1992), p. 582.

19 Dave Harstad, "Correspondence" section, *Rolling Stone,* 16 April 1992, p. 6. After mentioning R.E.M. to a colleague recently, he asked me if I meant now, "or back when they were good." When he heard a recent recording, "Fretless," on the soundtrack to *Until the End of the World* (1992), the same person assumed it to be their early work. In assuming that a good R.E.M. recording had to be an early one, he seems to have been responding as much to image as to the group's music.

20 Quoted in Michael Azerrad, "Nirvana," *Rolling Stone*, 16 April 1992, p. 38.

21 See John Leland, "Rap and Race," *Newsweek*, 29 June 1992, pp. 46–52.

22 Quoted in Brian Cross, *It's Not About A Salary: Rap, Race and Resistance in Los Angeles* (London and New York: Verso, 1994), pp. 186 and 197.

23 Shusterman, "The Fine Art of Rap," *Pragmatist Aesthetics*, pp. 210–11 (emphasis added).

24 Tricia Rose, *Black Noise: Rap Music and Black Culture in Contemporary America* (Hanover and London: Wesleyan University Press, 1994), pp. 23–25.

25 Quoted in Charles M. Young, "Who's Back," *Musician* 129 (July 1989), p. 67.

26 For another recognition of the necessity of "compromise" in rock music, see the interview with Robert Wyatt and Bill Nelson by Mac Randall, "Tough Guys Don't Dance," *Musician* 166 (August 1992), p. 47.

27 See Simon Frith, "The Industrialization of Music," in *Music for Pleasure: Essays in the Sociology of Pop* (New York: Routledge, 1988), pp. 11–23, and the longer argument of *Sound Effects: Youth, Leisure, and the Politics of Rock 'n' Roll* (New York: Pantheon Books, 1981).

28 Quoted in Andrew Doe and John Tobler, *The Doors in Their Own Words* (New York: Perigee Books, 1991), pp. 19–20. Morrison and Manzarek quotations identified as 1969 and 1978, respectively, but no sources given.

29 A classic account of the vicious cycle of debt incurred in recording, touring to promote records so that more records can be made, leading to more debt, is the story of the rise and fall of Commander Cody and the Lost Planet Airmen as chronicled by Geoffrey Stokes, *Star-Making Machinery*, a phrase that crops up in Joni Mitchell's "Free Man in Paris" (1973).

30 See Mac Randall, "Tough Guys Don't Dance," pp. 46–47, on the financial plight of Wyatt and Nelson.

31 Quoted in Scott Isler, "David Bowie," *Musician* 106 (August 1987), p. 68.

32 Quoted in Edna Gunderson, "Forging New Unity Along with Album," *USA Today*, 9 November 1992, p. 2D.

33 A pioneering examination of the relationship between commerce and meaning in rock music is Frith, *Sound Effects*.

34 Quoted in Florindo Volpacchio, "The Mother of All Interviews: Zappa on Music and Society," *Telos* 87 (Spring 1991), p. 128. Interview conducted 16 May 1991.

35 See Greil Marcus, "Notes on the Life and Death and Incandescent Banality of Rock 'n' Roll," *Esquire*, August 1992, pp. 67–75. Marcus, while a fine critic, has always viewed rock through a romanticist conceptual framework, as this essay makes clear.

36 In *Sexual Personae*, Paglia offers parallels between Elvis Presley and Lord Byron; most are physical similarities such as their early deaths and enlarged hearts.

37 Simon Frith, "Popular Music 1950–1980," in George Martin, ed., *Making Music* (New York: William Morrow and Company, 1983), p. 24.

38 Compare the scanty list of twelve songs identified as "Greatest 50s Protest Songs" with the forty identified in each of the following decades, in Dave Marsh and Kevin Stein, *The Book of Rock Lists* (New York: Dell/Rolling Stone Press, 1981), pp. 440–43.

39   Nik Cohn, *Pop from the Beginning* (New York: Weidenfeld and Nicholson, 1969), p. 133.

40   Carl Belz, *The Story of Rock,* 2d ed. (New York: Oxford University Press, 1972), p. 64.

41   Schultze et al., *Dancing in the Dark,* p. 155.

42   Quoted in Isabelle Anscombe and Dike Blair, *Punk* (New York: Urizen Books, 1978), p. 10.

43   Dave Marsh, *The Heart of Rock and Soul* (New York: Plume, 1989), pp. 474–75.

44   Charles White, *The Life and Times of Little Richard* (New York: Harmony Books, 1984), p. 84.

45   David Crosby and Carl Gottlieb, *Long Time Gone* (New York: Doubleday, 1988), pp. viii and 36–37.

46   John Lennon, quoted in David Sheff and G. Barry Golson, *The Playboy Interviews with John Lennon and Yoko Ono* (New York: Berkley Books, 1981), pp. 170–71.

47   John Lennon quoted in Jann Wenner, *Lennon Remembers* (San Francisco: Straight Arrow Books, 1971), p. 70; interview conducted in December 1970.

48   "Working Class?" *Daily Worker,* 7 September 1963, p. 5.

49   Zappa's testimony was in conjunction with the PMRC flap; the question was raised by Senator Hawkins. See "Record Labeling," Senate Hearing 99–529 (Washington: U.S. Government Printing, 1986), p. 61.

50   See Kristine McKenna, "Sting," *Rolling Stone,* 15 October 1992, p. 116.

51   See Chris Mundy, "Random Notes," *Rolling Stone,* 21 January 1993, p. 9.

52   Mick Jagger quoted in A. E. Hotchner, *Blown Away: The Rolling Stones and the Death of the Sixties* (New York: Simon and Schuster, 1990), p. 47. Original source of quotation not given.

53   Quoted in Matt Resnicoff, "Roger Waters: The Last Pink Floyd Story," *Musician* 170 (December 1992), p. 41.

54   Quoted in Geoffrey Stokes, *Rock of Ages,* p. 376.

55   Charlie Gillett, *The Sound of the City* (New York: Outbridge & Dienstfrey/Dutton, 1970), p. 36; Gillett's source is an interview with Presley in the British *Hit Parade* (January 1957).

56   Quotation of Marion Keisker, who was present at the sessions; Ed Ward, in *Rock of Ages* (New York: Rolling Stone Press/Summit Books, 1986), pp. 78–79.

57   Quoted in Geoffrey Stokes, *The Beatles* (New York: Rolling Stone Press/Times Books, 1980), p. 45.

58   Quoted in Max Weinberg with Robert Santelli, *The Big Beat* (New York: Billboard Books, 1991), p. 162.

59   Quoted in John Howell, *David Byrne* (New York: Thunder's Mouth Press, 1992), p. 43.

60   Roger Sessions, *Questions About Music* (New York: W. W. Norton, 1970), p. 11.

61   Marcus, "Notes on the Life and Death."

62 Monroe C. Beardsley, "Is Art Essentially Institutional?" in *The Aesthetic Point of View,* ed. Michael J. Wreen and Donald M. Callen (Ithaca and London: Cornell University Press, 1982), p. 127.

63 Schultze et al., *Dancing in the Dark,* p. 164. For other examples, see Ben Goertzel, "The Rock Guitar Solo: From Expression to Simulation," *Popular Music & Society* 15:1 (Spring 1991), pp. 91–101, and Bob Doerschuk, ed., *Rock Keyboard* (New York: Quill/Keyboard, 1985). Doerschuk prefaces interviews from *Keyboard* magazine with introductions and chapter headings that announce his allegiance with Romanticism as a mode of understanding rock keyboards.

64 Robert Pattison, *The Triumph of Vulgarity* (Oxford: Oxford University Press, 1987), p. 63.

65 Ibid., pp. 188 and 196. Pattison's main source on the topic of vulgarity is John Ruskin's position in volume 5 of *Modern Painters* (London: 1860).

66 Ibid., p. xi.

67 Ibid., p. 10.

68 Quoted in James Henke, p. 41.

69 Ibid., p. 64.

70 For a discussion of the complicated role of race in rock music, see Steve Perry, "Ain't No Mountain High Enough: The Politics of Crossover," in Simon Frith, ed., *Facing the Music* (New York: Pantheon Books, 1988), pp. 51–87. See also Nelson George, *Buppies, B-boys, Baps & Bohos: Notes on Post-Soul Black Culture* (New York: HarperCollins, 1992).

71 See Andy Hamilton, "The Aesthetics of Imperfection," *Philosophy* 65 (1990), pp. 323–40, and Ted Gioia, *The Imperfect Art* (New York: Oxford University Press, 1988), pp. 19–49.

72 Billie Holiday with William Dufty, *Lady Sings the Blues* (New York: Penguin, 1984), p. 39. (Holiday's autobiography was first published in 1956.) There is a certain irony here for anyone who wants to fit Holiday into the romantic archetype, since she is talking about commercial songs by white composers.

73 See Peter Kivy, *Sound Sentiment* (Philadelphia: Temple University Press, 1989), chapters 3–5; this incorporates his earlier book *The Corded Shell.*

74 See Simon Frith, *Sound Effects* (New York: Pantheon, 1981), pp. 202–234.

75 Attempts to legitimize rock by association with folk music first arose among rock critics; see Simon Frith, " 'The Magic That Can Set You Free': The Ideology of Folk and the Myth of the Rock Community," *Popular Music,* vol. 1, ed. Richard Middleton and David Horn (Cambridge: Cambridge University Press, 1981), pp. 159–68.

76 Peter Wicke, *Rock Music: Culture, Aesthetics and Sociology,* trans. Rachel Fogg (Cambridge: Cambridge University Press, 1990), chapters 5 and 7. See also Simon Frith and Howard Horne, *Art into Pop* (New York: Methuen & Co., 1987), chapter 2.

77 Friedrich Kerst and Henry Edward Krehbiel, eds., *Beethoven: The Man and the Artist, as Revealed in His Own Words* (New York: Dover Publications, 1964), p. 46; Beethoven wrote the remark in 1823.

78 Kerst and Krehbiel, *Beethoven*, pp. 51 and 61, respectively.

79 Langdon Winner, "The Strange Death of Rock and Roll," in Greil Marcus, *Rock and Roll Will Stand* (Boston: Beacon Press, 1969), p. 50.

80 Ben Shahn, *The Shape of Content* (New York: Vintage Books, 1957), p. 12.

81 Nietzsche, *Will to Power*, trans. Walter Kaufmann and R. J. Hollingdale (New York: Vintage/Random House, 1968), p. 429 (section 811).

82 Jeremy Bentham, "Reward Applied to Art and Science," *The Works of Jeremy Bentham*, ed. John Bowring, vol. 2 (New York: Russell & Russell, 1962), p. 253.

83 R. G. Collingwood, *The Principles of Art* (Oxford: Oxford University Press, 1958), p. 119.

84 Milton Babbitt, "Who Cares If You Listen?" *High Fidelity Magazine*, February 1958, p. 126. Babbitt uses the title "The Composer as Specialist" in all reprintings.

85 Milton Babbitt, "The Unlikely Survival of Serious Music," in Milton Babbitt, *Words About Music*, ed. Stephen Dembski and Joseph N. Straus (Madison: University of Wisconsin Press, 1987), pp. 164, 180, and 183.

86 Shahn, "Artists in Colleges," *The Shape of Content*.

87 Ezra Pound, *ABC of Reading* (Norfolk, Conn.: New Directions, n.d.; originally published 1934), p. 61. Pound's concerns about poetry have recently resurfaced; see Dana Gioia, *Can Poetry Matter?* (St. Paul, Minn.: Graywolf Press, 1992).

88 Quoted in Josef Woodard, "Frank Zappa," *Musician* 96 (October 1986), pp. 26–27.

89 My thanks to Paul Koonce for getting me to think about this objection.

90 George Kubler, *The Shape of Time* (New Haven: Yale University Press, 1962), p. 10.

8 *Sign O' the Times: Ideology and Aesthetics*

1 John Street, *Rebel Rock: The Politics of Popular Music* (Oxford and New York: Basil Blackwell, 1986), p. 169.

2 Susan McClary and Robert Walser, "Start Making Sense! Musicology Wrestles with Rock," in Simon Frith and Andrew Goodwin, eds., *On Record: Rock, Pop, & the Written Word* (New York: Pantheon, 1990), p. 281. McClary and Walser refer to musicology, but I do not think they are misrepresented by extending it to aesthetics.

3 Dick Hebdige, *Subculture: The Meaning of Style* (New York: Methuen, 1979), p. 129.

4 Terry Eagleton, *Literary Theory: An Introduction* (Minneapolis: University of Minnesota Press, 1983), p. 133.

5 John Fiske, *Understanding Popular Culture* (Boston: Unwin Hyman: 1989), p. 130.

6 Hebdige, pp. 11–13.

7 Timothy J. Clark, "The Painting of Modern Life," in Francis Fascina and Jonathan Harris, eds., *Art in Modern Culture: An Anthology of Critical Texts* (New York: Harper Collins, 1992), p. 43.

8 Hebdige, pp. 54–59.

9   John Storey, *An Introductory Guide to Cultural Theory and Popular Culture* (Athens, Ga.: University of Georgia Press, 1993), pp. 121–22.

10 Fiske, *Understanding Popular Culture*, pp. 10–21. See also Richard Dyer, *Heavenly Bodies* (London: British Film Institute, 1987).

11 Ibid., and Kristine McKenna, "A Monster Called Sting," *Rolling Stone*, 1 September 1983, p. 14.

12 John Fiske, *Reading the Popular* (Boston: Unwin Hyman, 1989), chapter 5, and Susan Bordo, " 'Material Girl': The Effacements of Postmodern Culture," *Michigan Quarterly* 29 (Fall 1990).

13 John Shepherd, *Music as Social Text* (Cambridge: Polity Press, 1991); Simon Frith and Angela McRobbie, "Rock and Sexuality," and Simon Frith, "Afterthoughts," both in Simon Frith and Andrew Goodwin, eds., *On Record: Rock, Pop & the Written Word* (New York: Pantheon, 1990), pp. 371–89 and 419–24.

14 Roger Taylor, *Art, an Enemy of the People* (London: Harvester, 1988), p. 56.

15 Niall Stokes, "The Making of a Legend," in Niall Stokes with Liam Mackey, eds., *Three Chords and the Truth* (New York: Harmony Books, 1989), p. 28.

16 John McGowan, *Postmodernism and Its Critics* (Ithaca and London: Cornell University Press, 1991), p. 25.

17 Janet Wolff, *Aesthetics and the Sociology of Art*, 2d ed. (Ann Arbor: University of Michigan Press, 1993), p. 84. See Arnold Berleant, *Art and Engagement* (Philadelphia: Temple University Press, 1991), and David Novitz, *The Boundaries of Art* (Philadelphia: Temple, 1992). Feminist aesthetics deserves some of the credit for the shift Wolff celebrates; e.g., Mary Devereaux, "Oppressive Texts, Resisting Readers and the Gendered Spectator: The New Aesthetics," *Journal of Aesthetics and Art Criticism* 48 (1990), part of a special issue devoted to Feminism and Traditional Aesthetics.

18 Ibid., and Peter Bürger, *Theory of the Avant-Garde*, trans. Michael Shaw (Minneapolis: University of Minnesota Press, 1984), chapter 3. Bürger's category of bourgeois art is roughly equivalent with modernist conceptions of art, with the crucial difference that Bürger is intent on exposing the social formation of art's autonomy that lies at the heart of the modernist concept.

19 Lydia Goehr, *The Imaginary Museum of Musical Works* (Oxford: Oxford University Press, 1992), p. 161.

20 Wolff, "The Ideology of Autonomous Art," in Leppert and McClary, *Music and Society*, pp. 1–12.

21 Bürger, p. 51.

22 Pierre Bourdieu and Alain Darbel with Dominique Schnapper, *The Love of Art: European Art Museums and Their Public*, trans. Caroline Beattie and Nick Merriman (Stanford: Stanford University Press, 1990), p. 37.

23 Quoted in Dave Marsh, *Born to Run: The Bruce Springsteen Story* (New York: Dell Publishing, 1981), pp. 219–20.

24 Fiske, *Understanding Popular Culture*, p. 49.

25 Rose Rosengard Subotnik, "The Role of Ideology in the Study of Western Music," in *Developing Variations* (Minneapolis: University of Minnesota Press, 1991).

26   Simon Frith, "Towards an Aesthetic of Popular Music," in Leppert and Mc-
     Clary, *Music and Society,* pp. 133–49. See Wolff, *Aesthetics and the Sociology
     of Art,* p. 23.
27   Ibid., p. 170.
28   Stephen Wright, "The Big No," *Esquire,* July 1994, p. 60.
29   Bourdieu, *Distinctions,* p. 41. He appears to take his basic categories from
     Kant in structuring his research.
30   Immanuel Kant, *The Critique of Judgment,* trans. Werner S. Pluhar (Indiana-
     polis: Hackett Publishing, 1987).
31   Alfred Lessing, "What Is Wrong with a Forgery?" *Journal of Aesthetics and Art
     Criticism* 23 (1965).
32   Jameson, *The Ideologies of Theory,* p. 115.
33   "The idea of a white blues singer seems an even more violent contradiction
     of terms than the idea of a middle-class blues singer" (Amiri Baraka [LeRoi
     Jones], *Blues People* [New York: Quill, 1963], p. 148). See also Joel Rudinow,
     "Race, Ethnicity, Expressive Authenticity: Can White People Sing the Blues?"
     Journal of Aesthetics and Art Criticism 52 (Winter 1994), pp. 127–37.
34   Baraka, p. 148.
35   John Shepherd, *Music as Social Text* (Cambridge: Polity Press, 1991), p. 214.
36   Lawrence Grossberg, "Rock and Roll in Search of an Audience," in James Lull,
     ed., *Popular Music and Communication,* 2d ed. (Newbury Park: Sage Publica-
     tions, 1991), p. 169.
37   Leslie Dunbar, *Reclaiming Liberalism* (New York and London: W. W. Norton,
     1991), p. 39.
38   Ludwig Wittgenstein, *Philosophical Investigations,* trans. G. E. M. Anscombe
     (Oxford: Basil Blackwell, 1976), pp. 128e and 49e.
39   Anita Silvers, "The Artworld Discarded," *The Journal of Aesthetics and Art
     Criticism* 34 (Summer 1976), p. 448, and Richard Conniff, "Ireland on Fast-
     Forward," *National Geographic* 186:3 (September 1994), p. 7.
40   Quoted in Jon Bream, "Babes by the Book," *Minneapolis/St. Paul Star Tribune,*
     18 August 1994, p. 3E.
41   Sarah Ferguson, "The Comfort of Being Sad," *Utne Reader* 64 (July/August
     1994), p. 60.
42   Dave Marsh, *The First Rock & Roll Confidential Report* (New York: Pantheon
     Books, 1985), p. 286.
43   Niall Stokes, "Introduction," *Three Chords and the Truth,* p. 5.
44   Bud Scoppa, liner notes to Joe Cocker, *Classics, Volume 4* (A&M Records,
     1987), emphasis added.
45   See Robin Denselow, *When the Music's Over: The Story of Political Pop* (Lon-
     don and Boston: Faber and Faber, 1989).
46   For a critique of the theoretical assumptions that such persons are both gender-
     less and self-sufficient, see Alison Jaggar, *Feminist Politics and Human Nature*
     (Totowa, N.J.: Rowman & Allanheld, 1983), pp. 31–42.
47   Terry Eagleton, *Ideology: An Introduction* (London and New York: Verso,
     1991), p. 61.
48   Street, *Rebel Rock,* chapter 9.

49 Leppert and McClary, p. xiii.

50 This formulation is from Patricia Waugh, *Practicing Postmodernism/Reading Modernism* (London and New York: Edward Arnold, 1992), p. 43. Subsequent quotations from Fredric Jameson, *Postmodernism, or, the Cultural Logic of Late Capitalism* (Durham: Duke University Press, 1991), chapter 1.

51 Fredric Jameson, *The Ideologies of Theory: Essays 1971–1986* (Minneapolis: University of Minnesota Press, 1988), p. 104.

52 Andrew Goodwin, "Music Video in the (Post) Modern World," *Screen* 28:3 (1987), pp. 38–40.

53 Lawrence Grossberg, *We Gotta Get Out of This Place*, p. 209.

54 Ibid., pp. 206–7.

55 Eagleton, *Ideology*, p. 61. See also Fascina, p. 92.

56 Grossberg, *Gotta Get Out*, pp. 225 and 234.

57 Grossberg, "Rock and Roll in Search of an Audience," p. 169.

58 Daniel Bell, *The Cultural Contradictions of Capitalism* (New York: Basic Books, 1976), pp. 21–22.

59 L. T. Hobhouse, *Liberalism* (New York: Oxford University Press, 1964), p. 19 (emphasis added).

60 McGowan, *Postmodernism and Its Critics*, p. 41. For poststructuralist and communitarian critiques of this conception of the autonomous individual, see McGowan and Charles Taylor, *Multiculturalism and "The Politics of Recognition"* (Princeton: Princeton University Press, 1992).

61 Anthony Scaduto, *Bob Dylan: An Intimate Biography* (New York: Ballantine, 1973), p. 205.

62 Simon Frith, "Rock and the Politics of Memory," Sohnya Sayres et al., eds., *The 60s Without Apology* (Minneapolis: University of Minnesota Press, 1984), p. 66.

63 Quoted in Andrew Doe and John Tobler, *The Doors: In Their Own Words* (New York: Perigee Books, 1991), pp. 89 and 94.

64 David Fricke, "Courtney Love: Life After Death," *Rolling Stone*, 15 December 1994, 108.

65 Ibid., p. 61.

66 Quoted in David Fricke, "Thurston Moore," *Rolling Stone*, 22 September 1994, p. 115.

67 Quoted in Paul Zollo, "Me'Shell NdegéOcello," *Musician* 190 (August 1994), p. 26 (emphasis altered).

68 Quoted in Dennis Cooper, "Real Personal," *Spin* 10:7 (October 1994), p. 132. Compare with Kurt Cobain: "I'm a spokesman for *myself*. It just so happens that there's a bunch of people that are concerned with what I have to say" (Azerrad, "Inside the Heart," p. 39).

69 Michael Azerrad, "Inside the Heart and Mind of Kurt Cobain," *Rolling Stone*, 16 April 1992, p. 39.

70 Gina Arnold, quoted in Greil Marcus, "Come As You Are," *Rolling Stone*, 2 June 1994, p. 56.

71 In *Paul Simon: Born at the Right Time* (WNET/American Masters Special; commercial release by Warner/Reprise, 1992).

72   Quoted in Steve Perry, "Replacements Rule (In Spite of Themselves)," *Musician* 124 (February 1989), p. 67.

73   Charles Aaron, "Kurt Cobain," *Spin* 10:9 (December 1994), p. 84. Asked to vote for "Artist of the Year," some *Spin* readers sarcastically proposed Picasso and van Gogh.

Selected Bibliography

Adorno, Theodor W. *Aesthetic Theory*. Trans. C. Lenhardt. New York: Routledge & Kegan Paul, 1982.

Adorno, Theodor W. *Introduction to the Sociology of Music*. Trans. E. B. Ashton. New York: Seabury Press, 1976.

Adorno, Theodor W. *Philosophy of Modern Music*. Trans. Anne G. Mitchell and Wesley V. Blomster. New York: Seabury Press, 1973.

Alperson, Philip, ed. *What Is Music?* New York: Haven, 1988.

Attali, Jacques. *Noise: The Political Economy of Music*. Trans. Brian Massumi. Minneapolis: University of Minnesota Press, 1985.

Barthes, Roland. *Writing Degree Zero*. Trans. Annette Lavers and Colin Smith. New York: Hill & Wang, 1968.

Beadle, Jeremy J. *Will Pop Eat Itself?* London and Boston: Faber and Faber, 1993.

Beardsley, Monroe C. *Aesthetics: Problems in the Philosophy of Criticism*. 2d ed. Indianapolis: Hackett Publishing, 1981.

Belz, Carl. *The Story of Rock*. 2d ed. Oxford and New York: Oxford University Press, 1972.

Bloom, Allan. *The Closing of the American Mind*. New York: Simon and Schuster, 1987.

Bosanquet, Bernard. *Three Lectures on Aesthetic*. London: Macmillan, 1931.

Bourdieu, Pierre. *Distinction: A Social Critique of the Judgment of Taste*. Trans. Richard Nice. Cambridge, Mass.: Harvard University Press, 1984.

Bürger, Peter. *Theory of the Avant-Garde*. Trans. Michael Shaw. Minneapolis: University of Minnesota Press, 1984.

Chapple, Steve, and Reebee Garofalo. *Rock 'n' Roll Is Here to Pay: The History and Politics of the Music Industry*. Chicago: Nelson-Hall, 1977.

Collingwood, R. G. *The Principles of Art*. Oxford: Oxford University Press, 1958.

Copland, Aaron. *Music and Imagination*. Cambridge, Mass.: Harvard University Press, 1952.

Danto, Arthur. *The Transfiguration of the Commonplace*. Cambridge, Mass.: Harvard University Press, 1981.

DeCurtis, Anthony, ed. *Present Tense*. Durham: Duke University Press, 1992.

Durant, Alan. *Conditions of Music*. Albany: State University of New York Press, 1984.

Eagleton, Terry. *Ideology: An Introduction*. London and New York: Verso, 1991.

Eagleton, Terry. *Literary Theory: An Introduction*. Minneapolis: University of Minnesota Press, 1983.

Eisen, Jonathan, ed. *The Age of Rock*. New York: Random House, 1969.

Eisenberg, Evan. *The Recording Angel*. New York: Penguin Books, 1988.

Ennis, Philip H. *The Seventh Stream: The Emergence of Rocknroll in American Popular Music*. Hanover and London: Wesleyan University Press, 1992.

Fiske, John. *Television Culture*. New York: Methuen, 1987.

Fiske, John. *Understanding Popular Culture*. Boston: Unwin Hyman, 1989.

Flanagan, Bill. *Written in My Soul*. Chicago and New York: Contemporary Books, 1987.

Frith, Simon. *Music for Pleasure: Essays in the Sociology of Pop*. New York: Routledge, 1988.

Frith, Simon. *Sound Effects: Youth, Leisure, and the Politics of Rock 'n' Roll*. New York: Pantheon, 1981.

Frith, Simon, and Andrew Goodwin, eds. *On Record: Rock, Pop, & the Written Word*. New York: Pantheon, 1990.

Garofalo, Reebee, ed. *Rockin' the Boat: Mass Music & Mass Movements*. Boston: South End Press, 1992.

Gillett, Charlie. *The Sound of the City: The Rise of Rock and Roll*. New York: Outbridge & Dienstfrey/Dutton, 1970.

Goehr, Lydia. *The Imaginary Museum of Musical Works*. Oxford: Oxford University Press, 1992.

Goodman, Nelson. *Languages of Art*. Indianapolis: Hackett, 1976.

Grossberg, Lawrence. *We Gotta Get Out of This Place: Popular Conservatism and Postmodern Culture*. New York and London: Routledge, 1992.

Hatch, David, and Stephen Millward. *From Blues to Rock*. Manchester and New York: Manchester University Press, 1987.

Hebdige, Dick. *Subculture: The Meaning of Style*. London and New York: Methuen, 1979.

Hein, Hilde, and Carolyn Korsmeyer, eds. *Aesthetics in a Feminist Perspective*. Bloomington: Indiana University Press, 1993.

Heylin, Clinton, ed. *The Penguin Book of Rock & Roll Writing*. New York: Viking, 1992.

Higgins, Kathleen Marie. *The Music of Our Lives*. Philadelphia: Temple University Press, 1990.

Ingarden, Roman. *The Work of Music and the Problem of Its Identity*. Trans. Adam Czerniawski. Berkeley and Los Angeles: University of California Press, 1986.

Jahn, Mike. *The Story of Rock from Elvis Presley to the Rolling Stones*. New York: Quadrangle, 1975.

Jameson, Fredric. *The Ideologies of Theory: Essays 1971–1986*. Minneapolis: University of Minnesota Press, 1988.

Jameson, Fredric. *Postmodernism, or, The Cultural Logic of Late Capitalism*. Durham: Duke University Press, 1991.

Kivy, Peter. *Sound Sentiment: An Essay on the Musical Emotions*. Philadelphia: Temple University Press, 1989.

Leppert, Richard, and Susan McClary, eds. *Music and Society: The Politics of Composition, Performance, and Reception*. Cambridge: Cambridge University Press, 1987.

Levinson, Jerrold. *Music, Art, & Metaphysics*. Ithaca: Cornell University Press, 1990.

Lipsitz, George. *Time Passages: Collective Memory and American Popular Music*. Minneapolis: University of Minnesota Press, 1990.

Loder, Kurt. *Bat Chain Puller*. New York: St. Martin's Press, 1990.

Marcus, Greil. *Lipstick Traces*. Cambridge, Mass.: Harvard University Press, 1989.

Marsh, Dave. *The Heart of Rock and Soul*. New York: Plume Books, 1989.

Martin, George, ed. *Making Music*. New York: William Morrow, 1983.

McGowan, John. *Postmodernism and Its Critics*. Ithaca and London: Cornell University Press, 1991.

Meyer, Leonard B. *Music, the Arts, and Ideas*. Chicago and London: University of Chicago Press, 1967.

Moore, Allan F. *Rock: The Primary Text*. Buckingham and Philadelphia: Open University Press, 1993.

Paglia, Camille. *Sex, Art, and American Culture*. New York: Vintage Books, 1992.

Paglia, Camille. *Sexual Personae*. New York: Vintage Books, 1990.

Pattison, Robert. *The Triumph of Vulgarity*. Oxford: Oxford University Press, 1987.

Raffman, Diana. *Language, Music, and Mind*. Cambridge, Mass. and London: MIT Press, 1993.

Rose, Tricia. *Black Noise: Rap Music and Black Culture in Contemporary America*. Hanover and London: Wesleyan University Press, 1994.

Russolo, Luigi. *The Art of Noises*. Trans. Barclay Brown. New York: Pendragon Press, 1986.

Savage, Jon. *England's Dreaming: Anarchy, Sex Pistols, Punk Rock and Beyond*. New York: St. Martin's Press, 1992.

Scruton, Roger. *The Aesthetic Understanding*. London and New York: Methuen, 1983.

Sessions, Roger. *The Musical Experience of Composer, Performer and Listener*. Princeton: Princeton University Press, 1950.

Shepherd, John. *Music as Social Text*. Cambridge: Polity Press, 1991.

Shusterman, Richard. *Pragmatist Aesthetics: Living Beauty, Rethinking Art*. Oxford and Cambridge, Mass.: Blackwell, 1992.

Street, John. *Rebel Rock: The Politics of Popular Music*. Oxford and New York: Basil Blackwell, 1986.

Subotnik, Rose Rosengard. *Developing Variations: Style and Ideology in Western Music*. Minneapolis: University of Minnesota Press, 1991.

Toop, David. *Rap Attack 2: African Rap to Global Hip Hop*. Boston: Consortium Press, 1992.

Walser, Robert. *Running with the Devil: Power, Gender, and Madness in Heavy Metal Music*. Hanover and London: Wesleyan University Press, 1993.

Ward, Ed, Geoffrey Stokes, and Ken Tucker. *Rock of Ages: The Rolling Stone History of Rock & Roll.* New York: Summit Books/Rolling Stone Press, 1986.

Weinberg, Max, with Robert Santelli. *The Big Beat.* New York: Billboard Books, 1991.

Weinstein, Deena. *Heavy Metal: A Cultural Sociology.* New York: Lexington Books, 1991.

Wicke, Peter. *Rock Music: Culture, Aesthetics and Sociology.* Trans. Rachel Fogg. Cambridge: Cambridge University Press, 1990.

Wolff, Janet. *Aesthetics and the Sociology of Art.* 2d ed. Ann Arbor: University of Michigan Press, 1993.

Index

Abbey Road (Beatles), 97
Abdul, Paula, 28
Abstract expressionism, 78
Achtung Baby (U2), 49, 90
Ackerman, Diane, 99
Acoustic properties, 111–14. *See also* Noise
Addison, Joseph, 140
Adolescence, 128–29. *See also* Youth culture
Adorno, Theodor W.: aesthetic theory of, 154–61, 166–69, 211, 213, 248 n.19, 249 n.44, 250 n.73; appraisal of, 161–73, 215, 249 n.40; influence of, 150–54, 247 n.3, 249 n.54; Marcuse and, 251 n.91; on jazz, 150–61; on popular culture, 155–65; on recordings, 169; on success of mass culture, 157–59, 210
Adrenalize (Def Leppard), 90
Aerosmith, x, 94, 96–97, 123, 201
African American musicians, ix–x, 3, 7, 69, 129, 131, 154, 171, 182, 187, 196, 216, 224, 241 n.62; appropriation from, 96, 165, 176, 196, 198–99, 217, 219–20, 258 n.33
Aldrich, Virgil: on primary and secondary materials, 73–75
Allen, Rick, 90
Allison, Jerry, 85
Allman Brothers Band, 170
Allographic art. *See* Musical work(s)
All Things Must Pass (George Harrison), 86

Allusion, 95–98, 221. *See also* Sampling
Altamont (concert), xii
American Bandstand, vii, 133
American Prayer, An (Jim Morrison), 86
Am I Not Your Girl? (Sinéad O'Connor), 63
Amnesty International, 220
Amplification, 108–11, 113–14, 119–24
A&M Records, 190
Anderson, Laurie, 221
Anka, Paul, vii
Anna Karenina (Tolstoy), 71
Anthem of the Sun (Grateful Dead), 49, 82
Anthrax, 99
A.P. (Alternative Press), 181
Apocalypse Now (film), 24, 172
Appel, Mike, 17, 21, 34
Arc (Neil Young), 49
Aristotle, 128, 165
Arlen, Harold, 6
Armstrong, Louis, 5, 149, 156, 162, 170–71, 197
Aronoff, Kenny, 136
Arousal theory, 140–43
Arrangement: musical, 11, 19, 91
Arrested Development, 54, 81
Artforum, 219
Art of Noise, The, 99
Art of Noises, The (Russolo), 114–18
Art music. *See* Classical music
Astral Weeks (Van Morrison), 3–4, 136
Attali, Jacques, 150, 159, 232 n.7, 249 n.41; on noise, 101–3, 106, 241 n.9

Theodore Gracyk is Associate Professor of Philosophy
at Moorhead State University in Minnesota and author
of numerous articles on aesthetics. The first recording he
ever purchased was the Who's *Quadrophenia*.

Library of Congress Cataloging-in-Publication Data
Gracyk, Theodore.
Rhythm and noise : an aesthetics of rock / Theodore
Gracyk.
Includes bibliographical references and index.
ISBN 0-8223-1734-6 (cl : alk. paper). —
ISBN 0-8223-1743-5 (pa : alk. paper)
1. Rock music — History and criticism. 2. Music — 20th
century — Philosophy and aesthetics. 3. Popular
culture — History — 20th century.   I. Title.
ML3534.G7 1996
781.66 — dc20   95-44601CIP   MN